Memory in the Real World

Second Edition

Gillian Cohen

The Open University, Milton Keynes, UK

Psychology Press

An imprint of Erlbaum (UK) Taylor & Francis

Copyright © 1996 by Psychology Press
an imprint of Erlbaum (UK) Taylor & Francis Ltd.

Psychology Press, Publishers
27 Church Road
Hove
East Sussex, BN3 2FA
UK

British Library Cataloguing in Publication Data
A catalogue record for this book is available from the British Library

  ISBN 0–86377–728–7 (Hbk)
  ISBN 0–86377–729–5 (Pbk)

Typeset by J&L Composition Ltd, Filey, North Yorkshire
Printed and bound in the United Kingdom by TJ Press (Padstow) Ltd.

To my Mother

Contents

Preface to the Second Edition

Since the first edition of *Memory in the Real World* was published in 1989 there has been a vast amount of new research into everyday memory. This new edition has been extensively updated and extended to include the latest work in all areas and to highlight the most important trends. It aims to provide a comprehensive state-of-the-art review to integrate different topics with each other and with the cognitive theories that underpin them. The controversy about the "bankruptcy" of everyday memory and, more generally, the value of naturalistic research as opposed to traditional laboratory methods is outlined and the views of both critics and defenders are evaluated. The current trend toward convergence of the two approaches is discussed. There is a detailed appraisal of the methodology of everyday memory research and a critical evaluation of its theoretical status.

The book brings together studies on many different topics, such as memory for plans and actions; memory for names, faces, and voices and advances in modelling person recognition; memory for routes and maps; conversations and stories; autobiographical experiences; and childhood events. Further chapters focus on memory for general knowledge and the long-term maintenance of knowledge. The section on metamemory includes new explanations of the feeling of knowing, and the chapter on memory for specialist domains such as chess, computer programming, dinosaurs, and bar-tending now includes new sections on the nature of expertise and on memory for music. Emphasis is also given to memory for internal mental events, such as thinking and re-remembering, and there is a new section on memory and dreams. Current attempts to bring dreaming within the framework of current cognitive theories are considered. Topics that have recently attracted attention, such as the false memory syndrome, memory for health events, and social remembering, are included.

This new edition spells out the links between naturalistic and applied studies and the models, and theories that support them. There is particular emphasis on the different types of mental representation that are required for different domains of everyday memory. In each area, the book shows how theoretical frameworks such as schemas, scripts, mental models, and production systems, and concepts such as encoding specificity, implicit memory, and rule-based and case-based reasoning, are needed to explain and interpret the findings and observations derived from the study of memory in the real world. The final chapter presents some general models of memory systems to see how far they can incorporate everyday memory and analyses the special characteristics that are needed if memory in the real world is to function efficiently.

1 The Study of Everyday Memory

HISTORICAL BACKGROUND: 100 YEARS IN THE LABORATORY

Psychologists have been studying memory for over a hundred years but a great deal of this time has been spent in the laboratory using formal experimental techniques to answer theoretical questions about the general principles that govern the mechanisms of memory. In its relatively short history psychology has often seemed to proceed by a series of reactions discarding one approach in favour of a new one, and then swinging back again to revive and reinstate the original ideas. This kind of oscillation is especially evident in the study of memory.

Around the turn of the century, psychologists began to react against the kind of philosophical, introspective approach exemplified in William James' (1890) reflections on memory. In an attempt to give psychology a status of genuine scientific respectability, the objective experimental methods employed by Ebbinghaus (1885) were enthusiastically adopted and developed. The majority of these experiments were concerned with verbal learning. A typical experiment of this kind tests memory performance in situations where a few of the relevant factors are isolated and rigorously controlled and manipulated. All the myriads of other factors that may normally influence memory in everyday life are deliberately excluded. Using stimuli such as nonsense syllables that are almost entirely devoid of meaning and of previously acquired associations, the experimenter controls the number, duration, and timing of the presentation of these stimuli. The subjects are carefully selected and instructed; the environment is standardised; the delay before recall is fixed and the mental events that occur during this retention interval are controlled as far as possible. Finally, the instructions for recall are presented and the experimenter can record the number and type of items that are recalled, and the order and timing of the responses.

Experiments like these reveal the limits of memory capacity and define the constraints that govern the system. Some general principles have emerged which have proved robust and reliable, and which generalise across a range of experimental situations. For example, the division of memory into a short-term store and a long-term store is widely accepted, and phenomena such as the bow-shaped curve of serial learning, the rate of decay, the role of rehearsal, and the effects of interference and of retention interval are well established. Research of this kind, often referred to as "traditional laboratory research" or TLR, has accumulated over many years and still continues. However, over the last two decades there has been a marked change of direction in the study of memory.

The Winds of Change

At the first conference on Practical Aspects of Memory in 1978, Ulric Neisser gave a talk entitled "Memory: What are the important questions?" in which he dismissed the work of the past hundred years as largely worthless. This talk was undoubtedly a milestone in the psychology of memory. Neisser believed that the important questions about memory are those that arise out of everyday experience. We ought, he claimed, to be finding out how memory works in the natural context of daily life at school, in the home or at work. We should be finding out what people remember from their formal education; why some people have "better" memories than others; why we remember some things and not others; and how we remember such diverse things as poems and town layouts, people's names, and events from our childhood. The traditional laboratory experiments, according to Neisser, have failed to study all the most interesting and significant problems and have shed no light on them. He claimed that the experimental findings are trivial, pointless, or obvious and fail to generalise outside the laboratory. He advocated a new approach, concentrating on the detailed examination of naturally occurring memory phenomena in the real world, and paying special attention to individual differences. According to this approach, psychologists should adopt an ethological approach studying human memory in the same way that ethologists study animal behaviour in the field. Neisser proposed that memory research should have *ecological validity*. By this he meant that it should apply to naturally occurring behaviour in the natural context of the real world. Interestingly, by the end of this conference Neisser had become aware that many of the "important" and "ecologically valid" questions were already being explored.

Precursors of the Change

It would be quite wrong to suppose that research into everyday memory only began abruptly as a result of Neisser's talk. Rather, he articulated a trend that had been slowly gathering strength over a long period. Long ago, both Galton (1883) and later Bartlett (1932) had addressed themselves to important questions about the rich and complex functioning of memory in natural contexts. Their ideas were allowed to lapse for many years but ecologically valid research began again both in Britain and in the United States during the Second World War. There was a new growth of applied psychology, when answers were urgently sought to practical questions about human performance in tasks like air traffic control (Broadbent, 1958), work on production lines (Welford, 1958) or morse code operation (Keller, 1953). Research into topics like these broadened the scope of memory research and awakened interest in how memory functions in natural contexts outside the laboratory.

More recently, the new school of cognitive psychology that evolved in the late 1960s adopted a much broader and more speculative approach to memory research than that of the traditional verbal learning experiments. Researchers confronted problems about memory strategies, and these led them to investigate many of the phenomena that characterise the use of memory in everyday life, such as, for example, the use of imagery and mnemonics (Paivio, 1969), the tip-of-the-tongue phenomenon (Brown & McNeill, 1966) and the advantages of categorical organisation (Mandler, 1967).

Kihlstrom (1994), reviewing the achievements of cognitive psychology in the last 30 years, argued that major advances have been made during this period and important general principles have been formulated and established. These include the principles of organisation and of encoding specificity; the role of schematic processing and reconstructive processing; and the importance of pre-existing knowledge, beliefs, and expectations. These examples illustrate the way that laboratory research using strict experimental methods had already begun to move away from the tradition of studying memory for items of information stripped, as far as possible, of meaning, context, and personal significance. What Kihlstrom called the "cognitive revolution" brought about a new willingness to examine memory for richer and more meaningful material and to explore the individual's attempts to relate the to-be-remembered information to previously stored knowledge. By 1978 the winds of change were already beginning to blow, and Neisser voiced ideas that had already begun to take shape. Nevertheless, the rapid growth of everyday memory research since then is proof that his forceful expression of these ideas has undoubtedly had great influence.

Neisser's ideas had an enthusiastic reception and the wind of change has blown more and more strongly since 1978, bringing with it a rapidly accumulating, richly varied, and extremely interesting body of research into everyday memory. Indeed, this new wave of interest in the more practical aspects of cognition is not confined to the study of memory alone. Ecological validity has become something of a catchword and vigorous efforts are underway to relate many areas of cognitive psychology more closely to the mental activities of ordinary people going about their daily lives. Problems such as how doctors decide on a medical diagnosis or how gamblers decide to place their stakes; how juries assess the credibility of a witness; the skills involved in holding conversations, planning routes, and recognising disguised faces are among the many topics being studied. In 1994, when the third conference on Practical Aspects of Memory was held, it was apparent that, since Neisser's original talk, a very wide variety of naturally occurring memory phenomena ranging from memory for grocery lists and television news broadcasts to memory for school field trips and dietary intake have attracted the attention of psychologists.

NEW DIRECTIONS

The Backlash

Neisser's ideas were so strongly stated, and his condemnation of traditional research on memory as irrelevant was so sweeping and so extreme, that it was perhaps inevitable that a backlash would develop. In 1989 Banaji and Crowder published a counter-attack "The bankruptcy of everyday memory". They argued that in many studies of everyday memory ecological validity is in inverse relation to generalisability. The study of memory in naturally occurring situations necessarily entails abandoning control over the encoding and storage stages. For example, in testing memory for classroom learning or memory for the details of a real traffic accident or a summer vacation, the researcher has no control over the original experience. There is no way of knowing how effectively the information was encoded and there is no control over the experience of the subjects during the interval between encoding and retrieval. Banaji and Crowder (1989) argued that, in consequence, the results cannot be generalised from one situation to another.

The limitations and problems inherent in everyday memory research stem from weaknesses in the methodology. How can we draw conclusions about what causes people to forget something in everyday life when we have no control over potentially relevant factors? Consider, for example, memory for faces. In the real world, the researcher has no control over the initial learning phase; the degree of attention paid to the face when it was encountered; the number and duration of encounters; the importance and affective quality of the encounters; and the number and similarity of the faces encountered during the intervening period. How, then, can we infer what causes X to forget Y's face? The combination of lack of control and, in some cases, the absence of a strong theoretical framework, means that everyday memory research is in danger of producing only a mass of interesting, but uninterpreted, observations and untested speculations. Because of these problems some researchers are inclined to dismiss everyday memory research as "soft" psychology, in contrast to the rigour and precision of the traditional experimental methods. Banaji and Crowder (1989) concluded that everyday memory research has failed to "deliver" any new theories, to add explanatory power, or to develop new methods that have the necessary rigour and precision. This scathing article provoked a spirited defence from everyday memory researchers.

The crux of the debate centres on the issues of control and generalisability. Without some form of control, either experimental or statistical, generalisability is weak and Banaji and Crowder believe it is better to sacrifice ecological validity and to maintain control and ensure generalisability. On the one hand, everyday memory researchers believe that traditional research fails to generalise from the laboratory to real life. On the other hand, traditionalists claim that everyday memory research also fails to generalise because uncontrolled factors are allowed to vary freely.

The Defence of Everyday Memory

In spite of this attack, everyday memory research is here to stay. As Neisser (1991) has said, "the genie is out of the bottle" and it is not going to go back in. There are several lines of defence. Researchers (e.g. Loftus, 1991; Conway, 1991) have pointed out that some aspects of memory can only be studied in natural settings. One example is the retention of information over very long time spans. There is no way of finding out how well people remember what they learned in school or how well they remember the layout of cities they lived in long ago without emerging from the laboratory into the real world. Moreover, such studies, as we shall see in later chapters, have produced replicable and useful findings and show retention functions that are interestingly different from those obtained over shorter time spans in laboratory experiments. Another example of a type of memory that can only be studied in natural settings is "passive remembering" (Spence, 1988), which consists of memories that come to mind unbidden, triggered by the natural context or by preceding thoughts. Because these memories are involuntary they cannot, by definition, be elicited in the laboratory. It would also be impossible, for ethical reasons, to do experiments to study the effects of severe stress on memory, but studies of naturally occurring post-traumatic stress syndrome have been very valuable.

A second argument in favour of everyday memory research is that phenomena occurring in laboratory experiments are not necessarily reproduced in real life. For example, the retention of real world knowledge does not conform to the retention functions that are typically found in experiments. Sometimes, similar phenomena are found in both types of research, but it is clear that different theoretical explanations are needed. Conway (1991) cites the fact that in the laboratory the recency effect, whereby the last few items in a list are the best remembered, is explained in terms of the operation of short-term memory. But in real life, rugby players show a recency effect for recall of games they have played (Baddeley & Hitch, 1977) and people generally show recency effects for books they have read or films they have seen over many months (Hitch & Ferguson, 1991). Clearly, short-term memory cannot be involved and a different explanation is required. These examples show how the scope of theories generated by laboratory research does not necessarily extend to real life situations.

Researchers also defended studies using special groups of subjects, such as the elderly or those who are brain-damaged, who may not be representative of the general population. It was pointed out that studies of amnesics have shed light on implicit memory (memory that is not consciously accessible, but which is nevertheless revealed by indirect testing) and on memory for names; and studies of prosopagnosics have constrained theories of face recognition. It is one of the advantages of studying memory in the real world that it takes more account of individual differences. Differences of age, culture, sex, personality, and socioeconomic and educational background are important factors in everyday memory performance. Laboratory studies have often seemed to operate on the assumption that all human beings behave in the same way, basing generalisations on tests carried out on a fairly homogeneous sample of young college students. Once the researcher emerges into the real world, the great range and variety of human responses to the same situation has to be confronted. However, Banaji and Crowder's criticisms (1989) did not apply to the use of special groups in well-controlled studies. Their main objection is to studies lacking controls.

Defenders of everyday memory (e.g. Conway, 1993) have also pointed out that the most rigorous methodology of the laboratory is no guarantee that the results will be of interest or will generalise beyond the experimental paradigm. It is possible to design experiments that conform to the highest standards of control and produce elegant quantitative data, but which only show how subjects respond in that particular experimental paradigm and shed no light on how memory functions in any other situations. The defenders also noted that an important function of everyday memory research is to identify phenomena that can then be followed up more carefully in the laboratory. For example, Cohen and Faulkner (1986a) used diary records of naturally occurring name blocks to confirm that elderly people report experiencing greater difficulty in remembering names and then went on to design experimental analogues to explore this phenomenon with better control of the variables.

The Convergence

This last point underlines the fact that although researchers were still arguing vociferously about the respective merits of everyday memory research and traditional laboratory research, the two methodologies were quietly converging. This convergence has come about for several reasons. Many issues are now being tackled by using both methods in a complementary fashion. Theories and findings derived from laboratory experiments direct the search for analogues in everyday life and the findings that orginate from naturalistic studies are followed up in rigorous experiments so that what might be called a hybrid methodology has become commonplace.

A good example of this kind of hybridisation comes from the studies of eyewitness testimony (see Chapter 4), where the effects of leading questions or misinformation identified in simulations of real world events have been further explored in carefully controlled experiments designed to test hypotheses about the mechanism of memory distortion. Similarly, studies of face recognition move freely between the real world of identification line-ups and analytic experiments testing the effects of specific variables such as inversion of the face.

Another reason for the convergence is that, in the course of the argument about whether everyday memory research should be considered as bankrupt or as a goldmine, it has become apparent that it is often difficult to decide whether a particular study is an example of everyday research or not. It proves difficult to formulate a clear definition of what constitutes everyday memory research. If everyday memory research is to have maximum ecological validity, this entails that the behaviour and the context of its occurrence should not be tampered with or distorted in any way, but this is rarely feasible. In fact, there is a continuum from studying performance in a memory task that is as natural as possible, like observing shoppers in a supermarket and noting how many items they forget to buy (Anschutz, Camp, Markley, & Kramer, 1985), to studying performance in a task that is entirely artificial, like having subjects try to memorise a string of unrelated letters while simultaneously repeating "the-the-the" (Wilding & Mohindra,1980). In between these extremes, are laboratory experiments that mimic everyday situations, and studies of everyday behaviour that incorporate some constraints and controls. Klatzky (1991) pointed out that laboratory experiments like, for example, those on text comprehension, may use meaningful material and may have practical applications. And everyday studies, like some of those testing eyewitness memory, have involved subjects witnessing artificially staged incidents under controlled conditions. The distinction is by no means clear-cut.

Kihlstrom (1994) concluded that there has been real convergence due to movement on both sides. He believes that laboratory research has become more open to what can be learned from everyday life settings and more willing to address practical questions, whereas everyday memory research has become more aware of the need to build in methodological controls. This second edition of *Memory in the real world* reflects the convergence of theoretical and applied research and aims to show how they fit together and how each sheds light on the other. Nevertheless, despite the move toward convergence and the growth of hybrid methodologies, everyday memory research does have distinguishing features.

CHARACTERISTICS OF EVERYDAY MEMORY RESEARCH

Function and Context

Among the characteristic features of everyday memory research is its emphasis on the functional aspects of memory. It views memory as part of a repertoire of behaviour designed to fulfil specific goals. Autobiographical memory functions to build and maintain personal identity and self-concept; prospective memory functions to enable an individual to carry out plans and intentions; spatial memory functions so that an individual can navigate in the environment, and so on. Bruce (1985) stated that ecological memory research must ask how memory operates in everyday life, identifying causes and processes; what functions it serves; and why it has evolved both ontogenetically and evolutionarily in this way.

Everyday memory is context-bound, not context-free. The kind of things people remember in everyday life include a great variety of different items such as, for example, remembering a shopping list or a recipe, remembering to telephone a relative or to fill up the car with petrol, recounting the arguments put forward at a meeting or the plot of a play seen on television, or the amount of a bill that has to be paid. All these experiences are embedded in a rich context of ongoing events and scenes; they are influenced by a lifetime of past experiences, by history and culture, by current motives and emotions, by intelligence and personality traits, by future goals and plans. It is probably impossible to take all these factors into account, but everyday memory research does recognise the importance of the context in which an event occurs. Instead of discounting context, everyday memory researchers exploit the way that reinstating the context can facilitate retrieval. People remember details of an event they witnessed when they are reminded of aspects of the context such as the scene, or the preceding or succeeding events (see the account of the cognitive interview in Chapter 4).

Everyday memory research also emphasises the fact that remembering usually occurs in a social context and that one of its main functions is to serve interpersonal communication. Memory is not just a private data bank; it is shared, exchanged, constructed, revised and elaborated in all our social interactions. The importance of this aspect of memory emerges strongly from studies of the role of memory in conversation (see Chapter 9).

Its emphasis on function and on the social and situational context allows ecologically valid everyday memory research to bridge the gap between basic and applied research and many practical applications have been developed. The findings can provide useful guidelines on how to structure a lecture or to frame instructions for using a gadget, to shape the advice a doctor gives to a patient, and how to maximise compliance of patients in keeping appointments, how to devise memory therapy and memory aids, and how to design road signs and physical environments.

Incidental Learning

Everyday memory research also differs from most traditional memory research in that the remembered information has often been learned incidentally rather than intentionally. This is an important difference that underlines the fact that everyday memory research is essentially about the norms and habits of memory function rather than being concerned with the limits of capacity. It is about what people choose to remember, or happen to remember, rather than what they are capable of remembering when pushed to the limits of their ability.

The traditional laboratory experiment typically tests intentional memory and is concerned with establishing the limits of capacity. The primary aim of this type of research is to infer the nature of the mechanism, to deduce general principles, and to construct and test theoretical models. It is probably true to say that, in everyday life, naturally occurring memory tasks rarely tax capacity to its limits.

The Correspondence Metaphor

Koriat and Goldsmith (1996) encapsulated the characteristics of traditional laboratory research in terms of what they call "the storehouse metaphor", as opposed to everyday memory research, which they think of in terms of the "correspondence metaphor". According to the storehouse metaphor, traditional laboratory research conceptualises memory as a storage space occupied by discrete units or items of information. The essence of this approach lies in counting these units: memory is assessed in terms of quantity, of how many units are remembered, and what factors influence the amount of remembered information. By contrast, everyday memory research fits the correspondence metaphor, which stresses the importance of the degree of correspondence between the original input and what is remembered. Thus everyday, memory research is concerned with memory quality, with how accurately, reliably and completely memory preserves reality. According to this view, forgetting is not a matter of losing a number of items of information but of loss of correspondence, or deviation from reality. The correspondence metaphor carries with it the implication that memories should be considered holistically: Memory components are interrelated into complex wholes so that loss of accuracy in one part may affect the whole. This line of thinking makes a lot of sense when applied to memory for conversations, places, people and complex events. Koriat and Goldsmith's valuable insight has highlighted one of the most important current trends in everyday memory research—the emphasis on memory accuracy motivates and informs a great deal of current research. Their experiments have also shown that, whereas the quantity of responses (that is, the number of items retrieved) is usually not under conscious control, the accuracy of responses can be strategically controlled. Subjects can opt to be absolutely correct or only approximately correct. The factors that govern strategic control of accuracy are of great importance in evaluating witness memory.

METHODS OF EVERYDAY MEMORY RESEARCH

Everyday memory research employs a wide range of different methods but these can be divided into two groups. The first draws its data from self-reports and relies on introspective evidence; the second involves the use of experimental methods which may be more, or less, naturalistic.

The Validity of Introspective Evidence

Self-reports seem to provide a simple way of finding out how people's memories work in everyday life by asking them. The researcher can record people's own observations about the way their memories function, collecting reports from individuals about the things they remember and the things they forget; the tricks and devices they use to prop up memory; the particular circumstances that are associated with success or failure. The use of self-reports may involve collecting oral histories and reminiscences. Or it may involve the administration of formal questionnaires about memory. Subjects may be asked to supply self-ratings of their own memory ability, or they may be asked to think aloud while they solve problems and produce a verbal protocol, or they may be asked to keep a diary recording the occurrence of memory phenomena such as absentminded lapses. All these procedures rely on introspection.

The recent use of introspective evidence by psychologists is another example of the way the history of psychology exemplifies a kind of swings and roundabouts progression, with ideas being enthusiastically adopted, then discredited, and then reinstated. Early psychologists like Wundt and Freud based their theories on the introspections of their subjects or patients, but during the Behaviourist period (roughly from the 1920s to the 1950s), only overt measurable behavioural responses were considered admissible as evidence. The importance, and even the existence, of mental events were discounted.

However, the advent of cognitive psychology in the 1960s brought renewed interest in covert, unobservable mental processes such as imaging, reasoning, deciding and planning. Psychologists also realised that memory performance varies with the kind of strategy that is adopted. For example, differences between young and elderly subjects are not necessarily due to an age-related deterioration in memory ability, but may arise entirely because the elderly group use a less efficient strategy (Cohen & Faulkner, 1983). Once this possibility is recognised, it becomes important to determine what strategy is being used. Although it is to some extent possible, with carefully designed experiments, to infer the nature of covert thought processes and covert strategies from the nature of the overt responses that are made, the subject's own introspections can provide valuable corroboration or can suggest alternative hypotheses. Introspective methods have been brought back into use and are now employed extensively in studying aspects of cognition like problem-solving and decision-making as well as everyday memory.

This resurrection of introspective methods has not been without its critics (Nisbett & Wilson, 1977). They argued (p.231) that "there may be little or no direct access to higher order cognitive processes". In particular, they claimed that causal reports, that is reports about the causal influences on judgements and responses, are very inaccurate and are based more on people's preconceptions than on what actually influenced them. People may, for example, be unable to report accurately on what actually influenced their choice of a particular brand in a supermarket.

It is generally acknowledged that many of the very rapid mental processes that underlie activities like perceiving a complex scene, recognising a word, or speaking a grammatical sentence are simply not accessible to conscious awareness. Another mental process, which takes place without conscious awareness, is the so-called *pop-up* phenomenon described in

Chapter 5, p.128. You may have the experience of finding that you cannot recall something, such as a person's name, although this may be a name that you know quite well. Such a retrieval block may persist, despite your best efforts, for hours or even days. Then, when you have given up and are thinking about something quite different, the forgotten name suddenly pops up into consciousness. In this situation, people are usually unable to report anything about the mental processes that produced the pop-up. Introspection fails to yield any information. In such cases, people are conscious of the end-product of the mental operations, but not of the processes themselves. Nobody can introspect and make verbal reports about what is going on below the level of consciousness, and much of mental activity is unconscious.

Nevertheless, there are some thought processes that do take place consciously, and with some effort and practice, people can become quite good at describing them. This is particularly true of the so-called slow processes—long drawn out mental processes like working out solutions to tricky problems or attempting to reconstruct a personal memory from childhood. Self-reports are more accurate if they are concurrent with the mental events being described because delay tends to introduce distortion. Reports that are produced afterwards are less likely to be accurate. The researcher must also avoid giving any hints that might bias the report by indicating what is expected of the subject (Ericsson & Simon, 1980). Even so, some mental events may be difficult or impossible to express in words, or, in some cases, the act of trying to verbalise what is going on in the head may interfere with or change the nature of the mental activity under scrutiny. Trying to introspect about how you read silently, for example, will almost certainly change the way you read, causing you to read more slowly and in a more word-by-word manner than you usually do when you are not thinking about it.

Nisbett and Wilson (1977) made a distinction between mental processes that, in their view, are not accessible to consciousness, and mental products that are accessible. The role of unconscious processes in determining behaviour has been conceptualised recently, not by Freudian principles, but by the connectionist approach in which mental events are represented by patterns of activation in networks distributed across brain areas.

The relaxation of interacting connectionist structures into patterns happens relatively quickly and automatically, below the surface of consciousness. We are conscious only of the end states, not of the means of getting there. As a result, in this view of the mind, our explanations of our own behaviour are always suspect, for they amount to stories made up after the fact to explain the thoughts that we already have. (Norman, 1988, p.117).

Others (e.g. White, 1988) have argued that the distinction between unconscious processes and conscious products is difficult to make. In any case, Nisbett and Wilson admitted that products can include personal history; the present focus of attention; current sensations and emotions; plans and intentions; and the intermediate stages in a series of mental operations. These are just the sort of things that researchers want to know about, so this admission provides ample justification for the use of introspection. From the point of view of everyday memory research, the inaccessibility of mental processes, as opposed to products, is not so severe a handicap as it might seem. Everyday memory research, as will be apparent in later chapters, tends to be concerned more with the content of memory—the mental representations—than with the mental processes.

Introspective evidence is sometimes considered "soft" in contrast to the hard objective evidence derived from overt responses in experiments. In fact, the difference between them is greatly exaggerated. Consider, for example, an experiment in which the subject is asked to read a text. After reading the text, the subject is shown a word displayed on a computer screen and has to decide if it had occurred in the text and respond "yes" or "no" accordingly by pressing a response key. Compare this with an introspective study in which the subject is asked to examine a childhood memory and decide if it is vivid or not. Both tasks involve inspecting memories and making decisions about them. Both tasks rely on introspection. In the experiment, the use of computers and timers gives the appearance of greater objectivity and masks the fact that what is being measured is a judgement based on introspection.

Nevertheless, even if it is admitted that the distinction between introspective and objective evidence is blurred, issues about the validity and reliability of introspective evidence will not go away. The relationship between conscious thought and subconscious or unconscious thought is one of the major issues confronting cognitive psychology at the present time.

The Phenomenological Approach

Nisbett and Wilson's admission that products of mental processes are accessible to consciousness legitimises studies that use a phenomenological approach to study memory quality. The method typically involves asking subjects to examine their own memories and to report the characteristics of these memories and this may be combined with experimental manipulations. In studies of this kind Johnson, Foley, Suangas, and Raye (1988), Suangas and Johnson (1988), and Johnson (1988) asked subjects to rate the sensory qualities, emotionality, amount of spatial and temporal detail and amount of supporting context in designated memories, such as the memory of wrapping a parcel. The variables that were manipulated included whether the memory was of a real event that had actually occurred or of an event that had only been imagined; the recency of the events; and the amount and type of rehearsal. The experimenters then compared the ratings of memory qualities. The phenomenological reports of these qualities were validated by the fact that they varied systematically with whether the memory was real or imagined and with the recency of the event and the type of rehearsal.

Similar studies have used the phenomenological approach to compare the vividness of autobiographical memories from different decades of the life span (Cohen & Faulkner, 1988a) and to examine the special qualities alleged to characterise the so-called flashbulb memories for dramatic public events (Conway et al., 1994; Cohen, Conway, & Maylor, 1994). Of course, phenomenological reports of this kind may sometimes be influenced by preconceptions. Subjects may be aware that recent memories or highly emotional memories "ought" to be more vivid and their reports may reflect such beliefs rather than the phenomenological evidence. It is up to researchers to try to discriminate carefully between the effects of preconceptions and of genuine phenomenological qualities.

Verbal Protocols

Verbal protocols are a record of what people say when they are asked to think aloud as they perform a task. For example, when people are asked to try to recall some event from their past lives, they can be asked to verbalise the processes of search. Their speech is recorded and later transcribed so that the mental processes that are reported can be analysed. The use of verbal protocols is a form of concurrent introspection. Concurrent introspection has certain advantages over retrospective introspection in that there is less opportunity for editing and rationalising the report, and less chance of forgetting some of the mental processes. The protocol reveals the temporal sequence of mental operations, and the location and duration of the pauses in verbalisation convey information about the choice points. It is especially useful as a research tool for studying complex tasks of fairly long duration that involve operations that are easy to verbalise. So, for example, a practised subject can report the reasoning processes underlying the selection of a chess move. One disadvantage of using verbal protocols is that they are necessarily incomplete and they give no indication of what has been omitted. As already noted, some mental processes are not accessible to conscious introspection. Unconscious processes cannot be reported and unspoken thoughts remain mysterious. Another disadvantage is that individual subjects may differ in the ease and spontaneity with which they can produce a running commentary on their thinking, and in the level of detail they report, so individual differences in the underlying thought processes may be obscured by individual differences in the spoken commentary. Verbal protocols may also be inaccurate if subjects are trying to please the experimenter or to present themselves in a good light. They may not like to reveal the confused and muddled state of their mental processes and may tidy up the reported version so as to seem more impressive. Nisbett and Wilson (1977) have emphasised the shortcomings of verbal protocols, but Ericsson and Simon (1980) have defended the use of concurrent introspections and they have proved to be an informative way to study problem-solving and planning (see Chapter 2, pp.47–49).

Surveys, Questionnaires, and Self-ratings

It is worth discussing the use of questionnaires at some length as many examples will be found in later chapters. Several different kinds of questionnaire can be distinguished. One type of memory questionnaire is a straightforward test of general factual knowledge and asks questions like "What is the date of the battle of Waterloo?" or "Who was the composer of Rigoletto?" This kind of memory test is used to plot the retention of knowledge over time, or to investigate differences in memory ability between different groups, or changes in memory ability that occur as a result of ageing, trauma, or dementia.

Another type of questionnaire is used in survey research to obtain information about people's activities, experiences, and opinions. For example, surveys may ask people how often they travel by bus or how many units of alcohol they consume each week, and are used primarily in developing public policies. However, Jobe, Tourangeau, and Smith (1993) underlined the fact that the design of survey research draws on current theories of memory and the results contribute to our understanding of everyday memory. A study of memory for dietary intake (Smith, Jobe, & Mingay, 1991) illustrated how far principles discovered in the laboratory— such as the effects of retention interval, the use of generic schemas to aid retrieval, and the organisation of items into related categories—were spontaneously implemented in a natural setting.

Another type of questionnaire has been called a metamemory questionnaire because it queries beliefs or judgements about memory. Metamemory questionnaires are not tests. They are more like opinion surveys. Questions in metamemory questionnaires take a variety of different forms. Some are self-assessment questions that ask people to assess their own memory abilities by choosing the appropriate rating (e.g. Very Good, Good, Fair, Poor, or Very Poor) in response to questions like "How good is your memory for the words of songs or poems?" or "How good is your memory for routes to places?" Alternatively, subjects may be asked to assess the frequency of certain specified lapses of memory, as in "How often do you forget appointments?" or "How often do you want to tell a joke, but find you cannot remember it?", by rating the frequency of occurrence as Very Often, Often, Occasionally, Rarely, or Never. In other types of metamemory questionnaire people are asked to predict their own performance in forthcoming tests. As well as asking for ratings of memory ability, metamemory questionnaires may ask subjects what memory strategies, mnemonics, or reminders they employ; or whether they have detected any changes over time in their memory ability; or what beliefs and expectations they have about the way that memory works in general.

Self-assessments of memory ability are based on direct first-hand experience of success and failure in a wide range of everyday tasks over a long period. It seems reasonable, therefore, to assume that people should know about their own memory performance and be able to assess it accurately, but many researchers (e.g. Morris, 1984) have expressed serious doubts about the validity of self-ratings. These ratings have proved to have high reliability (i.e. if subjects are asked to work through a questionnaire, and it is then administered again at a later date, there is a strong correlation between the original and the repeat ratings). However, validity appears to be low, because when the subjective ratings are correlated with scores on objective psychometric tests of memory ability, such as digit span (the number of digits that can be repeated back immediately after presentation of a list), or free recall of word lists, the correlations are low or nonexistent. For example, self-rated ability to remember telephone numbers correlates with digit span at only 0.4, and self-rated ability to remember faces correlates with tests of ability to recognise photographs of faces at 0.3 (Herrman, 1984). Several reasons for this low validity have been identified:

(1) Self-assessments may reflect a person's self-image rather than his or her performance, and be distorted by modesty or pride. Self-assessment is also known to be influenced by anxiety, depression and personality (Rabbitt, Maylor, McInnes, Bent, & Moore, 1995).

(2) The Metamemory Paradox may operate, so that people who make most errors are least likely to report them because they forget they have occurred.

(3) Individual variation in the opportunity for error may also distort results. For example, some individuals may assess their memory for faces as excellent, but have few demands made on it because they seldom meet many new people. Differences in the opportunity for error may explain why elderly people paradoxically report fewer memory lapses overall than the young. Yet nobody supposes that their memory is better. Similarly, the

fact that men report fewer lapses than women may be because some items in the questionnaires refer to shopping, and men do less shopping (Rabbitt et al., 1995).

(4) Using memory aids like diaries, address books, shopping lists, or knotted handkerchiefs may protect an individual from memory failures, so that few actually occur, even though memory is poor.

(5) Questions that ask "How often" or "How good" are ambiguous unless they specify a reference point. Providing an objective scale (e.g. instructing the subjects that "often" should be taken to mean about once a week) or specifying comparisons (e.g. How good are you as compared with an average person of your own age?") helps to increase precision.

(6) Response biases may operate that inflate or reduce estimates of frequency. For example, the elderly may be anxious about the possibility of cognitive deterioration and be sensitised to errors. Zelinski, Gilewski, and Thompson (1980) found that whereas young people's self-assessments were quite unrelated to their test scores, elderly people's ratings had greater validity.

(7) Low correlations between psychometric tests and self-assessments may be due simply to the fact that they are measuring different things. If so, it becomes necessary to ask which type of memory ability—the kind assessed by subjective reports or the kind measured by formal tests—is most important or relevant.

(8) The knowledge that people are asked about in questionnaires may be implicit, so that they do not have explicit awareness of this knowledge. For example, in recognition tests that test implicit memory, people may do better than they thought they would.

The factors that govern the everyday performance on which self-assessments are based are different in so many ways from the factors that operate in formal laboratory tests that the lack of agreement is not surprising. The subjective memory beliefs expressed in self-assessment questionnaires should be validated against objective observations of everyday performance, rather than against laboratory tests. Some researchers (e.g. Broadbent, Cooper, Fitzgerald, & Parkes, 1982; Sunderland, Harris, & Baddeley, 1983) have tried to check the validity of self-assessments by having a partner or close relative provide a parallel set of ratings. If I rate my tendency to lose objects as very rare, this can then be checked against my partner's observations. In the case of normal intact subjects these third-party ratings correlate only weakly with self-ratings, but for neurological patients the concordance is much higher. One reason for this discrepancy may be that in normal people the number of memory failures is relatively small. What is wanted, however, are more studies correlating self-assessments with ecologically valid tests that are close analogues of everyday situations, such as some of the tests in the Rivermead Behavioural Memory test battery (Wilson, Cockburn, & Baddeley, 1985) or Martin's (1986) study in which she validated subjects' ratings of their own ability to keep appointments with objective records of how often they had missed appointments while serving on the subject panel.

The technique of meta-analysis, which combines the data from numerous separate but similar studies and thereby increases the number of data points and the power of the analysis, has also been used to strengthen the validity of conclusions about memory ability based on questionnaires (Hultsch, Hertzog, & Dixon, 1987). Meta-analysis has become increasingly popular as a theoretical tool and is now applied to many different types of research, but there are serious doubts about the legitimacy of this procedure. Lepper (1995, p.412) questions the "fundamental premise . . . that studies that differ in their specific manipulations, procedures, and measures can be compared in terms of a single 'unbiased' and 'objective' index of effect size". Meta-analysis often combines and gives equal weight to good and poor studies, lumping together weak and strong effects and negative and positive results. In Lepper's view it can produce an illusion of quantitative precision by ignoring important qualitative differences.

Despite some doubts about their validity, self-assessment questionnaires have proved valuable in a number of ways. They have clearly indicated that people view their own memories as a set of specific abilities with specific strengths and weaknesses. Memory is not seen as being "good" or "bad" overall. Instead, people recognise that they may be good at remembering some things and poor at others. Self-assessment questionnaires provide a "profile" of memory ability that is considered more revealing than overall scores (Chaffin & Herrman, 1983).

These profiles have produced evidence for individual differences in memory style. Sehulster (1988) claims to have identified three factors in memory ability. A verbal factor includes memory for words, stories, facts, and jokes. An autobiographical factor includes memory for personal experiences, emotions, dreams, scenes, smells, and music. The third factor is prospective memory, which is essentially memory for things that have to be done, and includes memory for actions, plans, anniversaries, paying bills, appointments, etc. Sehulster has developed a typology of memory that characterises individuals according to their pattern of scores on these three factors. Factor analysis has been widely used to search for underlying structures in the memory abilities reported in questionnaire responses. Unfortunately, the results of different studies have disagreed about the number and nature of the constituent factors. Pollina, Greene, Tunick, and Puckett (1992) identified five dimensions of everyday memory in young adults: distractibility, misdirected actions, spatial/kinaesthetic memory, interpersonal intelligence and memory for names. Others have found either more or fewer. Richardson and Chan (1994) noted perceptively that everyday memory dimensions tend to be domain-specific. Intercorrelations between items on the questionnaires tend to be weak and subjective reports reflect specific memory abilities in domains such as memory for faces, actions, or routes, and fail to reflect global processes of remembering and forgetting.

As well as being used to differentiate individuals, questionnaires also provide an instrument for examining differences between groups like the young and the old (Cohen & Faulkner, 1984; Perlmutter, 1978) or studying changes over time following head injuries (Sunderland et al., 1983). And, in general, it is useful to know what people think about their memories because beliefs and expectations about memory performance (even if they are not accurate) affect many aspects of everyday behaviour, including people's preferences, the kind of tasks they are willing to tackle and the way they respond to information dissemination. Richardson and Chan (1995) concluded that "these subjective reports provide meaningful accounts of a particular individual's experience of learning and remembering in their daily life" (p.188).

Despite some reservations and difficulties, if self-report data derived from protocols and questionnaires are used and interpreted with care and caution, they can be a valid and valuable source of information about memory in everyday life.

Naturalistic Experiments

The other main approach to the study of everyday memory retains the experimental method, but attempts to devise experiments that are more naturalistic, more ecologically valid or representative of real life than the traditional laboratory experiment. Typically, such experiments involve testing people's memory for more natural material, such as stories, films, or maps, instead of the traditional lists of nonsense syllables, letters, or digits. In some cases, they may test memory for events that occurred naturally in the subject's daily life rather than for material selected and constructed by the experimenter. Thus, for example, researchers have studied college teachers' ability to remember the names or faces of their former students (Bahrick, 1984a) or John Dean's ability to remember conversations with Nixon (Neisser, 1982a). In other examples, naturalistic experiments may involve testing memory for specially constructed materials, but are carried out in natural environments outside the laboratory, such as Baddeley's (1982) study, which tested deep-sea divers' ability to remember information while they were on the sea-bed.

The naturalistic experiment is essentially a compromise in which the researcher tries to ensure the task and conditions are as close to those that obtain in real life as possible, while at the same time imposing enough control and standardisation of the procedure so that definite conclusions can be drawn from the findings. The aim is to ensure that memory in the more structured research context preserves the essential aspects of memory in the natural context. Of course, an experimental procedure can never be exactly the same as a real life situation. A certain amount of ecological validity must be sacrificed to ensure that manageable and informative results are produced. The researcher must classify and compare; must exclude or ignore some variables and focus on others; must impose some form of measurement or testing; must interpret the findings and extract generalisations from them. In doing so, it is inevitable that the natural context of the memory act is changed to some extent. Using experimental methods also affects the subjects' behaviour. In an experiment, subjects know they are being tested. They may be anxious, bored or eager to impress, and the material, or task, is liable to be more simplified and more orderly than real events.

Cognitive Modelling

It may seem that computer models are too abstract, generalised and artificial to represent memory in real world settings, but this is not the case. Hayes-Roth and Hayes-Roth (1979) developed a model, described in Chapter 2, that simulated planning errands. Burton and Bruce (1992) implemented a model that simulates the difficulty of retrieving people's names. These and other computer models represent very simplified versions of the real world analogue and are designed to suggest detailed mechanisms that could subserve the same functions and produce the same phenomena.

Another approach to the study of everyday memory relies on neuropsychological evidence. The relationship between types of memory impairment and their effects on memory function in everyday life can throw light on the mechanisms involved (Parkin, 1987). However, the focus of this book is on normal memory function, and neuropsychological research lies outside its scope.

CONCLUSIONS

As the two kinds of memory research, in the world of the laboratory and in the real world, continue to coexist and converge, it becomes increasingly clear that the relationship between memory in the laboratory and memory out in the real world is one of cross-fertilisation. The two approaches are not really antagonistic. Baddeley (1993) concluded that the hostilities between researchers working in different traditions constitute a phoney war. The consensus view now is that laboratory research and everyday research are complementary. They exert a useful and mutually beneficial influence on each other. Laboratory research is enriched and extended; everyday research is disciplined and guided.

As Baddeley and Wilkins (1984) have pointed out, everyday memory research provides a testing ground for the theories and findings that have resulted from 100 years of laboratory experiments. Studies of everyday memory test the range of situations to which the laboratory based findings apply. Do they generalise to the real world? Can they be applied to naturally occurring phenomena? This relationship between the two approaches works to ensure that the laboratory experiments are not sterile. Laboratory research has a tendency, left to itself, to become incestuous, endlessly exploring its own paradigms. Everyday research acts as a corrective to this tendency by opening up new lines of inquiry. The functional questions about what memory is for, which arise in the everyday context, provide a better basis for laboratory research than theory-building for its own sake.

The benefits do not flow in one direction only. Everyday research also draws heavily on what has been learned in the laboratory. Although the results obtained in the laboratory are unlikely to be precisely replicated in the real world, some of the general principles, the organising concepts, and the distinctions and classifications derived from traditional studies can be carried over and used to give shape and structure to research on everyday memory. Throughout the chapters that follow, the studies of everyday memory that are described illustrate the debt that everyday memory research owes to the traditional approach. The findings are commonly interpreted in terms of these general principles even if the fit is, at times, rather loose. Distinctions like those between episodic and semantic memory or attentional and automatic processes or constructive and copy theories are frequently employed. Models such as schema theory and production systems are applied and concepts such as levels of processing, metamemory, and scripts are used to make sense of the data and supply a guiding framework for further research. It would be unrealistic to suppose, however, that the data from everyday memory research is going to fit very neatly and precisely into the theoretical models it borrows. Because of the complex and wide-ranging nature of the topics studied it is not to be expected that any one model should be able to account for all of the findings. The extent to which everyday memory research has borrowed and adopted the theories generated by traditional laboratory research underlines the fact that everyday memory research itself has so far been relatively unsuccessful in developing strong predictive theories of its own. In this respect, the critics appear to be vindicated.

In addition to the rapprochement between traditional memory research and everyday memory research, the naturalistic approach has helped to reduce the gulf between cognitive psychology and social psychology. Memory research that takes place in a real world context cannot possibly ignore social factors. This is particularly obvious, when social and cognitive psychologists come together in the study of collaborative remembering.

A LOOK AHEAD

In the chapters that follow different aspects of everyday memory are loosely grouped together according to the type of memory function. These groupings are often rather arbitrary because, in practice, different types of memory function overlap and interact in most everyday activities. Chapter 2 examines memory for actions and includes monitoring ongoing sequences of actions, remembering what to do and when to do it, and planning how to carry out complex actions. Chapter 3 concentrates on the use of visual memory and includes remembering maps and routes, and remembering the location and appearance of objects. Chapter 4 is concerned with memory for events including the testimony of witnesses and memory for dramatic public events. Chapter 5 is about memory for people. This chapter includes memory for faces and for voices and a section on memory for proper names, which turns out to be a distinct and peculiar type of memory. Chapter 6 focuses on autobiographical memory for personal experiences. Of course, memory for personal experiences includes remembering places and faces, objects and events. Chapter 7 discusses memory for knowledge including general knowledge and metaknowledge, which is concerned with knowing what we know. These kinds of knowledge, though not so obviously "everyday", are nevertheless used in many daily activities. Chapter 8 deals with memory for expertise and specialist knowledge, such as expertise in chess and music and how these affect performance, and Chapter 9 is concerned with verbal memory, with remembering spoken information and written information. Chapter 10 focuses on memory for internal mental events and discusses reality monitoring, which is the ability to distinguish between real and imagined events, and the role of memory in dreams, a topic of increasing interest to cognitive psychologists. Readers may be surprised to find that these internally generated events are considered to be an important aspect of memory which is not confined to processing externally derived stimuli and generating external responses. This emphasis is because, in real life, as opposed to laboratory experiments, one of the main functions of memory is to support reflections, daydreams, plans, evaluations, and reasoning that take place covertly and may never issue in any identifiable response. Another important point to bear in mind is that naturally occurring memories are very often memories of memories rather than memories of the originally perceived objects and events. In everyday life, re-remembering is more common than first time or one-off acts of remembering.

In each of these chapters, the findings, observations and phenomena are described, and cognitive models and theories are introduced where relevant to show how these can help to explain and illuminate the workings of memory in the real world. More comprehensive accounts of these theories can be found elsewhere. Here they are presented only in enough detail to show how they apply to real world memory. In the explanation and interpretation of memory function, common sense intuitions are frequently invoked. Everyday memory research is an area where common sense has a good deal to contribute. In particular, where theory or data offend against common sense it is a powerful indication that they should be carefully re-examined.

2 Memory for Intentions, Actions, and Plans

THE ROLE OF MEMORY

Traditional studies of memory focused primarily on verbal memory but the current concern with memory in real life situations brings with it a new emphasis on memory for actions. Norman (1988) has identified seven stages of action, and memory has a role at each of these stages:

(1) forming the goal—deciding on the desired outcome;
(2) forming the intention—deciding to do something to achieve the goal;
(3) specifying the action or action sequence—deciding how to do it—formulating the plan;
(4) executing the action or actions;
(5) perceiving the state of the world, especially perceiving the effects of the action;
(6) interpreting the state of the world; and
(7) evaluating the outcome in respect to the initial goal.

In Norman's formulation, these seven stages form a continuous cycle, but in real life they may be spread over a long period of time with delays between each stage so that memory is involved in linking each stage to the others, and the goal must be held in mind throughout all the stages.

The first three stages are concerned with intentions and plans. Before embarking on an action sequence that is novel or complex, we usually spend some time thinking what we are going to do, how best to achieve the goal, in what order to perform the individual actions and how much time and effort will need to be allocated to the task. Memory is involved in formulating such plans, holding the elements and sequence in mind while the plan is being assembled, evaluated, revised, and implemented. For large-scale plans like how to start a business or write a book we would not rely on internal memory alone, but would employ external aids in the form of written schedules and memos. Less ambitious plans, like packing for a holiday or organising a party, may be formulated in memory. When it comes to implementation of the plan, the component actions are assembled in some form of output buffer and the memory system monitors the output of actions from the buffer to ensure that the plan is implemented correctly. When the effects of the actions are perceived and evaluated the original goal must be retrieved to see if it has been achieved. Thus, memory is involved at every stage of intentions, plans, and actions.

PROSPECTIVE MEMORY

What is Prospective Memory?

Everyday memory does not only consist of a record of past events. As well as remembering what has happened in the past, we also use memory, as Norman's analysis has emphasised, to store intentions and plans. Most importantly, we need to remember to actually perform the intended actions, and memory is also involved in keeping track of ongoing actions and of the actions we intend to carry out in the future. This type of memory is known as prospective memory. Everyday memory research lays particular emphasis on memory functions, and remembering to carry out daily tasks is one of the most basic of these functions. If this kind of memory is impaired people are very severely incapacitated.

Retrospective memory involves remembering events experienced in the past, but prospective memory is memory for a future act. Prospective memory includes remembering a plan of action (i.e. what to do) and also remembering to do it. In most cases, the planned action has to be performed at a specified time, or within some time limits, so prospective memory also involves remembering when to perform the act. In everyday life, prospective memory is almost continuously active. We go through the day employing prospective memory to remember to pay the gas bill; to phone a relative; to buy more cat food; to raise a point at a meeting; to look up a reference in the library; and so on. In some cases, failures of prospective remembering may have serious, or even catastrophic, consequences. The safety of many people may depend on the prospective memory of pilots, doctors, and those in charge of machinery.

A major point of interest is the relationship between prospective and retrospective memory. Baddeley and Wilkins (1984) have pointed out that, in practice, the distinction between the two kinds of memory is not absolutely clear-cut because prospective memory necessarily includes some elements of retrospective memory. In remembering my plan to phone my mother, I also remember, retrospectively, her number and how to use the phone, and not to call while she is watching her favourite televison programme. However, despite this overlap between the two kinds of memory, there are numerous distinguishing features (West, 1984). Prospective memory differs from retrospective memory at the encoding stage, as prospective plans are usually self-generated and do not involve initial learning, but the difference between the two is perhaps more marked at the retrieval stage. In prospective memory, the amount of information that has to be remembered is usually small. You need only remember to post the letter, call the plumber, or whatever. In most retrospective memory tasks the amount of information that has to be recalled is much greater.

Some studies have also shown that prospective memory ability and retrospective memory ability show signs of dissociation. Kvavilashvili (1987) found no significant correlation between retrospective and prospective memory. In her study those subjects who were good at the prospective task of remembering to give a message to the experimenter were not necessarily good at recalling the content of the message, and vice versa. Wilkins and Baddeley (1978) actually found a negative correlation. They designed a prospective memory study to simulate remembering to take pills at a specific time. Subjects had to press a button on a small box at 8.30 a.m., 1.00 p.m., 5.30 p.m. and 10 p.m. each day for 7 days. The apparatus in the box recorded the time of each button press. Lateness of response increased across the 7 days, and across each day, with early responses being more accurate than later ones, perhaps because, later in the day, competing activities were distracting. The same subjects were also given a retrospective memory test of free recall of lists of unrelated words. It emerged that those who had good retrospective verbal memory did poorly on the prospective task, a phenomenon labelled the "absentminded professor effect". The same evidence of dissociation is also evident in studies of the effects of ageing on memory. Cockburn and Smith (1988) reported that tests of prospective memory are particularly sensitive to ageing. They administered the Rivermead Behavioural Memory Tests, a battery that includes both prospective and retrospective tests. The two prospective items were remembering to make a new appointment and remembering to ask for the return of a personal possession given to the tester at the start of the session. These prospective tasks were particularly likely to show an age deficit. Huppert and Beardsall (1993) used the same test battery with groups of normal elderly people and patients with varying degrees of dementia. Their results suggested that a discrepancy between performance on retrospective and prospective tests may be an indicator of early dementia.

Studies of memory following brain injuries have also shown that the underlying neuropathology associated with deficits in prospective memory may be different from those associated with retrospective memory deficits. Shimamura, Janowsky, and Squire (1991) have identified prospective memory deficits with damage to the frontal lobes which are also involved in planning, decision-making, the inhibitory control of irrelevant actions, and the sequencing and monitoring of activity (Kimberg & Farah, 1993).

Although there are logical and functional differences between prospective and retrospective memory, it is by no means clear that prospective memory is a distinct and separate memory system. It is not too surprising that prospective memory for taking medicine does not correlate strongly with the kind of retrospective memory involved in recall of word lists from long-term memory because these are very different tasks. When the tasks are more similar a different result emerges. Hitch and Ferguson (1991) compared prospective and retrospective memory in a study that tested the ability of members of a film society to recall, retrospectively, the names of films they had seen in the past and to recall, prospectively, the names of films they intended to see in the future. The two kinds of memory showed interesting correspondences. Retrospective memory for past films showed the usual recency effect with better recall of more recent films. As shown in Fig. 2.1, prospective memory for future films showed an analogous proximity effect. Films that would be seen sooner were better remembered.

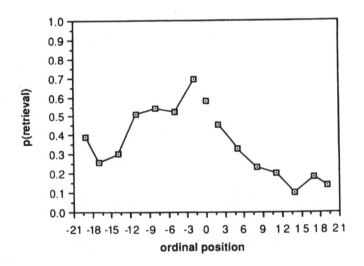

FIG. 2.1.   Proportion of films retrieved as a function of ordinal position in subjects' film diaries (zero = current film; negative numbers = past films; positive numbers = future films). (from Hitch & Ferguson, 1991). Reproduced with permission.

For both past and future films, memory was inversely related to the total number of films and there was a small but significant correlation between an individuals's retrospective and prospective memory. It is still not clear, therefore, how far prospective memory should be regarded as a distinct and separate memory system.

Types of Prospective Memory

Prospective memory is probably much too broad a category to be useful. As research in this area progresses, distinctions between different types of prospective memory are being made. One obvious distinction is between self-imposed prospective tasks, and prospective tasks imposed by someone else. Another distinction is between prospective plans that are routine plans, and involve remembering to perform habitual, often-performed, routine actions; and prospective plans that are novel plans and involve novel actions or novel modifications of familiar actions, such as performing familiar actions at different times or in novel contexts. A prospective plan may be for a single isolated action, or it may be part of a complex network of related plans. Some prospective plans are highly specific and detailed (e.g. going to a particular shop and buying a particular brand of cat food), and others are vaguer and more general (e.g. do the shopping). This distinction is one of level of formulation.

This point about specificity also applies to the timing, as well as the content, of the plan. Prospective memory involves time-monitoring as well as remembering. Ellis (1988) distinguished between "pulses" and "steps". A pulse is a prospective plan that specifies an exact time at which it must be implemented (e.g. 3.15 on Tuesday afternoon). A step is a much more indefinite plan (e.g. before the library closes; next time I see him; after I've finished everything else I have to do today). Ellis found that pulses are better recalled than steps, are judged to be more important, and people are more likely to use an external memory aid such as a diary to remind them of pulses. Consideration of variations in the specificity of timing leads on to a further distinction that rests on priority. Some plans are of vital importance and have high priority; others are much less important and have low priority. It is not necessarily the case that a prospective plan is implemented if it is remembered. Different plans may compete with each other for implementation time. Busy people have whole sets of prospective plans waiting to be implemented. Some will be postponed, some will be truncated, and some will be discarded altogether.

Einstein and McDaniel (1990) have distinguished between two kinds of prospective memory on the basis of the cues that trigger retrieval. Time-based prospective memory requires performance either at a specific time or after some period of time has elapsed. In event-based prospective memory the action is cued by a an object, person, or event (e.g. putting on your coat reminds you to take it to the cleaners). Time-based prospective memories are generally harder to remember because the passage of time has to be monitored and remembering is self-initiated, whereas in event-based prospective memory the reminder is supplied by the context—there is some kind of external event which cues the prospective memory. Einstein and McDaniel (1991) showed that elderly people showed no deficit in event-based memory but were poorer at time-based tasks and the distinction receives further support from a study by Sellen, Louie, Harris, and Wilkins (in press). Their subjects had to remember to press a button on a badge either at specified times or when they were in specified places. In the time-based prospective memory task the subjects averaged 33% hits but in the place-cued version (which counts as an event-based task) they achieved 52% hits.

All these differences between various types of prospective memory are significant because they are likely to influence its efficiency. Both theoretical and common sense considerations suggest that novel, high-priority event-based plans that are part of a network of related plans are more likely to be remembered.

Methods of Studying Prospective Memory

Devising methods for studying prospective memory presents a challenge. The methods that have been adopted include questionnaires, naturalistic experiments and laboratory experiments. Questions about prospective memory have often been incorporated in a number of questionnaires, for example, "How often do you forget to keep appointments?" or "How often do you forget to take things with you when you go out?" or "How often do you forget to say something you intended to say?" Problems about the validity of self-assessments of this kind were discussed at greater length in Chapter 1, p.15–19. One difficulty is that subjects may not always be aware of failures of prospective memory. Of course, failure to implement some plans is noticed because it brings serious consequences or earns bitter reproaches, but other failures may well pass unnoticed. In an experimental prospective memory task, Wilkins and Baddeley (1978), in their pill-taking study, noted that although subjects remembered when they had performed planned actions, they tended to be unaware of omissions. This finding suggests that self-assessment of prospective memory is likely to be inaccurate.

Several studies have reported that elderly people assess their prospective memory as better than young people assess theirs (Harris & Sunderland, 1987). Logically, this could arise if elderly people more often fail to notice their errors, or, having noticed them at the time, they forget about them later, but Martin (1986) concluded that they were essentially accurate in their self-assessment. She found that an elderly group rated their memory as better than a young group for keeping appointments, paying bills, and taking medicine. Objective records of their attendance at appointments confirmed their superiority. However, questionnaire responses do not reveal how far successful prospective remembering was due to the use of external reminders and how far the respondents relied on their own memory. The apparent superiority of elderly people could also arise if their life style is more relaxed so that the demands on prospective memory are less severe for them than for the young. All these factors make questionnaire responses unlikely to be an accurate reflection of prospective memory ability.

The method that provides more objective evidence of success or failure is the naturalistic experiment. Researchers on prospective memory set subjects a specific task, such as remembering to post a postcard or make a phone call to the experimenter at a designated time. This method allows the experimenter to vary factors such as the retention interval; the number and spacing of the to-be-remembered actions; and the incentives that are offered for successful performance. Sometimes, prospective memory tasks are incorporated in an interview (West, 1984). In her study, remembering to keep the interview appointment was one test of prospective memory. Subjects were also told at the beginning of the interview that they should remember to locate a folder and hand it to the interviewer at the end of the session.

A number of problems can arise with naturalistic experiments like these. Although the experimenter can manipulate some of the relevant variables, there is no way of controlling other, potentially relevant, variables operating during the retention interval, such as the amount of rehearsal and the number of competing tasks. Maylor (1990) used a telephone call task and later debriefed subjects about the strategies they had used. She classified these as conjunction cues (mentally linking making the phone call to another routine event), external cues (using notes, diaries, alarm clocks), and internal cues (relying on memory, rehearsing the task, mentally reviewing a schedule). The older subjects did less well than the young group, but only when they were relying on internal cues. Thus, the results of the experiment were misleading unless the underlying strategies were disclosed and taken into account.

Experiments like these are examples of ones that have high ecological validity, retaining a close resemblance to the naturally occurring tasks of everyday life, but in so doing they sacrifice the element of control and are therefore difficult to interpret. Another problem is that the number of observations (e.g., the number of telephone calls made or postcards posted) per subject is low, making the data difficult to interpret.

Laboratory studies of prospective memory suffer from different problems (see Kvavilashvili, 1992, for a review). West (1986) designed an experiment varying the load on prospective memory. She required subjects to carry out a sequence of up to 14 actions (such as put the comb on the table, put the toothbrush in the bag) and recorded omission errors and order errors for young and older subjects. There was a clear age deficit in ability to carry out the longer-action sequences. However, the task is a very artificial one. In everyday life people seldom need to memorise 14 unrelated actions. A number of recent studies have built prospective memory tasks into a text-processing paradigm (e.g. Evans, Wilson, & Baddeley, 1994). For example, subjects must remember to underline certain target words in the text, to put a tick at the end of a page, to get up, and to switch off the room lights at the end of a passage. Other experimenters have embedded a prospective task into a short term-memory task (e.g. Einstein & McDaniel, 1990). Here, the primary task is to study a list of words for subsequent recall; the prospective task is to press a key when a target word occurs. It is arguable, however, whether such tasks are a fair test of prospective memory or whether they are tests of the allocation of attention between a primary task and a secondary task.

Even when a laboratory study of prospective memory involves a naturalistic task, the unfamiliar environment of the laboratory may affect the results. Ceci, Baker, and Bronfenbrenner (1988) studied the behaviour of children who had to remember to take cakes out of the oven after 30 minutes. As shown in Fig. 2.2, the frequency and pattern of clock-checking was significantly different when the task was performed at home and when it was performed in the laboratory. At home, the children checked the clock often in the first 10 minutes but then only infrequently until the last few minutes.

Ceci et al. (1988) suggested that the children used the frequent initial checks to calibrate their subjective psychological clock with the objective external clock and then were able to rely on internal monitoring. This interpretation was confirmed by the fact that the same calibration strategy was evident even if the clock was made to run faster or slower than normal. In the laboratory, clock-checking was 30% more frequent and showed a different pattern, increasing in frequency across the 30-minute period. This study is important because it demonstrates that an interesting strategy for time-based prospective remembering was only revealed in naturalistic conditions. Clearly, conclusions about prospective memory are highly sensitive to the particular methodology that is used.

Prospective Memory Efficiency

Much of the research on prospective memory has been concerned with identifying the factors that promote successful remembering or induce failure. The nature of the prospective task is one of these factors, but other

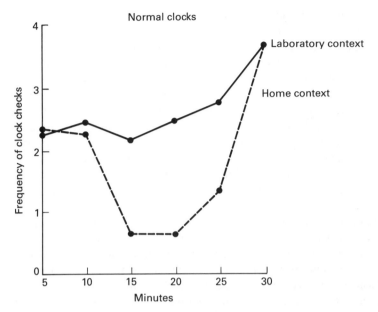

FIG. 2.2. Children's frequency of monitoring a clock during cooking in a laboratory and home context (from Ceci, Baker, & Bronfenbrenner, 1988). Reprinted by permission John Wiley & Sons Ltd.

important determinants arise from how the task is encoded and the kind of strategies, reminders, and cues that are used. Meacham and Leiman (1975) gave people postcards to post back at varying intervals up to 32 days later. Half the subjects were given coloured tags to hang on their key chains as a reminder, and there was some evidence that this improved performance. McDaniel and Einstein (1993) have demonstrated that cues that are highly distinctive and specific are most effective. A real life example is the loud beeping signal that reminds me to turn off the car lights when I park.

However, many people spontaneously devise their own reminders. Moscovitch (1982) suggested that the superior performance of the elderly in some prospective memory tasks is due to increasing reliance on external reminders. Elderly people are known to make more use of written reminders in diaries and notes, and Harris (1980) also reported that middle-aged women made extensive use of reminders such as calendars and wall charts to remember family birthdays and social commitments. Other people make knots in handkerchiefs, leave objects where the eye will fall on them, or write in biro on their hands. Differences in the extent to which people devise internal and external reminders, and use them efficiently, may underlie observed differences in prospective task performance between individuals, age groups, or sexes.

Another important factor in prospective memory is motivation. This operates in two ways, affecting both compliance and memory. For a prospective act to be performed, the actor must not only remember to perform it, but also must be willing to perform it. A patient may remember a hospital appointment, but not feel like going, or may remember to take prescribed medication, but decide not to take it. These are examples where poor motivation, rather than a failure of prospective memory, has caused a failure of compliance. But the level of motivation may also affect whether the prospective act is remembered. It is a truism that very important appointments are rarely missed. When a job interview is make-or-break, you get there on time. A high level of motivation may ensure that an elaborate reminder system is set up and the sequence of events is carefully planned and frequently rehearsed.

These common sense observations have been confirmed experimentally. Meacham and Singer (1977) gave subjects eight postcards to post back one a week for eight weeks. One group was offered a cash incentive for posting on time, which produced a small improvement in performance. Poon and Schaffer (1982) asked subjects to phone in 25 times over a 3-week period at specific times. Although a cash incentive had no effect on the proportion of calls remembered, the payment did improve the accuracy of timing for the elderly subjects but not for the young subjects. The effects of experimental manipulation of motivation by incentives is not very striking, but it seems probable that self-generated motivation in naturally occurring prospective memory tasks is a more powerful factor.

Other factors that are potentially relevant have so far received little attention. These include emotion and personality traits and states such as levels of anxiety and stress, and the effects of fatigue and illness. Cockburn and Smith (1994), in one of the few studies that have addressed these problems, found a complex relationship beween level of anxiety and performance on a prospective memory task. Their findings suggested that both low and high levels of anxiety can be beneficial, but intermediate levels produce more failures. At this level there is sufficient anxiety to produce errors but not enough to induce the extra effort needed to over-come them. Searleman and Gaydusek (1989) also reported that people with Type A personalities, who are highly conscientious, tense, competitive worriers, are better at prospective memory tasks.

Another factor that has been studied experimentally is timing. Time factors such as the length of the retention interval, the time of day, and the regularity of target times have been manipulated. By analogy with retrospective memory, and in line with the proximity effect in Hitch and Ferguson's (1991, p.28) study of memory for films, it would be expected that prospective memory would decline as the retention interval increased. However, Wilkins (1976) varied the retention interval in a postcard task from 2 to 36 days, but found no effect of increasing delay. This finding reinforces the view that prospective memory does not operate like retrospective memory. Harris and Wilkins (1982) studied the effect of response spacing. Subjects were asked to hold up a card at 3- or 9-minute intervals while watching a film. They found no effect of response spacing and no effect of the stage of the film. The interesting finding in this study was that subjects sometimes forgot to make the response even though they had checked the time within the previous 10 seconds. In this situation, with the competing activity of watching the film, it was difficult to hold prospective intentions in mind even for a very short time. Everyday life often involves concurrent tasks, and we are often distracted from our prospective intentions as, absorbed in one activity, we forget to interrupt it and do something else. The amount and type of concurrent activity are likely to be important factors in naturally occurring prospective memory. Ellis and Nimmo-Smith (1993) noted that their subjects reported more rehearsal of future intentions when their concurrent task required little attention, and common sense suggests that busy people with a lot on their minds might perform differently from those with a more relaxed schedule.

Prospective memory efficiency is also affected by the relationship between goal and action. Studies that are indirectly relevant to prospective memory were carried out by Lichtenstein and Brewer (1980) and Brewer and Dupree (1983). They were investigating memory for actions that had already been performed, rather than memory for future actions. They proposed that goal-directed sequences of actions are organised within an overall plan schema. Within the plan schema, the actions are linked by the *in-order-to* relationship to an overall goal. In their example, the actor takes keys from pocket in-order-to unlock the door in-order-to open the door in-order-to go into the house. The overall goal, at the top of the goal hierarchy, is getting into the house. In a recall test, actions higher up in the goal hierarchy were remembered better than those lower down, and actions that did not relate directly to the main goal (e.g. putting keys back into pocket) were also less well remembered. They concluded that plan schemas have a strong influence on recall of actions. Brewer and Dupree, in a further series of experiments, were able to clarify the role of plan schemas. Their results indicated that, over time, information about actions was progressively lost from the hierarchy in a bottom-up direction, but the plan schema was used to reconstruct the whole action sequence at the retrieval stage. In everyday life, prospective plans are commonly embedded within each other. For example, my plan to remember to buy some eggs is embedded in a higher-order plan to make a birthday cake. If prospective plans are like retrospective actions in being better remembered when they are embedded in a plan schema, then experiments on prospective memory may be underestimating everyday ability by using isolated tasks that do not form part of a plan schema.

Theoretical Perspectives on Prospective Memory

Prospective memory is closely related to the theoretical principles and models of mainstream memory research. One theoretical issue concerns the nature of the memory representation for future actions. Koriat, Ben-Zur, and Nussbaum (1990) argued that if the representation is verbal then memory should be better if tested by verbal recall than when tested by actual performance. If the representation is enactive or motoric then memory should be better when tested by performance. The results of their experiments showed that when subjects had to remember a series of actions, the perform mode of recall was superior. This superiority was especially evident if the subjects knew in advance that they would be asked to perform the actions. Koriat et al. (1990, p.577) concluded that "the encoding of future tasks entails an internal symbolic enactment of the tasks which enhances memory", but did not rule out the possibility that the representation may include a mixture of verbal, imaginal, and enactive elements. The nature of the representation is crucial because the effectiveness of a cue in triggering retrieval of a prospective memory depends on the relationship between the cue and the representation. In line with the principle of encoding specificity (Tulving & Thomson, 1973), a representation of locking the door that includes an image of the bunch of keys lying on the kitchen table is more likely to be activated when the keys are seen.

Like Koriat et al., Vallacher and Wegner (1987) also concluded that there are multiple representations of a given action or action sequence and that these multiple representations are organised hierarchically with the general goal at the highest level and specific details at the lower levels. Thus, the same action sequence may be represented at different levels as "seeing if someone is home", "pushing the doorbell", and "moving the index finger". The dominant control moves up and down the levels as the action sequence is in progress and is affected by the difficulty, familiarity, and complexity of the action. For actions that are easy and familiar, control tends to remain at the higher level; for difficult, unfamiliar actions, control shifts to the specific details at the lowest level. The level at which an intended action is represented is likely to affect the success or failure of prospective memory. High-level representations may be too general to be triggered by specific cues. A high-level general intention like "give a party" is less likely to be cued by an external event or object than a lower-level specific intention like "buy the drinks" or "invite John". The cognition-action link between the cognitive representation of action and overt behaviour is not yet fully understood.

Interestingly, Goschke and Kuhl (1993) have reported an "intention-superiority effect". Subjects read passages of text describing simple activities. Some of these actions had to be executed later and some had to be recalled. Words from the to-be-executed items were recognised faster than words from the to-be-recalled items and this effect was attributed to a heightened level of persisting activation for intentions.

Another theoretical issue concerns the mechanism of prospective memory. The idea that the central executive component of working memory schedules, controls and monitors actions can be applied to prospective memory. This account is also consistent with the concept of a Supervisory Activating System (SAS), proposed by Norman and Shallice (1986), which acts to maintain goals and resist distractions, and is also capable of interrupting and changing ongoing behaviour in accordance with the prevailing context. Norman and Shallice have identified the frontal lobes of the brain with the operation of the SAS. The frontal lobes are responsible for planning, organising, and controlling actions, and patients who have sustained damage to the frontal lobes show a *frontal lobe syndrome* that includes increased distractability and inability to allocate attention effectively. Although they perform normally on many cognitive tests, these patients are distinguished by a disabling inability to organise their daily lives. Shallice and Burgess (1991) tested three patients with severe frontal lobe damage on a range of tasks including analogues of real life planning. The Six Element Task required them to schedule and carry out two sets of three different tasks (dictating a route, solving 35 arithmetic problems, and writing the names of 100 pictured objects) within 15 minutes. Relative to control subjects, the patients were unable to allocate their time between the tasks. The Multiple Errands Task required them to carry out eight different errands (buying a loaf, buying throat pastilles, writing down the name of a shop, etc.) in a shopping precinct. Again the patients performed very poorly, breaking the rules and failing to complete the tasks, and although they were able to memorise the instructions, they seemed unable to organise their performance. Shallice and Burgess (1991) identified deficits in formulating, modifying, and evaluating an overall plan, and for creating triggering markers for the individual tasks within the plan. Goldstein, Bernard, Fenwick, Burgess, and McNeil (1993) reported very similar patterns in the performance of another patient with unilateral frontal lobectomy. The relationship demonstrated in these studies between frontal lobe damage and impaired prospective memory is consistent with the theoretical model in which these functions are controlled by the Supervisory Attentional System, or the central executive component of working memory.

ABSENTMINDEDNESS AND SLIPS OF ACTION

Errors of prospective memory involve failing to carry out a plan or to comply with an instruction to do something. These can be distinguished from absentmindedness and slips of action. As defined by Norman (1981), a slip is an error that occurs when a person does an action that is not intended. Errors of this kind arise during the performance of an action sequence. So, absentminded slips of action usually take the form of doing the wrong thing, whereas errors of prospective memory take the form of forgetting to do it at all.

Slips of action are a common experience in daily life and occur both in speech and in nonverbal behaviour. In this chapter we will be concerned with errors in nonverbal actions. We all find ourselves, from time to time, doing things like pouring coffee into the sugar bowl, throwing cheques into the waste-paper basket, or driving towards one destination when we actually intended to go to quite a different one. By analysing the nature and incidence of these kinds of slips, researchers have been able to infer some of the characteristics of the mechanisms that control the performance of action sequences.

Classifying Slips of Action

Reason (1979) asked 35 volunteers to keep a diary record of their slips of action. In two weeks the diaries yielded 400 of these slips, and Reason was able to identify several different categories of error.

(1) *Repetition errors*: Forgetting that an action has already been performed and repeating it, e.g. "I started to pour a second kettle of boiling water into the teapot, forgetting I had just filled it". Reason called these "storage failures" and 40% of his corpus consisted of repetition errors of this kind.

(2) *Goal switches*: Forgetting the goal of a sequence of actions and switching to a different goal, e.g. "I intended to drive to a friend's house but found myself driving to work instead" or "I went upstairs to fetch the dirty washing and came down without the washing, having tidied the bathroom instead". These slips (which Reason called "test failures") formed 20% of his corpus.

(3) *Omissions and reversals*: Omitting or wrongly ordering the component actions of a sequence, e.g. filling the kettle but failing to switch it on, or putting the lid on a container before putting something in it. In Reason's study 18% of the errors were of this kind.

(4) *Confusions/blends*: Confusing objects involved in one action sequence with those involved in another sequence, e.g. taking a tin-opener instead of scissors into the garden to cut flowers. Or confusing the actions

from one sequence with actions from another sequence, as in the case of a woman who reported throwing her earrings to the dog and trying to clip dog biscuits on to her ears. In these cases, there has been crosstalk between two programmes and different action sequences have been confused with each other. About 16% of errors in Reason's study were confusions.

Although the diary records produced good descriptive evidence for the occurrence of these different types of error, the reported incidence of each kind may not be a very accurate record of actual incidence. A particular kind of slip may be reported as more frequent because it is more disruptive and therefore more noticeable. Slips that involve confusions are likely to be particularly memorable because they tend to produce rather ludicrous results, but other slips of action may go unnoticed.

Automatic and Attentional Processes

Some characteristic features have been identified from the classification of slips. The most important finding is that slips of action occur predominantly with highly practised, overlearned, routine activities. Making cups of tea and coffee, for example, are activities that give rise to many of the reported slips of action. This is partly because actions that occur very frequently provide more opportunities for slips to occur. However, the predominance of errors in making tea and coffee is not just evidence of a national obsession, but also arises because these are routine, repeated actions. To understand the underlying mechanism, researchers have applied the distinction between *automatic* and *attentional processes* formulated by Shiffrin and Schneider (1977). Highly practised actions become automatic and can then be carried out according to pre-set instructions, with little or no conscious monitoring. Reason and Mycielska (1982) called this mode of action control an "open loop" system.

Automatic, or open loop, processes differ from attentional, or "closed loop", processes. Attentional processes are under moment-to-moment control by a central processor, which monitors and guides the action sequence, modifying performance according to feedback about changes in external circumstances and internal needs and intentions. A good example of this distinction between automatic and attentional processes occurs when you are driving a car. Emerging from a road junction is (or ought to be) an attentional process. The traffic must be scanned, distances and speeds assessed, and the driver is consciously thinking about the actions that need to be implemented. In contrast, for the practised driver, changing gears is an automatic process. The actions involved do not need to be consciously monitored, and can usually be carried out successfully while the driver is attending to something quite different, like chatting to a passenger or calculating petrol consumption. Automatic action sequences have the advantage that they can be carried out while the conscious mind is free to engage in other parallel activities. However, automatisation can lead to slips of action. Even automatic actions may need intermittent attention to keep them on the right track, and slips of action occur if attention is not shifted to the ongoing action at a critical point in the sequence.

Predisposing Conditions

An action sequence (or programme) that is in frequent use is "stronger" than one that is used less often. There is a tendency for a stronger programme to take over from a weaker programme, particularly if some component stages are common to both, and this type of slip is sometimes known as a "strong habit intrusion" or a "capture error". Slips of action often occur at junctions where two programmes share a particular component and there is an involuntary switchover to the stronger programme. William James (1890) describes these switchovers as "strong habit intrusions". In his example, a person went into the bedroom to change his clothes, took off one garment, and then got undressed completely and went to bed. The stronger "going to bed" programme took over from the "changing clothes" programme because both shared the common components of entering the bedroom and removing the jacket. The types of slip classed as Goal Switches and Confusions may both occur because of strong habit intrusions.

Another predisposing condition, besides automaticity and competition from stronger habits, has been identified by Reason (1984). Any form of change in a well-established routine is liable to produce errors. In one of his examples, someone who had decided to give up sugar on cornflakes sprinkled it on as before. In the same way, the ex-smoker's hand goes to his pocket to take out the cigarettes that are no longer there.

In addition to these predisposing circumstances, there are predisposing internal states. Some individuals are much more prone to make these kinds of errors than other people, but many people find that slips of action increase with tiredness, illness, or stress. Broadbent et al. (1982) developed the Cognitive Failures Questionnaire (CFQ) to serve as an index of an individual's susceptibility to slips of action, as well as other failures of memory and perception. Respondents were asked to assess the frequency with which they experienced specific examples of cognitive failure, for example "Do you forget whether you've turned off the light or fire, or locked the door?" on a 5-point scale ranging from Never to Very Often. Broadbent et al. established that CFQ scores were not related to performance on tests of immediate and delayed memory, or to perception as measured by performance on a word identification task. Martin and Jones

(1984) later attempted to establish whether CFQ scores were related to any other aspects of cognitive ability, or to personality traits and internal states. They found that CFQ scores correlated significantly with ability to perform two tasks at the same time, indicating that poor ability to deploy attention and allocate processing resources effectively is associated with frequent slips of actions as well as other forms of cognitive failure. CFQ scores were also related to forward digit span, which tests ability to maintain a set of items in the correct serial order. This ability is also involved in carrying out action sequences, and the kind of slips classified as omissions and reversals arise as a result of breakdown in the maintenance of the correct serial order for components in an action sequence. Besides these measures of cognitive ability, Martin and Jones also reported an association between frequent cognitive failures and high anxiety, and cited studies by Parkes (1980) comparing nurses working on high-stress wards and low-stress wards, which suggested that cognitive failures are related to vulnerability to the effects of stress.

Just as the level of representation may be an important factor in failures of prospective memory, it can also underlie slips of action. Norman (1988) suggested that some slips are "description errors" and are caused because the action has been ambiguously represented in memory. In one of his examples, someone who threw a dirty shirt into the toilet instead of into the laundry basket had apparently represented the action too generally as "throw object into an open container".

Theoretical Perspectives

Both Reason (1984) and Norman (1981) have developed explanatory models of action control to account for absentminded slips of action. Common to both models is the concept of an *action schema* similar to those described by Vallacher and Wegner (1987). An action schema is a knowledge structure representing the sensorimotor knowledge that constitutes an action sequence. Schemas are linked together in related sets, and several action schemas may be operative simultaneously. Schema theory is described in more detail in Chapter 3, pp.76–82, and the theoretical models of slips and errors are reviewed by Berry (1993).

Reason's Model

In Reason's model there are three levels of control. At the schema level, control is by automatic pre-programmed instructions built into the schemas; the activation of a particular schema initiates the action sequence. Schemas can be activated by sensory information or by another, already active schema. At this level, activation is influenced by recency and frequency of use. Schemas that have been implemented more recently or more frequently (the "strong habit" schemas) have lower thresholds and are more easily activated. The second level of control in Reason's model is the Intention system, which generates goals, and can also activate the schemas that are appropriate for achieving these goals. The Intention system assembles plans, monitors ongoing activity and corrects errors. It has a limited capacity, so that only one plan is maximally active at any one time. At the third level, the Attentional control system acts to energise or suppress the activation of particular schemas, deploying attentional resources in accordance with the goals of the Intention system. Reason conceptualises the complete set of schemas as a "cognitive board" on which attentional resources in the form of an "attentional blob" are moved around and may be concentrated on one particular schema or diffused over several, as shown in Fig. 2.3.

In this model, some action sequences require little or no attentional resources. These are the automatic, open loop, schema-driven ones. Other, higher-level, closed loop action sequences involving complex decision-making require much more attention. Slips of action result from the faulty deployment of attention. For example, the allocation of attention may be too fixed and narrowly concentrated on a very limited number of schemas. This model is mainly a descriptive one and does not generate novel predictions.

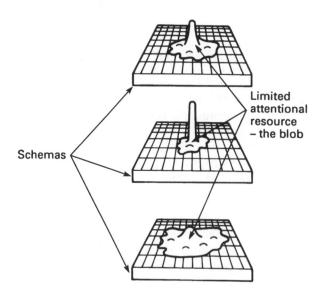

FIG. 2.3. The cognitive board with attentional resources more or less concentrated (from Reason, 1984).

The GEMS Model

More recently, Reason (1990) has outlined the Generic Error Modelling System (GEMS). This system distinguishes between *skill-based slips* in which actions are not executed as planned, *rule-based mistakes*, and *knowledge-based mistakes*. Whereas skill-based slips are failures of monitoring, rule-based mistakes and knowledge-based mistakes are problem-solving failures that do not involve attentional failures. Rule-based mistakes arise because the wrong rule is selected from the stored repertoire, but knowledge-based mistakes arise when the individual has no rule-based solution adequate to deal with the problem. Rule-based mistakes may take the form of applying a good rule in the wrong situation, or using a poor rule. Knowledge-based mistakes may reflect a lack of relevant knowledge or an inaccurate mental model of the problem. This analysis has been able to provide an account of a wide range of errors from pouring the tea into the sugar bowl to nuclear power plant disasters like Chernobyl.

Norman's Model

Norman's (1981) model emphasised the hierarchical organisation of schemas, which work together in organised groups, as in Fig. 2.4.

He called the highest level "parent schemas". These correspond to global intentions or goals (like "having a cup of tea"). Subordinate level "child schemas", or subschemas, correspond to component actions necessary to achieve the overall goal (like "getting out the teapot" or "boiling water"). The activation level of each schema is determined by internal events (plans, needs, intentions) and by external events (the current situation). Each schema also has a set of triggering conditions that must be fulfilled for it to be implemented. These consist of external events and circumstances. A given schema operates when the activation level is above threshold, and the current situation matches the triggering conditions. So,

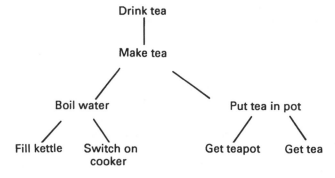

FIG. 2.4.   A hierarchy of action schemas for making tea.

in the tea-drinking example, the intention to have a cup of tea activates the whole set of schemas related to this goal, and the state of the boiling water might constitute the triggering conditions for initiating the teapot-filling subschema.

Slips of action result, according to Norman's model, from faulty specification of the overall intention, faulty activation of the schemas, or faulty triggering. Particular examples of slips can be classified in terms of these causes. The specification of the intention to go to work may be inadequate if it fails to specify the intended form of transport, and could result in getting into the car when you meant to take the bus. Strong habit intrusions or goal switches, like driving to the wrong destination, can be explained as faulty activation. So, for example, the frequently used "going to work" schemas are more highly activated and may take over from the less frequent, less activated "visiting a friend" schemas. In Norman's terminology, this is a capture error. Tidying up the bathroom instead of fetching the washing is also a case of faulty activation. The mess in the bathroom matches the triggering conditions for the bathroom-tidying schema and causes it to be activated. Norman called this kind of slip a data-driven error because the switch originates from externally cued activation. Reversals and repetitions occur when the triggering of an action sequence is faulty, and blends or confusions result if two different schemas are triggered simultaneously. Slips are not always due to competing schemas, but may result if activation is inadequate or fizzles out. In this case, you may be found standing in a room and wondering why you went there, and what you intended to do there. The original intention is no longer activated. Or, you may simply omit to perform the intended action—forgetting to collect your coat from the cleaners, or failing to turn off the electric fire. The activation is insufficient to sustain the performance of the actions. The key feature of Norman's model was the idea that action sequences can be represented at different levels, from a global, general representation of the overall goal at the highest level to specific subordinate actions at the lowest level.

Norman's model and the original version of Reason's model obviously have a good deal in common. In Norman's model, the postulated mechanism for action control is able to account for the different types of error that are observed. Reason's model does not offer such a fine-grained explanation. However, his claim that slips of action can be ascribed to faulty deployment of attention is supported by Martin and Jones' (1984) finding that ability to divide attention efficiently is related to the incidence of slips.

Heckhausen and Beckman (1990) have stressed the need to integrate slips of action into a general theory of intentional behaviour. In their view, actions are guided by mentally represented intentions of two kinds, goal intentions and instrumental intentions. The latter are further subdivided into initiation, implementation, and termination intents. They also distinguish between two control modes. Processing with a wide goal span encompasses a range of overlapping or unrelated activities and is automatic and unconscious; in processing with a narrow goal span all attentional capacity is absorbed by the current ongoing activity. Narrow goal span is associated with unfamiliar and difficult actions. They found that most slips of action occurred with wide goal control and could be categorised in terms of the initiation, implementation or termination phase of action. Their model is similar to Reason's but lays more emphasis on the role of intents and includes problems in terminating actions.

Although many of the examples of slips of action are of trivial everyday actions, similar slips, which may have catastrophic consequences occur in driving, flying planes, operating machinery, medicating patients, and so on. Important lessons about training procedures, the design of equipment, the avoidance of fatigue, and the development of effective cues can be derived from theoretical analyses of slips of action and mistakes such as GEMS (Reason, 1990). Applied psychology and theoretical cognitive psychology are interdependent in this area.

PLANNING

What is Planning?

Prospective memory involves remembering what to do and when to do it. Planning and mental rehearsal are concerned with *how* to do it. As defined by Hayes-Roth and Hayes-Roth (1979), a plan is the "predetermination of a course of action aimed at achieving some goal". According to Battman (1987, p.4), a plan is "an ordered set of control statements to support the efficiency of actions and the preparation of alternative actions for the case of failure". In everyday life, people spend a lot of time planning how to do things. This is particularly true when a prospective task is a novel or complex one involving a sequence of actions, and when decisions have to be taken about which actions will produce the best results. People plan journeys and holidays; what to buy for dinner and what to plant in the garden; how to play a hand of bridge or behave at a job interview. Those actions that are unplanned are very simple or very routine ones, automatic, unconscious actions or purely impulsive actions. For most people a high proportion of their daily activities involve some degree of planning.

Mental practice is a form of planning that consists of mentally simulating an action sequence. This has been found effective in assisting acquisition and enhancing performance in a wide variety of skills and sports such as golf, skating, and diving (Annett, 1991).

Planning is also a type of problem-solving by mental simulation, envisaging the circumstances and running through possible actions, evaluating the consequences, and selecting the optimal actions and the optimal order for executing them. Planning depends on memory. Knowledge derived from past experience and stored in long-term memory must be retrieved and used in formulating possible plans, and in constructing representations of hypothetical events. A working memory buffer store is needed to hold tentative or incomplete plans while these are being evaluated or revised.

Individual Differences in Planning

It is common knowledge that people differ in the amount of planning they habitually do. We all know people who rush into things without stopping to think at all, and others who obsessively think through every detail before embarking on a course of action. There has been little formal investigation of these differences so far. Giambra (1979) analysed the content of daydreams (defined as thought unrelated to the current task), and found that for all age groups the majority of daydreams were of the type he called "problem-solving" and involved planning future activities. Young males were the exception to this generalisation: They had more daydreams of love and sex than of problem-solving. Females of all ages had more problem-solving daydreams than males. This finding has also emerged from a questionnaire used in a pilot study by Cohen and Faulkner (unpublished). Females reported spending more time on mental planning; they planned in more detail, and formulated more alternative plans in case of difficulties. Elderly people also reported more planning than young people. The reasons underlying these differences are not clear, but probably include personality, level of anxiety, work load, and the importance of efficient performance.

The Travelling Salesman Task

Battman (1987) studied the planning involved in the "travelling salesman problem". He was interested primarily in the function of planning and also in individual differences in planning. Battman argued that planning entails an investment of time and effort. It is therefore only cost-effective if it improves efficiency and/or reduces anxiety in the execution phase. But planning is not always helpful. If the plan is inadequate, or if circumstances change, it may be a positive disadvantage.

Battman compared the performance of two groups of subjects in a version of the travelling salesman task. Subjects had to act as chain store supervisors, visiting 10 stores in one day. Three of the visits had to be made at pre-arranged times, plus or minus 10 minutes. Subjects had to make decisions about marketing or finance at each store. They had access to a map and information about average between-store travel times and the average time needed to handle a problem within a store. In addition, they could change any of the appointment times, provided this was done at least 25 minutes beforehand. Arriving early for an appointment meant wasting time; arriving late entailed making a second visit. One group of subjects were instructed to plan before beginning the task. They could fix intermediate goals and write out a schedule of visits. The other group were not instructed to plan ahead.

The subjects with plans performed more efficiently. They kept more appointments punctually, completed more visits, spent less time driving between stores, and made more use of the ability to change appointments. As well as these indices of efficiency, level of stress was monitored during performance. The findings differed according to the intelligence of the subjects. High-IQ subjects who planned were more stressed on the first trial, but benefited on later trials. Planning was cost-effective for them because it improved efficiency and reduced anxiety. For low-IQ subjects planning brought no reduction in anxiety. Planning did increase their efficiency, but keeping to the plan was effortful, and a high level of stress was maintained. Battman concluded that generating and executing a plan can, in some circumstances, be more demanding than simply responding in an *ad hoc* way and "making it up as you go along". Most of us can probably think of people we know who are meticulous planners, but who clearly suffer a good deal of agitation in trying to execute these plans.

Planning Errands

A detailed study of planning by Hayes-Roth and Hayes-Roth (1979) used verbal protocols to study the way people plan a day's errands. The subjects' task was to produce a plan for completing as many as possible of the errands listed below, moving around the hypothetical town shown in the map (Fig. 2.5).

"You have just finished working out at the health club. It is 11.00 and you can plan the rest of your day as you like. However, you must pick up your car from the Maple Street parking garage by 5.30 and then head home. You'd also like to see a movie today, if possible. Show times at both movie theatres are 1.00, 3.00, and 5.00. Both movies are on your 'must see' list, but go to whichever one fits most conveniently into your plan. Your other errands are as follows:

- pick up medicine for your dog at the vet
- buy a fan belt for your refrigerator at the appliance store
- check out two of the three luxury apartments
- meet a friend for lunch at one of the restaurants
- buy a toy for your dog at the pet store
- pick up your watch at the watch repair shop
- special order a book at the bookstore

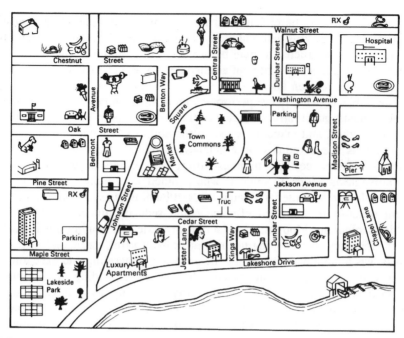

FIG. 2.5.   The town map for the errand planning task (from Hayes-Roth & Hayes-Roth, 1979).

- buy fresh vegetables at the grocery store
- buy a gardening magazine at the newsstand
- go to the florist to send flowers to a friend in hospital."

Figure 2.6 (pp.50–51) reproduces one of the verbal protocols. This typical subject started by defining the goal and tasks and classifying errands as high-priority or low-priority. He begins sequencing the errands from the start point, forming clusters of errands based on priority and on adjacency. There are frequent revisions of the plan, and at a later stage, some sequencing backward in time from the final errand (picking up the car at 5.30). The mental simulation of one stage of the plan guides the later stages, and consists in mentally timing the actions and inferring the consequences. Planning occurs at different levels of abstraction, sometimes involving specific items and sometimes higher-order clusters.

Hayes-Roth and Hayes-Roth noted that planning was opportunistic. The subject did not formulate an overall global plan and then proceed to fill in the stages by successive refinements, but jumped about between levels with many shifts and changes. Instead of being controlled in a top-down direction by higher-order principles and pre-set goals, the plan was under multidirectional control, many decisions being influenced on a moment-to-moment basis by new facts that came to light as planning proceeded. Planning was incremental, with tentative decisions becoming gradually firmer, and alternative plans were considered in parallel.

The cognitive model they formulated to represent these aspects of the planning process included a working memory buffer, which they call the *blackboard*, where different forms of knowledge interact. The different kinds of knowledge include:

(1) Knowledge of the overall task (the metaplan).
(2) A set of possible actions, procedures for implementing them and outcomes (plans).
(3) A list of desirable attributes (such as quick, adjacent) for these plans (plan-abstractions).
(4) A knowledge base of specific data about errand routes and locations. The model also has an executive for taking decisions and for allocation of resources. A computer simulation of this model produced a protocol broadly similar to that produced by a human subject, but the computer's plan was more feasible. It sacrificed more of the low-priority errands and, unlike the human subject's plan, it could have been completed in the available time.

In the errand-planning task the problem lies in selecting and ordering actions. The constraints are mainly of time and distance and the task involves a number of goals that are interdependent, a knowledge base that is equivalent to long-term memory, and the blackboard for carrying out evaluations and decision processes that is equivalent to working memory.

Theoretical Perspectives

Planning, like prospective memory and carrying out action sequences, depends on the operation of working memory and the allocation of attention and also on the way plans are represented in memory.

Types of Representation

The types of representational system that are current in cognitive psychology today fall into three basic types. These are propositional, analogical and procedural (Rumelhart & Norman 1985). In propositional systems knowledge is represented as a set of symbols arranged to constitute statements of facts or rules. Much of the factual knowledge used in planning is represented as propositions. For example, the knowledge that you can get a bookstore to order books for you or that restaurants serve lunch between 12.30 and 2 p.m. can be represented propositionally.

1. Let's go back down the errand list. Pick up medicine for the dog at veterinary supplies. That's definitely a primary, anything taking care of health. Fan belt for refrigerator. Definitely a primary because you need to keep the refrigerator. Checking out two of three luxury apartments. Its got to be a secondary, another browser. Meet the friend at one of the restaurants for lunch. All right. Now, that's going to be able to be varied I hope. That's a primary though because it is an appointment, something you have to do. Buy a toy for the dog at pet store. If you pass it, sure. If not, the dog can play with something else. Movie in one of the movie theatres. Better write that down, those movie times, 1, 3, or 5. Write that down on my sheet just to remember. And that's a primary because it's something I have to do. Pick up the watch at the watch repair. That's one of those borderline ones. Do you need your watch or not? Give it a primary. Special order a book at the bookstore.

2. We're having an awful lot of primaries in this one. It's going to be a busy day.

3. Fresh vegetables at the grocery. That's another primary. You need the food. Gardening magazine at the newsstand. Definitely secondary. All the many obligations of life.

4. Geez, can you believe all these primaries?

5. All right. We are now at the health club.

6. What is going to be the closest one?

7. The appliance store is a few blocks away. The medicine for the dog at the vet's office isn't too far away. Movie theatres—let's hold off on that for a little while. Pick up the watch. That's all the way across town. Special order a book at the bookstore.

8. Probably it would be best if we headed in a southeasterly direction. Start heading this way. I can see later on there are a million things I want to do in that part of town.

9. No we're not. We could end up with a movie just before we get the car. I had thought at first that I might head in a southeasterly direction because there's a grocery store, a watch repair, a movie theatre all in that general area. Also a luxury apartment. However, near my parking lot also is a movie, which would make it convenient to get out of the movie and go to the car. But I think we can still end up that way.

10. All right. Apparently the closest one to the health club is going to the vet's shop. So I might as well get that out of the way. It's a primary and is the closest. We'll start . . .
   [The experimenter mentions that he has overlooked the nearby restaurant and flower shop.]

11. Oh, how foolish of me. You're right. I can still do that and still head in the general direction.

12. But, then again, that puts a whole new light on things. We do have a bookstore. We do have. OK. Break up town into sections. We'll call them northwest and southeast. See how many primaries are in that section. Down there in the southeast section, we have the grocery store, the watch repair and the movie theatre. In the northwest section we have the grocery store, the bookstore, the flower shop, the vet's shop, and the restaurant.

13. And since we are leaving at 11.00, we might be able to get these chores done so that some time when I'm in the area, hit that restaurant. Let's try for that. Get as many of those out of the way as possible. We really could have a nice day here.

14. OK. First choose number one. At 11.00 we leave the health club. Easily, no doubt about it, we can be right across the street in 5 minutes to the flower shop. Here we go. Flower shop at 11.05. Let's give ourselves 10 minutes to browse through some bouquets and different floral arrangements.

FIG. 2.6. Thinking aloud protocol; from the errand-planning task (from Hayes-Roth & Hayes-Roth, 1979).

Procedural representations encode knowledge about how to perform actions like making appointments or ordering books, and this knowledge is stored in the form of a set of procedures. Procedural knowledge must necessarily be involved at the stage when planned actions are executed.

Analogue representational systems are ones in which the objects and events being represented map directly on to the representation. An analogue representation is more like a copy of the real thing. Some kinds of information involved in planning might be better represented analogically. An analogical representation of the spatial lay-out of the town allows relations like next to, nearest to, to be read off directly, and hypothetical moves can be evaluated in terms of locations and distances. The same information could be represented propositionally, but the analogical form has certain advantages. Analogical representations are dynamic: They are readily transformed, rotated, and dismantled. They can be constructed from different viewpoints, they can represent change and movement, and they are specific and determinate. Whereas propositions are truth functional (i.e. they are either true or false), analogical models can be hypothetical. These characteristics of analogical representations are well suited to mental planning tasks, but they also have some shortcomings. It is not easy to see how some kinds of information can be represented in an analogue form.

Temporal and causal factors, quantifiers like "all", "some", "several", and relations like negation are easier to represent propositionally.

It is important to note that these different forms of representation are not mutually exclusive. Different aspects of the real world may be represented in different ways, and a particular object or event may be represented in different ways at different times. It is a reasonable assumption that the memory representations used in planning are of more than one kind.

Hybrid Models

These difficulties can be solved by adopting a hybrid model combining both kinds of representation. Kosslyn (1981; Kosslyn et al., 1992) incorporates both propositions and analogue imagery in his model. He postulates a "deep representation", which stores propositional knowledge in long-term memory. Also in long-term memory there is what Kosslyn calls a "literal representation", consisting of sets of coordinate points. From the deep and literal representations, a "surface representation" in the form of an analogue spatial image can be generated as a temporary visual display, and there are processes that can scan the image, and can expand, contract, or rotate it. This kind of multiple representation model is well suited to the demands of planning, particularly plans that involve spatial judgements.

Another form of multiple representation has been proposed by Johnson-Laird (1983). He writes "What we remember consists of images, models, propositions and procedures for carrying out actions" (p.447). The central component in this set of representations is the *mental model*. Mental models "play a central and unifying role in representing objects, states of affairs, sequences of events, the way the world is, and the social and psychological actions of daily life. They enable individuals to make inferences and predictions, to understand phenomena, to decide what action to take and to control its execution, and, above all, to experience events by proxy" (p.397).

According to Johnson-Laird, mental models are representations that constitute a working model of the real world, although they may be incomplete or simplified. They are derived from perception and from verbal information. Mental models may be physical or conceptual. Physical mental models are analogue in form and can represent relations, space and time, change, and movement. Conceptual mental models can represent more abstract features such as negation. Mental models are specific, but can be used to represent hypothetical states of affairs. They are intermediate between propositions and images because they represent a mapping, or interpretation, of propositional representations and can be used to generate images. Mental models, as described by Johnson-Laird, are not fixed structures, but dynamic models that can be constructed as and when they are required, and this makes them particularly well suited to planning because they are able to simulate dynamic actions and events. In this, they appear to have the advantage over the images in Kosslyn's model which only represent static scenes and objects, and are limited in the kind of transformations they can undergo. Cognitive processes like planning appear to require a hybrid form of representation that is dynamic and that can represent hypothetical states of affairs. Mental models fulfil these criteria better than other systems of representation.

CONCLUSIONS

In this chapter we have considered several aspects of memory for plans and actions, including the ability to execute plans, and the slips that occur when actions are not executed according to plan; the ability to remember to implement prospective plans; as well as how and why people make plans. All these topics relate to naturally occurring behaviour in everyday life, but each has been illuminated and interpreted by the application of formal theories of working memory, attentional mechanisms, and representation developed in the context of traditional laboratory experiments. Nevertheless, the fit between the theories and performance in applied everyday settings seems to be largely based on intuition rather than being confirmed by experimental testing. In most cases, examples of planning or slips of action have been carefully observed, analysed, and described, and then a theoretical model has been invoked that seems relevant to the phenomena under study. So far, there has not been much attempt to generate predictions from the models and test them systematically. It is worth noting that whereas most forms of everyday memory described in later chapters are primarily supported by long-term memory, memory for plans and actions relies primarily on working memory, in particular the operation of the central executive component. In consequence, it is especially vulnerable to the effects of ageing and frontal lobe damage.

3 Memory for Places: Routes, Maps, and Object Locations

FUNCTIONS AND CHARACTERISTICS OF SPATIAL MEMORY

Spatial memory encodes information about location, orientation, distance, and direction. In everyday life it has numerous functions. It enables us to remember places and to remember how to find our way around. We can recognise places as familiar and recall routes from one location to another. We can devise novel routes or short cuts for reaching a goal. Spatial memory is also used for locating objects, and for remembering how to find things, which may range from landmarks along routes such as a service station on the motorway, to objects lying around the house such as a pair of spectacles. Memory for scenes and for the layout of objects within scenes mediates our interaction with the immediate environment. All these functions involve knowledge of the spatial layout of the environment.

Spatial representations in memory allow us to mentally revisit known places; to work out and evaluate routes without actually travelling; to search for objects and scan possible locations mentally without actually going and looking. Spatial memory also has the characteristic that, although it may be partitioned into small local segments, these segments are linked together into larger configurations. Space is not inherently hierarchical, but Neisser (1988) suggested that we tend to represent it mentally as nested hierarchical structures with local representations nested inside global ones. This structure enables us to locate, for example, a particular restaurant in a particular street, but also within a district, city, and country. Cognitive space is relational. Every element is related to every other.

Bryant (1992) has argued that we have a separate spatial representation system that is independent of other memory systems. Neisser (1988) also speculated that spatial memory could be a specific memory module and there is ample neuropsychological evidence (e.g. Marshall & Halligan, 1995) for dissociations of spatial memory from verbal memory so that, following strokes or traumas, patients may perform normally in tests of verbal memory but be impaired in tests of spatial memory, or vice versa. It is apparent, however, that the kind of spatial ability that is measured in psychometric tests in the laboratory, or by the clinician, is not very similar to the kind of spatial ability required in everyday life. Kirasic (1991) devised a series of tests to examine spatial memory for the layout in both a familiar and an unfamiliar supermarket. The tests were scene recognition (identifying photographs taken in the supermarket); distance ranking (for the distances of specified items from a specified start point); route execution (walking the shortest route to pick up seven different items); and map placement (placing pictures of items in the correct locations on a floor plan of the super-market). Subjects also performed a battery of psychometric tests of spatial ability such as the Form Board, Cube Comparison, and Building Memory tests. Correlations between the supermarket tests and the formal psycho-metric tests were very weak. A similar result emerged when Simon, Walsh, Regnier, and Kraus (1992), in a study of elderly subjects, measured neighbourhood knowledge (assessed by map-drawing) and neighbourhood use (assessed by number and length of trips in the area). They also administered formal tests of spatial ability including learning spatial environments from films or models. Only one of these tests proved a significant predictor of neighbourhood knowledge and only one predicted neighbourhood use.

Why should there be this disparity? Spatial cognition in everyday life is operating in a far richer environment. Instead of being employed in an arbitrary and pointless task it is goal-directed. Another important charac-teristic of spatial cognition as it is exercised in real world tasks, is that the spatial environment is related to the self. The self is present as the traveller of routes, the observer of scenes, the searcher for objects, so that spatial knowledge in natural settings is almost invariably self-referential. Numer-ous studies have shown that self-referential memory is usually superior to memory that is not self-referential (Eysenck, 1992), so the psychometric tests, which are not self-referential, may underestimate people's spatial ability in natural conditions.

MEMORY FOR ROUTES

Navigating in the Environment

In this section we begin by considering spatial memory in relation to remembering places and navigating around the environment. In everyday life people have to find their way about within buildings, within cities, or across country. They may be pedestrians or they may be using various forms of transport. They may be equipped with maps, or instructions, or be relying on memories of previous experience. The most important variables in navigation tasks are scale, complexity, and familiarity. In finding your way around your own home, or following a daily route to shops in the next street, the environment is familiar, small-scale, and relatively simple. These are very different problems from finding your way when driving through a strange city or walking through mountainous country, where the environment is large-scale, unfamiliar, and complex.

In a simple, small-scale, familiar environment, navigation is a matter of following routes that are remembered as a set of paths, with specific directions and specific distances, linking known landmarks. It is unlikely that you will get lost. Problems only arise if you emerge from a building or a shopping centre by an unfamiliar exit and have difficulty reorienting yourself with respect to the known routes. Or, if you have learned a route in one direction only, it will be unfamiliar if you need to traverse it in the reverse direction. In this case, landmarks must be recognised from different viewpoints and changes of direction transposed.

In a less familar, larger-scale urban environment, navigation becomes more complex. It may involve finding short cuts or new routes. In this case, the kind of spatial ability required includes orientation and making spatial inferences. To work out a quick way to the station, or to reorient yourself after your known route is blocked by a newly imposed one-way restriction, you have to be able to orient yourself in respect to your destination: To remember the spatial relationships that hold between alternative routes and to infer, for example, that if the station is at two o'clock from your present position, a sequence of turns, such as right-left-right, will bring you approximately to its location. In this situation, you can get lost if your spatial inferences are based on inaccurate estimates of distances and directions.

Following directions in an unfamiliar environment presents different problems. You may be given route instructions such as "Go past the post office, take the first right and then turn left at the town centre". To map this description on to the scene in front of you requires that you be able to recognise the landmarks that are described. You have to match the buildings you encounter against your mental representation of a post office. You can get into difficulties deciding whether a particular configuration of roads and buildings answers the description "town centre", or whether a narrow entry should be counted as a turning or not.

Navigating in a strange environment may involve following a map instead of following route instructions. To match the actual environment to the mapped representation you have to abstract and simplify in order to extract the essential skeleton of the road layout from the cluttered scene in front of you. Of course, if the map you are following is in memory, you may get lost because your memory is inaccurate. If the map is available in front of you, you may still make navigation errors if you cannot match it to the area you are travelling through, as, for example, when the map omits minor roads.

Observations of naturally occurring navigation behaviour are too hapha-zard to yield much insight into the mental representations and mental processes that underlie memory for places. To gain greater understand-ing, psychologists have used a variety of methods including experiments that range from naturalistic, ecologically valid situations to more artificial tasks and self-assessment questionnaires.

Individual Differences in Memory for Routes

Most people would agree intuitively that individuals vary very consider-ably in navigational ability. Some have a poor sense of direction. Put them in a maze or an unfamiliar town and they have little idea which direction they have come from, or which direction they should be heading for. Some are notoriously poor map readers and car drivers are tempted to risk trying to study the A–Z while driving, rather than rely on their guidance. Other people have a good sense of direction and a good track record as successful navigators.

One study that attempted to analyse these differences was carried out by Kozlowski and Bryant (1977). They examined the relationship between self-assessed "sense of direction" and a variety of performance measures. They asked students to rate their own sense of direction on a 7-point scale ranging from very poor to very good. The performance measures included pointing to the location of buildings on the campus when these buildings could not be seen from the room where testing took place; estimating distances; pointing to the location of nearby cities; and filling in the location of six buildings on an incomplete map of the campus. Self-assessed sense of direction correlated significantly ($r = 0.49$) with the accuracy of pointing to campus buildings, and with the accuracy of distance estimates ($r = 0.65$), but was not related to accuracy of pointing to cities.

Kozlowski and Bryant considered the possibility that the subjects with a good sense of direction might be performing better because they were more familiar with the campus environment, rather than because they had superior spatial ability. To test this, they walked subjects through a maze of underground service tunnels beneath the campus from a start point to an end point and back again. Subjects were divided on the basis of their self-assessed sense of direction into good and poor groups. On return to the start, they had to point to the location of the end-point. In this unfamilar environment, there was no difference between good and poor groups on the first trial, but on later trials those with a good sense of direction improved more than the poor group. Kozlowski and Bryant concluded that this kind of directional orientation is not automatic but requires effort, attention, and repeated exposures. Those with a "good sense of direction" are those who are able to benefit from experience and acquire an accurate cognitive map.

Besides performing better on these tasks, those with a good sense of direction also rated themselves as better at giving and following directions; at remembering routes experienced as a passenger in a car; at remembering written directions and as liking to read maps and to find new routes to places. It is not clear, however, whether a sense of direction can be regarded as a unitary ability that mediates performance in a variety of spatial tasks, or a constellation of different abilities (such as visuospatial memory, ability to estimate angular relations and distances, ability to visualise, and spatial reasoning) that reinforce each other.

MEMORY FOR MAPS

A study by Thorndyke and Stasz (1980) focused on individual differences in ability to acquire knowledge of an environment by studying maps. In this task, subjects studied a map and had to memorise the absolute and relative positions of the named objects and places shown, so that they could draw the map from memory in a recall test. After six study-test trials, they were also asked to solve some route-finding problems from memory. The two maps used, a town map and a country map, are shown in Figs. 3.1 and 3.2, respectively.

Three of the subjects were experienced in the use of maps. DW was a retired army officer who had taught recruits to use field maps. FK was a retired air force pilot experienced with military maps, and NN was a scientist who worked with geographical data and cartography. Five other subjects were inexperienced with maps. Both expert and novice subjects were asked to verbalise the strategies they used while studying the maps and their verbal protocols were recorded and analysed. An extract from one of the protocols is shown in Fig. 3.3.

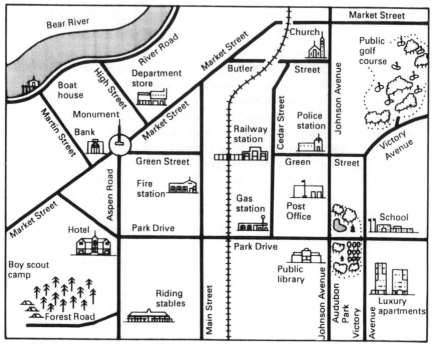

FIG. 3.1. The town map (from Thorndyke & Stasz, 1980).

The task revealed large individual differences. On trial 5, the best subject (DW) scored 100% and the poorest scored 19%. Surprisingly, the expert subjects did not necessarily outperform the novices. Although DW was outstandingly good, FK was 6th out of the 8 subjects and NN was the poorest of all. The verbal protocols revealed that different acquisition strategies were associated with good map learning. Good and poor learners differed in three ways.

(1) *Allocation of attention*: Good learners partitioned the map into areas and focused attention on one area at a time before shifting to a fresh one. The protocol in Fig. 3.3 exemplifies this homing-in strategy. Poor learners adopted a more diffuse global approach, trying to learn the whole map at once.

(2) *Encoding strategies*: Good learners reported using visuospatial imagery to encode patterns and spatial relations. Poor learners used no imagery, and relied on verbal rehearsal of named elements or verbal mnemonics.

(3) *Evaluation*: Good learners tested their own memory to find out how they were doing and then focused on areas they had not learned. Poor learners did not do this efficiently.

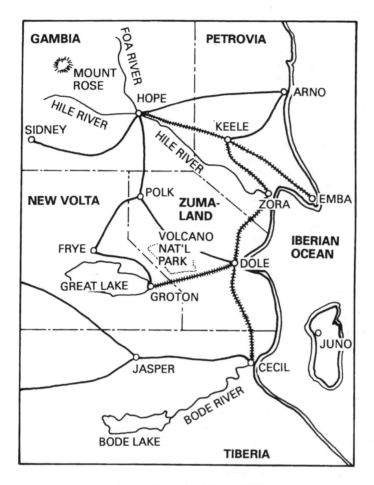

FIG. 3.2.   The country map (from Thorndyke & Stasz, 1980).

Learning from Maps

In a second experiment Thorndyke and Stasz tested the effects of instructing subjects to use the more effective techniques. Those subjects who had
high scores on tests of visual memory benefited from the training, but those
with poor visual memory failed to improve. Neither the greater experience
of the expert subjects, nor training in optimal strategies was sufficient to
guarantee efficient map learning. A good visual memory appeared to be a
prerequisite. However, Gilhooly, Wood, Kinnear, and Green (1988) sus-
pected that the failure of the experts to show superior skill might be due to
the fact that the maps used in these tests were simplified planimetric maps
without contours, which gave little scope for the exercise of expertise.

1. Um. First I notice that there's a railroad that goes up through the middle of the map.
2. And then, the next thing I notice is there's a river on the top left corner, and let's see.
3. There's a main street and . . . I guess I'd try and get the main streets first.
4. That would be Market and Johnson and Main. Try to get the relationship of those.
5. On these two streets, they both start with an M.
6. Then I'd just try to get down the other main streets, that, uh,
7. Victory Avenue comes below the golf course, and
8. then goes straight down and
9. becomes parallel with Johnson, and . . .
10. I guess I'd try to learn the streets that are parallel first, parallel to each other.
11. Just try to remember which, in which order they come.
12. I guess with this one I could, since there's a sort of like a forest, I could remember that this is Aspen, and um,
13. let's see, and Victory, I guess I could relate it to the golf [course], winning the golf [match].

FIG. 3.3.   A verbal protocol from a subject studying the town map (from Thorndyke & Stasz, 1980).

When they compared the ability of groups of experts and novices to remember contour maps they found that the experts were better at remembering contour features, although there was no difference between the groups when memory for noncontour features like place names, roads, and buildings was tested. Trained map-readers do have superior memory for the more specialist aspects of maps.

Rossano and Hodgson (1994) tested the hypothesis that people learn maps in a global-to-local fashion and they also compared the effectiveness of different learning strategies. Subjects learned the "five countries" map shown in Fig. 3.4 in one of four different learning conditions.

In the ad lib condition subjects studied the map in their own way; in the imagery condition they were told to form a mental picture so that they would be able to draw the map; in the story condition they read a story about a plague spreading across the countries; and in the verbal condition they were asked to make up phrases to describe the location of the elements in the map. Map-recall scores showed that, as predicted, countries were remembered better than provinces, which, in turn, were better remembered than cities confirming that map learning was global-to-local. The imagery instructions were most effective in improving recall.

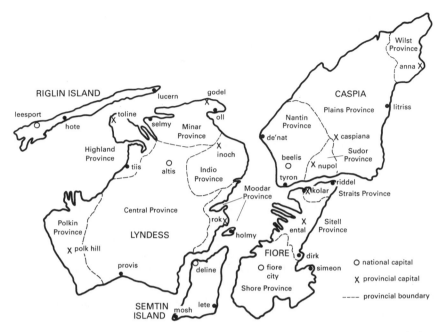

FIG. 3.4.   The five countries map (from Rossano & Hodgson 1994). Reprinted by permission John Wiley & Sons Ltd.

Map Knowledge and Route Knowledge

It is fortunate, perhaps, for those who are no good at it, that studying a map is not the only way to acquire knowledge of the environment. It can also be learned directly from the experience of moving around. Thorndyke and Hayes-Roth (1982) set out to compare the kind of spatial knowledge that results from these two modes of learning. They tested two groups of subjects for their knowledge of a large complex building. The map-knowledge group learned from floor plans. The navigational, or route-knowledge group was composed of people who worked in the building. Each group included people at two different levels of experience. A series of tests were administered.

(1) *Distance*: (a) Estimate the straight-line distance between two named locations, and (b) estimate the route distance (walking from one location to the other).

(2) *Orientation*: (a) Point to the location of one place when standing at another location, and (b) point to the location of one place while imagining yourself standing at some other location.

(3) *Location*: Mark designated locations on an incomplete plan.

Route-knowledge subjects were better at estimating route distances and at orientation. Map-knowledge subjects were better at estimating straight line distances and marking locations. Thorndyke and Hayes-Roth concluded that map knowledge (sometimes called survey knowledge) is good for representing global relationships and gives direct access to distance and location information. It provides a *bird's-eye view*, but this is difficult to transform into a different view. Navigational knowledge is based on sequentially organised procedural knowledge acquired by traversing the routes, and results in a *ground-based view*. However, the results suggested that route knowledge can be used to generate map knowledge. Mental simulation of navigation (i.e. imagining yourself walking around) yields information about routes, distances, and locations, and information about orientation and straight-line distance can be computed from route knowledge. Comparison of subjects with high and low experience suggested that with increasing experience, navigationally acquired route knowledge undergoes qualitative changes, becoming more flexible. Thorndyke and Hayes-Roth (1982) claimed that this ground-based view becomes effectively translucent, so relationships between points can be "seen" despite intervening obstructions. The best all-round performance in this experiment was achieved by the highly experienced navigators.

The distinction between route knowledge and map knowledge is not hard and fast. If Thorndyke and Hayes-Roth are correct in claiming that route knowledge is transformed into map knowledge with experience, there must be transitional stages in between, and experience confirms that one kind of spatial knowledge can be converted into the other. You can derive a route from studying a map, and you can construct a map from knowledge of routes. However, we can still distinguish between the two kinds of knowledge. Route knowledge is typically small-scale knowledge of local areas, acquired episodically from personal navigational experiences. It is represented from a ground-based, egocentric point of view in terms of sequentially organised procedures for getting from one point to another. Map knowledge is larger-scale, and represents global spatial relations topologically from a bird's-eye point of view.

Using a different paradigm, Tversky (1991) also differentiated between route knowledge and map or survey knowledge. In her experiments the two kinds of knowledge are exemplified in different forms of verbal description. Route descriptions take the reader on a mental tour presenting information sequentially and relating it to the traveller's own body position (left, right, in front, behind). Survey descriptions take a perspective from above and describe the locations of landmarks in terms of canonical directions (north, south, east, west), as in the following extracts from examples of descriptions of a resort area shown in Fig. 3.5.

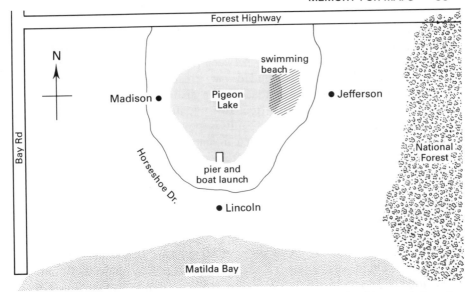

FIG. 3.5.   Map of resort area (from Taylor & Tversky 1992). Reprinted by permission of Academic Press, Inc. and the author.

Route Description

. . . to reach the Pigeon Lake area drive south along Bay Road until you reach, on your left, the point where the Forest Highway dead-ends into Bay Road. From this intersection, you can see in the distance that Bay Road continues to Matilda Bay . . . You turn left on to Forest Highway and travel about 40 miles until on your right you reach Horseshoe Drive. Horseshoe Drive is the only road you can take to get into the Pigeon Lake region. Turning right onto Horseshoe Drive you see on your left, Pigeon Lake . . .

Survey Description

. . . The resort area is bordered by four major landmarks: the National Forest, Matilda Bay, Bay Road, and the Forest Highway. The eastern border is made up of the National Forest . . . the southern border is made up of Matilda Bay. Two major roads, Bay Road and the Forest Highway form the other two borders of the region. Bay Road runs north–south along the western border of this region . . . (Tversky, 1991, p.111)

Tversky was interested in whether these two kinds of descriptions produced different mental representations or whether both produced a common perspective-free representation. Subjects in her experiments read detailed descriptions (either route or survey) of fictitious environments and afterwards made true/false judgements about statements. True statements were either verbatim statements about the location of landmarks extracted from the text, or they were inference statements containing information which could be inferred from the text. The results showed no difference in speed or accuracy between route and survey descriptions, so Tversky and colleagues concluded that, irrespective of the perspective of the description, the reader constructs a spatial mental model of the environment that is perspective-free. Her findings contrast with those of Thorndyke and Hayes-Roth (1982). It is possible that perspective-free representations are constructed when a spatial layout is learned from a verbal description and that learning from maps or from navigation gives rise to representations that retain the perspective of the input.

Mental Representation of Spatial Information

The mental representation of spatial information may take a number of different forms. Although Tversky's (1991) results suggested that map knowledge and route knowledge result in the same form of mental representation, Bartram and Smith (1984) considered that map knowledge is propositional and route knowledge is procedural. However, both introspective evidence and some of the experimental results suggest a role for analogue representations. The subjective experience of consulting a mental map seems more like looking at a pictorial or graphic representation than reviewing a set of propositions. Remembered routes are experienced as a series of pictorial images. Remembered maps are a mental analogue of real maps. Kosslyn's (1981) theory of mental imagery (outlined in Chapter 2) suggests that both propositional and pictorial representations coexist. According to his model, long-term spatial knowledge is stored as propositions, and as sets of coordinate points, and these representations can be used to generate a temporary analogue visual display. The analogue display represents orientation, direction and distance in a form that allows judgements of relative position and relative distance to be read off directly from the display.

Just as, according to this view, map knowledge can be represented both propositionally and also, temporarily, in picture-like analogue displays, so route knowledge may also have multiple forms of representation. You may have a set of procedures that, if executed, will enable you to walk from home to the station. This knowledge can also be represented visually as a series of mental pictures showing the roads and landmarks. If you were asked to describe the route, you could convert your knowledge into a verbal description, and there is no reason why this route knowledge should not also be stored as propositions.

The representation of spatial knowledge, like the representation of plans, discussed in Chapter 2, can also be characterised, as Tversky (1991) argued, in terms of mental models. Johnson-Laird offers this demonstration of the way people can construct a mental model of spatial layouts from descriptions. The extract in Fig. 3.6a is from Conan Doyle's story *Charles Augustus Milverton* (quoted from Johnson-Laird, 1983, pp.158–159).

Tversky's experiments, described earlier, were designed to reveal the nature of the representation constructed from verbal descriptions of spatial environments. She found that verbatim statements were verified more rapidly and accurately than inference statements, and concluded from this that readers must retain a verbal or propositional representation of the surface form of the language of the text. However, inference statements appeared to be verified by reference to a perspective-free spatial mental model. This characteristic of being perspective-free is incompatible with an image representation, as images instantiate a particular viewpoint, but can be accommodated by a mental model. Thus, she found evidence for both types of mental representation, mental models, and verbal or propositional representations.

Franklin and Tversky (1990) have suggested that spatial mental models are constructed using a spatial framework, or frame of reference. When the observer is positioned in a three-dimensional scene, he is in an egocentric frame with three dimensions, left/right, front/back, and head/foot, defined by the observer's body. Verification experiments have shown that these three dimensions are not equally available. The head/foot dimension usually dominates and people can locate objects on this dimension faster and more accurately, probably because it is the most stable. As the observer moves around the scene, left and right, front and back, may shift, but the head and foot dimension usually remains unchanged (unless one turns somersaults). Alternatively, an allocentric frame of reference, with canonical dimensions, may be useful for encoding the relations of static objects to each other. Spatial mental models differ from images in several ways. They are particularly suited to representing routes because they can incorporate temporal and causal relations as well as spatial ones and because they can represent a dynamic sequence of scenes.

Verbal descriptions do not, as a rule, specify space as completely and precisely as maps, models, or actual experience. Descriptions may be indeterminate in that they fail to specify the distances between objects or they use indeterminate expressions like "A is beside B", which leaves their relative positions unspecified. This type of indeterminate information can be represented mentally as a set of propositions but not as an image or mental model where information has to take a determinate form.

Tversky (1991) concluded that people encode multiple different kinds of representations of spatial information and this view is widely accepted. It is likely that several factors determine which type of representation dominates. One factor is the form of the input, whether it is a map, a verbal description, or a visual or navigational experience. Another factor is the

With our black silk face-coverings, which turned us into two of the most truculent figures in London, we stole up to the silent, gloomy house. A sort of tiled veranda extended along one side of it, lined by several windows and two doors.

"That's his bedroom", Holmes whispered. "This door opens straight into the study. It would suit us best, but it is bolted as well as locked, and we should make too much noise getting in. Come round here. There's a greenhouse which opens into the drawing room".

The place was locked, but Holmes removed a circle of glass and turned the key from the inside. An instant afterwards he had closed the door behind us, and we had become felons in the eyes of the law. The thick, warm air of the conservatory and the rich, choking fragrance of exotic plants took us by the throat. He seized my hand in the darkness and led me swiftly past banks of shrubs which brushed against our faces. Holmes had remarkable powers, carefully cultivated, of seeing in the dark. [!] Still holding my hand in one of his, he opened a door, and I was vaguely conscious that we had entered a large room in which a cigar had been smoked not long before. He felt his way among the furniture, opened another door, and closed it behind us. Putting out my hand I felt several coats hanging from the wall, and I understood that I was in a passage. We passed along it, and Holmes very gently opened a door upon the right-hand side. Something rushed out at us and my heart sprang into my mouth, but I could have laughed when I realized that it was the cat. A fire was burning in this new room, and again the air was heavy with tobacco smoke. Holmes entered on tiptoe, waited for me to follow, and then very gently closed the door. We were in Milverton's study, and a portière at the farther side showed the entrance to his bedroom.

It was a good fire, and the room was illuminated by it. Near the door I saw the gleam of an electric switch, but it was unnecessary, even if it had been safe, to turn it on. At one side of the fireplace was a heavy curtain which covered the bay window we had seen from the outside. On the other side was the door which communicated with the veranda. A desk stood in the centre, with a turning-chair of shining red leather. Opposite was a large bookcase, with a marble bust of Athene on the top. In the corner, between the bookcase and the wall, there stood a tall, green safe, the firelight flashing back from the polished brass knobs upon its face.

Here is a simple plan of the house with the veranda running down one side of it:

The question is: which way did Holmes and Watson make their way along the veranda—from right to left or from left to right?

FIG. 3.6a.   A spatial problem from a story by Conan Doyle (from Johnson-Laird, 1983). Copyright 1983 AAAS.

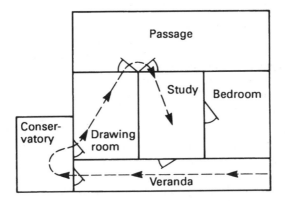

FIG. 3b. The solution showing Holmes' and Watson's route.

function of the representation, for example, whether it is used for comput-
ing distance or relative locations, for finding short cuts or retracing known
routes, for moving the furniture around or finding a parking space.

Spatial Information-processing: Inferences and Estimates

Spatial information processes include both the construction of the representation and processes of consultation that occur when information is
extracted from the memory representation. When information is explicitly
represented, it may be read off directly, but when information is not
explicit in the representation, processes of spatial inference and spatial
transformation are needed to extract it. The relative positions of some
objects, their relative distances, and orientations may be unspecified or
indeterminate but this information can often be inferred.

In propositional representations, spatial locations may be hierarchically
arranged, so, for example, the proposition "Scotland is north of England"
is superordinate to "Edinburgh is in Scotland" or "Newcastle is in
England". The information that Edinburgh is in Scotland is, in our
example, already stored as a proposition and can be accessed directly.
The information that Edinburgh is north of Newcastle is not stored
directly, but is implicit and can be inferred by logical deduction from
this set of propositions.

Spatial inferences are not always accurate, however. Stevens and Coupe
(1978) asked subjects to judge the relative positions of one city to another
(e.g. Reno to San Diego). The errors that were made showed that subjects
derived their answers by inferences from superordinate propositions that
express the spatial relationship between Nevada and California. Because
Nevada lies east of California, they assume (wrongly) that Reno lies east of
San Diego. Similarly, in the United Kingdom, if people are asked whether

Bristol lies east or west of Edinburgh, they tend to infer (again wrongly) that Bristol must be west because it lies on the west coast and Edinburgh lies on the east coast.

Information about distance and orientation can also be inferred when it is not stored directly. Byrne (1979) asked subjects to estimate walking distances between pairs of locations in and around the town of St. Andrews, Scotland. These included short routes and longer routes; routes in the town centre and routes in the suburbs; straight routes and routes with changes of direction. People tended to overestimate the short routes, those with more changes of direction, and the town centre routes where there were more landmarks. Byrne concluded that distance estimation was based on the number of identifiable segments in the route. The larger the number of segments, the greater the estimated distance.

Byrne also tested subjects' ability to draw from memory the angles between the roads at familiar junctions. The results showed that all types of angles were normalised towards the right angle. Inaccurate estimates of angles would necessarily distort inferences about direction and orientation, so this tendency would explain why it is that short cuts do not always take you to your intended destination. Memory for places, and being able to find your way around, depend on the accuracy and completeness of the mental representation of spatial knowledge and, also, on the processes employed to read out or compute the required information.

MEMORY FOR OBJECTS AND OBJECT LOCATIONS

In everyday life, memory for objects has two main functions. The first involves object identification. We rely on memory representations to identify and classify objects, to recognise what they are and what category of objects they belong to. The second function involves memory for the location of objects. Because we are constantly moving around in our environment and changing the locations of the objects with which we interact we need to remember where objects are, and we also need to be able to recognise them when we have found them. This latter point may seem obvious and trivial but research has shown that memory for the visual appearance of common objects is sometimes very imprecise and poorly specified. This may explain why people looking for a mislaid object can fail to "see" it when it is in plain view.

Landau and Jackendoff (1993) drew on their analysis of language to gain insight into spatial cognition and, in particular, into the nature of representation of objects and places. Interestingly, they concluded that there may be distinct separate spatial cognitions systems for representing "what" and "where". The descriptions used to refer to objects when concerned with their identity (the what system is engaged) use rich and complex terminology to describe their shape and surface. When the same objects are in the role of landmarks or reference points (the where system is engaged) descriptions are restricted to very schematised features. Rather similarly, Tversky (1995) has developed a theory of memory for the visuospatial world that distinguishes between memory for figures, objects or elements of a scene, and memory for the spatial relations between them. There is also some neurological evidence of double dissociations between object recognition ability and ability to localise objects in space and in relation to each other (Farah, Hammond, Levine, & Calvanio, 1988) which supports the view that these are separate systems. Nevertheless, in everyday life the business of finding mislaid objects seems to involve both kinds of spatial cognition.

Memory for Object Location

Losing Objects

Forgetting where you put something, misplacing or losing objects, is a common and frustrating experience in everyday life. The lapse of memory may be only temporary. The moment when you realise you cannot remember where you parked the car is usually short-lived and the memory is recovered quite soon. In other cases, forgetting is complete, the memory is never recovered and the missing object may never be located. The questions of interest are why we sometimes forget an object's location, and how we set about trying to find missing objects. Several different causes of error in object location can be distinguished.

(1) *Absentmindedness*: The object has been put in an unusual, unintended place by mistake, and the subject does not remember putting it there.
(2) *Updating errors*: The object has been put in one of several familiar places. The subject has memories of putting it in all of these places on different occasions, but cannot remember which memory is the most recent one.
(3) *Detection failures*: The object has been put in its proper place. The subject looks there, but fails to detect it.
(4) *Context effects:* Tversky (1995) has pointed out that memory for locations is relative to other contextual elements in the scene and to a higher-order frame of reference (such as the walls of the room, or a map of the world) and these may introduce distortions. For example, Gestalt principles of grouping and common fate may mean items are remembered as closer together than they really were.

In trying to locate missing objects there are also several different kinds of search strategy that can be employed.

(1) *Action replay strategy*: The subject tries to reconstruct mentally the sequence of actions, and so retrieve the memory of placing the object.

(2) *Mental walk strategy*: The subject can generate visual images of locations in which the object might be placed and mentally inspect these locations to see if the object is present.

(3) *Reality monitoring strategy*: The subject can generate images of putting the object in various possible locations, and employ the reality-monitoring criteria described on pp.285–286 to judge whether any of these correspond to reality.

(4) *Physical search*: Instead of mental searching for the object, the subject can physically search possible locations.

Tenney (1984) administered a "lost and found" questionnaire to young and elderly subjects. She expected to find that elderly people misplaced objects more often than the young, and she generated two preliminary hypotheses about why we lose things. The first hypothesis attributed such incidents to memory problems. Tenney suggested that elderly people might be more absentminded than the young, and lack of attention to ongoing activities would cause them to put objects down inadvertently in unintended places. Tenney's second hypothesis attributed object loss to detection failures. She suggested that elderly people might have more difficulty in finding objects because of perceptual difficulties caused by sensory handicaps, or poor search strategies. Subjects were asked to report any incidents of losing objects occurring within a two-week period. Approximately 30% of the subjects experienced such an incident, but young and elderly subjects did not differ in the number of incidents reported.

The Absentminded Hypothesis.   Subjects were also asked to supply self-ratings on an absentmindedness scale. Although there was again no age difference, object losers (unsurprisingly) rated themselves as more absent-minded than those who had not lost any objects. The absentminded hypothesis received further support from the fact that in 62% of the incidents the objects were left in unintended places and in 58% of these cases the subject had no recollection of ever having put the object there. Tenney divided the misplaced objects into common objects (misplaced by more than one subject) and unique objects (misplaced by only one subject). Common objects included pen, pencil, chequebook, keys, money, glasses, watch and jewellery. Although it is not clear from her data exactly how many incidents involved common objects, it does seem as if a substantial number of incidents occurred in the course of routine activities handling routine objects. In these circumstances, failures of memory for object location can be interpreted in the same way as slips of action (see Chapter 2, p.38). They occur during routine activities that are under automatic control. Because of the lack of conscious attentional monitoring, the action of misplacing the object is not adequately encoded in memory, and the object's location cannot be recollected later. This kind of explanation fits those cases when the subject has no memory of putting the object in the place where it is eventually found.

The Perceptual Hypothesis.   Tenney (1984) found that some of the object-losing incidents fitted the perceptual hypothesis. Elderly subjects reported a higher incidence of cases where object-misplacing involved defective search or failure of detection, but even young subjects reported some occasions when they found the object in plain sight (6.8%), in a place where it was usually kept (21.5%), or in a place where they had already looked (23.75%). Although it seems odd that people should fail to find an object when it is in its usual place, this is obviously quite a common experience. Sometimes, of course, the object may be partly concealed or obscured by other objects, but when an object is in plain sight it may be undetected if memory for the object's appearance is incomplete, inaccurate, or based on an inappropriate orientation. Failures of object detection may therefore be linked to the process of mental rotation. When searching for an object, the searcher generates a visual image of the missing object in the expected location and looks for a match. If the target object is at an unusual orientation (fallen over, lying askew) it will not match the visual image unless either image or stimulus is mentally rotated into alignment. Failure to carry out the appropriate mental rotations could account for cases when objects in plain view are not found. Tversky (1995) has pointed out that many objects have a "canonical" view. Teapots and horses are easiest to recognise when seen sideways on but for clocks and telephones the frontal view is canonical.

The Memory-updating Hypothesis.   Another explanation, not suggested by Tenney (1984), also rests on the fact that many misplaced objects are those that are handled very frequently. This hypothesis suggests that when you try to recall an object's location, the problem is one of correctly dating the memory that is retrieved. You may remember putting the car keys on the hall table, or the chequebook in the desk drawer, but is this the memory from the last, most recent time you used the keys or chequebook? Or is it derived from some previous occasion?

Bjork (1978) reminded us of the importance of updating in every sphere of everyday life. You need to remember where you parked the car today, not last week. You need to know your current car's registration number, not the number of the car you had before. You need to know what are trumps in the hand of bridge you are playing now. Bjork also pointed out that very many jobs, from short-order cook to air traffic controller, require continual memory updating. Effective management of any enterprise requires accurate updating of information about supplies, orders, personnel, etc. There is a very general need to forget, erase, or override information that is no longer current, and replace it with the most recent version. When we make mistakes about object locations, it is often because this updating process has failed and we retrieve an outdated memory.

Bjork distinguished two mechanisms of updating: *destructive updating* whereby earlier versions are completely destroyed, and *structural updating* whereby earlier versions are preserved but order and recency information is built into the series by some structural principle. In his experiment, the task tested memory for paired associates. The stimulus word remained the same, but was paired with a different response word on each trial (e.g. Frog-Rope; Frog-Plum, etc.). As well as testing total recall of all the response words, the task tested updating by asking subjects to recall the most recent response word. Subjects were given different instructions. In the *destructive updating condition*, they were told to imagine writing the words on a blackboard, erasing the previous response word, and filling in the new one on each trial. In the *ordered rehearsal condition,* they were told to rote rehearse the items in order of presentation. In the *structural updating condition,* they were given a story line to connect the items, and in the *imagery condition,* they had to form a mental picture relating the items (e.g. a frog with a rope), then undo the picture and replace the old item with the new one on each trial (e.g. replace the rope with a plum). Subjects reported that they were unable to carry out the destructive instructions. The structural condition produced the best updated recall of the most recent item, but total recall was poor in this condition, indicating that some destruction of earlier items may have occurred.

Where Did I Park?

Remembering where you parked the car is usually a problem of updating. You can probably recall parking it in several places and can image the car in each of these. But which is today's memory? As Bjork's (1978) subjects reported, although it is often useless in everyday life to remember outdated information, we do not seem to be able to erase it at will. Various strategies can be employed to cope with the car parking problem. I tend to use an action replay strategy. When I cannot remember where I parked the car today I trace back through a sequence of activities (Which direction did I come from as I approached the building I work in? Did I arrive early, when the nearest parking slots would have been vacant?) In effect, I supply a story line in order to identify the most recent of my parking memories. By elaborating the memory in this way I can place it in the right temporal context.

Da Costa Pinto and Baddeley (1991) studied memory for car parking in Cambridge in a series of experiments. Their findings showed a clear recency effect and suggested that both decay over time and interference from repeated parking events affected recall. Both factors affect the discriminability of the target memory from other parking events. This study is consistent with the interpretation of the recency effect offered by Baddeley and Hitch (1993). They suggested that the advantage for recent events derives from two factors; an implicit priming factor causes gradually declining activation and so makes the most recently presented items easiest to reactivate (they call this the "light bulb analogy"), and an output factor such that there is an explicit strategy of retrieving the last items first. The parking study is an elegant demonstration of the way in which naturalistic research can be used to test the scope and generalisability of theoretical concepts.

Lutz, Means, and Long (1994) also carried out a naturalistic study of memory for car parking in which 32 university staff were asked to indicate on a map the exact space in which they had parked that day and the three preceding days. Accuracy of recall was good for the same day but declined for the previous days. For the same day, 88% of the staff were accurate within three spaces but for the most remote day only 58% maintained this level of accuracy. Some individuals made wild errors, even forgetting which parking lot they had used. Subjects used a variety of strategies to help them remember where they had parked. The most popular strategy was to eliminate the problem by sticking to a favourite parking spot. Other commonly used strategies were relating the car to a visual landmark or mentally retracing the action. Both these strategies seemed to include a strong imagery component and few subjects reported encoding the information verbally. The decline in memory for parking on previous days suggests that these outdated memories may fade fairly rapidly and so lose their power to interfere with the most recent memory.

Memory for a Common Object

Memory representations of objects need to be sufficiently precise and fine-grained to support the kinds of discriminations that are usually made. We need to be able to discriminate between an apple and a pear, and possibly between a William pear and a Conference pear, but we may not need to discriminate between one banana and another. There is a case for arguing that memory representations of common objects are only as precise and accurate as they need to be. It has been noted that people are often unable to report the layout of numbers on a telephone dial or pad and that even typists cannot reconstruct the keyboard. Nickerson and Adams (1982) confirmed experimentally that people have surprisingly poor memory for the visual appearance of common objects. They asked 20 subjects to draw each side of a US one cent piece. Out of a total of 8 features (4 on each side), the mean number of features correctly reproduced was only 3, and nearly half of these were mislocated. Nickerson and Adams considered the possibility that performance was poor because, although people often need to recognize coins, recall is rarely required. However, on a recognition test, where subjects had to select the correct version from 15 drawings of different versions, only half the subjects were correct. More recently, Richardson (1992) tested people's ability to recall the orientation of the monarch's head on British coins and found there was there was a bias to recall the profile incorrectly as facing left. He suggested that people develop a left-facing schema from their experience with the orientation of the head on stamps and erroneously apply this to coins.

Foos (1989) found that elderly people were particularly poor at recognising coins and telephone dials. Thirty percent of young adults identified the correct drawing of a coin and 40% identified the correct layout of the telephone dial. None of the elderly subjects identified the coin and only 7% identified the dial. However, in spite of their poor performance, the elderly were more confident in their responses. It seems that people only remember enough of the visual properties of objects to be able to make the quite gross discriminations required in everyday life. In the case of coins, knowing the size, shape, and colour of metal is sufficient and it is unnecessary to know anything about the inscriptions and symbols on the coin faces. If memory for the visual appearance of other common objects is similarly vague, it is not so surprising that people sometimes fail to find an object that is in its proper place.

MEMORY FOR SCENES

Another aspect of memory for objects is invoked when instead of having to remember the location of a particular object, you are asked to remember all the objects present in a particular scene. Brewer and Treyens (1981) tested people's ability to remember objects in a room. The rationale and interpretation of this experiment was based on schema theory, so it is necessary to outline the main principles of schema theory first.

Schema Theory

Schema theory is able to provide a theoretical explanation of considerable generality for many phenomena in everyday memory. It can account for the fact that many of our experiences are forgotten, or are reconstructed in a way that is incomplete, inaccurate, generalised, or distorted. Schema theory emphasises the role of prior knowledge and past experience, claiming that what we remember is influenced by what we already know. According to this theory, the knowledge we have stored in memory is organised as a set of schemas, or knowledge structures, which represent generic knowledge about objects, situations, events, or actions that has been acquired from past experience.

Bartlett (1932) introduced the idea of schemas to explain why, when people remember stories, they typically omit some details, introduce rationalisations and distortions, and reconstruct the story so as to make more sense in terms of their own knowledge and experience. According to Bartlett, the story is "assimilated" to pre-stored schemas based on prior knowledge. These processes are described in more detail in Chapter 9, p.260. Although for many years Bartlett's ideas were neglected, in recent years schemas have been given a central role in memory.

Schemas represent all kinds of generic knowledge from simple knowledge such as the shape of the letter "A", for example, to more complex knowledge such as knowledge about political ideologies or astrophysics. Like the action schemas described on p.43, knowledge schemas may be linked together into related sets, with superordinate and subordinate schemas. So, for example, the schema for "table" would be linked to schemas for "furniture", "rooms", and "houses". A schema has slots that may be filled with fixed compulsory values, or with variable optional values. A schema for a boat would have "floats" as a fixed value, but has "oars" and "engine" as variable values. Schemas also supply default values. These are the most probable or typical values. If you are thinking about some particular boat, and you cannot remember the colour of the sails, the boat schema might supply the default value "white" as being the most probable value to fill the colour slot. "Schema" is used as a general term to cover all kinds of general knowledge. More closely specified versions of schemas are called *scripts*, which consist of general knowledge about particular kinds of events, or *frames*, which consist of knowledge about the properties of particular objects or locations. Scripts are discussed in more detail in Chapter 6.

Pre-existing schemas operate in a top-down direction influencing the way we encode, interpret and store the new information coming in. According to schema theory, new experiences are not just passively "copied" or recorded in memory. A memory representation is actively constructed integrating the old generic information in the schema with new information from the current input using processes that are strongly influenced by schemas in a variety of ways, as outlined by Alba and Hasher (1983).

(1) *Selection*: The schema directs attention and guides the selection of what is encoded and stored in memory. Information that is relevant to whichever schema is currently activated is more likely to be remembered than information that is irrelevant.

(2) *Storage*: A schema provides a framework within which current information relevant to that schema can be stored.

(3) *Abstraction*: Information may undergo transformation from the specific form in which it was perceived to a more general form. Specific details of a particular experience tend to drop out, whereas those aspects that are common to other similar experiences are incorporated into a general schema and retained.

(4) *Normalisation*: Memories also tend to be distorted so as to fit in with prior expectations and to be consistent with the schema. They are sometimes transformed toward the most probable or most typical item of that kind. People may remember what they expected to see rather than what they actually saw. An example of the way schemas may influence memory for common objects by normalisation comes from a study by French and Richards (1993) who found that when subjects were asked to draw a clock with Roman numerals from memory after examining it for one minute, 10 of the 14 subjects represented the 4 as IV. In fact , all clocks and watches with Roman numerals represent the 4 as IIII. In this striking example schema-based memory of the normal form of representation overrode the perceptual experience.

(5) *Integration*: According to schema theory, an integrated memory representation is formed that includes information derived from the current experience, prior knowledge relating to it and default values supplied by the schema.

(6) *Retrieval*: Schemas may also aid retrieval by providing cues. People may search through the schema in order to retrieve a particular memory. When the information that is sought is not represented directly, it can be retrieved by schema-based inferences. (If you know that John has measles, you can infer, from your measles schema, that he won't come to the party).

Brewer and Tenpenny (personal communication, 1996) in a similar analysis of schema mechanisms list directing attention, providing a framework, integrating old and new information, and guiding retrieval, but add two further mechanisms, distinctiveness and verification. A schema provides a background against which new information not consistent with the schema becomes distinctive. This mechanism renders a pig in the living-room more distinctive and more memorable than the same pig in the farmyard. The schema also supplies a criterion for verifying new episodic information. If it is inconsistent with the schema it needs to be double-checked (is it really a pig in the living-room?).

The most important prediction from schema theory is that what is normal, typical, relevant, or consistent with pre-existing knowledge will be remembered better than what is unexpected, bizarre, or irrelevant. However, intuitively, this prediction is not entirely convincing and the results of experimental testing have not always supported it. Critics of schema theory have pointed out that it often seems to be what is odd or unusual that tends to remain in memory. To account for this finding, schema theory has been modified in a somewhat *ad hoc* fashion to create a schema-plus-tag model in which the memory representation is composed of generic information derived from the schema plus the novel, deviant, or unexpected information that is appended in the form of a tag (see Chapter 6, p.141 for more details of this model). Alternatively, Brewer and Tenpenny's distinctiveness mechanism provides a more convincing account of the tendency to remember what is bizarre.

Memory for Objects in a Room

Brewer and Treyens (1981) set up an experiment that tested the predictions from schema theory. Subjects were called one at a time to serve in an experiment. When they arrived they were asked to wait in a room and left there alone for 35 seconds. They were then called into another room and given the unexpected task of recalling everything they had seen in the first room. This first room was arranged to look like a graduate student's office, and contained 61 objects. Some of the objects were schema-relevant, that is, they were objects people would expect to find in such a room, such as a table, typewriter, coffee pot, calendar, posters, etc. Other objects were schema-irrelevant (e.g. a skull, a toy top, a piece of bark). A different set of subjects were asked to rate all the objects on two scales, a schema-expectancy scale and a saliency scale. For the schema-expectancy scale, they rated "how likely the object would be to appear in a room of this kind". For the saliency scale, they rated how noticeable the object was.

The mean number of items correctly recalled was 13.5 per subject. Responses included some items, such as books and telephone, that had not actually been present, but were probable in the context. These had been inferred from the schema. Recall correlated with both schema expectancy ratings and with saliency ratings. That is, the most probable items and the most noticeable items were most often remembered. Items that formed part of the room itself, like walls and doors, were also frequently recalled. Brewer and Treyens refer to these as *frame objects*. Table 3.1 lists the items that were most frequently recalled.

It is clear that, contrary to the predictions of schema theory, bizarre objects, with low schema expectancy, like the toy top and the skull, were also recalled quite frequently. The results also demonstrated the normalising influence of schemas on memory for location. When subjects were asked to recall the exact location of objects in the room, they tended to shift the objects toward a canonical location. For example, a note pad was

TABLE 3.1
Items Recalled in an Experiment Testing Memory for Objects in a Room

Object	No. Subjects[a]	Object	No. Subjects
Chair (next to desk)	29	Frisbee	3
Desk	29	Jar of coffee	3
Wall[b]	29	Poster (in addition to those in room)[c]	3
Chair (in front of desk)	24	Screwdriver	3
Poster (of chimp)	23	Snoopy picture	3
Door[b]	22	Rotary switches	3
Table (worktable)	22	Cactus	2
Shelves	21	Cardboard boxes	2
Ceiling[b]	16	Coffee cup[c]	2
Table (with coffee)	15	Computer cards	2
Skinner box	14	Papers on bulletin board	2
Child's chair	12	Pens[c]	2
Door[b]	12	Pot (for cactus)	2
Light switch[b]	12	Solder	2
Toy top	12	Vaccuum tube	2
Brain	11	Window[c]	2
Parts, gadgets (on worktable)	11	Wires	2
Swivel chair	11	Ball[c]	1
Poster on ceiling	10	Brain (in addition to that in room)[c]	1
Books[c]	9	Brick	1
Ceiling lights[b]	9	Computer surveys (on floor)	1
Poster (of food)	9	Curtains[c]	1
Typewriter	9	Decals on walls[c]	1
Bulletin board	8	Desk (in addition to those in room)[c]	1
Clown light switch	8	Doorknob[b]	1
Coffee pot	8	Eraser	1
Skull	8	Fan	1
Mobile	7	Glass plate (covering desk)[c]	1
Road sign	7	Globe	1
Calendar	6	Hole in wall (for pipe)	1
Wine bottle	6	Homecoming button	1
Football-player doll	5	Lamp[c]	1
Jar of creamer	5	Magazines	1
Pipe (cord)	5	Nails[c]	1
Postcards	5	Packets of sugar	1
Tennis racket	5	Paper (on desk chair)	1
Blower fan	4	Scissors	1
Coloured patterns on ceiling lights	4	Screws[c]	1
Piece of bark	4	Teaspoon	1
Papers on shelf	1	Picnic basket	1
Pencil holder[c]	1		
Pencils[c]	1		
Filing cabinet[c]	3		

(Continued)

TABLE 3.1
(Continued)

Object	No. Subjects[a]	Object	No. Subjects
Pliers[c]	1	Umbrella	1
Saucer	1	Wrench	1
Telephone[c]	1		

[a] Maximum number of subjects = 30.
[b] Frame object.
[c] Inferred object, i.e. an object not in the office.

From Brewer and Treyens (1981).

remembered as being on the desk when it was really lying on the seat of a chair.

Brewer and Treyens' experiment showed that people remember objects that are typical, normal, and consistent with the currently active schema better than objects that do not fit the schema. Schema-consistent objects are more likely to be encoded; they are better retained because they are stored in a permanent framework, and they are more likely to be retrieved by schema-guided search processes. The experiment also provided evidence of schema-induced errors. People remembered the expected objects whether they actually saw them or not, and they remembered things in their expected places when they were elsewhere.

However, the experiment also shows that schemas are not the only factor at work. Saliency, as well as schema-expectancy, affected what was remembered. Very noticeable objects were more likely to be recalled. Brewer and Treyens (1981) did not distinguish between perceptual saliency and the kind of distinctiveness conferred by incongruity, but the results suggested that some objects, such as the skull, were remembered because they were bizarre and incongruent in that setting. These objects benefit from what Brewer and Tenpenny (personal communication, 1996) subsequently called the distinctiveness mechanism. Other studies (e.g. Mäntylä & Backman, 1992) have found that memory for schema- inconsistent information in a visual scene may actually be superior to memory for schema-consistent information. In everyday life, if you ask someone to recall the contents of a kitchen or a garage that they have just seen, you might also find that they remember any very distinctive, surprising, or peculiar objects better than the highly probable, schema-consistent objects. Note, however, that even if people tend to remember whatever is *not* consistent with the schema, this still implies the existence of a schema. The results of this experiment conform to Brewer's (1994) view that the primary way that schemas facilitate recall is by guiding the retrieval process to locate new episodic information for recall, and the primary reason why schemas induce errors is because the new episodic information is integrated with the old generic information and the two cannot always be distinguished.

Brewer and Treyens' finding that memory for the *position* of items in a room was influenced by stored knowledge about where things ought to be has also been noted by Mandler and Parker (1976). They showed people pictures of organised scenes and unorganised scenes as shown in Fig. 3.7, and asked them to reconstruct these scenes from memory, either immediately afterwards or one week later.

The organised scene was reconstructed much more accurately, but when testing was delayed for a week, there was an interesting difference in the accuracy of placement on the vertical dimension and the horizontal dimension. Vertical positions were better remembered. Mandler and Parker (1976) suggested that vertical placement is predictable from stored knowledge of spatial relations. We know that pictures are on walls, and are higher than chairs, which are on the floor, but horizontal placement is not predictable and there is no way of guessing whether the flowerpot should be on the left or right of the television set.

CONCLUSIONS

These studies give clear evidence that memory for object location is strongly influenced by stored schemas that have been constructed by generalising over past experience about what kinds of objects are found in which locations. More generally, although spatial memory may be a separate system, it does not operate independently of other kinds of memory, but interacts with knowledge about the nature and function of objects and knowledge about people and their activities. Studies of memory for maps, routes, and layouts have suggested that spatial memory is not tied to one form of representation. People can construct multiple different forms of representation and can translate one form into another to meet the demands of the current task.

If this chapter has seemed to emphasise the fallibility and weaknesses of spatial memory for places and object locations, this is partly a reflection of research techniques rather than an objective evaluation. Researchers deliberately contrive tasks with a level of difficulty that ensures a substantial proportion of errors simply because the nature of the errors and the pattern of incidence yield more information about the underlying mechanism than successful performance can reveal. These experiments do not give much idea of how well memory functions in the real world. Memory efficiency in everyday life needs to be judged in the street, not in the laboratory. In ordinary circumstances, efficiency is determined by values and costs, by

FIG. 3.7. Examples of an organised scene (top) and an unorganised scene (bottom) (from Mandler & Parker, 1976).

the trade-off between effort and accuracy. Destructive updating is economical in storage and makes for easier retrieval than keeping superseded or falsified memories in store, but it carries penalties in that old versions cannot be reinstated if new ones are discredited. Schemas are a powerful device for making the most of what we remember. They supply information that is missing, and allow us to make inferences and to reconstruct what has been forgotten. These benefits are also accompanied by some disadvantages. Mistakes and distortions occur. The way memory functions in everyday life is in the nature of a working compromise between the conflicting demands that are made on the system.

4

Memory for Events: Eyewitness Testimony and Flashbulb Memory

EYEWITNESS TESTIMONY

This chapter is concerned with memory for events that have been witnessed. Eyewitnessing differs from many other aspects of everyday memory in that accuracy is of much greater importance. For many everyday purposes memory does not have to be exact. We remember the gist of conversations; we have a rough idea of the spatial layout of a town; we can recall the salient points of a political issue. In these and other situations, there is a level of detail which is not relevant for most purposes. Many people deliberately make the decision not to clutter up their memory with details like names and addresses or times of trains but prefer to rely on being able to look these up. In everyday life it is rarely necessary for memory to be one hundred per cent accurate and complete. Examinations and eyewitness testimony are among the exceptions.

How Accurate are Eyewitnesses?

How accurately can people recall witnessed events? Failures of reality monitoring (discussed in Chapter 10, p.283) show that people are sometimes unable to distinguish in memory between what they have actually perceived, and what they have only heard about or imagined. Brewer and Treyens' (1981, p.79) experiment testing memory for objects in a room showed that the influence of schemas sometimes induces people to "remember" nonexistent objects, and List (1986) showed similar effects of pre-existing schemas on memory for events. Subjects in her experiment watched a video showing eight different acts of shop-lifting being carried out. Each of the sequences contained some elements people had previously rated as high in probability in a shop-lifting scenario, and some rated as low in probability. When the viewers' memory for these events was tested one week later, the influence of a shop-lifting schema was clearly evident because they remembered more high-probability elements than low-probability ones, and they also made more high-probability errors. That is, they falsely remembered events that had not actually occurred, but which were rated as highly likely to occur during shop-lifting. As well as containing schema-induced inaccuracies and distortions, memory for witnessed events also tends to be very incomplete. In everyday life situations, if an event is not very remarkable people may not be paying much attention to it, and may simply fail to see what is going on.

Eyewitness testimony is an area of research that has very obvious and important applications: It has a fundamental role in the administration of criminal justice. It is also one of the areas of everyday memory research that is very closely related to theoretical issues and theoretical constructs developed in the laboratory. In consequence, it provides an excellent illustration of the symbiotic relationship between the two approaches that was outlined in Chapter 1.

Eyewitness Testimony

Loftus and her colleagues (1979a) have carried out a detailed examination of eyewitness testimony in an extensive series of experiments. The main thrust of their research has been to demonstrate that memory for an event that has been witnessed is highly malleable. If someone is exposed to new information during the interval between witnessing the event and recalling it, this new, post-event information may have marked effects on what they recall. Loftus has interpreted the results as showing that the original memory can be modified, changed or supplemented.

These findings are of great practical importance in a legal context, when the credibility of a witness is at issue. Loftus has claimed that the witness' memory can be altered by the type of questions posed during questioning by police or lawyers. Leading questions, misinformation, or even quite subtle implications can introduce errors into the witness' subsequent recall of the event and this finding has very important implications for the kind of interviewing procedures which should, and should not, be employed. There is considerable controversy, however, about exactly what happens to the original memory in these circumstances. For example, McCloskey and Zaragoza (1985) have disputed Loftus' claim that the memory is changed, and have argued that misinformation biases the way that people respond to questions, but does not affect the original memory.

Eyewitness Testimony Experiments

Effects of Misleading Information

Eyewitness research relies on naturalistic experiments. These experiments typically consist of three phases. In the first phase, the subjects are asked to view a film or a series of slides depicting an event such as a car accident. Of course, this is rather different from the real life situation, when witnessed events are not necessarily the focus of deliberate and sustained attention, and people do not usually know, or even guess, that they will be asked to recall the event later. In the second phase, the subjects are exposed to post-event verbal information about the event they have seen. This might take the form of being asked questions or being asked to read a narrative description of the event. In the third phase of the experiment, memory for the original event is tested by further questions, or, if Phase 1 consisted of a slide sequence, then the memory test in Phase 3 may be a forced-choice picture recognition test in which pairs of slides are shown. One member of each pair is "old" (i.e. it occurred in the original Phase 1 presentation) and one of the pair is new. The subjects have to pick out the picture that is old.

The critical factor in these experiments is the nature of the post-event information presented in Phase 2. At this stage the subjects are divided into two groups. For the control group, the post-event information is *consistent* with the witnessed event (i.e. true). For the other group (the misled group) the post-event information is *misleading* (i.e. false). For example, in one experiment (Loftus, 1975), after all the subjects had witnessed a film of a car accident, post-event information for the control group included the question "How fast was the white sports car going when it passed the Stop sign?". The misled group were asked "How fast was the white sports car going when it passed the barn while travelling along the country road?". In the original film, the car did pass a Stop sign, but there was no barn. Hence, the mention of a barn was misleading because it implied its existence. In Phase 3, when all the subjects were questioned about the accident seen in the film, 17% of the subjects who had been exposed to the false information in the misled condition reported seeing a barn. Less than 3% of those in the control condition made this mistake. According to the Loftus interpretation of these results, the original memory of the event is supplemented with the false post-event information. The nonexistent barn is added to and integrated with the original memory representation of the event.

Further experiments have demonstrated that, as well as inserting nonexistent items into a memory representation, false information may transform the memory, deleting some elements and replacing them with others. In an experiment by Loftus, Miller, and Burns (1978) subjects viewed a set of 30 colour slides of a car accident. One group of subjects saw a version with a red Datsun stopped at a Stop sign. The other group saw a version with the Datsun stopped at a Yield [Give Way] sign, as shown in Fig. 4.1.

In Phase 2, subjects answered 20 questions about the accident. Half the subjects in each group were asked "Did another car pass the red Datsun while it was stopped at the Stop sign?" and half were asked "Did another car pass the red Datsun when it was stopped at the Yield sign?" So, overall, for half the subjects the post-event information was consistent with what they had seen and for half it was conflicting. Twenty minutes later, both groups received a forced-choice recognition test. Fifteen pairs of slides were presented, and subjects had to choose which one of each pair corresponded to the original version they had seen. The critical pair of slides were those shown in Fig. 4.1. Seventy-five percent of the subjects who had received consistent information in phase 2 made the correct choice. Only 41% of those who received conflicting post-event information were correct. Loftus interpreted this result as showing that a witness's memory of an event can be transformed by false post-event information.

Leading Questions

In other studies Loftus demonstrated that quite subtle differences in the wording of questions can influence the responses of a witness. After seeing a film of a multiple car accident, subjects were asked either "Did you see *a* broken headlight?" or "Did you see *the* broken headlight?" The question with the definite article "the" (implying that there was a broken headlight) elicited more positive answers. In a study by Loftus and Palmer (1974)

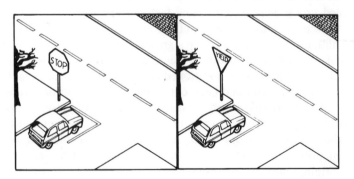

FIG. 4.1.   The red Datsun at a Stop sign (left) and at a Yield sign (right) (from Loftus, Miller, & Burns, 1978).

subjects were asked "About how fast were the cars going when they smashed into each other?". Alternative versions of the question used the verbs "collided", "bumped", "contacted", or "hit". Subjects who received the "smashed" version estimated a higher speed, and were more likely to answer "yes" to the question "Did you see any broken glass?", even though no broken glass was shown. These effects show that people are sensitive to the presuppositions and implications underlying the questions they are asked, and that their responses can be manipulated by the wording of the questions.

 ## Resistance to Distortion

Witnesses are not always easily misled. In some cases, their memory for the original event resists distortion. Further experiments have revealed some of the conditions and some of the factors that make witnesses more, or less, suggestible. One factor is public commitment. Subjects who make a public statement of what they recall before being exposed to false information are much less likely to change their recollection. Whether this is because verbalisation "fixes" the original memory and makes it more resistant, or because they are unwilling to contradict themselves is not clear.

Another factor is the plausibility of the false information. People resist attempts to mislead them more successfully if the false information is "blatantly incorrect". Loftus (1979b) showed subjects a series of slides showing a man stealing a large, bright red wallet from a woman's bag. When accuracy of perception was tested by an initial set of questions immediately afterwards, 98% of subjects had perceived the colour of the wallet correctly. They then read a narrative description of the event (allegedly generated by a psychology professor to enhance its credibility). One version of the narrative contained "subtle" errors such as errors about the colour of items that were only peripheral in the original event and not important. Another version contained, in addition, the "blatantly incorrect" statement that the wallet was brown. The final test showed that all but two of the subjects resisted this blatantly incorrect information, and continued to remember the wallet as red, but many subjects were misled by the false information about peripheral items. Thus, memory for obviously important information, which is accurately perceived at the time, is not easily distorted. The colour of the wallet was correctly remembered because the wallet was the focus of the event, not just a peripheral detail, and because its colour was correctly noted at the initial viewing. The experiment also demonstrated that, once witnesses recognise one piece of misleading information as false, they become more distrustful and are less likely to be misled by other false information.

Loftus and Greene (1980) tested memory for a staged event, rather than a film. This involved a man entering a classroom, picking up a book, and arguing with the professor. Misleading versions of the questions in phase 2 incorporated a critical question with the false presupposition that the man had a moustache. When the false presupposition was embedded in a subordinate clause ("Did the intruder, who was tall and had a moustache, say anything to the professor?") more subjects were misled and subsequently remembered the intruder as having a moustache than when the false presupposition was contained in a simpler sentence ("Was the moustache worn by the intruder light or dark brown?"). In the first version, the nonexistent moustache is tacked onto the question "by the way". In the second sentence, where it is the main point of the question, the attempt to mislead is too obvious and is less successful. To be effective, misleading information must be plausible, not too obvious, and come from an authoritative source that has not been previously discredited.

Time factors also influence the effects of false information. In the Loftus, Miller, and Burns (1978) study, the final test was given one week after the viewing, but the interval between the viewing and the false information in Phase 2 was varied. The number of subjects who resisted the misleading information fell from 50% when the false version followed immediately after the viewing the accident, to 20% when the false information was delayed for one week and presented just before the final test. False information has more effect if the original memory has had time to fade.

Factors Affecting Accuracy

A number of factors have been shown to affect witness accuracy. One such factor is the level of stress experienced by the witness at the time of the event. However, the precise effects of stress are still controversial. Some researchers (e.g. Kassin, Ellsworth, & Smith, 1989) have argued that the effects follow the well-known Yerkes–Dodson law so that very low levels of arousal produce poor memory and very high levels of emotional stress also have a detrimental effect on subsequent recall. According to this view moderate levels of stress produce the best recall. If the event is highly dramatic, observers are more likely to pay attention, but stress induced by frightening or emotional events can make their subsequent recall less reliable (Buckhout, 1982). This view received support from a study by Loftus and Burns (1982). They found that subjects who viewed a film showing a very violent version of a crime in which a boy was shot in the face had impaired memory for the events preceding the violence. Other studies have revealed a phenomenon known as "weapon focus". When an individual is attacked with a weapon, attention seems to be focused exclusively on the gun or knife so that not much other information is remembered.

In contrast with these findings, researchers such as Christianson and Hubinette (1993) have carried out a field study examining eyewitness memory for real events and have reported that high levels of stress can produce memories that are accurate, detailed, and long-lasting. They questioned 110 witnesses who, between them, had witnessed 22 bank robberies. Some of the witnesses had been bystanders whereas others, classed as victims, had been the bank tellers who were being threatened. Both victims and bystanders answered questions about the event and supplied ratings of their own emotions. Although there was no correlation between emotionality ratings and recall, the victims did remember more than the bystanders. Fifteen months after the event, the victims still showed accurate recall of details about the actions, clothing and weapons of the bank robbers. Christianson and Hubinette suggested that good recall of a highly stressful experience is characteristic of real events and that contrary findings were largely based on laboratory experiments using filmed or staged events. This interesting discrepancy illustrates the importance of collecting data from real, naturally occurring events. Laboratory simulations cannot, for ethical reasons, reproduce the level of stress generated by real events and cannot have the same impact as a real experience.

Another factor which may influence witnesses' accuracy is consequentiality. When people are acting as subjects in an experiment, even if they are doing their best to co-operate, they know that nobody's life and liberty hangs on their responses. In this situation, the consequentiality of memory accuracy is low. The question arises, then, whether people are more accurate if they believe that their responses will have serious consequences. Foster, Libkuman, Schooler, and Loftus (1994) produced evidence suggesting that consequentiality does have an effect. Their subjects viewed a video of a bank robbery and were then asked to identify one of the robbers in a line-up. Half the subjects were told that it concerned a real robbery and their responses would influence the trial: The other subjects did not receive this information. The results showed that the manipulation of consequentiality did affect recall, with men being influenced more than women. Consequentiality, like emotional stress, is another factor that is difficult to induce experimentally, so we may speculate that witness memory for real life events may be more accurate than laboratory findings suggest.

Memory accuracy also varies with the age of the witness. It is generally, although not invariably, found that the recall of child witnesses is less accurate and less complete than adults. Ceci and Bruck (1993) have noted that child witnesses are more suggestible than adult witnesses so that it is especially important to avoid leading questions or biasing information. A study by Flin, Boon, Knox, and Bull (1992) compared recall by children aged 5–6 years, 9–10 years and adults interviewed after 1 day and after 5 months. The results showed no age difference at 1 day, but after 5 months, although the adults had no significant forgetting, the children had forgotten a considerable amount. The researchers stressed the conclusion that the long delays in the legal system before children are questioned in court have damaging effects on their value as witnesses. Davies and Flin (1988) reviewed the evidence for the accuracy of child witnesses for two kinds of information, event information (a verbal report of an incident) and identity information (the physical appearance of persons involved). They noted that for events, younger children tend to recall less information than older children or adults, but there is little, if any, age difference in accuracy. Errors are more likely to occur for peripheral details, for events that are not understood, and when questioners over-prompt the children. Reviewing the evidence for suggestibility in children, they stressed that children are more likely to resist misleading suggestions about central aspects of an event and cited a study by Goodman, Aman, and Hirschman (1987) in which children aged from 3 to 6 years were questioned about a visit to a medical centre for inoculations. The children resisted leading questions such as "Did the man kiss you? Did he hit you?" and were accurate in their report of the central events. Davies and Flin concluded that some instances of suggestibility arise from social conformity, rather than from restructuring of the memory, as children may revert to the truthful answer later. In general, child witnesses have more difficulty with identity information than with event information. In producing a description, younger children produce fewer details, although these are generally accurate, but for all age groups questioning tends to elicit more inaccuracies. Overall, Davies, and Flin inclined to the view that the differences between child and adult witnesses have been exaggerated and that there is a strong case for the legal admissibility of the testimony of young children. (For a discussion of false memory syndrome, which is also concerned with the veracity of children's memory, see Chapter 6, p.163)

There is also evidence that elderly people are more susceptible than younger adults to misleading information. Cohen and Faulkner (1989) showed a film of a kidnapping incident to middle-aged and elderly subjects. Following the film, they read a narrative account of the episode. For the control subjects, the narrative was accurate and for the "misled" group it contained misleading information. After a brief delay all the subjects answered questions about the film. Suggestibility was assessed by comparing controls with those who had received the misleading information within each age group. The proportion of elderly who made errors based on the false misleading information, relative to elderly controls, was significantly greater than the proportion of middle-aged making similar errors. Yarmey (1984) has also reported that eyewitness memory in elderly people is less accurate and less complete. In one striking example, 80% of an elderly group omitted to report that an attacker brandished a knife, whereas only 20% of the younger group omitted to report this. To summarise the effects of age, the largest differences betwen misled and control subjects are found in 5- to 10-year-olds and in those over 65 years. Herrmann (1991) has also reported differences based on occupation. She found that artists, architects, and salespeople were among those most easily misled, whereas college students were among those least likely to be misled. Interestingly, Leippe and Romanczyk (1987) distinguish between two components of witness credibility: honesty and the ability to remember. Stereotypically, both children and the elderly are perceived as being more honest but as having faulty memories.

Before we leave the issue of eyewitness accuracy it is worth noting an interesting current debate about the relationship between confidence and accuracy. Numerous studies have failed to find any significant relationship, a finding which is grossly counterintuitive. Most of us would expect, intuitively, that greater confidence would be linked to greater accuracy. Gruneberg and Sykes (1993), in a recent critique, suggest three reasons why the absence of any relationship is an artefact of the typical experimental paradigm. First, they argue that the claim has been based on between-subject designs whereas, logically, within-subject designs should be used. Second, they point out that most experiments are designed to produce a high probability of errors in order to generate enough variance in the data. This means that, in these studies, the level of confidence is generally fairly low. In everyday life, the relationship of confidence to accuracy is likely to be strongest when confidence is high and the event is very salient. If a person is absolutely positive that her mother was run over by a car, there is a high probability that she is correct. Finally, they note that, in everyday life, the confidence-accuracy relationship may be increased by additional supporting evidence. Someone may be sure that a car accident occurred at 4.45 p.m. because he knows that he left a football match at 4.40 p.m. and saw the accident after walking a distance that takes 5 minutes. In laboratory experiments this kind of supporting information is not available. In the light of these arguments it seems that the view that there is no relationship between confidence and accuracy may need to be modified.

It appears that, of the factors considered above, stress, consequentiality and confidence levels tend to be distorted by the experimental paradigm so that experimental results do not correspond to real life situations. As these discrepancies become apparent the limits to the generalisability of experimental findings must be recognised.

INTERVIEWING WITNESSES

The Cognitive Interview

Among the factors that exert a powerful influence on the amount and accuracy of the information witnesses can recall is the technique of interviewing. It has always been obvious that some interviewers are more effective than others. Geiselman, Fisher, Mackinnon, and Holland (1986) codified some of the principles that, if put into practice, can maximise accurate recall, and developed the "cognitive interview". In the original version four principles were instantiated in instructions to the witness:

(1) Mentally reinstate the context of the target event. Recall the scene, the weather, what you were thinking and feeling at the time, the preceding events, etc.
(2) Report every detail you can remember even if it seems trivial or irrelevant.
(3) Report the episode in several different temporal orders moving backwards and forwards in time.
(4) Try to describe the episode as it would have been seen from different viewpoints, not just your own.

The interview follows a fixed sequence. After the first two instructions the witness supplies a narrative report followed by directed questions and then the procedure is repeated with the third and fourth instructions. The principles of reinstating the context and reporting every detail can be linked to encoding specifity theory. Each strategy is calculated to elicit more cues that may have been associatively encoded with relevant details of the event and may thus serve to retrieve more information. The principles of varying the sequential order and the viewpoint relate to reconstruction theories of memory by forcing the witness to construct a new description of the event that might then be recognized as correct. Information that was only implicit in the original description might become explicit in one of the reconstructions. Geiselman et al. tested the cognitive interview by comparing it with standard interviewing techniques. Subjects viewed a film of a violent incident. Two days later they were questioned using either the standard or the cognitive interview. Subjects who received the standard interview recalled on average 29.4 correct items of information; subjects receiving the cognitive interview recalled 41.2 correct items; and the two types of interview did not differ in the number of errors.

Numerous further studies using the cognitive interview have produced information gains varying from 10% to 98% but averaging between 25% and 35% (Bekerian & Dennett, 1993). The effect of the cognitive interview is robust and reliable although the size of the effect is so variable and depends on many factors. Its success depends on witness co-operation and it is thought to be less effective when the witness is highly emotional. A revised version of the cognitive interview lays more emphasis on principles (1) and (2) and on the value of listening skills and repeated attempts at recall. Altogether, the revised cognitive interview includes 13 basic skills.

(1) Establishing rapport.
(2) Listening actively.
(3) Encouraging spontaneous recall.
(4) Asking open-ended questions.
(5) Pausing after responses.
(6) Avoiding interrupting.
(7) Requesting detailed descriptions.
(8) Encouraging intense concentration.
(9) Encouraging the use of imagery.
(10) Recreating the original context.
(11) Adopting the rememberer's perspective.
(12) Asking compatible questions.
(13) Following the sequence of the cognitive interview.

Fisher, Geiselman, and Amador (1989) trained a group of detectives in Florida in the use of the revised cognitive interview and examined their performance interviewing real victims and witnesses. Comparison of their performance before and after training showed a 47% gain in information elicited; comparison of untrained and trained detectives showed a 63% improvement with training.

These studies provide a striking illustration of the fact that witnesses remember a great deal more than they report. Just as their memory can be changed or distorted by leading questions and misinformation, it can also be recovered intact by skilled and sympathetic questioning.

THEORETICAL PERSPECTIVES

The Fate of the Original Memory

When people are misled by false post-event information, what has happened to the original memory? This is a question of considerable theoretical interest. Does misinformation impair the ability to retrieve the original memory or does the stored memory trace itself undergo some transformation or weakening? There are several possible answers.

(1) *The vacant slot hypothesis* claims that the original information was never stored at all, so the false post-event information is simply inserted

into a vacant slot in the memory representation. Loftus and Loftus (1980) reject this possibility on the grounds that 90% of subjects who are tested immediately after witnessing the event, and are not exposed to any post-event information, are correct.

(2) *The coexistence hypothesis* states that both the original version and the false post-event version coexist as two competing alternatives. When tested, subjects usually respond with the false version because it has been presented more recently, and is therefore more accessible. This hypothesis implies that even if subjects produce the false version when memory is tested, the original correct version is, in principle, recoverable.

(3) *The demand characteristics hypothesis* also claims that both memories coexist, but argues that they are equally accessible. According to this hypothesis, people respond with the misleading information because they think this is what is demanded of them, not because it is more accessible. Loftus et al. (1978) tested this hypothesis by asking subjects in a final debriefing to recall *both* the original and the false versions, but very few could do so.

(4) *The substitution hypothesis* states that the false post-event information displaces, or transforms the original memory representation, which is then irrecoverably lost. This hypothesis is the one favoured by Loftus. It assumes a destructive updating mechanism (see p.74). Both the coexistence and the substitution hypotheses contain the "would-have-remembered" assumption, that is, they assume that subjects would have remembered the original version correctly if their memory had not been interfered with by the false post-event information.

(5) *The response bias hypothesis* put forward by McCloskey and Zaragoza (1985) claims that misleading post-event information has no effect on the original memory, but simply biases the response. They argue that, in most of the experimental paradigms, people have forgotten the original information by the time it is tested. When people respond with the false information, they are not *remembering* wrongly, they are just choosing the most recently mentioned item.

(6) *The source monitoring hypothesis* has been suggested by Johnson, Hashtroudi, and Lindsay (1993). They link the effects of misleading information in the standard experimental paradigm to failures of source-monitoring. When subjects are shown a visual sequence of events followed by verbal misinformation and a test of memory for the visual information, they are being asked in the memory test to discriminate between information from the visual source and information from the verbal source. When they claim to have seen things mentioned in the false verbal suggestions they are making a source-confusion error. The source-monitoring framework makes a distinction between memory for information and memory for

its source, so this explanation does not entail that the original memory itself is impaired, only the memory of its source.

Further evidence for and against these hypotheses is reviewed next. Some support for the source-monitoring hypothesis comes from an experiment by Lindsay and Johnson (1989). Subjects received pictorial information followed by post-event verbal information with or without misleading suggestions. At test, half the subjects had a yes–no recognition test in which they had to decide which items had been in the picture and which had not. The others had a source memory test in which they had to indicate the source (picture, verbal narrative, or both) of any items they recognised. Lindsay and Johnson predicted that, when subjects were forced to attend to the source of the information, they would not make errors based on the misleading verbal information. They found, as predicted, that subjects in the yes–no test were misled and claimed to have seen things that were only in the text, but subjects in the source memory test showed no suggestibility effect at all. It seems, therefore, that at least some of the effects of misleading information can be explained as failures of source-monitoring.

On the coexistence hypothesis, the original memory should be recoverable, but both the substitution hypothesis and the response bias hypothesis claim that the original memory is not recoverable. This issue about the recoverability of the original memory has been investigated by studying the effects of warnings. If people are given false information, and then warned that this information was inaccurate, are they able to disregard it and reinstate the original memory? In addition to the theoretical issue about the fate of the original memory, this question also has important practical implications. For example, can jurors discount the evidence given by a witness who is subsequently discredited? Greene, Flynn, and Loftus (1982) found that a warning given after the false information produced no significant improvement in the memory of the misled subjects relative to those who were not warned. The warned subjects seemed unable to disregard the discredited false information and recover the original memory.

Bekerian and Bowers (1983) produced evidence favouring the coexistence hypothesis. They presented slides of a car accident (as in Loftus et al., 1978) showing either the Stop or the Yield sign. Half the subjects received misleading information in Phase 2. In the recognition test, pairs of slides were either presented in the original sequence, or, as was done in the Loftus et al. (1987) experiment, the slides were presented in a random order. The random order produced the typical misled effect. Of the control subjects, 94% made the correct choice on the critical pair, but only 60% of the misled subjects were correct. However, presentation in the correct sequence elicited almost as many correct responses from the misled subjects (87%) as from the controls (85%). Bekerian and Bower argued that the original information had not been lost, and looking at the slides in the correct sequence provided enough cues to make it accessible. However, McCloskey and Zaragoza (1985) failed to replicate this result, so the status of this finding is in doubt. It is worth noting, however, that when the original and misleading alternatives are in direct contradiction, the coexistence hypothesis is, in common sense terms, rather implausible, because it suggests that people go around believing two contradictory things at the same time.

If the original memory is still intact and recoverable, it is certainly not very easily reinstated. Loftus (1979a) gave her subjects a $25 incentive to respond correctly, but the percentage of misled subjects who chose the correct alternative did not increase. Another way to test whether the original memory is intact is to offer subjects a second guess. On the coexistence hypothesis, people whose first response was the misleading information should be able to make the correct choice from among the remaining alternatives on their second guess. Loftus (1979a) reported an experiment in which subjects saw, in Phase 1, a man reading a green book. The misleading information in Phase 2 described the book as yellow. On test, the alternatives offered were green, yellow, or blue. Misled subjects whose first choice was yellow were only at chance level on their second choice, showing that their memory of the original colour could not be recovered. On the whole, the evidence for recoverability of the original memory is too slight to give much support to the coexistence hypothesis.

McCloskey and Zaragoza (1985) and Zaragoza, McCloskey, and Jamis (1987) have challenged the substitution hypothesis. Reassessing the experimental findings to take account of the probabilities of choosing different responses by pure guessing, they saw no reason to conclude that the misleading information has any effect whatsoever on the original memory. They argued for the response bias hypothesis, claiming that a high proportion of subjects in both control and misled groups forget the original item. To make this clearer, suppose that, in a two-choice test, 50% of the control group remember the original item and choose correctly. The other 50% have forgotten and are forced to guess. Of these, half will make the correct choice by chance, so, altogether, 75% of the control group will be correct. In the misled group, 50% will also remember the original item and be correct. But the 50% who have forgotten will be biased to choose the false alternative because it was mentioned in the misleading information. Because of this bias, fewer than half will choose correctly, so the total number of subjects who are correct in the misled group will necessarily be smaller than in the control group.

McCloskey and Zaragoza demonstrated that if the response biasing factor is removed, misled subjects perform as well as controls. In their procedure, control and misled subjects both witnessed an event with a man using a hammer. Misled subjects read a misleading narrative account describing the tool as a screwdriver, whereas controls were given a narrative that did not mention the tool. In the test phase, the choice was between a hammer and a wrench. The misleading false alternative was not offered as a choice, so no response bias could operate. If the false mention of a screwdriver had impaired or altered the original memory of the hammer, fewer misled subjects would choose "hammer". In fact, misled and control groups did not differ. Both were about 70% correct. From this result, McCloskey and Zaragoza concluded that misleading information does not affect the original memory. However, Loftus and Ketcham (1991) remains unconvinced by their arguments.

The fate of the original memory therefore remains controversial at present. It may be transformed or rendered inaccessible, the source may be misremembered or the memory may be lost altogether. It may be replaced with a false memory or a false response bias. There is, in fact, no good reason to suppose that original memories should always suffer the same fate. Given that Loftus has shown that susceptibility to misleading information varies with different circumstances, it is a reasonable conclusion that the fate of the original memory might also vary, being sometimes lost and sometimes changed. It is also arguable that the issues would be clearer if researchers distinguished more carefully between the effects of misleading information on memories, and its effects on beliefs and on reports. Whatever may be its effect on memory, it is undeniable that misleading information changes what witnesses report.

FLASHBULB MEMORIES

Flashbulb memory is a special case of witness memory. It is the term given to the unusually vivid and detailed recollection people often have of the occasion when they first heard about some very dramatic, surprising, important, and emotionally arousing event. Hearing the news that President John Kennedy had been shot, the bombing of Pearl Harbour, the first landing on the moon, or, more recently, the Challenger shuttle disaster, are among the examples that have been studied. Flashbulb memories typically encode what is called the "reception event" rather than the event itself. That is, they encode the circumstances in which the person first received the news and usually include the place, who was present at the time, what activities were going on, the affect occasioned by the event, and the source of the news. Once formed, flashbulb memories are apparently long-lasting and unchanged over time. Flashbulb memories are also distinguished by their phenomenological quality. They seem to have the peculiarly vivid character of an actual perception—what Brown and Kulik (1982) call "live quality"—and tend to include seemingly irrelevant and trivial details. However, there is considerable controversy about whether so-called flashbulb memories are different from other memories of events that are distinctive and personally significant. Are flashbulb memories special? There is also debate about how they originate and about the kind of information they incorporate.

Brown and Kulik (1982) suggested that there is a special neural mechanism triggered by high levels of emotion, surprise and consequentiality. This mechanism, they claimed, causes the whole scene to be "printed" on the memory. Such a mechanism would have obvious evolutionary advantages ensuring that the organism retains a vivid memory of the circumstances surrounding a potentially dangerous event. However, this account has been challenged by Neisser (1982c) and McCloskey, Wible, and Cohen (1988). Neisser has argued in favour of a reconstructive theory, claiming that flashbulb memories are simply ordinary memories preserved by frequent rehearsal and retelling after the event, rather than special processes activated at the moment itself. They are not necessarily true or accurate because they are the product of successive reconstructions. According to this view, the perceived importance of the event is a crucial factor because it gives rise to frequent rehearsal, but surprise and emotion are not necessary for the memory formation. So, whereas Brown and Kulik stress the importance of factors, such as emotion, present at the time of encoding, Neisser's reconstructive account places the emphasis on subsequent rehearsal.

Much of the debate has centred on whether flashbulb memories can be shown to be unusually accurate. If flashbulb memories can be shown to be inaccurate this tends to support Neisser's view. Neisser has cited cases where flashbulb memories recounted in great detail and good faith turned out to be inaccurate when independently checked. In his own recollection of hearing the news of Pearl Harbour in December 1941, he remembered that he was listening to a baseball game on the radio when the programme was interrupted by a newsflash. Neisser believed this memory must have been a fabrication because no baseball games are broadcast in December. However, Thompson and Cowan (1986) have discovered that a football game was actually broadcast at the relevant time, so Neisser's memory was inaccurate, but not completely wrong. McCloskey et al. (1988) also challenged the view that flashbulb memories have special qualities. Using a technique known as double assessment, they tested subjects' memory for the explosion of the space shuttle Challenger a few days after the event and again about nine months later. They found inconsistencies between the two accounts and clear evidence of forgetting. In a similar double assessment study, Neisser and Harsch (1992) obtained similar results. On the basis of these findings they have argued that the strong claim that flashbulb memories are 100% accurate and immune to forgetting must be discarded. Against this view, others (e.g. Schmidt & Bohannon, 1988) have pointed out that no attempt was made to check on the emotional impact of the event on the subjects. It is possible, therefore, that those who showed forgetting may have had a lower level of emotional response and never encoded a true flashbulb memory. Brown and Kulik (1982) always maintained that flashbulb memories are only formed if the event is of high personal importance to the individual. In support of their view, they showed that the incidence of flashbulb memories varied systematically with personal involvment and perceived consequentiality. Black Americans had more flashbulb memories than white Americans for the deaths of Martin Luther King and Malcolm X. In any case, in the McCloskey et al. study only 8% of the subjects showed forgetting and a remarkable 92% retained complete and accurate memories over the nine month interval.

The weaker claim that flashbulb memories are significantly different from ordinary memories has also been challenged. As McCloskey et al. (1988) have pointed out, ordinary memories can also be accurate and long-lasting if they are highly distinctive, personally significant, and interesting. For these memories the observed level of recall can be explained by frequent rehearsal and there is no need to postulate a special mechanism. So are flashbulb memories really different? Rubin and Kozin (1984) argued that so-called flashbulb memories are not essentially different in character from other vivid memories. They found that subjects rated some events of personal importance, such as graduating from high school, or an early romantic experience, as having flashbulb clarity and the vividness of these memories was also related to rated values for surprise, emotionality, and consequentiality. Their findings failed to reveal any features that would clearly distinguish flashbulb memories from other vivid autobiographical memories.

Wright (1993) has also argued that flashbulb memories show evidence of schema-based reconstruction in the same way that ordinary memories do, so that there is no need to postulate a special mechanism. He studied memory for the Hillsborough disaster, a tragic event in 1989 when 95 people were crushed to death in a football stadium. He tested three different groups of people after 2 days, 1 month, and 5 months. Subjects tested after 5 months' delay were more likely to recall hearing the news with their families and on television and judged it to be more important both personally and socially. Wright concluded that their memory for the event had been reconstructed to fit a schema or stereotype, but it is difficult to be sure that between-group differences of this kind are really due to reconstructive processes introducing changes over time, rather than simply reflecting differences in the way the groups originally experienced the event.

A multinational study by Conway et al. (1994) sought evidence for flashbulb memories by investigating people's memory for learning the news of the resignation of the British prime minister Margaret Thatcher. Using a double assessment test-retest procedure they established that over 86% of British subjects had complete and accurate recall that met the criteria for flashbulb memory nearly one year later. By contrast, only 29% of nonBritish subjects had flashbulb memories. Analysis of ratings and questionnaire responses supplied by the subjects showed clearly that flashbulb memory formation was associated with high levels of emotional response, interest in politics, and the level of importance attached to the event. Most nonBritish subjects, who were not particularly interested or excited by the event, showed normal forgetting of the details. These results suggest that both memories for dramatic public events and vivid memories for highly significant personal experiences may receive special encoding that can only be triggered by emotion and consequentiality. In the absence of these causal factors memories do not have flashbulb quality.

Brown and Kulik (1982) based their claim that a special mechanism exists for flashbulb memories on the fact that they have a canonical structure. People remember *Location* (where they were); *Activity* (what they were doing); *Source* (who told them); *Affect* (what they felt); and *Aftermath* (what happened next). However, according to Neisser (1982c) there is no need to postulate a special mechanism to explain these uniformities because they are the product of "narrative conventions", the traditional schemas that govern the format for story-telling. If schema theory can explain the canonical form of flashbulb memories and frequency of rehearsal can explain why they are selectively well-preserved, there is no need to invoke a special "print" mechanism. For Neisser, these special memories are primarily of social and cultural importance and function as "benchmarks" in the history of the individual.

Other researchers have studied developmental aspects of flashbulb memory in order to throw some light on the causal factors. Winograd and Killinger (1983) were interested in the development of flashbulb memories, and in whether dramatic events experienced by young children would be remembered in the same way as these events appear to be remembered by adults. They used subjects who were between the ages of one and seven at the time of John Kennedy's assassination and testing took place 16 or 17 years after this event. The subjects were asked questions about location, activity, the effect on those around them, the aftermath, how often it was discussed and any additional details. They plotted recall as a function of age at the time of the event using two different criteria for recall. The lenient criterion was satisfied if the subject claimed to be able to recall the event and could supply information in answer to one of the questions. The stricter criterion was satisfied only when four questions could be answered. It is clear from Fig. 4.2 that older children were more likely to remember the event and to recall more details about it.

The information most frequently recalled was location (90%), followed by activity (77%), source (70%), aftermath (43%) and other details (26%). The results did not support Neisser's (1982c) view that the vividness of flashbulb memories is produced by frequent rehearsal because very little rehearsal was reported by any of the children. Moreover, if recall depends on reconstruction subsequent to the event, it is difficult to see why the age at encoding has such a strong effect on retention. The absence of flashbulb memories in the younger children seems more likely to be due to neuro-logical immaturity or to their inability, due to lack of knowledge, to realise the importance of the event or to be surprised by it. Pillemer (1992) studied children's memory for a dramatic event when a fire broke out at their preschool and police and fire-engines arrived. Two weeks later two groups of children aged 3½ and 4½ years were asked questions about the event. Both groups recalled details of the event, but the older group were able to supply additional information about their location at the time, the emotion aroused by the event, and the cause of the fire. Retested 7 years later, only the older group had long-term memory for the event showing flashbulb character-istics. This finding therefore supports Winograd and Killinger's (1983) conclusion that a process of maturation occurring about the age of 4 years is a prerequisite for flashbulb memory formation.

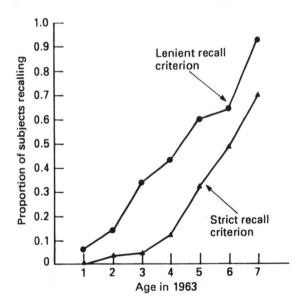

FIG. 4.2.   The proportion of subjects who could recall President Kennedy's assassination as a function of age at the time of the event (from Winograd & Killinger, 1983).

At the other end of the developmental spectrum, Yarmey and Bull (1978) investigated age differences in memory for the Kennedy assassination 12 years after the event and found that those aged 66 years and over had poorer recall of the event. A similar trend was noted by Cohen et al. (1994) who examined age differences in the incidence of flashbulb memories for the Thatcher resignation. Although 90% of young subjects had flashbulb memories, only 42% of the elderly group met the criterion. A possible interpretation of this finding is that lowered levels of arousal associated with aging are insufficient to trigger the special encoding mechanism necessary for flashbulb memory formation.

The flashbulb memory debate is still far from resolved. It is clear that some memories do exhibit remarkable persistence, clarity and detail. Some of the factors associated with the formation and maintenance of these super-memories have been identified, but whether it is necessary to postulate a special mechanism, or whether they can be explained in terms of normal memory processes, is still disputed. Conway (1995) maintained that the evidence for flashbulb memories is compelling and argued that they can be distinguished from other autobiographical memories. Autobiographical memories are actively constructed at retrieval and thus have a dynamic changeable quality in contrast to flashbulb memories that are fixed and highly durable. Flashbulb memories, in Conway's account, are more detailed and vivid, more holistic and integrated, than most autobiographical memories, and the formation of flashbulb memories is dependent on the preconditions of surprise, emotion, importance, and consequentiality. Conway's book provides a state-of-the-art review of studies of flashbulb memory and the theoretical controversy surrounding it as well as a well-argued case for regarding flashbulb memories as "special".

CONCLUSIONS

In this chapter, the studies of eyewitness testimony have focused on the fallibility and inaccuracy of memory and its susceptibility to misleading information and suggestions but this may not be a true reflection of witness memory. Koriat and Goldsmith (1996) have shown that memory accuracy can be greatly enhanced if tests abandon the forced-choice format and allow people the option of not responding to questions when they do not know the answers. Many experimental tests of eyewitness memory have used forced-choice recognition, which has the effect that although more questions are answered more answers are incorrect. Moreover, experimental tests are deliberately designed to be difficult. If pilot testing shows that subjects are producing near ceiling performance the experiment is redesigned to make it more difficult. For these reasons, experiments may not give a true picture of how well memory functions in the real world. We noted, for example, that the effects of high levels of stress and the confidence-accuracy relation are not the same in laboratory experiments as they are in field studies. By contrast with the studies of eyewitness testimony that stress the inaccuracy of memory, the flashbulb memory studies give evidence of remarkable levels of accuracy. Perhaps one reason for this is that flashbulb memory studies, unlike many of the eyewitness testimony experiments, test recall of real events.

Research on eyewitness testimony, and, in particular, the cognitive interview, has provided striking evidence that, like an iceberg, nine-tenths of everyday memory is submerged. When the right cues are supplied people can be helped to recall more information than they thought possible. This phenomenon relates to the theoretical distinction between implicit memory, which exists without conscious awareness, and explicit memory, which is consciously recollected. A great deal of memory for events is implicit and the cognitive interview technique works to make it explicit. The work with the cognitive interview shows clearly that we can remember more if we try harder: As well as generating more cues this technique pushes people to make more effort. Of course, mistakes and distortions do occur. Reconstructions may be inaccurate, particular details may be lost, and the unexpected may be disregarded. If flashbulb memories are accurate and long-lasting copies, rather than reconstructions, they are only encoded at the cost of some emotional distress. In general, the level of memory accuracy in particular situations is determined by a complex combination of motivational and affective factors and the operating characteristics of the mechanisms of encoding, storage, and retrieval.

5

Memory for People: Faces, Voices, and Names

Memory for people is a crucial element of everyday life, both in social interaction and in work and family life. Memory for people differs from memory for objects in a number of ways. One of the most important differences is that person recognition demands identification at the level of the individual, whereas for object recognition it is often sufficient to identify the category. We commonly recognise someone as John Smith or as our next-door neighbour, but we recognise an apple as an apple, not as a particular apple. Recognising people as individuals allows us to behave consistently to the same person and differently to different people, but it is usually unnecessary to tune our behaviour so finely for individual apples. Although memory for faces and memory for voices and for names form separate sections in this chapter, remembering people in everyday life involves all these as well as information about their physical appearance, the context in which we encounter them, and their biographical details. It makes more sense to think of memory for people as a single system in which all this information is integrated.

MEMORY FOR FACES

Memory for faces is an area of research that provides ample refutation of the critics of everyday memory. Strong theoretical advances have been based on the convergence of studies of face-processing in the laboratory, everyday performance in natural situations, and patterns of neurological impairment. Each line of research has informed and illuminated the others.

Remembering Faces in Everyday Life

How Important are Faces?

Remembering faces is a skill that is in daily use, but in real life we are not often called on to recognise people by their faces alone. Faces are rarely seen in isolation, even in photographs. We recognise people, not faces. Information about a person's identity is supplied by body build, clothes, gait, voice, and the context in which the person is encountered, as well as the face. We know very little about the relative contribution of these different aspects of personal identity to the recognition process, but mistakes and difficulties of identification suggest they are important cues. Clothes and context are both liable to change, and therefore ought to be less reliable as cues, but experience suggests that we do rely on them to a considerable extent. It is hard to recognise your bank manager at the disco or your dentist in evening dress. Young and Bruce (1991) called this the Little Red Riding Hood effect—even wolves can seem like grandmothers if they are in the right cottage and wearing the right clothes.

In contrast to the real life situation, many of the experiments that test face-recognition ability use still photographs of isolated faces, taken out of context, and stripped of all the additional information that normally accompanies a face. In real life we are rarely required to recognise isolated faces in this way. Although you may sometimes be asked to identify a person whose photograph or portrait is shown to you, there would usually be some visible background or contextual information. Unlike photographs, real faces are three-dimensional and dynamic and these characteristics yield a great deal of additional information. Face recognition in natural situations can exploit a much wider and richer range of cues and is therefore more likely to be successful.

Face Identification, Face Recognition, and Face Recall

How good is our memory for faces? In everyday life, this ability is tested in different ways, by face identification, face recognition, or (more rarely) face recall.

Face identification entails being able to look at a person's face and say who it is; being able to remember the person's name or some details about the person, or the circumstances in which the person was previously encountered. In the case of full identification, all this information is remembered, but sometimes you may only remember some of it. For instance, you may remember all about a person but may be unable to recall the name.

Face recognition, as distinguished from identification, occurs when you recognise a face as one that you have seen before. Familiar faces are usually identified as well as recognised, but recognition may sometimes occur without identification, as when you know that a face is familiar but cannot recall who it is. Recognition without identification is a form of face memory that is commonly tested in experiments. Subjects are shown a set of photographs, and are later required to recognise these as familiar, discriminating them from novel, unfamiliar faces. In everyday life, however, this type of face memory is relatively useless. To behave appropriately toward someone, it is necessary to know more about them than just that they seem vaguely familiar.

Face recall occurs in everyday life when you try to describe a face verbally to someone else, when you try to draw a face from memory, or when you try to "picture" a face by forming a mental image of it.

We know from our own experience that people seem to vary in face-memory ability quite considerably, so that it is difficult to say what level of performance should be considered normal. The incidence of errors varies with the degree of familiarity. Identification failures for faces that are well known do sometimes occur, but they are usually temporary mistakes due to misleading circumstances, such as changes of appearance, seeing someone in an unusual context, or poor visibility. Confusions may happen if a person is very similar in appearance to someone else, but such errors do not usually persist with prolonged inspection. With less well-known faces, identification failures are more common. It is quite easy to forget the face of someone you have only met casually, seldom, or a long time ago. Recognition is affected by familiarity in the same way as identification. Although it is relatively rare for someone to fail to recognise a well-known face, it is not so unusual when the face is unfamiliar. Face recall is not so often required of us in everyday life. When we need to describe a person to someone else, with the intention of enabling the hearer to identify that person, we do not usually supply much detail about the face. We generally describe age, height, build and any very distinctive features (e.g. "curly red hair", "beard" or "glasses") rather than giving a comprehensive description of the face. However, more complete and accurate recall is sometimes required, as when witnesses are asked to describe suspects to the police or to construct a photofit.

Naturalistic Studies of Memory for Faces

Ecological Validity

Studies by Bahrick (reported by Bahrick, 1984a) highlight the differences between the traditional laboratory experimental test and more realistic assessment of memory for faces. In his study, the same students were used as subjects in both types of test. In a traditional type of paradigm, they were first shown photographs of 20 target faces for 5 seconds each, and were later tested for ability to recognise them. In the recognition test, the faces were presented in sets of 10, with each set containing 2 target faces and 8 distractors (new faces that had not been seen before). The mean percentage of correct recognitions was 29%. In the realistic assessment, the target faces were those of classmates on a course who had met 40–45 times over a 10-week period. The distractor faces were those of students at the same university who were not classmates. Subjects had to pick out the photographs of their classmates. Recognition acuracy was 38%. Performance on the realistic task was significantly better and performance on the two tasks was not significantly correlated.

Bahrick noted that the tasks differed mainly in the degree of control over motivation and attention. In the laboratory version, subjects studied the faces for a fixed time, learning was intentional, and the amount of interference was controlled. In these conditions, performance reflects learning capacity and encoding strategies. In the realistic situation, learning was incidental and there was no control over the amount of exposure or the degree of attention paid to the classmates' faces. Even though the overall duration and type of interaction were to some extent standardised by the classroom situation, some of the target faces might have acquired social or emotional significance for some of the subjects. In ordinary everyday circumstances, the frequency of encounter and the nature of the interaction must be powerful factors in determining how well a face is remembered. Another difference between the studies was that the faces of fellow students were seen from many different angles and with different expressions, whereas the faces in the laboratory experiment lacked dynamic information.

In another realistic study of memory for faces, Bahrick tested the ability of college teachers to recognise photographs of their students and former students. The amount and duration of contact was constant (3–5 times a week for 10 weeks), but the time elapsed since the last encounter was varied. In a face-recognition task, the teachers had to pick out each of the target students' faces from four distractors, and in a face-identification task they had to name the faces. In the recognition task correct responses waned from 69% at 11 days' delay to 48% after 1 year, and were at chance after 8 years. When face identification was tested, and teachers had to name the faces, scores were, predictably, much lower. Memory for faces, even ones that are well known at some period, fades if time passes without further encounters. No doubt the continuing waves of new faces that teachers experience contribute to this effect.

Everyday Errors of Person Recognition

In the same way that Reason and Mycielska (1982) collected slips of action and attempted to infer the underlying mechanism, Young, Hay, and Ellis (1985) studied naturally occurring errors in recognising people and developed a model of person recognition based on an analysis of the types of error that were reported. Twenty-two people kept diaries of the errors they made and the difficulties they experienced over an eight-week period. The most common types of error were:

(1) *Failure to recognise a person* (114 cases). Most of these incidents involved people who were not very familiar, but in some few cases the person was well known and these lapses are difficult to account for.

(2) *Mistaking one person for another* (314 cases). Most of these mis-identifications were very quickly corrected and involved mistaking an unfamiliar person for a familiar one on the basis of similarities of hair, build, or clothing.

(3) *Failure to remember who someone was* (233 cases). In these cases the person seemed familiar but the diarist could not remember who it was. Most of these incidents involved meeting people who were not very well known in an unexpected context (e.g. "I was walking along the streets when I saw a person who looked familiar. At first I thought she was an assistant in the library, but I wasn't sure. Gradually I became convinced she was. I would have recognised her instantly in the library").

(4) *Incomplete recall* (190 cases). Another common type of error was failure to remember some details about the person (usually the person's name), although enough information was remembered for an identification to be made. In most of these cases, the diarist could recall the person's occupation (e.g. "I saw a poster advertising a film. I knew what films the actress was in and knew she does a lot of Beckett, but it was another minute before I could remember her name").

Other, less frequent, errors included being unsure who a person was, giving the wrong name to a person, and various combinations of different types of error. Diarists also reported incidents in which they noted the resemblance of one person to another, although no error was made. The subjects in this study reported that, although many different kinds of information were used in person recognition, they relied mostly on facial features. Incomplete recall and mistaken identification were types of error that often involved people known through the media, rather than from personal acquaintance.

Line-ups and Photofits

Accuracy of person recognition takes on much greater importance in the legal context where many miscarriages of justice have resulted from misidentification. As the diary study showed, errors and mistakes of recognition are particularly likely to occur when the person to be recognised is not well known and has perhaps only been briefly glimpsed. These factors often affect the accuracy of identification when witnesses are asked to identify a suspect in a line-up. In addition, there are several other aspects of the line-up situation that influence the witness' ability to recognise the criminal. Fruzetti, Toland, Teller, and Loftus (1992) pointed out that, although the witness may be told that the suspect is not necessarily present in the line-up, there is a tendency to believe that the police would not go to the trouble of arranging a line-up unless they had a good suspect to put in it. Thus the task becomes a multiple-choice recognition test and a witness is liable to select whoever best matches their memory of the criminal. In these circumstances, the size and composition of the line-up is critical. Nontargets should be similar to the target in appearance and clothing so that they cannot be eliminated immediately and the suspect selected by default rather than by genuine recognition. It has also been suggested that presenting one member of the line-up at a time, rather than simultaneously, reduces the number of false positive identifications. Additionally, witnesses should be instructed that a high degree of certainty is required before a suspect is identified.

Read (1995) distinguished between perceptual knowledge and contextual or semantic knowledge and investigated the contribution of each to person identification. In the first experiment, 121 retail store clerks were asked to identify target shoppers with whom they had interacted in a photo line-up. Read manipulated three variables, the length of the interaction; the similarity of the target's appearance in the original encounter and in the photo line-up; and the presence or absence of the target in the line-up. The results showed that false positive identifications increased when the interaction was longer, especially if the target was not in the line-up, and confidence in these misidentifications also increased with the length of the interaction. On Read's interpretation, the longer interaction increased contextual knowledge of the target causing an overestimation of perceptual knowledge. That is, people think they should be able to identify someone when they know more about them. In a further experiment, the target was a new class assistant briefly introduced to groups of students. All groups had the same perceptual experience but some groups received additional contextual information about the target (that he had mislaid exam scripts, that he had completed a hypnotic stop-smoking programme). This enhanced contextual knowledge was associated with twice as many false positive identifications responses in a target-absent line-up. Knowing more about the class assistant made people more confident that they could identify him and more likely to make false identifications. A third experiment again examined target identification by store clerks. Following encounter with the target, one group were induced to rehearse contextual knowledge about the interaction; another group were induced to rehearse perceptual knowledge. In this experiment enhanced contextual knowledge produced more false positives when the foils were highly similar. In sum, these experiments show that people infer their ability to make an identification from their level of contextual knowledge and tend to be overconfident when contextual knowledge is high. It follows that, in real life situations, witnesses' accuracy may be impaired when contextual knowledge is boosted by thinking and talking over the circumstances of the encounter.

Whereas line-ups test person recognition, witnesses are sometimes required to recall the appearance of suspects. The witness may be helped to construct a likeness using photofit. Photofit consists of sets of photographed features (hair, eyes, nose, mouth, and chin), which the witness selects and puts together like a jigsaw. Research (e.g. Davies & Milne, 1985) has shown that, although they bear a general resemblance to the target face, the resulting composites are seldom very good likenesses. Better results are achieved using systems based on computer graphics such as E-fit (Electronic Facial Identification Technique). The witness' verbal description is matched against a library of features and a seamless composite is constructed and displayed on screen. The shape, size, position, and darkness of individual features can then be adjusted. This system has several advantages. Instead of selecting features in isolation from each other, features are always seen in the context of the whole face; configurational information is represented as well as individual features; and subtle adjustments can be made. Although E-fit is a relatively recent technique it appears to be produce better likenesses (see Fig. 5.1).

In addition, E-fit may provide a better method of assessing people's ability to recall faces. Testing recall by Photofit or by verbal descriptions forces the witness or subject to decompose their memory image and produce a feature by feature reconstruction. E-fit operates more holistically and this may be an advantage if the memory representation is also a holistic one.

Factors Affecting Face Recognition

Familiarity

Several of the factors that affect the accuracy of recognition have already been noted. Not all faces are equally easy to recognise. It is fairly obvious that faces that are highly familiar and have been seen many times are easier to recognise than unfamiliar faces. Experiments have shown that face memory is superior if a face is seen in a variety of different poses (Ellis & Shepherd, 1992) rather than repeated exposures of the same pose. In

FIG. 5.1. Photograph of Tony Blair, together with an E-fit composite constructed from memory (supplied by Heidi Oldman, Department of Psychology, University of Leicester).

everyday life, faces that are more familiar are ones that have been seen from many different viewpoints.

Distinctiveness

The everyday intuition that highly distinctive faces are easier to remember than faces that are ordinary and typical has also been experimentally confirmed (Valentine & Bruce, 1986; Valentine & Moore, 1995). In the Valentine and Bruce study, subjects were shown photos of familiar (i.e. famous) and unfamiliar people and asked to rate each face for how well it would stand out in a crowd. On the basis of these ratings the faces were classified as distinctive or as typical. Different subjects were then shown the faces in a mixed sequence and asked to respond as fast as possible whether each face was familiar or not. The average response time was significantly faster for the distinctive faces. This finding is consistent with the results of studies investigating the effects of caricature. Rhodes, Brennan, and Carey (1987) used a computer program to exaggerate the features of line-drawings of faces and found that the resulting caricatures were easier to recognise than the originals. Because caricature enhances distinctiveness this result confirms the conclusion that distinctive faces are easier to recognise than typical ones. The effects of attractiveness are less clear-cut. Some researchers have reported that attractive faces are easier to remember and others have reported the opposite result.

Stereotypes

There is also some evidence that memory representations of faces are influenced by stereotypes (Yarmey, 1993). He showed videos of 30 unfamiliar white males, aged 25–30 years, to 240 students and asked them to rate personality characteristics for each one and to select which person was most like a mass murderer, a sexual assault felon, an armed robber (the bad guys) and a clergyman, a doctor and an engineer (the good guys). There was considerable consensus as to which targets fitted which roles, so it appears that people do believe that facial appearance is linked to personality traits and, as Yarmey points out, this means that, in a legal context, judgements about criminality may be biased by the physical appearance of suspects. However, evidence that recognition was influenced by stereotypes was weak. There was no difference in the recognition hit rates for the faces classed as good guys and those classed as bad guys, but there was a higher level of confidence in the recognition of the good guys.

Theoretical Perspectives of Face Recognition

Representations of Faces in Memory

In discussing the use of Photofit we noted that it seems difficult to recall a face by producing a feature-by-feature description. This observation is in accord with a growing body of evidence that suggests that faces are represented holistically, or configurally, rather than as a list of features. In an experiment designed to explore this issue Tanaka and Farah (1993) asked subjects to learn names for faces. Some of the faces were normal and in some conditions the faces were scrambled (see Fig. 5.2). For example, subjects learned that a face constructed (using Mac-a-Mug computer software) with a particular combination of features was called Larry. At test, they were asked to: (a) identify a single feature such as Larry's nose when seen as one of a pair of isolated noses; (b) identify Larry's face when seen as one of a pair of normal faces differing only in the nose; and (c) identify Larry's face when seen as one of a pair of scrambled faces, again differing only in the nose.

Tanaka and Farah argued that if facial features are represented separately, then memory for a particular feature should be as good when it is seen in isolation as when it is seen in the context of the whole face. If faces are represented configurally, then it should be more difficult to recognise isolated features. The results showed that features learned in the context of a whole normal face were better recognised when seen in a whole normal face. Although this advantage did not hold for scrambled faces or when the faces were upside down. The conclusion is that normal faces are represented configurally in memory but the representation of scrambled or

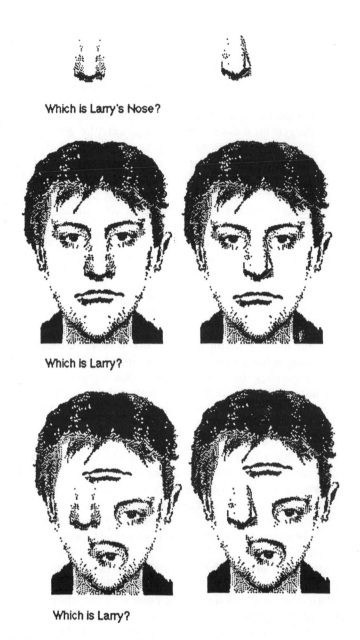

Which is Larry's Nose?

Which is Larry?

Which is Larry?

FIG. 5.2.   Examples of test pairs with isolated noses (top), noses set in normal face contexts (middle) and in scrambled faces (bottom) (from Tanaka & Farah, 1993).

inverted faces is different. Yin (1969) reported that recognition of faces was peculiarly difficult when they are inverted and this effect has been interpreted as due to the fact that inversion disrupts the configural processing normally used for upright faces. By contrast, object recognition seems to involve specific parts or features being represented and processed separately and is not so much affected by inversion.

Despite the evidence that faces are represented configurally, features also seem to play some part in face recognition. There is evidence, for example, that some features are more salient than others. Subjects spend more time looking at some features when memorising a face; recognition is more disrupted by changing some features than by changing others; and a face with a highly distinctive feature is more easily recognised. Experiments (Ellis, Shepherd, & Davies, 1979) suggest that, in recognition of familiar faces, features in the inner part of the face (eyes, nose, and mouth) are more important than features in the outer part (hair and face shape). However, for unfamiliar faces there is no difference. These findings indicate that the mental representation of a face undergoes some change as the face becomes more familiar. Ellis and Shepherd (1992) suggested that the more expressive inner features become more important as we get to know a person. Further evidence that familiar faces and unfamiliar faces are represented differently comes from the finding that recognition of unfamiliar faces is disrupted by changes of view, whereas recognition of familiar faces is unaffected.

Valentine (1991) has suggested a form of representation that explains why distinctive faces are easier to recognise than typical ones. He postulates a multidimensional face space. The dimensions of this space include both features like colour of hair and size of nose, and more holistic characteristics like overall face shape. A particular face is represented by its location in the multidimensional space. Typical faces that share many of the same values on these dimensions (e.g. blue eyes and brown hair) will be clustered together; distinctive faces that have unusual values on dimensions (e.g. auburn hair and green eyes) will occupy an area where few other faces are located. According to this model, identifying a face involves locating it in the multidimensional space so, obviously, it is easier to pick out a distinctive face in a relatively empty area than a typical one in a crowded area.

Models of Face Recognition

Models of face recognition have been based on a rich mixture of information derived from everyday observations and information derived from experimental testing. As more information has accumulated, the models have evolved to take account of new findings. The diary study by Young et al. (1985) gave rise to a sequential stage model of person recognition shown in Fig. 5.3.

From their data, Young et al. (1985) concluded that person recognition is a graded process with levels of recognition varying from "seeming familiar" to full identification. They proposed a model in which the first stage consists of face-recognition units (FRUs), which contain representations of the physical appearance of known faces. At this stage a face that matches one of the stored representations is judged to be familiar. Activation of an FRU allows access to the next stage, a person-identity node (PIN), which stores biographical information, such as the person's occupation and nationality. Activation of the PIN allows access to the final stage where there is a further store holding additional information and the person's name.

The sequential organisation of the stages explains both the types of error that do occur and the types of error that do not occur. Person recognition may succeed at one level, but fail to reach a higher level. For example, as Young et al. (1985) found, biographical information about a person may be recalled without name recall if the PIN, but not the final stage is activated.

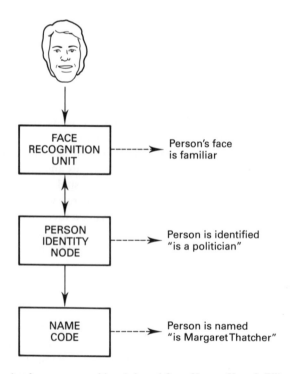

FIG. 5.3.   Levels of person recognition (adapted from Young, Hay, & Ellis, 1985).

You may know who someone is, but may not be able to remember his or her name. However, failures of recognition in which the name of a person is recalled but not the biographical information (you know someone's name but cannot remember who it is) do not occur. In everyday life, and in the model, the name code cannot be accessed unless the PIN has been activated. Recognition mistakes occur if the physical information causes the wrong face-recognition unit or the wrong person-identity node to be activated.

There is considerable evidence from experiments with normal subjects and from neuropsychological cases to support the basic form of this model. In reaction time studies (e.g. Young, McWeeny, Ellis, & Hay, 1986) subjects respond fastest when asked to decide if a face is familiar (a decision made at the first, FRU, stage). They are slower to decide if a face is the face of a politician (a decision that requires access to the PIN stage), and slowest of all to retrieve the person's name. In another study, where the response requirements were carefully matched, Johnston and Bruce (1990) asked subjects to decide if two faces were both dead or both alive (a PIN decision) or whether the two faces were both called John or both called James. Consistent with the model, the naming decision took longer than the dead or alive decision.

Neuropsychological cases have been observed that reflect the stages in the model. The patient EST described by Flude, Ellis, and Kay (1989), could recognise famous faces as familiar and recall biographical information about them but could not retrieve their names. The patient ME, described by De Haan, Young, and Newcombe (1991), performed normally in making familiarity judgements but could not retrieve any personal details or names. These cases show that earlier stages may be intact when later stages are impaired.

The Bruce and Young (1986) model is an elaboration of the earlier stage model, retaining the same basic components but integrating them within a broader framework of other functions of facial information and different ways of recognising people by their names or voices. This model is shown in Fig. 5.4.

The initial stage of structural encoding converts the input face to a description that is independent of the particular viewpoint and expression. In addition to the person-identification route of FRU, PIN, and name generation, which is retained from the earlier model, there are three independent modules operating in parallel. Expression analysis yields information about the person's mood and feelings, facial speech analysis carries out lip-reading: and directed visual processing selectively processes information, such as age, sex or race, that does not require identification of the person. Again, there is neuropsychological evidence that supports the model. Dissociations have been reported by Campbell, Landis, and Regard

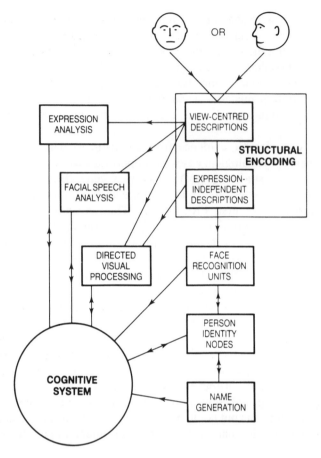

FIG. 5.4.   A model of face recognition (adapted from Bruce & Young, 1986). Reprinted by permission of The British Psychological Society and the author.

(1986) in which one patient had impaired expression analysis but intact lip-reading and another patient had the opposite pattern of impairment. In further elaborations of the Bruce and Young model additional identification routes allow the PINs to be accessed from spoken or written names or from voices.

Further theoretical developments were prompted when neuropsychological cases came to light in which patients were performing in ways that are difficult for the Bruce and Young (1986) model to explain. Briefly, there was evidence that, in a patient called PH, higher-level information about person identity or name was subconsciously available even though there was complete failure at the first stage of familiarity judgements. According to the model there should be no access to identity or name information should take. The researcher later asked the shop assistant/bank clerk to participate in a voice-identification test. In this situation, when testing was anticipated, identification was at chance level after 4 hours delay. Memory for voices is clearly not as good as our intuitions may suggest. Strange voices are unlikely to be recognised after a delay unless the listener has made a deliberate effort to commit the voice to memory, and even when the listener has tried to remember the voice, recognition is poor after two or three days.

However, in some circumstances people can remember a speaker's voice for hours or days and this is an indication that memory for the surface form of utterances is not necessarily lost as rapidly as psycholinguists such as Sachs (1967) have argued (see Chapter 8). Palmeri, Goldinger, and Pisoni (1993) in a series of experiments showed that detailed information about a speaker's voice is retained in long-term memory. Recognition memory for spoken words is superior if the words are repeated in the same voice rather than in a different voice, and this "same-voice advantage" persists over a considerable time. Their experiments suggested that retention of voice characteristics is an automatic process because it was unaffected when the processing demands were increased by increasing the number of different speakers.

Voices, as we already noted, have been integrated within the Bruce and Young (1986) and the Burton and Bruce (1992) models of face recognition, with a separate input route accessing the PINs so that the model does represent the role of the voice in making judgements about identity. However, as well as conveying information about a person's identity, voices carry information about age, sex, and national, regional, and social origins, and we also tend to make judgements about character on the basis of voice. Harmey (1993) in his study of stereotypes for faces and voices found that there were significant correlations between rated voice characteristics and rated personality traits. For example, high voices were associated with weak personalities and soft voices with submissive personalities. Voices may express mood, affect, and emotions even more clearly than faces. These considerations suggest that further routes for voice expression analysis (mirroring the route for facial expression analysis) and for directed voice-processing of semantic information need to be incorporated in the model. Voice recognition also parallels face recognition in that neuropsychological studies (e.g. Van Lancker, Cummings, & Kreiman, 1989) have shown cases of phonagnosia, a specific deficit for voice recognition associated with damage to the right parietal lobe, and similar to prosopagnosia, the specific deficit for faces. Van Lancker, Cummings, Kreiman, and Dobkin (1988) also reported double dissociations of the ability to recognise familiar voices and the ability to discriminate between two unfamiliar voices, thus confirming the experimental finding that these are different abilities.

unless the face is judged familiar. Yet this patient did appear to have some weak activation of names and biographical information (see De Haan et al., 1987, for details). These findings are difficult to reconcile with a strictly sequential stage model.

In response to this evidence, Burton, Bruce, and Johnston (1990) and Burton and Bruce (1992) developed the Interactive Activation and Competition (IAC) model. This model reformulates the central identification route of the Bruce and Young model in a parallel connectionist format. The stages are replaced by three separate pools of units. The face-recognition units are activated by the presentation of a familiar face. The PINs are identity-specific nodes, one for each known person. In effect, the person is represented at the PIN, which receives activation from the associated FRU, and also from other systems (not shown in Fig. 5.5), which process the written or spoken name and the voice. The semantic information units that store both names and biographical information are accessed from the PINs. Units in different pools are linked by bidirectional excitatory connections. As can be seen in Fig. 5.5, a particular semantic unit such as "politician", might be linked to several different PINs.

The most important features of the IAC model are that there is no longer a separate store for names and that familiarity decisions are made at the PINs rather than at the FRUs. Access to the different pools of units is no longer in strict sequence and units can be activated to a subthreshold level. The model can therefore explain the performance of patients like PH who have access (at least to some extent) to name and identity information for people they cannot recognise as familiar. The IAC model has the further advantage that it has been fully implemented and has simulated the experimental findings and also generated new predictions.

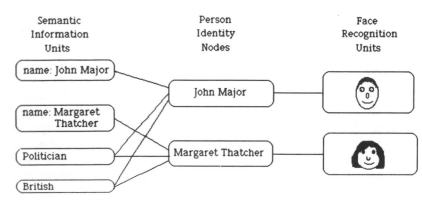

FIG. 5.5. Basic components of the Interactive Activation and Competition (IAC) model of face naming (adapted from Burton & Bruce, 1992).

Good face recognisers

Individual Differences in Memory for Faces

Although there are many parallels between the way faces are recognised and the way objects are recognised, there is considerable evidence that face recognition is a "special" ability with specific mechanisms dedicated to face-processing. Patients suffering from prosopagnosia may show preserved object recognition although they are unable to recognise faces, and there have been a few cases of people who can recognise faces but have trouble with objects. The conclusion is that there are specific face-processing modules but that the processes involved are not unique; similar processes are involved in recognising animals, flowers, and objects.

Many researchers have commented on the wide spread of individual differences in face-memory tasks, and this conforms with our everyday experience. People often make the unlikely boast that they never forget a face, or regret their poor ability to remember faces. However, Woodhead and Baddeley (1981) found that people's self-ratings of their own ability to recognize faces in everyday situations bore no relationship (r = −0.05) to their performance in a laboratory face-recognition experiment. Either people are very bad at assessing their own ability, or the formal face-recognition experiment tests abilities quite different from those exercised in everyday life. However, people who do well at one laboratory task perform consistently well across a variety of other experimental tests of face memory, and are also good at other tests of visual memory, such as picture recognition. It has proved difficult, however, to obtain clear and consistent results to show what characteristics define a good face-recogniser. Face memory is poorer in childhood and in old age. There is a clear trend whereby face recognition improves from the age of about five years up to adulthood. Chung and Thomson (1995) reviewed a number of possible explanations for this developmental trend and concluded that the amount of facial information that is encoded increases with age, and that there is greater efficiency in encoding both featural and configural information. There are also some gender differences in face recognition. Women are sometimes superior, but only at recognising women's faces (Goldstein & Chance, 1971). Finally, face recognition has sometimes been found to correlate with measures of field dependence (Ellis, 1975). On the whole, however, research has little to say about why some people are better than others at remembering faces, and little to offer in the way of suggestions as to how we could train people to improve their face-recognition skills. Laboratory experiments using artificial material, such as photographs presenting disembodied faces divorced from any social or situational context for only a few seconds, are posing problems that are very different from those encountered in the real world.

MEMORY FOR VOICES

In everyday life situations, voices may play a part in [...] when we detect a familiar voice across a crowded roo[m ...] ence leads us to believe that our ability to remember v[...] not unusual to pick up the phone and immediately rec[...] friend who has not been heard from for many years. A [...] totally unexpected and there are no contextual cues to a[...] are still able to identify the speaker. On other occasion[...] to put a name to the voice, but yet be confident that i[...] and not the voice of a stranger.

Clifford (1983) contrasted these situations with th[...] which a witness, or a victim, has heard an unfamilia[r ...] commission of a crime and is asked to identify it late[r ...] once-heard voices is not nearly as good as identification[...] Bricker and Pruzansky (1966) found that people we[re ...] identifying the familiar voices of people they worked [...] trasts with the findings from experiments using strange[...] experiment by McGehee (1937), 740 listeners heard a [...] being read aloud. Recognition tests were given after inter[vals ...] 1 day to 5 months. In the recognition test, five differen[t ...] original passage and listeners had to identify which voi[ce ...] before. Recognition accuracy was 80% for a delay of up [...] after 2 weeks, 51% after 3 weeks, and 35% after 3 mon[ths ...] study (1993), he compared recognition accuracy after p[...] sisting of face, face plus voice, and voice alone. Both fa[...] voice scored hit rates of 0.99, but for voice alone hit rates [...] high false positive rate.

Clifford's review also indicates that the accuracy of voi[ce ...] slightly reduced if the speech sample is small and is seriou[sly ...] distortions, such as whispering. In an experiment design[ed ...] effects of delay, target voices uttered the sentence "I will [...] the National Westminster Bank at 6 o'clock tonight". In [...] test there were two target voices and 22 distractors. Traine[d ...] as subjects. Recognition accuracy declined from 55% at 1[0 ...] to 37% at 2 weeks' delay.

Clifford pointed out that naturally occurring situations[...] experimental situation in that the listener is not forewarned[...] will be required to recognise the voice. Forewarning appe[ars ...] substantial difference to performance. In a naturalistic s[...] tested the ability of shopkeepers and bank clerks to recog[nise ...] of a male stooge who entered the bank or shop, introd[uced ...] explained that he had lost his chequebook and card, and ask[ed ...]

MEMORY FOR NAMES

When people are recounting their personal experiences, or when they are quizzed about things that have happened to them, it is noticeable that memory seems to be particularly fallible for the recall of people's names, and it is quite common to hear people, especially as they get older, complaining that they have a poor memory for names. Everyday experience suggests that, although we seldom forget the names of objects, we often forget the names of people or places, so that memory for proper names appears to differ from memory for common nouns.

Experimental studies of memory for names have asked subjects to recall the names of people they have known personally or of famous people, and have probed the retrieval strategies used in this situation. Other experiments have focused on subjects' ability to learn new names. Naturalistic studies have been concerned with naturally occurring lapses of name recall, and have used diaries and questionnaires to analyse the failures of name recall that occur in everyday life when you meet someone, or want to talk about someone, but cannot remember his or her name. Neuropsychological studies have investigated cases of patients with selective deficits for proper names, and, more recently, evidence of double dissociations for object names and proper names has been reported (see Cohen & Burke, 1993, for a review).

Experimental Tests: Retrieval of Known Names

Names of Classmates

Williams and Hollan (1981) asked four subjects between the ages of 22 and 37 to recall as many names of their schoolfellows as possible. Over a series of test sessions, spread over 2 weeks and amounting to up to 10 hours, the number of names retrieved ranged from 83 (the poorest subject's score) to 214 (the best subject's score). Recall was cumulative and new names were still being retrieved in the final session, even though subjects had earlier been convinced that they could not recall any more. Persistent searching produced names that had seemed inaccessible. Verbal protocols were recorded so that the retrieval processes could be analysed.

Several different kinds of retrieval process could be identified. Subjects first tried to narrow down the search context by concentrating on a particular location, activity, or time. For example, they searched within contexts like the general science class, the lunch queue, school dances, or neighbourhood friends, often using pictorial imagery as they searched. Contextual information was used to construct and enrich a description of the target person, as in:

"I'm trying to remember the name of this guy who used to—Art—He was in our 10th grade art class—He would also bring a whole lot of people to—At his house was the first time I heard a Jefferson Airplane album."

"I remember this girl who used to play the oboe, and it was junior year, she was our age—or was she older?"

In these examples, the subject is constructing a description, or target specification. General knowledge schemas about school activities and customs and what clothes were worn are used to define the context and to enrich the description. The more complete the description the greater the chance of retrieving the name. Subjects sometimes recalled only fragments of a name, such as the first letter or syllable, and then generated a list of candidate names with these characteristics. One of these might then be recognised as the target name. Groups of names from within the same context were sometimes recalled in batches.

In line with a model outlined by Norman and Bobrow (1979), there was evidence for three stages of retrieval: formation of the initial specification, matching a retrieved name against this specification, and evaluating the match (deciding whether the name was correct). It is an obvious, but significant, point that in this task, when the subjects were simply asked to recall names, what they actually recalled was primarily the people, and only secondarily the names. Apparently, names are not accessed directly, but only indirectly, via the contextual and personal identity information.

Names of Teachers

Whitten and Leonard (1981) carried out a similar study, asking college students to recall the names of their schoolteachers, one from each of the 12 school grades. They were particularly interested in studying the effects of order of retrieval. If past experiences are chronologically organised in memory, then retrieval might be best achieved by searching along the temporal dimension. Whitten and Leonard set out to compare the efficacy of forward-ordered search (beginning with the first year at school), backward-ordered search (beginning with the last year), and randomly ordered search. They reasoned that forward-ordered search might be most efficient because it would benefit from a primacy advantage and from the coincidence of order of retrieval with order of experience. Backward-ordered search, however, would have the advantage of recency effects. They found that subjects who were instructed to recall in backward order were more successful, recalling more names correctly, and recalling them more rapidly, than subjects in either the forward or the random conditions.

From these results, Whitten and Leonard concluded that event memories are not accessed independently. If they were stored and accessed as separate and independent units then a random order of search would have been equally successful. Instead, memories are interdependent, with memories that are adjacent in time sharing the same context of occurrence and being retrieved together. In backward search, the starting point is the most recent period (the last year in school) and is therefore most easily recalled. Once this is accessed it aids recall of the next-to-last item that shares some of the same context, and so on, in a reverse chain.The verbal protocols recorded during retrieval showed a variety of other strategies in addition to chronological search. As in the Williams and Hollan (1981) study, subjects focused their search on particular locations or particular academic subjects. Some teachers were remembered for distinctive physical attributes ("she was a gigantic woman with a scar on her neck"); some were linked to landmark events in the pupil's own life such as changing schools or moving house; and some were associated with the emotional responses they evoked.

Although Whitten and Leonard's findings demonstrated the superiority of backward search, this result may be specific to this kind of task. Teachers' names, and the order in which they occur, are arbitrary, but many autobiographical episodes are sequentially determined, each being causally related to a prior episode. It is a reasonable assumption that a "begin at the beginning" strategy would be better for recall of these causally related events. Recall of the different jobs I have held, for example, might be more easily accomplished in a forward order because the nature of the later jobs was determined by the nature of the earlier ones. Moreover, it should be noted that the superiority of backward search may be linked to the age of the subjects. Older people, whose school-days are more distant, may exhibit different patterns of recall.

Names of Entertainers

Read and Bruce (1982) analysed the memory blocks that occur when attempts at name recall are initially unsuccessful. Their subjects were tested repeatedly for the recall of names of entertainers from theatre, film, and television. Recall was cued by either a photograph of the entertainer or an identifying description, such as "He created the role of Charley's Aunt on Broadway". A total of 497 memory blocks occurred that were ultimately resolved either by remembering the name, or by recognising it when four alternatives were presented.

When each cue was initially presented the subjects were asked to give a "Feeling of Knowing" (FOK) rating of 1 (the name has come to me immediately); 2 (it is on the tip of my tongue); 3 (it is not on the tip of my tongue, but I feel I know it and can get it after some thought); 4 (it is not on the tip of my tongue, and though I feel I know it I don't think I can get it); or 5 (I simply do not know the name). Read and Bruce examined the relationship between these FOK judgements, and the time actually taken to resolve the name blocks. They found that the stronger the FOK the sooner the name was likely to be recalled, and the more likely it was to be recalled by the subject's own unaided search. (The nature of the FOK is discussed at length in Chapter 7, p.192).

Subjects' reports indicated that 21.5% of the blocks were accompanied by partial recall of the name (e.g. length, component letters, or component sounds). Retrieval processes included generating additional contextual information, using visual and auditory imagery, and running through lists of plausible names. Memory blocks are occasionally resolved when the forgotten name suddenly comes to mind at a time when no conscious attempts at retrieval are being made, and the subject is thinking of something quite different. Spontaneous pop-up retrievals of this kind were relatively rare in Read and Bruce's study (5.3%), and the mechanism underlying pop-up recall is disputed. Norman and Bobrow (1976) argued that pop-ups are the product of continuing unconscious search processes, the hunt for the missing name being continued without conscious awareness. Read and Bruce (1982) disagreed with this interpretation, and believe that pop-ups occur as a result of search processes that were originally conscious, but have been forgotten, and so cannot be reported. Alternatively, the pop-up may be triggered by an environmental cue. An example of this kind occurred in a study by Cohen and Faulkner (1986). A subject had forgotten the surname "Bell". Hours later, having consciously abandoned the search, she heard the clock strike and the name popped up. Sometimes an internally generated cue may induce a pop-up, as when a train of thought on a completely different topic fortuitously provides an association that triggers the missing name. However, pop-up often seems to happen without any identifiable external cue. Whatever the underlying process, the subjective experience of pop-up as a spontaneous event is a compelling one when it occurs.

Experimental Tests: Learning New Names

In these experiments, subjects are presented with face-name pairs, or with descriptions and names, and are tested for ability to recall the names. Cohen and Faulkner, in their 1986 study, tested recall of information from fictional minibiographies. Subjects heard, for example: "James Gibson is a policeman who lives in Glasgow and wins prizes for ballroom dancing", and later attempted to fill in blanks in a written version of this biography. Recall of first names and surnames was poorer than recall of place names, occupations, and hobbies.

McWeeny, Young, Hay, and Ellis (1987) also confirmed experimentally that names are harder to remember than occupations. They were concerned to test possible explanations for the difficulty of retrieving names. The following explanations were considered:

(1) *Arbitrariness*: Occupations might be easier to recall than names because context and visual appearance can give clues to a person's occupation, but not to his or her name. This is because names are only arbitrarily related to their referents. Although the characteristics of sex and nationality are contingently related to some first names, there are no characteristics that are necessarily related to them. Names like Ann or John are arbitrary in that the person I know as Ann (or John) might equally well have been called by another name.

(2) *Frequency*: Names may be retrieved less frequently than other information about a person.

(3) *Imageability*: Names are often not easily imageable, and are also less meaningful than occupations.

All these factors, which might favour recall of occupations, were systematically eliminated in an experiment by McWeeny et al. (1987). Subjects viewed 16 photos of middle-aged men's faces one at a time and were told each man's name and occupation. The faces were presented without visible background or clothing to eliminate any contextual cues; frequency of names and occupations was matched and, in some examples, the same word (e.g. Baker or Potter) was interchanged so that it sometimes functioned as a surname and sometimes as an occupation. When this was done, imageability and meaningfulness were equated. Even when these factors were controlled there was a vast difference betwen memory for names and memory for occupations. The percentage of trials on which subjects recalled occupation but not name (75%) far exceeded the trials on which they recalled names but not occupations (5%).

Cohen (1990) has argued that proper names are difficult to recall because they are meaningless and arbitrary. Her subjects learned to associate faces with names and occupations or with names and possessions. She found that if occupations or possessions were rendered meaningless by using nonsense words, then recall of these was as poor as recall of names. In "Mr Hobbs has a dog" the dog was remembered better than Mr Hobbs, but in "Mr Hobbs has a blick" there was no difference between Hobbs and blick. If a meaningless name was paired with a meaningful occupation ("Mr Ryman is a baker") then the occupation was superior; but if the name was meaningful and the occupation meaningless ("Mr Baker is a ryman") the result was reversed and the name was recalled better. Price and Cohen (unpublished) found that when subjects were permitted to generate and assign names to faces themselves, choosing names that suited the faces, recall of the name was substantially improved. So, when the name-face link was made less arbitrary and more meaningful, it was easier to remember the names.

Naturally Occurring Name Blocks

Reason and Lucas (1984) carried out a diary study designed to investigate naturally occurring occasions when memory for a word is blocked and people experience a "tip-of-the-tongue" (TOT) state. When this kind of incident occurs, people are temporarily unable to remember a word, although it is one they know and feel they ought to be able to remember, but for the moment it is tantalisingly out of reach. In these cases, the direct automatic retrieval process fails and a laborious attentional search must be instituted. The corpus of data collected by Reason and Lucas included blocking of both common words and proper names, but the high proportion of proper names (77%) confirms that blocks are particularly likely to occur for names.

In a similar study, Cohen and Faulkner (1986) asked subjects to record details of any name blocks they experienced during a two-week period. There were large individual differences in the frequency of blocks. The incidence was higher in elderly people, and subjects also reported that more blocks occurred when they were feeling tired, stressed, or ill. The majority (68%) of blocks were for names of friends or acquaintances, and most of these were rated as well-known names, which were usually easy to retrieve. Although this seems counterintuitive, the same finding also emerged from the Reason and Lucas (1984) study. It is perhaps partly due to the fact that there are more opportunities to forget names that are in frequent use. This fluctuating availability of well-known names suggests that retrieval failure results from dynamic variations in the retrieval process, rather than defective encoding or storage. In Cohen and Faulkner's data, names of famous people accounted for 17% of the blocks; only 7% were names of places; and 8% were other proper names such as brand names, book titles, and names of pop groups.

Most of the blocked names were eventually remembered without recourse to external aids like looking it up, or asking someone else, although 62% took more than an hour to recall, and in some cases several days elapsed before the name came to mind. When name recall was blocked, subjects were almost invariably able to remember all the personal identity information they had ever known about the target person, such as biographical details, physical appearance, and the nature of previous encounters. Partial information about the name itself was also recalled in 56% of cases. Typically, this consisted of phonological or orthographic features or name fragments, such as the first letter, first syllable, or name length. Occasionally attributes of the names such as "pretty", "uncommon" or "foreign" were also remembered.

When elderly people suffered name blocks they tended to report that they experienced a complete mental blank, with no names at all coming to mind. However, when younger subjects attempted to retrieve a blocked name, they often found that other names came to mind instead of the target. These nontarget candidates were nearly always recognised as being incorrect, but were persistent and difficult to set aside. They were often phonologically similar to the target name (e.g. *Sylvia* instead of *Cynthia*, or *Ken* instead of *Kevin*). Sometimes the nontarget candidates were contextually related to the target name (*Carter* instead of *Reagan*). Reason and Lucas (1984) also recorded that candidate names were elicited on 59% of blocks. They describe these nontarget items as "blockers" that impede access to the target, but Cohen and Faulkner's (1986) subjects reported that in the process of rejecting nontarget candidates they sometimes retrieved additional information about the target name. When several nontarget candidates were elicited, these could be graded as more or less similar to the target. In one example, the target name was *Kepler*. The first letter and first vowel sound were retrieved. Candidates, in order of occurrence, were *Keller, Klemperer, Kellet*, and *Kendler*. All of these were rejected, but *Keller* was recognised as being closest to the target, and the additional information that the target name was foreign came to light during evaluation of the candidates. Nontarget candidates may sometimes be stepping stones toward recall, rather than blockers.

Jones (1989) has reported an experiment specifically designed to test whether these nontarget candidate words (he calls them interlopers) obstruct or facilitate target retrieval. He presented word definitions (e.g. for the target word "Anachronism", "something out of keeping with the times in which it exists") and each definition was accompanied by an interloper. Interlopers were related to the target word in either sound or meaning or both or neither. Because more TOT states resulted when the interloper was similar in sound to the target than when it was not, Jones argued that these phonologically similar interlopers obstructed target retrieval. However, interlopers supplied by the experimenter may not have the same effect as candidates that emerge spontaneously within the subject's own memory.

When people were trying to resolve name blocks they used a variety of different kinds of retrieval strategies. These included:

(1) Generating names to fit partial information. If you know that the target name is a short name for a female beginning with A, you can search through all the names you know that fit that specification (Ann, Alice, etc.).

(2) Generating candidates from the relevant context. If the target name

is that of a politician, you can search through all the names of politicians you can remember.

(3) Trying to enrich the target description by reliving past encounters with the target person.

(4) Trying to induce a pop-up. This strategy was rare, but one subject described trying to "force up" the name of the author John Braine by rapidly repeating aloud the title of his book, "Room at the Top by ????"

It is not clear which strategies have the best success rate. Reason and Lucas (1984) reported 30.4% spontaneous pop-up recalls in their study, but Cohen and Faulkner identified only 17%. However, elderly people frequently said they found that conscious search was self-defeating, and it was more effective to abandon it and hope for some serendipitous external cueing or spontaneous pop-up. Burke, Mackay, Worthley, and Wade (1991) also carried out a diary study and analysed TOTs for proper names, object names and abstract words. Like Cohen and Faulkner, they found that older adults experienced more blocks than young adults and they experienced more blocks for proper names, especially names of acquaintances, than for other words. They also noted that the probability of blocking was linked to the frequency and recency of use of the name. Names that had not been used frequently, or not for a long time, were more likely to be blocked.

Neuropsychological Studies

There have been several reports of patients with selective deficits for proper names. McKenna and Warrington (1980) noted deficits for people's names, and Semenza and Zettin (1989) studied a patient who had a deficit for both people's names and geographical proper names. These deficits are remarkably "pure" in that they occur in conjunction with normal performance on other language tasks and with ability to recall detailed personal information and semantic information about the targets. More recently, however, cases have been reported (e.g. Semenza & Sgaramella, 1993) in which the opposite pattern of deficit was observed. Some ability to use proper names was preserved when ability to name objects was severely impaired. These cases imply that person-naming and object-naming are independent processes that can be independently damaged.

Models of Memory for Proper Names

Several models have been proposed to account for the special difficulty in recalling proper names in terms of the way they are represented and processed.

The Sequential Stage Model

The Bruce and Young (1986) model shown in Fig. 5.4 on p.120 explains why biographical information about a person may be recalled without access to the name, but the name of a person is not recalled without biographical information. Access to name information can only be achieved via the person-identity node. However, when this model is applied to naturally occurring name blocks it is apparent that it cannot account for all the observations without some modification. There are three kinds of blocks which require explanation:

(1) total blocks in which nothing can be recalled.
(2) partial blocks when contextually related wrong names are recalled; and
(3) partial blocks when phonologically related wrong names are recalled.

The model can account for total blocks because these may occur if the activation of the person-identity node is too weak to trigger the name node effectively. Blocks when contextually related wrong names are recalled can also be explained because these might occur if the target and the nontarget candidate share the same context or the same personal identity attributes, so that activation of the person-identity node triggers more than one name node. This is what may happen when you block out the name of someone's current girlfriend, and recall the name of his former girlfriend instead. However, in order to explain how phonologically similar nontarget candidates are elicited instead of the target name (*Sylvia* instead of *Cynthia*), the model needs to be extended to include associations between similar-sounding names. Then, if the target name node is only weakly activated, so that there is only partial recall of name fragments, these might activate other nontarget names that share the same fragments.

The model also fails to explain why there is a cueing asymmetry between the name node and the person-identity node, so that it is easier to remember the personal details when you are given the name than it is to remember the name when you are given the personal details.

The IAC Model and the Representational Model

The IAC model shown in Fig. 5.5 (p.121) explains the difficulty in retrieving proper names as due to their uniqueness. A proper name (first name and surname) is relatively unique. In the model it can be seen that although an occupation, like politician, can accrue activation from multiple connections, a proper name, like John Major, has only a single unique connection. Thus, names are harder to recall than other biographical, semantic information because they have a lower level of connectivity and so receive less activation. Cohen's Representational model (Cohen & Burke, 1993) provides an essentially similar explanation but substitutes meaninglessness for uniqueness as the crucial factor. On this explanation, meaningless terms, like names, lack connections to semantic associates, and thus receive insufficient activation to produce recall. Meaningful words, like object names, recruit activation from the many semantic associates to which they are linked. This Representational model explains why there is a gradient of difficulty that runs from names of acquaintances, to famous names, to geographical names. Famous names (like Napoleon) or place names (like the Taj Mahal) tend to have more semantic associations than names like Ann or Michael.

The Node Structure Theory

This detailed model of language perception and production has been extended to account for problems in memory for proper names (Mackay & Burke, 1990). Figure 5.6 illustrates the representation of "baker" the occupation, and "Baker" the proper name.

As can be seen, the lexical node for baker, the occupation, can receive activation from a number of semantic nodes representing information about bakers and converging on the node for baker. In contrast, the node for Baker, the family proper name, does not receive convergence of activation and is connected only by a single link to the semantic attributes of the named individual.

In all these models structural relations between items of information determine the extent to which activation converges on the target and summates. It is assumed that for successful recall activation must reach some threshold level. The architecture of the system is such that proper names have fewer connections and receive less activation than object names. In cases where the general level of activation is reduced, as may occur in old age, or disrupted, as in cases of brain damage, recall of proper names will suffer disproportionately. In normal people, the weaker activation of proper names would make them more susceptible to forgetting than object names.

CONCLUSIONS

Although the topic of memory for voices is still under-researched, great progress has been made in understanding the processes of face recognition and name recall. In both these areas, researchers using a wide range of different methodologies, including formal experiments, naturalistic observations, neuropsychologcal case studies, and computer simulations, have pooled their findings and sought to construct theoretical frameworks that take account of them all. The conclusions based on these converging

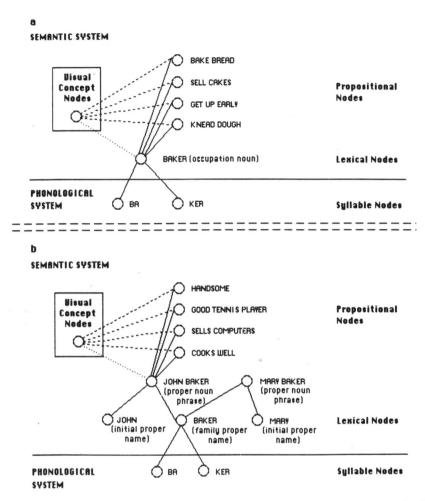

a

SEMANTIC SYSTEM

Visual Concept Nodes

BAKE BREAD
SELL CAKES
GET UP EARLY
KNEAD DOUGH

Propositional Nodes

BAKER (occupation noun)

Lexical Nodes

PHONOLOGICAL SYSTEM

BA   KER

Syllable Nodes

b

SEMANTIC SYSTEM

Visual Concept Nodes

HANDSOME
GOOD TENNIS PLAYER
SELLS COMPUTERS
COOKS WELL

Propositional Nodes

JOHN BAKER (proper noun phrase)   MARY BAKER (proper noun phrase)

JOHN (initial proper name)   BAKER (family proper name)   MARY (initial proper name)

Lexical Nodes

PHONOLOGICAL SYSTEM

BA   KER

Syllable Nodes

FIG. 5.6.   Basic components of the Node Structure (NST) model of proper name retrieval (from Mackay & Burke, 1990. In T.Hess (Ed.) *Aging and cognition: Knowledge organization and utilization.* pp. 1–51. North Holland). Reprinted by permission of the publishers and author.

approaches have, in consequence, an increased power and scope. It is apparent that memory for faces and memory for proper names constitute "special" systems in that they can be independently impaired. Both identification of faces and retrieval of proper names incur the added difficulty attaching to individuation. As opposed to tasks that only rely on classification, individuation requires an extra level of discrimination and precision so that, although it is easy to say something is a face, it is a great deal harder to decide whose face it is. Interestingly, both face recognition and name recall elicit a wide range of individual differences in ability. Although it is rare for normal subjects to score poorly in tests of object or word recognition, many people are not at all good at recognising faces or at remembering names, and the line between normal and pathological performance is blurred.

6

Memory for Personal Experiences: Autobiographical Memory

This chapter is concerned with how we remember the events and experiences that form our own personal history. Aspects of everyday memory that have already been discussed, such as memory for places and faces, objects and actions, are components within this broader framework. Memory for personal experiences comprises many different kinds of specific memories that together form the fabric of daily life and are recorded in autobiographical memory. However, before we begin to examine the nature of autobiographical memory in detail it is helpful to review some theoretical models for the representation of personal experiences.

THEORETICAL BACKGROUND

Theoretical ideas developed in the course of computer modelling have provided a useful and illuminating approach to understanding how people represent experiences in memory. Schank and Abelson (1977) and Schank (1982a) introduced the concept of a *script*, which is a particular kind of schema (see Chapter 2, p.41 and Chapter 3, p.76) representing knowledge about events and experiences.

Scripts

A script is a general knowledge structure that represents the knowledge abstracted from a class of similar events, rather than knowledge of any one specific episode. Thus, people have scripts for familiar experiences like eating in restaurants, going shopping, visiting the dentist, and so on. Through everyday experience everyone acquires hundreds of such scripts. An example is shown in Fig. 6.1.

A script consists of a sequence of actions that are temporally and causally ordered and are goal-directed. So you sit down *before* ordering; the waitress brings the food *because* you ordered it; you go to the cashier *in order to* pay; and the *goal* of the whole activity is to satisfy your hunger. The script also includes roles (e.g. the waitress) and props (e.g. the table, the menu), but notice it does not contain details about the kind of food, the decor, the company, or the size of the bill. These details belong to specific episodes, or what Brewer and Tenpenny (personal communication, 1996) call an instantiated script. When you remember a particular occasion, specific details can be inserted into the relevant slots in the general script. Scripts are broken up into subscripts, or scenes, which are hierarchically organised with a main action and subordinate action.

The concept of a script was originally designed to explain comprehension processes, so that, for example, when we hear that John went to a restaurant and had an omelette, we can fill out this brief account from the

---

Script:	Restaurant (the script header)
Roles:	Customer, waitress, chef, cashier
Goal:	To obtain food to eat
Subscript 1:	Entering
	move self into restaurant
	look for empty tables
	decide where to sit
	move to table
	sit down
Subscript 2:	Ordering
	receive menu
	read menu
	decide what you want
	give order to waitress
Subscript 3:	Eating
	receive food
	ingest food
Subscript 4:	Exiting
	ask for check
	receive check
	give tip to waitress
	move self to cashier
	move self out of restaurant

FIG. 6.1. The restaurant script (from Schank & Ableson, 1977).

stored knowledge in our restaurant script. Script elements function as default values, so that, unless told otherwise, we would infer from the underlying script that John sat down and that he paid a bill. The scripts allow us to supply missing elements and infer what is not explicitly stated. As well as guiding and enriching our understanding of events, scripts also provide an organising framework for remembering events. They explain the common observation that in remembering routine, familiar, often-repeated events we seem to have a generic memory in which individual occasions, or episodes, have fused into a composite. Looking back on schooldays, or bus-rides, or trips to the library, you may find that you cannot remember any specific occasion, but have only a generalised memory of what typically happens.

The psychological reality of scripts has been demonstrated in a study by Bower, Black, and Turner (1979). They asked students to generate the component actions that comprise an event, and list them in order of occurrence. The events they asked about were attending a lecture, visiting a doctor, shopping at a grocery store, eating at a fancy restaurant, and getting up in the morning. There was very substantial agreement about the component actions and their sequence, as can be seen in Fig. 6.2.

Subjects also agreed on how a given script was subdivided into scenes, and there was also evidence that they recognised that scripts were hier-archically structured with superordinate goals and subordinate goals. Bower et al. went on to study memory for written texts that were based on the scripts that had been generated. Subjects read either one, two or three different versions of a script. For example, the "visit to a health professional" script had a doctor version, a dentist version, and a chiro-practor version. Twenty minutes later the subjects were asked to write down as much as they could remember of each one. Each action they recalled was classified as stated (i.e. had been in the original text) or unstated (i.e. had been in the underlying script but had not been mentioned in the text). Of the actions recalled, 26% were unstated script actions. Moreover, when the actions in the text were in a disordered sequence there was a tendency to recall them in the familiar canonical order. These findings confirm the psychological reality of scripts and demonstrate their influence on memory.

The Schema-plus-Tag Model

In real life, events are not always routine repeated ones, and memories are not always generalised. Many events are unique one-off experiences. Some events are first-time ones, never experienced before, or novel deviations from more familiar experiences. It is clearly nonsense to suppose that these events are not memorable, and common sense observations suggest the

Attending a lecture	Visiting a doctor
ENTER ROOM	*Enter office*
Look for friends	CHECK IN WITH RECEPTIONIST
FIND SEAT	SIT DOWN
SIT DOWN	Wait
Settle belongings	Look at other people
TAKE OUT NOTEBOOK	READ MAGAZINE
Look at other students	*Name called*
Talk	Follow nurse
Look at professor	*Enter examination room*
LISTEN TO PROFESSOR	Undress
TAKE NOTES	*Sit on table*
CHECK TIME	Talk to nurse
Ask questions	NURSE TESTS
Change position in seat	Wait
Daydream	Doctor enters
Look at other students	Doctor greets
Take more notes	Talk to doctor about problem
Close notebook	Doctor asks questions
Gather belongings	DOCTOR EXAMINES
Stand up	Get dressed
Talk	Get medicine
LEAVE	Make another appointment
	LEAVE OFFICE

Note: Events in capital letters were mentioned by most subjects, items in italics by fewer subjects, and items in ordinary print by fewest subjects.

FIG. 6.2.   Script actions listed by subjects for the events of attending a lecture and visiting a doctor (from Bower, Black, & Turner, 1979).

contrary. The day you won the 100-metres sprint; the day little Johnny was sick in the doctor's waiting-room; the time you hadn't enough money to pay the restaurant bill; these are the occasions that stand out in your memory. The unusual or atypical event seems to be more memorable than the ordinary run-of-the-mill occasions.

Experiments have confirmed these intuitions. Just as in Brewer and Treyens' experiment (Chapter 3, p.79) the objects in a room were rated according to their schema-relevance, so actions can be graded as being more or less relevant to the current script. Sitting in a chair is a relevant action in the restaurant script, but standing on the table is not. Nakamura, Graesser, Zimmerman, and Riha (1985) compared ability to remember script-relevant and script-irrelevant actions. Students attended a 15-minute lecture that was specially staged. During the lecture, the lecturer performed

---

Relevant Actions
Pointing to information on the blackboard
Opening and closing a book
Moving an eraser to the blackboard
Handing a student a piece of paper

Irrelevant actions
Scratching head
Wiping glasses
Bending a coffee stirrer
Picking up a pencil off the floor

FIG. 6.3. Some of the relevant and irrelevant actions incorporated in a lecture (from Nakamura, Graesser, Zimmerman, & Riha, 1985).

a number of actions that varied in relevancy to the lecture script. Examples are shown in Fig. 6.3.

After the lecture, the students were given a recognition test in which they had to work through a list of actions, and identify those that had been performed by the lecturer. Irrelevant actions were recognised better than relevant actions, and the false alarm rate was three times higher for relevant actions than for irrelevant actions (i.e. subjects were much more likely to falsely claim that relevant actions had been performed when they had not).

These results have been interpreted in terms of the schema-plus-tag model. According to this model, the memory representation for a specific event consists of the instantiated script, which includes both script-relevant actions that actually occurred and script-relevant actions that were inferred, plus tags that correspond to the irrelevant, unexpected, or deviant aspects of the event. These distinctive tags are highly memorable, and serve as markers, or indices, for the retrieval of specific episodes. This modification of the original script model accounts for the way that novel or atypical occasions (like Johnny being sick on the doctor's carpet) seem to stick in memory.

Later research has suggested that the schema-plus-tag model is oversimplified. In a series of experiments by Brewer and Tenpenny (personal communication, 1996) subjects heard passages containing four types of item: script, instantiated script, irrelevant, and inconsistent. These items were either embedded in a familiar script or, for a group of control subjects, the same items occurred in a nonscript context. Examples are shown in Fig. 6.4.

After listening to the passages subjects performed either a free recall test or a recognition test in which the sentences from the passage were mixed with foil sentences. The results showed that for script items recall was good but recognition was poor, indicating that subjects rely on the

The script condition

A restaurant

Gordon decided to go out for dinner. He went in the front door of the expensive restaurant. He was seated by the waiter. *He noticed that his shoe had come untied and tied it.* (Irrelevant) He ordered a drink. *He looked at the menu.* (Script) *He ordered lamb chops.* (Instantiated Script) He looked around at the other patrons. He ate his salad. The waiter brought the main course. He ate slowly, enjoying every bite. *He walked through the forest.* (Inconsistent) He ordered dessert. He left a $5 tip. He went home quite pleased with his evening.

The nonscript control version

Gordon went to the first football game of the season. He put a new record on his stereo. He cleaned the blackboard. *He noticed that his shoe had come untied and tied it.* He went to the library. *He looked at the menu. He ordered lamb chops.* He dribbled the basketball. He chose a window seat. He studied for his German quiz. He took his toaster in to be repaired. *He walked through the forest.* He swore to tell the truth. He got the lawnmower. He replaced a red bulb that had burned out.

FIG. 6.4. Examples of a script and nonscript passage from experiments by Brewer and Tenpenny (personal communication, 1996). Reproduced with the permission of the author.

pre-experimental generic script to generate recall responses, but this is not adequate to distinguish between target and foil sentences in recognition. Reliance on the pre-existing script in recall was also reflected in the high rate (over 50%) of intrusions. Instantiated script items were also well recalled, and recall of these items in the script condition was far superior to the control condition although these cannot be derived from the pre-stored script. Brewer and Tenpenny argued that the script gave an advantage by guiding retrieval. Inconsistent items were well recalled and were also the most easily recognised and this is consistent with two schema-based mechanisms, attention and distinctiveness (see Chapter 3, p.78). Attention is directed toward items not consistent with the operative schema and these items also benefit from their distinctiveness in the context of the schema. As can be seen in Fig. 6.5 there was no sign of an advantage for inconsistent items in the control nonscript condition. Recall of irrelevant items was inferior to the other three item types, although the script condition was still better than the control condition, indicating that these items did stand out from the operative script. These results illustrate the extremely complex ways in which memory for elements of new experiences can be influenced by stored schemas and scripts.

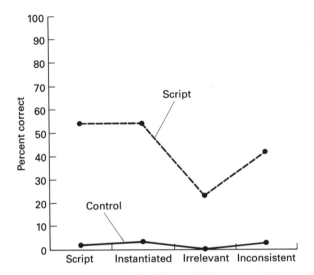

FIG. 6.5.   Recall scores for script and control conditions for each item type (from Brewer and Tenpenny, personal communication). Reproduced with the permission of the author.

Dynamic Memory: Scripts, MOPs, and TOPs

Developments and modifications of the original script model (Schank, 1982a, b) have focused on this relationship between generalised event knowledge and memory for specific episodes. Bower et al. (1979), noted in their experiment that people tended to confuse elements from different scripts in memory. The existence of confusions between actions occurring during the visit to the doctor and actions that occurred during the visit to the dentist suggested that there exists some memory structure that is common to both scripts. To account for this finding, Schank (1982a) proposed that memories can be organised at many different levels of generality. He also confronted another weakness of the original script model. He recognised the fact that people can understand and remember an enormous range and variety of different situations. The original model, in which each situation is interpreted by means of pre-stored knowledge about a pre-set sequence of actions, is at once too rigid and too cumbersome to cope with this fact. The number of scripts that would be required would be highly uneconomical to store and pre-compiled scripts would be too rigid to handle novel situations. Schank concluded that there must be higher level of representations that are abstract and general enough to fit novel situations. Another difficulty for Schank's original formulation is that life experiences do not conform so neatly to categorised and compartmentalised units as script theory implies. An experience of a picnic, for example, may involve eating and drinking, games, quarrels, minor injuries, thunderstorms, and many other elements that cannot be fitted into a single pre-compiled picnic script.

These observations led Schank to revise the original version of scripts and develop a model that is more dynamic, more flexible, and more economical. The main features of this version are:

(1) Memory structures are constantly reorganised in the light of new experiences and repetitions of previous experiences, and links between structures reflect similarities between different experiences.

(2) The new system is dynamic. Instead of using pre-stored, pre-compiled scripts to understand experiences and organise memories, memory structures are assembled as and when required. Different kinds of knowledge can be activated and linked up to create an appropriate representation for a particular occasion.

(3) Instead of replicating elements that are common to many scripts (like entering a building, paying, taking a seat, etc., which belong to the cinema script, the restaurant script, the doctor script, and so on), these common elements are each represented separately at a higher, more general level, and can be called in and incorporated into the current script when required. So the generalised actions like entering and paying can be activated when a memory structure for a visit to a restaurant is being created, but the restaurant script itself now contains only the actions that are specific to restaurants like calling a waitress, reading the menu, etc. This organisation, whereby generalised actions are common to different scripts, is more economical in storage and can account for the way people sometimes make confusions between related scripts.

(4) The higher-level generalised event representations have been called MOPs, short for Memory Organisation Packets. A MOP is a kind of high-level script that is linked to other related MOPs. In the picnic example, the memory of this particular picnic would involve weather MOPs, friendship MOPs, sports activities MOPs, and first-aid MOPs. The memory representation for this event would invoke general knowledge from all these MOPs as well as the standard picnic MOP.

(5) As in the Schema-plus-Tag model, nonstandard aspects of a particular occasion are stored as specific pointers, tags, or indices, which serve to retrieve the memory of a particular occasion. Standard occasions, or standard aspects of novel occasions, are absorbed into the relevant generalised event representations (the MOPs). The specific pointers provide the mechanism for the process Schank calls "reminding". You may be reminded of a particular episode by a friend who says "Do you remember the time David fell in the river? You know, the day we got caught in a thunderstorm. You must remember, we played frisbee in a field of cows."

The friend is *reminding* you of the event by activating successively the tags he thinks you are most likely to have used as indices.

(6) Within this new dynamic memory system a particular episode, like going to a party, can therefore be stored at several different levels of generality, as:

going to David's party last Saturday evening; *or*

going to parties; *or*

social interactions.

The system also allows for even more general, higher-level representations which Schank (1982a) has called TOPs or Thematic Organisation Points. Themes like "Getting what you want", "Achieving power", or "Failing to achieve a goal" are examples, and their existence is evident in conversational exchanges like the following:

"I just heard I didn't get the job".

"Bad luck. And I've failed my driving test again. Let's go and have a drink to cheer ourselves up."

The conversation illustrates how two disparate events can be organised under the high-level theme of Failures. These high-level structures allow us to recognise similarities and analogies between superficially quite different events. In Schank's own example of the Steak and the Hair Cut, a friend's complaint that his wife would not cook his steak rare enough reminds the listener of occasions when a barber would not cut his hair short enough. The events are related to the common theme of failing to get a service performed in a sufficiently extreme form.

Schank's theories were originally developed in the process of writing programs for computer modelling of language-understanding, rather than being designed to account for human memory in everyday life, but they have been modified and adapted so as to explain experimental findings and observations. Some aspects, such as the emphasis on the need for economy of storage, may be more appropriate for the computer than for the human brain. However, the later versions of the model provide what is, on the whole, a convincing account of how people remember the events they experience in daily life.

Episodic and Semantic Memory

Tulving (1972) distinguished between memory for personal experience and general world knowledge and considered these as two separate and distinct memory systems. According to this distinction *episodic memory* consists of personal experiences, and the specific objects, people and events that have been experienced at a particular time and place. *Semantic memory* consists of general knowledge and facts about the world. Table 6.1 shows the main features of the episodic-semantic distinction.

Tulving developed this distinction to clarify the difference between long term semantic knowledge and the kind of knowledge acquired in verbal learning experiments, where learning a specific list of words constitutes an "episode". The distinction has since been extended to autobiographical memory, where memory for personal experiences is classed as a subsystem of episodic memory. However, further consideration has blurred the edges of the episodic-semantic distinction. The two forms of knowledge are not separate, compartmentalised structures, but are in an interactive and inter-dependent relationship. Semantic knowledge is derived from personal experiences by a process of abstraction and generalisation. Episodic auto-biographical memories are interpreted and classified in terms of general semantic knowledge in the form of schemas and scripts. In later develop-ments of his theoretical distinctions Tulving (1985) labels memory for a specific event as *noetic* when we have no knowledge about how and why that event occurred in our past life. Episodic memories that do carry information about the context in which they were experienced by the self are called *autonoetic*.

AUTOBIOGRAPHICAL MEMORY

Autobiographical memories are episodes recollected from an individual's past life. The study of autobiographical memory has undergone a marked change in the last decade. Until then, the approach was almost exclusively psychoanalytic or clinical in orientation and diagnostic or therapeutic in aim. Recent studies, however, have adopted a cognitive approach and seek

TABLE 6.1
The Episodic–semantic Distinction

	Episodic	Semantic
Type of information represented	Specific events, objects, people	General knowledge facts about the world
Type of organisation in memory	Chronological (by time) or spatial (by place)	In schemas or in categories
Source of information	Personal experience	Abstraction from repeated experience or generalisations learned from others
Focus	Subjective reality: the self	Objective reality: the world

to interpret autobiographical memory within the theoretical framework of mainstream memory research. This undertaking is fraught with difficulty because of the great quantity and variability of the data. It is a daunting task to try to discover the general principles that govern the encoding, storage, and retrieval of personal experiences accumulated over their lifetimes by different individuals with different personal histories. Nevertheless, some progress has been made, at least in defining the questions that are of most interest, and in exploring methods of gathering the data.

What is Autobiographical Memory?

Autobiographical memory, or in Tulving's terminology autonoetic memory, is distinct from memories of other people's experiences, memories of public events, general knowledge, and skills. The defining characteristic of autobiographical memory is its relationship to the self: The remembered events are of personal significance and are the building blocks from which the self is constructed. Paradoxically, the self is both the experiencer and the product of the experiences. Autobiographical memories are long-lasting, perhaps because the self-reference that is characteristic of these memories is known to promote recall (Rogers, Kuiper, & Kirker, 1977). Conway (1990) provides a detailed and comprehensive survey of the literature on autobiographical memory.

Personal experiences are usually stored without a conscious intention to memorise them and give rise to memories that can be of several different kinds. We can identify several dimensions of autobiographical memory:

(1) Autobiographical memories may sometimes consist of biographical facts, for example, I may remember the fact that I was born in Liverpool without having any actual memory of having lived there. This kind of factual memory is what Tulving calls noetic and contrasts with the kind of autonoetic memory, which is experiential. For example, when I recall that I went to school in Wales I can relive the experience with associated sensory imagery and emotions.

(2) Brewer (1986) argues that memories vary in the extent to which they are *copies* or *reconstructions* of the original event. Some personal memories seem like copies because they are vivid and contain a considerable amount of irrelevant detail. However, some personal memories are not accurate, and, rather than being raw experiences, they sometimes incorporate the interpretations that are made with hindsight, which suggests they are reconstructed. It seems plausible that the noetic type of memory is more likely to be reconstructed.

(3) Autobiographical memories may be *specific* or *generic*, for example, I may remember eating lunch at a particular restaurant on a particular

occasion, or I may have a generic memory of family dinners. Neisser (1986) has also noted that a personal memory may be one that is representative of a series of similar events and has termed this type of blended memory "repisodic".

(4) Autobiographical memories may be represented from an *observer* perspective or from a *field* perspective. Nigro and Neisser (1983) found that when people examined their own memories some were remembered from the original viewpoint of the experiencer (the field perspective), but a larger number of memories seemed like viewing the event from the outside, from the point of view of an external observer. These "observer" memories cannot be copies of the original perception and must have been reconstructed. Nigro and Neisser reported that recent memories were more likely to be copy-type memories re-experienced from the original viewpoint, but older memories were more likely to be reconstructed ones seen from the observer's viewpoint. Robinson and Swanson (1993) replicated this finding and noted that field memories were more vivid. They asked students to recall personal memories from different periods of their lives, to report on the perspective of each memory, and to rate it for affect. In a later session they were asked to reinstate the memory in the original perspective or to recall it from the other perspective. Changing from a field to an observer perspective had the effect of diminishing affect. The findings showed clearly that it was possible to switch perspectives and most memories could be recalled in either the field or the observer mode, although it was harder to switch if the memory was old and not very vivid. The dynamic, unstable quality of autobiographical memory evidenced in this study is consistent with a reconstructive theory.

Functions of Autobiographical Memory

Robinson (1992) distinguished between intrapersonal and interpersonal functions. The most important intrapersonal function is the construction and maintenance of the self-concept and self-history. Memory for our own personal history is of great importance as it is an essential element of personal identity. To a considerable extent we are what we remember. If someone suffers, through trauma or disease, from loss of memory and cannot recall his or her own personal history, in a very real sense he or she loses his or her identity. This is why the practice of reminiscence therapy, whereby elderly people are induced to revive their own memories of the past and to reminisce about their youth, is found to be helpful in preserving a sense of identity. Autobiographical memory is also used intrapersonally to regulate moods. Judicious selection of appropriate memories may serve to maintain a happy mood or to improve a sad, depressed one.

Interpersonal functions of autobiographical memory include making friends and maintaining relationships. Self-disclosure is a means of increasing intimacy, of pooling experiences, of giving and receiving understanding and sympathy, and of "placing" ourselves in a given social and cultural context. People become friends by exchanging personal narratives.

Memory for personal experiences has other functions besides that of reinforcing personal identity and promoting friendships. It has been argued that memory for specific episodes has no real function in everyday life, and that behaviour is guided entirely by procedural and general semantic knowledge. However, everyday experience suggests that specific episodic memories can have a role in problem-solving. When we are confronted with a current problem, the general knowledge that has been abstracted from past experiences may not always be relevant, and it may be more useful to search back through autobiographical memory and review specific experiences with analogous problems (for a theoretical account of this process, see the section on case-based reasoning in Chapter 7, p.186). Autobiographical memories provide us with a store of "recipes" for handling current problems and current situations. We know how to behave in social and professional contexts, how to cope with practical problems like changing the wheel on a car or booking tickets for the theatre because we remember how it worked out last time we had a similar experience. Likes and dislikes, enthusiasms, beliefs and prejudices are also the product of remembered experiences. Finally, remembering what happened in the past helps us to predict what is likely to happen in the future.

Organisation and Structure

Autobiographical memories are not just a random collection but are grouped into related sets, organised and indexed so that they can be retrieved on demand, and a particular memory of a specific event has an internal structure of its own. Researchers have inferred the principles of organisation and the nature of the structure from studying the way people retrieve their memories. The consensus view emerging from a wide range of studies is that there are two principles of organisation, temporal and thematic. Personal memories may be chronologically organised in a temporal sequence, like the memories of schoolteachers in Whitten and Leonard's study (p.126), or in lifetime periods, sometimes called "extendures" (such as schooldays, college days, working in London, retirement, etc.). They may also be organised in themes such as illnesses, holidays, or parties. Specific episodes, it is claimed, are nested in a rough hierarchy within general events, which in turn are nested within higher-level themes and lifetime periods. So, for example, the specific episode "visiting the

Colosseum" is linked to the general event "holiday in Italy" and to the theme of "holidays" and the lifetime period of early married life. Retrieval may occur in a top-down direction in response to queries like "What holidays did you have when you were first married?" or in a bottom-up direction in response to "When did you visit the Colosseum?".

The order in which people free recall target events and the relative effectiveness of different instructions and different cues provide indications of the underlying organisation. Numerous studies have inferred the organisation of autobiographical memories by comparing the response times taken to retrieve personal memories to different cues. Subjects are supplied with a cue word and asked to respond as soon as a personal memory associated with the cue word comes to mind. Robinson (1976) compared the time taken to recall experiences involving an activity (e.g. throwing) or an object (e.g. car) with those involving an emotion (e.g. happy). He found that retrieval was slowest with emotion cues. This result suggests that people do not organise their memories in terms of the associated emotions. Robinson argued that this would be an inefficient form of organisation because many different experiences share the same emotions.

Reiser, Black, and Abelson (1985) investigated how script-like knowledge structures function in the organisation and retrieval of experiences. They compared the effectiveness of two different kinds of knowledge structure as a means of accessing personal memories. One kind of knowledge structure they called *Activities*. These are script-like structures consisting of knowledge about sequences of actions undertaken to achieve a goal, for example, eating in restaurants, shopping in department stores, or going to libraries. The other kind of knowledge structure they termed *General Actions*. These are MOP-like structures representing higher-level knowledge about actions that can be components in many different specific activities. So paying, sitting down, buying tickets are examples of General Actions that occur in many different scenarios.

Reiser et al. put forward the Activity Dominance Hypothesis predicting that Activities would be better retrieval cues than General Actions because accessing specific activities, such as eating in restaurants, generates many inferences about food, decor, and service that can serve as further cues for retrieval of specific experiences. General Actions are not "inference-rich" structures in this way. They do not constrain the area of search sufficiently and are too abstract to generate useful cues. To test their predictions, Reiser et al. asked subjects to recall specific personal experiences to fit an Activity cue such as "went out drinking" or "had your hair cut" and a General Action cue such as "paid at the cash register". They varied the order in which these two cues were presented. More experiences were successfully recalled and responses were faster when the Activity cue was first. In everyday terms, you would find it easier to remember an occasion when you had your hair cut than an occasion when you bought a ticket. Reiser and his colleagues concluded that retrieval involves two stages, first, establishing a context, like hair cuts, and second, finding an index or tag that identifies a particular experience within that context. Activities are knowledge structures at the optimal level of specificity. This is the level at which experiences are originally encoded, and is the level that provides the optimal context for search. This context-plus-index model is similar to the Schema-plus-Tag model (p.139) and to the account of retrieval processes given by Williams and Hollan (p.125).

Although the idea that there is an optimal level of specificity for search contexts is convincing, Reiser et al. (1985) only tested the efficacy of actions as retrieval cues, and did not compare actions with other cues such as locations or lifetime extendures, or the names of objects or emotions. Conway and Bekerian (1987) failed to replicate the findings of Reiser et al. and found that retrieval was facilitated when cued by lifetime period (e.g. schooldays, time at college), and suggested that people's memories of their own personal history are organised in terms of such periods. Moreover, Anderson and Conway (submitted) have pointed out an important flaw in the design of Reiser et al.'s experiment. When they presented a general action before an activity cue the temporal order of events was reversed. For example, when "finding a seat" (the general action cue) preceded "going to the cinema" (the activity cue) the actual order in which these events occur was violated. Anderson and Conway repeated the experiment selecting cues such as "parked the car" (general action) and "went to the cinema" (activity), which preserved the correct temporal order. They found no differences in the effectiveness of the two kinds of cue, but retrieval was faster when temporal order was preserved than when it was violated. They concluded that autobiographical memories are not indexed by activities or general actions but by themes and lifetime periods.

Barsalou (1988) has also questioned the "activity dominance hypothesis", which claims that personal memories are organised primarily in terms of activities. Using the same paradigm as Reiser et al., he compared the effectiveness of activity cues (watching television), participant cues (your mother), location cues (in the cafeteria), and time cues (at noon). Retrieval time was not affected by cue type or by cue order, but participant cues elicited the most memories. He noted that goals, like passing an exam or learning to drive, were good cues for retrieving memories. Barsalou also conducted a free-recall experiment in which students were asked to recall what they did last summer. The most frequently recalled events were extended events (taking a trip to Europe), and repeated events (playing tennis). Only 21% of the recalled events were specific episodes. Organisational clusters could also be discerned in the recall protocols. From these data Barsalou concluded that, as shown in Fig. 6.6, that the highest level of organisation is chronological. Barsalou calls this level of the hierarchy "extended-event time lines", which are analogous to extendures or lifetime periods. Several different time lines may overlap concurrently. According to Barsalou, summarised events are represented at lower levels in the hierarchy. The consensus view is that autobiographical memory is organised in this kind of hierarchy with interlocking structures of time periods and themes.

Diary Studies of Autobiographical Memory

Diary studies of autobiographical memory also shed some light on organisation. Linton (1982) undertook a systematic six-year study of her own memory for the events of her daily life. Each day she wrote on cards a brief description of at least two events that occurred on that day. Every month she reread two of these descriptions, which were selected at random from the accumulating pool, so that the retention period was varied. She then

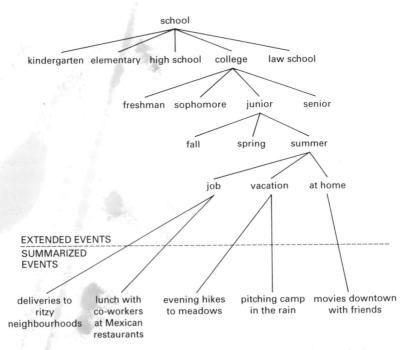

FIG. 6.6. Hierarchical organisation of autobiographical memories. Summarised events at the lower levels are nested in extended time lines (from Barsalou, 1988). Reprinted by permission of Cambridge University Press.

tried to remember the events described, to estimate the temporal order in which they occurred, and the date of each event. She also rated each memory for salience (importance) and for emotionality both at the time of writing the description and again at the time of recall.

Linton noted two types of forgetting. One form of forgetting was associated with repeated events, such as regular trips to attend a committee meeting in another town. Over time, memories of particular trips became indistinguishable from each other, and she found she had only retained a generic composite memory. The specific memory of a particular occasion had been absorbed into a generalised event memory, or, in other words, she had acquired a script for these events. This finding conforms to most people's own experience. Unique occasions are usually better remembered than repeated events, which blend into each other. A second type of forgetting also occurred. When she reread descriptions of some events she simply could not remember the event at all. Here it was not the case that similar events had been confused and amalgamated in memory, but that a single event had been forgotten. The number of events forgotten in this way increased steadily with each year of the study, and, after six years had elapsed, 30% of the events recorded had been totally forgotten.

A surprising feature of Linton's study was her failure to find any strong relationship between rated importance and emotionality, and subsequent recall. Common sense experience suggests that we remember important events, and those that roused strong passions better than those that were trivial or left us unmoved. However, Linton found that the emotionality and importance ratings she initially gave to an event did not correspond closely with those she gave later on with hindsight. It appears that the characteristics of an event at the time of encoding only affect memorability if the same qualities are still present at the time of recall.

To gain further insight into the way events are organised in memory Linton also studied strategies of recall. She tried to recall all the events that occurred in a designated month. Introspective monitoring of her own attempts at recall showed that many events were organised chronologically and were recalled by temporally ordered search. Some were organised in categories (themes) and were retrieved by working through named categories like parties or sporting activities. For events that were more than two years old, there was a shift away from chronological search toward a greater use of thematic search, reflecting a change in memory organisation. Linton's recall attempts also confirmed that events may be organised in terms of lifetime periods, which she called extendures, such as a job, a marriage, or living in a particular place. Within these extendures, specific events are embedded and can be accessed via the relevant extendure. The findings from Linton's diary study are therefore consistent with Barsalou's and Conway's view that memories are organised hierarchically, both chronologically and thematically. The results also emphasise the fragility of specific memories relative to higher-level general event memories.

Wagenaar (1986) employed similar methods in recording 2400 events of his daily life over a period of six years. He specifically recorded each event in terms of *who, what, where,* and *when* plus some critical identifying detail. This format had two advantages. He was able to determine which of these facts about an event were best retained, and also which facts provided the best cues for retrieving the rest of the information. He also rated the pleasantness, emotionality and saliency of each event. Saliency was defined as how often such an event might be expected to recur, so unique events were rated as highly salient, and routine events were rated low. Figure 6.7 shows the pro-forma for recording the events.

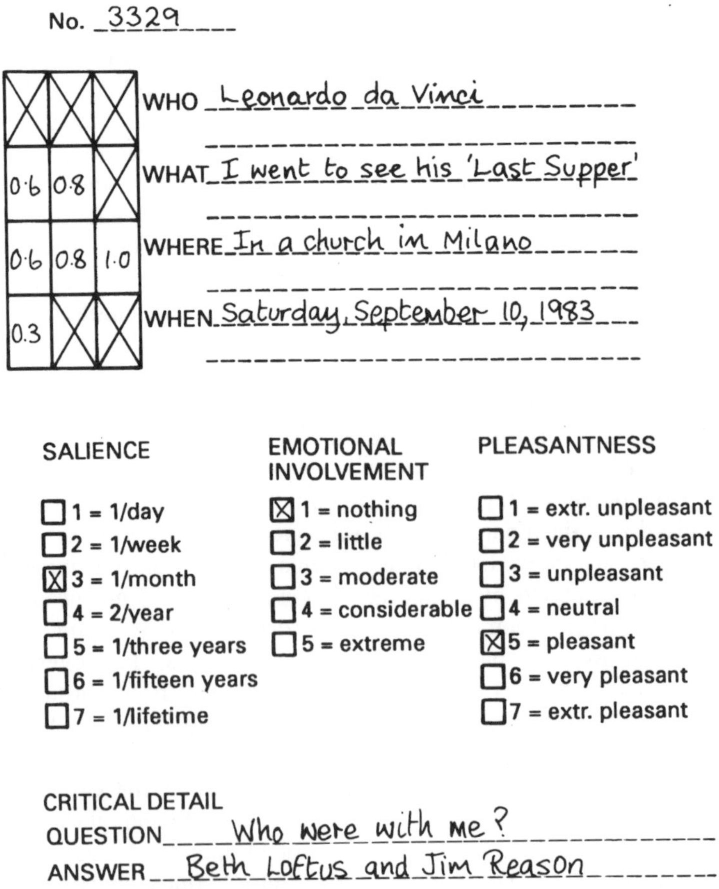

No. _3329____

WHO _Leonardo da Vinci_____

WHAT_I went to see his 'Last Supper'_

WHERE_In a church in Milano_____

WHEN_Saturday, September 10, 1983___

0·6 0·8
0·6 0·8 1·0
0·3

SALIENCE

☐ 1 = 1/day
☐ 2 = 1/week
☒ 3 = 1/month
☐ 4 = 2/year
☐ 5 = 1/three years
☐ 6 = 1/fifteen years
☐ 7 = 1/lifetime

EMOTIONAL INVOLVEMENT

☒ 1 = nothing
☐ 2 = little
☐ 3 = moderate
☐ 4 = considerable
☐ 5 = extreme

PLEASANTNESS

☐ 1 = extr. unpleasant
☐ 2 = very unpleasant
☐ 3 = unpleasant
☐ 4 = neutral
☒ 5 = pleasant
☐ 6 = very pleasant
☐ 7 = extr. pleasant

CRITICAL DETAIL
QUESTION____Who were with me ?_____
ANSWER __Beth Loftus and Jim Reason_____

FIG. 6.7. An example of a recorded event from Wagenaar's diary study (1986).

When memory was tested, each cue was presented in turn. For example, on trial 1 Leonardo da Vinci (the *who* cue) was supplied and Wagenaar had to try to recall *what* happened, *where*, and *when*. On trial 2, two cues were given; on trial 3, three cues; and on trial 4 all four cues were given and the question about the critical detail was posed. Cue order was varied systematically. The retention function showed that the percentage of questions answered correctly dropped over a four-year period from 70% to 35%. Recall increased with the number of cues provided. Pleasant events were remembered better than unpleasant or neutral ones, a finding sometimes known as the *Pollyanna principle*, but retention was also related to the other rated dimensions of salience and emotionality. The order of efficacy of the retrieval cues when presented singly was *what, where, who, when*. *What* was by far the most powerful cue and *when* was almost useless. Chronological information was often missing from the memory of the event, and could not be used as a search criterion. Wagenaar concluded that only a few landmark events were precisely dated in memory, and events were, on the whole, not filed in memory by dates. In everyday terms, it is unlikely that you will remember if I ask you what happened on 17 July four years ago, but if I tell you that you went to watch a tennis match you would probably remember who played, where it took place, at roughly what period of the year, and what happened. The failure to remember when events occurred may seem to be at odds with the claim made in other studies that memories are chronologically organised, but that claim was based on evidence showing organisation into the large chunks of time that constitute lifetime periods, not precise days and dates. However, the power of the *what* cue does suggest that the predominant form of organisation is thematic.

Internal Structure of Specific Memories

Anderson and Conway (1993) were interested in the internal structure of specific memories. Their subjects were asked to recall a memory and then to list details of that memory as fast as possible in one of four different ways: forward order of occurrence, reverse order, from the most central detail to the least central, or free recall. Production rates were fastest for free recall and for forward-order recall In the free-recall condition it was evident that the order of production was influenced by the personal importance and distinctiveness of particular details. Figure 6.8 shows that in free recall the details of the remembered event "meeting Angela" deviate from the chronological forward order with the important and distinctive detail "dancing with Angela" being reported earlier.

The general conclusion from this study again identified both temporal and thematic factors as organising principles.

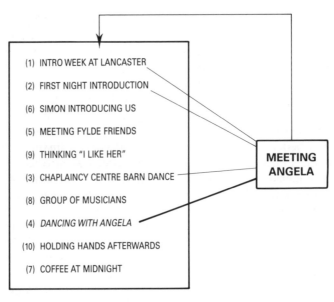

FIG. 6.8. Organisation of knowledge of a specific autobiographical memory. Memory details are listed in forward chronological order from top to bottom and numbers in parentheses denote ordinal position in the free recall output (from Anderson & Conway, 1993). Reprinted by permission of the authors.

Availability of Memories

An obvious question to ask is what kind of experiences people are most likely to remember from their past lives, and, conversely, what kinds of experiences they are most likely to forget. In ordinary everyday language we often speak of an experience as "unforgettable", and, in fact, we probably do have quite accurate intuitions about what kinds of events someone ought to be able to remember. If a person could not remember his or her own wedding, we would consider this abnormal; if he could not remember going to a party ten years ago we would not think this very unusual. However, remembering personal experiences is not always the result of effortful search and retrieval. Memories are sometimes spontaneously elicited by some cue such as a phrase, a smell, a tune, or when we are reminded of them by a similar current experience. Some memories come unbidden into consciousness. Salaman (1982) has described examples of these involuntary memories which are peculiarly vivid and emotional and have a strong feeling of immediacy. Spence (1988) described this kind of experience as "passive remembering", which is triggered by a particular context. Passive memories are not necessarily available on demand. More often, however, personal memories are deliberately sought and retrieved in response to a query, or for comparison with a current experience. It is clear from our discussion so far that autobiographical memories vary in availability; some are easy to retrieve and others are more elusive. Although organisation is one factor that influences availability, several other factors are also important.

The Distribution of Autobiographical Memories

It is well established that when people look back over their lives, memories from some parts of the life span are more readily available than from other parts. There is variability both in terms of quantity and quality so that memories from some periods may be more numerous and more vivid than those from other periods.

Studies that focus on the retention of autobiographical memories over time and on the distribution of memories across the life span have used different methods, and addressed different issues. Rubin, Wetzler, and Nebes (1986) have collated the results of a number of studies (e.g. Rubin, 1982; Crovitz & Schiffman, 1974) that used word-cueing and investigated the incidence of memories across the life span. With this method, subjects are presented with a list of cue words. For each cue word the subjects report the first autobiographical memory that comes to mind, and, after completing the list, they supply the date of each reported memory. So, given the cue word "plum", a subject may respond "I remember making plum jam" and identify this memory as 10 years old. In these studies, the number of memories elicited from each period of the life span is then plotted. Rubin et al. reported that the data fitted a retention function with a linear relationship between the log of memory frequency and the log of recency of occurrence: That is, the mean number of memories elicited declined as a function of the age of the memories; there were many recent memories and fewer remote ones. Thus, the main trend reflects the normal course of forgetting. However, superimposed on this retention function, Rubin et al. noted a "reminiscence peak", seen in Fig. 6.9, consisting of a disproportionate number of memories recalled from the period when the subjects were between 10 and 30 years old. The reminiscence bump is present for all subjects over the age of about 35 years and was replicated in data collected by Cohen and Faulkner (1988a), who pointed out that this peak was composed of highly significant life events that tend to occur at this period in life. Fitzgerald (1988) suggested that memories from early adult life are more elaborated because these events form part of a personal narrative that sets the developing self in a social and cultural context. A third component of the distribution of memories across the life span, not apparent in Fig. 6.9, is the small number of memories from the period when subjects were aged 0–5 years. This phenomenon, known as childhood amnesia, is discussed in the next section.

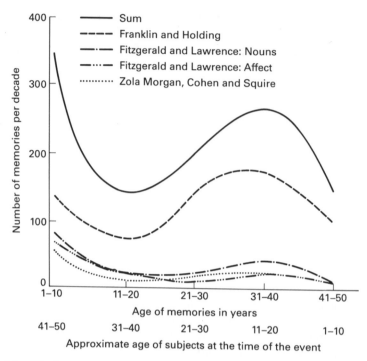

FIG. 6.9. Distributions of memories across the life span (from Rubin, Wetzler, & Nebes, 1986). Reprinted by permission of Cambridge University Press.

Further research has shown that the distribution of elicited memories across the life span is extremely sensitive to the method used. The recency effect observed by Rubin et al. (1986) was evident when subjects were asked to supply a memory for each of the word cues, and then go back through the memories they had produced and date them. Holding, Noonan, Pfau, and Holding (1986) asked their subjects to date each memory as it was produced, and found that this method produced a primacy effect, with memories being more numerous from the early part of the life span. They concluded that the dating process induced a chronological search. Cohen and Faulkner (1988a) did not use word-cueing, but simply asked subjects to produce and describe their most vivid memories. This technique also induced a forward-order chronological search through the life span and resulted in a preponderance of early memories. Thus, the incidence of memories from different parts of the life span varies according to the retrieval process being used. These methods do not test whether recent memories are better retained, or more easily elicited, than remote ones. They simply reflect the fact that when people retrieve memories by searching backwards through their past lives they produce more recent memories, and when they begin at the beginning and search forwards they produce more remote memories.

The accuracy and quality (as opposed to the incidence) of autobiographical memories is more consistently found to deteriorate with time elapsed. As in the studies by Linton (1982) and by Wagenaar (1986), and in Bahrick's (1984a) data on teacher's memory for their students (p.109), information is lost over time, and Cohen and Faulkner (1988a) also found that the self-rated vividness of autobiographical memories declined over time, with older memories being less vivid than recent ones. To summarise, it is clear that memory availability is influenced by age and time variables, including the length of time elapsed since the event, the age at which it was experienced, and the age of the person at the time of recall.

Event Characteristics

Some of the factors that tend to make an event memorable are characteristics of the event itself, and operate at the time of encoding. As we saw in the studies of flashbulb memory (pp.99–104), events that are personally important, consequential, unique, emotional, or surprising are liable to be better remembered. These variables tend to co-occur so that it is difficult to assess the relative contribution of each. Recall is also affected by variables that operate during retention, such as how frequently the event is talked about or thought about. Rubin and Kozin (1984) asked a group of students to describe three of their clearest memories, and to rate them for national importance, personal importance, surprise, vividness, emotionality and how often they had discussed the event. The most commonly reported events concerned injuries or accidents, sports, and encounters with the opposite sex. Memories that were more vivid also received higher ratings for importance, surprise, and emotionality. A study by Sehulster (1989) confirmed the role of importance and rehearsal in making events particularly memorable. Sehulster tested his own ability to free-recall details, dates, and casting of 284 opera performances seen over 25 years and checked his recall against the programmes. The importance of particular performances as rated by experts, and the amount of rehearsal opportunity, as estimated from the availability of tapes, books, and TV showings, correlated with recall of the content and casting of the operas but did not influence recall of dates.

Cohen and Faulkner (1988a) also reported that memory vividness correlated significantly with emotion, importance, and the amount of rehearsal. In their study, the relative power of these factors shifted with the age of the person who was remembering. For younger people, characteristics of the event itself, such as emotionality and importance, were the best predictors of memory vividness, but for elderly people the amount of rehearsal was the most powerful factor. The vividness of their remote memories was preserved because the events were often thought about and talked about. The events that were most often remembered were births, marriages, and deaths (22.2%), holidays (11.8%), trivia (8.2%), illness/injury (8%), education (8%), family (7.5%), war (6.1%), love affairs (5.1%), and recreations/sports (4.9%). Events in which the subjects were actors were remembered better than events in which they were only bystanders, and unique occasions and first times were remembered more often than generic events or last times.

A similar pattern was noted by Means and Loftus (1991) in a study of people's ability to recall health events such as visits to the doctor. Like Linton, in her diary study, they found that similar, recurring events like repeated visits for chronic conditions were recalled less well than nonrecurring one-off visits. The recurring events blended into a generic "repisode", which was hard to decompose, but serious health events, which can be presumed to be more personally important, were remembered better than trivial ones. Cohen and Java (1995) also tested recall of health events, including illnesses, symptoms, injuries, and visits to health professionals, by subjects who had kept health diaries for 12 weeks. Three months later only 47% of these events were recalled. An unexpected finding was that people aged over 70 years had better recall than younger subjects and this was attributed to the greater importance they attached to their health problems.

Despite the wide variation in the methods used and in the type of memories that were probed, these studies have produced converging results. Events are better recalled if they are unique, important, and frequently rehearsed. These conclusions are therefore well supported, if not particularly surprising.

FALSE OR TRUE? THE FALLIBILITY OF MEMORY

Research in autobiographical memory is complicated by the fact that most of the methods used are highly subjective, and rely on self-reports. There is often no way of checking whether the memories reported are veridical, but researchers have gone to considerable lengths to find ways of checking autobiographical memories. A person's recall of an event at one time can sometimes be checked against recall of the same event at a subsequent time, or against the recall of other people who may have experienced the same event. These methods have been used in the studies of flashbulb memory and eyewitness testimony reviewed in Chapter 4. For public memories there may be contemporary records, but for private memories tests of accuracy usually rely on the diary method, checking subsequent recall against the subject's own diary record.

Barclay and Wellman (1986) asked 6 adults to record 3 events every day for 4 months and then administered a recognition test after 3, 6, 9, 12, or 31

Original	Foil
_____ rode her bike through the park while I ran . . . I ran until I had to stop to get her out of the snow, walk her bike up a hill, etc. We were out an hour—it was beautiful out. Again it made me think how much I've enjoyed the city.	_____ rode her bike through the park while I ran . . . I ran until I had to stop to get her out of the snow, walk her bike up a hill etc. We were out an hour—it was a mess out. Again it made me think how hard it is to adjust to the city.

FIG. 6.10. An original memory and a foil where the evaluation has been changed (from Barclay & Wellman, 1986).

months. In the recognition test the original event descriptions were mixed with foil items that were of three different kinds. Some foils changed the description of the event, some changed the evaluation of the event, and some substituted a completely different event. Shown in Fig. 6.10 is one of the original memories and a foil that has changed the evaluation.

Hit rates for correct recognition ranged from 92% at the shortest interval to 79% at the longest, but false positive rates were high. Even for the completely different foils the false alarm rate was 22% and Barclay noted that false alarm rates were higher if the foil was semantically similar to the original event. He concluded that a process of schematisation takes place with details being lost and memories becoming generic.

Conway, Collins, Gathercole, and Anderson (1996) reported a study in which two people kept diaries recording both true and false events and thoughts over a period of five months. Seven months later they tried to discriminate between the true and false records. Correct recognition for true memories was high and was associated with conscious recollection of the event, but false memories produced a high rate of false positive responses that were not associated with a distinct recollection. Events were recognised better than thoughts. These studies illustrate the fallibility of autobiographical memory.

Reconstruction versus Copy Theories

The extent to which autobiographical memories are reconstructions or direct copies of the original event is related to the issue of accuracy. Barclay's (1993) ideas constitute a *Strong Reconstruction View* of autobiographical

memory. He believes that new versions of the past are continually reconstructed. According to this view people use their general knowledge and
past experience to make plausible inferences about what might have
happened. Reconstructed memories are therefore liable to conform to the
general character of the original event but to be inaccurate in specific
details.

Against this view, it is argued that memories often do contain specific
details that are accurate. Brewer (1988) favours a more moderate *Partial
Reconstructive View*. He gave his student subjects a beeper set to go off at
random intervals and asked them to record what they were doing, thinking
and feeling at that moment. Later, they were given recall and recognition
tests and asked to rate the extent to which they could re-experience the
event. He found that there was some degree of re-experiencing for the
majority of events and considered this was evidence against the strong
reconstructive position. The subjective feeling of re-experiencing is not a
guarantee that a memory has not been reconstructed but Brewer found that
accuracy, confidence, and degree of re-experiencing were highly intercorrelated.

Factors that Influence Accuracy

It is arguable that forced-choice recognition experiments that use foils
produce underestimates of the accuracy of autobiographical memory.
The events that were tested in these studies were relatively mundane and
trivial, and the foils were constructed so as to be confusing. In the ordinary
circumstances of everyday life, when people try to recall autobiographical
memories, they have the option of deciding they do not remember and so
are less likely to make inaccurate responses. In experimental situations,
when they are pushed into making yes/no responses to deliberately confusing items, it is not surprising that they make errors.

A number of factors have been identified that influence memory accuracy. It is commonly believed that highly stressful and emotional experiences leave indelible memories. Wagenaar and Groeneweg (1990)
examined this idea in their study of the memories of concentration camp
survivors. For 15 of the witnesses at the trial of Martinus De Rijke, a camp
guard, their testimonies had been collected in 1943–47 and were given
again in 1984–87. After 40 years, their experiences were generally well
remembered but there was a marked loss of specific but essential details
such as the names and appearance of torturers, and specific events such as
seeing a murder and being brutally treated. The missing information
appeared to be irretrievably lost and could not be recovered by cueing.
Generic information about the daily routine was well remembered. The
results of this study conform to the pattern found in more humdrum

memories and do not support the view that very emotional experiences are never forgotten.

A study by Conway (1990) highlights the fact that memories may be altered to conform with current beliefs and attitudes, a sort of hindsight bias. Before they took an examination he asked students to report their expected grade; how much importance they attached to doing well; the number of hours they spent in preparation; how well prepared they were; and how far they thought the grade they obtained would accurately reflect their knowledge and ability. Two weeks after the results of the examination were known they were asked to recall this information. Those who had grades worse than expected recalled working less hard; thought the grade less related to their true level of knowledge and ability; and thought the result less important than their original estimates. Those who did better than expected recalled the amount of work they had done correctly, but estimated the importance of the result more highly. Consistent with a reconstructive view, these findings suggest that personal memories are to some extent unstable and can be edited in the light of later experiences.

False Memories

It is well known that brain injuries can cause patients to confabulate, producing autobiographical memories that have no basis in fact. The borderline between confabulation and reconstruction is not absolutely clear as it is well known that normal adults may confabulate details of real memories, and, as we have seen in the studies of eyewitness testimony, memories may be contaminated by misleading information. However, the question that currently preoccupies many researchers is whether normal adults may produce completely false confabulated memories of events that never occurred at all. Interest in false memories has been amplified recently by the spate of cases in which adults claim to have recovered repressed memories of sexual abuse that occurred in childhood. Recovery of these memories usually takes place in the course of psychotherapy, and many researchers believe that the recovered events never took place, but have been implanted in disturbed and vulnerable people by the suggestions offered by the therapist. The phenomenon has been labelled the *False Memory Syndrome,* but it proves extremely difficult to find hard evidence to show that such memories are either true or false. To prove that the memory is true it would be necessary to have objective evidence that the abuse actually occurred, but this is usually lacking. Moreover, the existence of repressed memory, as distinct from normal forgetting, is itself controversial. Furthermore, a recent investigation by the British Psychological Society showed that in 134 out of 181 cases, memories of abuse were not suddenly recovered from total amnesia, but had been partially recalled previously over varying periods of time.

There has been a tendency, especially in the United States, for people to take up extreme positions, with some asserting that it is impossible to recover forgotten memories and attacking the concept of repression. The fact that some recovered memories, such as those involving being carried off by aliens in space ships, are intrinsically unbelievable, is cited in support of this position. On the other hand, some people claim that a wide variety of psychological problems such as depression and eating disorders are indicative of sexual abuse in childhood, and that sufferers can be helped to recover forgotten memories of this abuse.

A more balanced view is that it may be possible to recover repressed memories later in life but that most recovered "memories" probably never happened. Lindsay and Read (1994) argued that memory recovery therapy can lead clients to create illusory memories. We know from studies of eyewitness testimony and flashbulb memory (Chapter 4) that gross inaccuracies are not uncommon and that memory is highly suggestible. It has certainly been clearly demonstrated that it is possible to implant false memories in a subject who comes to believe the false memory with a high degree of confidence. Recent studies by Bruck, Ceci, Francouer, and Barr (1995) have demonstrated that children's memory for what occurred during a medical examination can be influenced by post-event suggestions (e.g. "He looked into your ear, didn't he?"). This study also demonstrated that the longer the time that had elapsed since the event, and the more often the suggestions were repeated, the stronger the effects of the suggestions. Loftus and Coan (in press) reported an experiment in which a 14-year-old boy was told by his brother of an event in which, when he was 2 years old, the boy had been lost in a shopping mall, found by a stranger and reunited with his parents. This event had never occurred. Over a period of days the boy became completely convinced that he remembered this episode and spontaneously supplied additional details. Ceci, Loftus, Crotteau, and Smith (in press) interviewed young children, repeatedly asking them if they had ever experienced particular events, some of which had really occurred and some of which were fabricated (e.g. "Did you ever get your finger caught in a mouse-trap and have to go to hospital to get the trap off?"). More than half the children produced false narratives with compellingly vivid details. Thus, it is clear that false memories can be implanted in someone who then genuinely believes the memory to be true. Whether this is what is happening in some of the cases when memories of sexual abuse are "recovered" is not yet established, but it is clear that it could be happening. The possibility that some "recovered" memories are illusory is made more likely by the techniques employed, because some forms of memory recovery therapy encourage clients to believe strongly in memories that are sketchy or consist only of vague feelings. Lindsay and Read (1994, p.318) concluded that "the creation of illusory memories of childhood sexual abuse is not merely an abstract possibility but rather a tragic reality". Nevertheless, most psychologists recognise that it is possible to retrieve forgotten memories of events that occurred long ago and that some recovered memories of sexual abuse may be true.

It is common for information to be lost from autobiographical memory, false details may come to be incorporated in true memories, and completely false memories can be implanted by suggestion. Yet these findings are not representative of the normal functioning of autobiographical memory. In ordinary circumstances, when we are not deliberately misled or influenced by suggestion, memories may be inaccurate in detail but are usually accurate in general terms.

MEMORY FOR DATES

The ability to date memories is crucial to chronological organisation. The idea that memories are organised on a temporal dimension and retrieved by some form of chronological search raises questions about the accuracy of subjective dating.

Rubin (1982) checked a sample of events that subjects had recalled and dated against their own diary records and found that 74% were correct to within a month. Brown, Rips, and Shevell (1985) pointed out that people seldom have a precise memory record of the dates of public events, so that dates are *estimated* rather than remembered. They suggested that estimation is based on the amount of information about the event that can be recalled. That is, people work on the assumption that information is progressively lost from memory over time, so the less that is remembered, the older the memory must be. Brown et al. asked subjects to date the month of 50 news events from 1977 to mid 1982. They selected some events that subjects would know a lot about, and some events they would know little about, and predicted that dates of high-knowledge events (like "President Reagan shot") would be shifted toward the present, and dates of low-knowledge events (like "25 die in California mud slides") would be shifted toward the past. The results conformed to the prediction. Dates of high-knowledge events were too recent by an average of 0.28 years, and dates of low-knowledge events were too remote by an average of 0.17 years. The number of propositions a subject could recall about an event was systematically related to the judged recency of the event.

People also estimate dates of public events using the strategy of relating the target event to autobiographical events or to some other, more easily dated public event. If a landmark event can be dated, and the temporal relationship of landmark to target is known, the target date can be estimated. For example, I can estimate the date of the Prince of Wales' wedding because I remember being on holiday in Switzerland at the time and seeing it on television in a hotel in the mountains, and I know the date of this holiday.

Loftus and Marburger (1983) confirmed that events are dated more accurately if a landmark is supplied as a temporal reference point. They noted that people usually overestimate the recency of events, especially ones that are very emotional and salient, a phenomenon known as *forward telescoping,* but this tendency was reduced by using landmarks. They compared responses to questions preceded by landmarks with responses to the same questions preceded by no landmark. In the No Landmark condition the questions were:

> "During the last six months—
> did anyone try to rob you?
> did anyone attack you with a weapon?
> did you report a crime to the police?
> did the failure to rescue the hostages in Iran occur?
> did you have a birthday?
> did you eat lobster?"

In the With Landmark condition, the same questions were preceded by

> "Since the eruption of Mount St. Helens did you —"
> *or*
> "Since last New Year's Day did you—"

or the subject was instructed to supply a personal landmark to use as a reference point when answering the question. Forward telescoping was reduced by the use of all of these landmarks. Rubin and Baddeley (1989) also found forward telescoping in their study of people's memory for visits to the Applied Psychology Unit in Cambridge, with the size of the error increasing systematically with the time elapsed since the visit. They explained the phenomenon of forward telescoping in terms of two main factors. First, errors are larger for older events so more of these will be shifted into a different period, whereas the small errors that occur for recent events are not sufficient to shift them outside the correct period. Second, the recency effect preserves the dates of recent events so these are less likely to be shifted backward. The combination of these factors makes it more likely that dating errors will be forward shifts.

Questions about the date of events may be important when medical histories are elicited. The patient's ability to recall the dates and ordering of episodes and symptoms and their frequency and intensity is crucial for diagnosis. Means, Mingay, Nigam, and Zarrow (1988) have pointed out that in chronic health conditions, recurring events blended into a generic memory and were difficult to decompose. Their study showed that when people were trained to link events to personal landmarks, like birthdays or holidays, recall improved. Cohen and Java (1995), in their study of memory for medical history, found that 50% of health events that occurred in the previous six months were dated accurately to within two weeks and there was no difference between forward and backward shifts in dating errors. However, this was a relatively short time period and subjects spontaneously used personal landmarks. Loftus (1987) has noted that accuracy of dating improves when two time frames are interrogated instead of one. Asking whether X occurred (a) in the last 6 months? and (b) in the last 2 months? forces people to be more accurate and precise than simply asking whether X occurred in the last 6 months.

Brown, Shevell, and Rips (1986) collected verbal protocols from subjects during date estimation. In this study, both political events (Cyrus Vance resigns) and nonpolitical events (Mount St. Helens erupts) were dated after lags of up to five years. Overall, 70% of the protocols contained temporal inferences of the kind "I know X happened just before Y and Y was about last autumn"; 61% of political events were related in this way to other political events and 31% to personal history. For nonpolitical events, 25% were related to public events and 50% to personal history. It was easier to "place" nonpolitical events within personally defined periods, such as college terms, and to place political events within publicly defined periods, such as the Reagan administration, but public and personal event histories were clearly interwoven and each provided a reference system for the other.

It follows from these findings that memories are dated more accurately if someone has a clearly defined time line. Skowronski and Thompson (1990) tested the hypothesis that women have a better developed temporal reference schema than men and are therefore better able to reconstruct the dates of past events. The idea behind this is that women are more concerned with keeping appointments, remembering the dates of birthdays and anniversaries, and more often keep personal diaries. In a meta-analysis of four dating studies they found that the dating accuracy of women was superior, although this difference is thought to be culturally induced rather than being a gender-specific difference.

CHILDHOOD MEMORY

There is a great deal of rather conflicting folklore on the subject of childhood memory. On the one hand, it is said that people remember very little of the experiences of their early years. On the other hand, some childhood memories appear to be retained with great vividness. Most people would agree that if they attempt to recall their personal history, they can retrieve a fairly continuous record for the years after the age of six or seven, but, for the period before this age, memories are sparse and fragmentary consisting of isolated vignettes of particular events. Freud (1916) described this phenomenon as "childhood amnesia".

Childhood Amnesia

The term "childhood amnesia" is used as a label for deficient recall, and does not necessarily imply that memory is completely lost. Initially, claims of childhood amnesia rested on clinical reports, anecdotes, and intuitions, but more recently there have been attempts to give a more precise definition and to provide an empirical demonstration. Wetzler and Sweeney (1986) pointed out that what needs to be demonstrated is deficient recall for the early childhood years that is independent of age at retrieval (current age) and of the length of the retention interval. That is, adults of all ages should exhibit a similar degree of childhood amnesia, and the loss of memory in the childhood years should be greater than would be predicted by the decay function, whereby forgetting increases with the passage of time. This approach concentrates on a quantitative criterion for childhood amnesia rather than on qualitative aspects of childhood memories. Figure 6.11 shows a hypothetical distribution of memories across a 20-year life

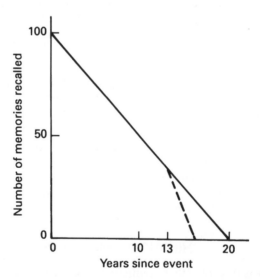

FIG. 6.11. The hypothetical distribution of memories across the lifetime of a 20-year-old subject. The solid line represents a linear function of normal forgetting; the broken line represents the accelerated forgetting due to childhood amnesia (from Wetzler & Sweeney, 1986). Copyright 1986 American Psychological Association. Reproduced by permission of the author.

span. Wetzler and Sweeney examined the data from several studies of autobiographical memory, and found distributions approximating closely to this hypothetical one, with accelerated forgetting (i.e. disproportionate loss of memories) for the years before age five.

Another way to probe this "dark age" is to ask people to produce their earliest memory. Dudycha and Dudycha (1941) noted that the average age for earliest memories was around 42 months and Halliday (personal communication) obtained a similar result with a mean of 39 months. Sheingold and Tenney (1982) focused on a specific episode that took place at a known age, the birth of a sibling. They interviewed 4-year-old children whose sibling had been born within the last year, and 8-year-olds and 12-year-olds whose siblings had been born when they were 4 years old. At interview, they were asked specific questions, shown in Fig. 6.12. The children's mothers were also questioned to provide confirmation of their answers. The 4-year-olds answered a mean of 13 questions out of 20 and, on average, 9 of their answers were confirmed by their mothers. The scores for amount recalled showed only minimal differences between children of different ages. The 12-year-old children remembered the event of 8 years

---

1. Who told you that your mother was leaving to go to the hospital?
2. What were you doing when you were told that she was leaving?
3. What time of day was it when she left to go to the hospital?
4. Who went with her? Did you go?
5. Who took care of you right after your mother left to go to the hospital?
6. What did you do right after your mother left?
7. How did you find out that the baby was a boy or girl?
8. Who took care of you while your mother was in the hospital?
9. What things did you do with that person while your mother was in the hospital?
10. Did you visit your mother while she was in the hospital?
11. Did you talk to your mother on the telephone while she was in the hospital?
12. How long did she stay in the hospital?
13. Who picked your mother and the baby up?
14. What day of the week did they come home?
15. What time of day was it?
16. What did you do when your mother and the baby arrived home?
17. What was the baby wearing when you first saw it?
18. What presents did the baby get?
19. Did you get any presents at that time?
20. How did you find out that your mother was going to have a baby?

FIG. 6.12. Questions about the birth of siblings used by Sheingold & Tenney (1982) (from Neisser, 1982b). Copyright 1982 W.H. Freeman & Co. Reprinted with permission.

ago as well as the younger children for whom it was more recent. For this highly salient event, there was almost no forgetting. Sheingold and Tenney also examined college students' memory for the birth of siblings and found a sharp discontinuity in memory between the ages of 3 and 5 years. Students who were younger than 3 years when their sibling was born recalled almost nothing about the circumstances, whereas those who were aged 4 at the time recalled an impressive amount of information. This discontinuity is reflected in Fig. 6.13.

Different studies therefore place the boundaries of childhood amnesia at different ages, ranging from 3 years (Sheingold & Tenney, 1982) to between 6 and 8 years (Freud, 1916). Moreover, Usher and Neisser (1993) have shown that some events are remembered from earlier in childhood than others. They compared the earliest ages of recall for four different events. For birth of a sibling and for being hospitalised the earliest age was 2 years, for death of a family member and for a family move the earliest age was 3 years.

A range of explanations for the phenomenon of childhood amnesia are on offer (White & Pillemer, 1979). According to the Freudian explanation, early memories are present but with the rejection of infant sexuality, memories are repressed and cannot be recalled to consciousness. The deficit is thus a retrieval failure. Freud identified those early memories which can be recalled as "screen" memories, fabricated to block out emotionally painful realities. Other theories attribute the dearth of early memories to inadequate encoding, neurological immaturity, or developmental changes in

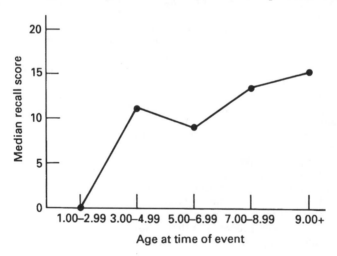

FIG. 6.13.   Amount recalled about the birth of a sibling as a function of age at the time of the event (from Sheingold & Tenney, 1982). Copyright 1982 W.H. Freeman & Co. Reprinted with permission.

cognitive mechanisms. It has been argued that very young children lack the linguistic ability to encode their experiences verbally, and lack the schemas within which they can represent and organise event memories (Schachtel, 1947). They may fail to use encoding strategies which elaborate and enrich the memory representation with semantic associations (Winograd & Killinger, 1983), or they may encode memories in ways that are inappropriate for the retrieval processes used at a later age. According to this explanation, developmental changes in coding and organisation produce a mismatch between the original coding and the subsequent retrieval cues. An example of this kind occurs when you try to remind a child of a particular event, such as a family trip to visit a relative. Your descriptions of the journey, the destination, and the relative, fail to evoke any memory in the child, but it turns out eventually that the child remembers the event in terms of the ice cream he or she was given at lunch. This type of example raises the possibility that we are underestimating the number of events that can be remembered from early childhood because we do not find the right triggers to elicit them. A more recent explanation of childhood amnesia has been offered by Perner (1992). He linked the ability to recall experiences to the development of "theory of mind". Children aged 3 and 4 years watched an object put into a box or were told what was inside and were later asked what was in the box and how they knew. Both age groups could recall the object but only the 4-year-olds could explain how they knew. The older children had developed the ability to relate their knowedge to what they had experienced and, in Perner's view, this marks the beginning of auto-noetic memory and and the end of childhood amnesia. This is an interesting idea that may gain ground with further testing. However, the likelihood is that there is no single explanation for childhood amnesia but that several factors are responsible.

Early Childhood Memories

Failure to recall early childhood memories in later life does not mean that young children cannot remember their experiences. There is growing evidence of impressive memory ability in very young children. This revelation is a testament to the value of naturalistic field studies undertaken in the context of the child's daily life. Formal laboratory experiments seriously underestimate children's ability (Baker-Ward, 1993). There are several reasons why this is so. Children's memory is idiosyncratic. What is memorable to a child is not necessarily what would strike an adult as memorable. Children remember what makes sense to them and fail to remember what does not make sense. Children's memory is also socially determined in that they tend to remember what they want to communicate. Hudson (1990) has developed a social interaction model of the development of autobiographical memory. Memories are jointly constructed, elaborated and shaped in conversation between mother and child, as in the example shown in Fig. 6.14, and children recall experiences better when their mothers have helped to provide a narrative format. Laboratory experiments cannot create the social and motivational conditions that facilitate memory in everyday life.

There is also evidence of implicit memory in preverbal infants as young as 9–21 months (McDonough & Mandler, 1994). Infants who have watched actions performed with a toy, such as listening to a toy telephone or feeding a teddy with a bottle, will imitate these actions at a later date, with the retention interval increasing with the child's age. Similarly, there are many parental anecdotes about young children who make straight for the cupboard where toys or biscuits are kept in a house they visited some time previously. These feats of implicit memory, although impressive, are obviously not equivalent to explicit recall.

Once language has developed it becomes possible to study explicit recall, and research on children's memory for events has centred on questions about the acquisition of scripts and the function of scripts in supporting memory. Following Schank and Abelson (1977), Nelson and Gruendel (1986) identified five features that define a script.

---

21 months Rachel and her mother:

M: Did you see Aunt Gail and Uncle Tim last week?
C: Yes, yes, Uncle Tim.
M: What did we do with Aunt Gail and Uncle Tim?
C: Said bye-bye.
M: You said bye-bye to Aunt Gail and Uncle Tim?
C: Yes, go in car, in car.
M: Tim went in the car?
C: Aunt Gail with Uncle Tim. (p.180)

Even at this early age, Rachel is contributing bits of information to this re-construction of an episode that mother and child experienced together in the recent past. Six months later she could initiate and guide the recall:

27 months

C: Do you remember the waves, Mommy?
M: Do I remember the waves? What about the waves?
C: I go in the waves and I build a sand castle. And do you remember we swimmed? I swimmed in the waves and we did it again.

FIG. 6.14. Joint construction of memories by a mother and child (from Hudson, 1990). Reprinted by permission of Cambridge University Press and the authors.

(1) Scripts are organised sequentially.
(2) They are organised around a central goal.
(3) They are generalised and include slots for variable elements.
(4) They are similar across individuals who share the same experience.
(5) They are consistent across repeated experiences.

Figure 6.15 shows examples of some of the scripts supplied by children of different ages in response to questions and prompts. Scripts for other events like getting dressed and going shopping were also elicited. These examples show that young children's event knowledge conforms to the defining features of scripts. Their scripts show temporal sequencing of actions, central goals, are consistent and are expressed in a general form. Older children produced longer scripts with more detail and elaboration. Younger children's scripts were similar in form, but more skeletal. This finding supports Winograd and Killinger's conclusion that developmental differences in amount recalled stem from differences in the degree of elaboration at encoding. Nelson (1991) also stressed the importance of scripts and general event memories which allow the child to anticipate the future and act appropriately in the present.

Hudson (1986) examined children's organization of memory for events within the framework of schema-plus-tag, or context-plus-index models, whereby specific autobiographical events are organised in long-term memory in terms of their relationship to general event representations. Routine, repeated events which conform to the same pattern are absorbed into a general event representation and are not remembered as distinct occasions. However, novel, unique or deviant occasions are retained as specific memories, although linked to the relevant general event representation. Autobiographical memories can therefore include a blend of specific knowledge about what happened on a particular occasion, and general knowledge which has been abstracted from past experience of similar occasions. Hudson pointed out that this form of representation is essentially a developmental one, as the general event representations are progressively built up out of accumulating specific event representations. She sought evidence for qualitative changes in children's memory for events reflecting this development. She expected to find age differences in the relative proportions of general event knowledge, and specific event knowledge.

In her first study, she examined three and five-year-olds' memory for specific episodes of routine events which occurred the previous day (e.g. "What happened when you had dinner at home yesterday?"). She also studied their general knowledge about this class of event (e.g. "What happens when you have dinner at home?") All the children produced more information in answer to the general dinner script question than in

Making Cookies

Well, you bake them and eat them. (3;1)

My mommy puts chocolate chips inside the cookies. Then ya put 'em in the oven . . . Then we take them out, put them on the table and eat them. (4;5)

Add three cups of butter . . . add three lumps of butter . . . two cups of sugar, one cup of flour. Mix it up . . . knead it. Get it in a pan, put it in the oven. Bake it . . . set it up to 30. Take it out and it'll be cookies. (6;9)

First, you need a bowl, a bowl, and you need about two eggs and chocolate chips and an egg-beater! And then you gotta crack the egg open and put it in a bowl and ya gotta get the chips and mix it together. And put it in a stove for about 5 or 10 minutes, and then you have cookies. Then ya eat them! (8;8)

Birthday Party

You cook a cake and eat it. (3;1)

Well, you get a cake and some ice cream and then some birthday (?) and then you get some clowns and then you get some paper hats, the animal hats and then and then you sing "Happy Birthday to you," and then then then they give you some presents and then you play with them and then that's the end and they go home and they do what they wanta. (4;9)

First, uhm . . . you're getting ready for the kids to come, like puttin' balloons up and putting out party plates and making cake. And then all the people come you've asked. Give you presents and then you have lunch or whatever you have. Then . . . uhm . . . then you open your presents. Or you can open your presents anytime. Uhm . . . you could . . . after you open the presents, then it's probably time to go home. if you're like at Foote Park or something, then it's time to go home and you have to drive all the people home. Then you go home too. (6;7)

Well, first you open your mail box and get some mail. And then you see that there's an invitation for you. Read the invitation. Then you ask your parents if you can go. Then you . . . uhm . . . go to the birthday party and after you get there you usually wait for everyone else to come. Then usually they always want to open one of the presents. Sometimes then they have three games, then they have the birthday cake then sometimes they open the other presents or they could open them up all at once. After that they like to play some more games and then maybe your parents come to pick you up. And then you go home. (8;10)

FIG. 6.15. Examples of scripts for making cookies and for birthday parties from children aged 3–8 years. (from Nelson & Gruendel, 1986).

answer to the specific episode question. There were no age differences in the relative proportions of general event knowledge and specific event knowledge in their answers. They had relatively little recall for the last occurrence of a routine event, but when asked to recall a novel event, such as a trip to the zoo or circus, their replies showed rich and detailed memory for these unique events.

In a second study, Hudson asked five and seven year olds about events which had been experienced a varying number of times. There was evidence that increasing familiarity with an experience produced increasing schematisation, with more general information and fewer particular details being reported. A further study examined children's memory for an untypical episode. New York children who made fairly frequent trips to museums were questioned about a particular trip to the Jewish Museum which was unusual. One year later, memory for this specific occasion was well retained, but it had not been incorporated into the general museum script, and this general museum script had not been modified by the novel experience. Hudson & Fivush (1991) asked the children to recall the museum visit again six years later and found they were still able to recall some details.

Hudson also found that recall of specific memories of particular occasions depended on the cues that were used. Those children who could not remember the Jewish Museum visit after one year when they were asked "What happened when you went to the Jewish Museum?" succeeded in recalling the occasion when asked about the archaeological activities which were shown in the museum. These children had filed the episode under an "archaeology" tag. This finding confirms the view that what seems like a loss of early memories may be due to a mismatch between the index or tag in the filing system and the retrieval cue. As children's experience increases, and their knowledge of the world accumulates, the indices they use to tag specific episodes are likely to approximate more closely to probable retrieval cues, thus reducing the chance of mismatches.

Taken together, these studies showed that the relationship between general event representations and specific event memories that characterises adult memory is apparent as young as three years old. Structurally and functionally, autobiographical memory in young children is equivalent to autobiographical memory in adults. Routine events are absorbed into the general script; unique events are stored separately. There was no evidence of age-related changes in this basic structure between the ages of three and seven, but there was evidence that changes in autobiographical memory occurred as a function of increasing experience rather than age, and affected content rather than structure.

In spite of this impressive evidence that children's memories are highly organised, many of the early memories that people report do not seem to fit this pattern. In Cohen and Faulkner's (1988a) study 21% of the events recalled from the first decade of the life span were categorised as Trivia. Whereas the other memories from this period were clearly linked to general event representations for school, family, holidays, pets, etc., these trivial memories were apparently unrelated to any script or general event knowledge. They were memories of isolated scenes that seemed relatively pointless and devoid of context, and were rated as low in emotionality, importance and frequency of rehearsal. Examples such as "sitting in the sandpit in the garden and looking at the sky through the leaves" or "walking along a road towards a beach" have the quality of scenes recalled from dreams. It is not clear why these memories should have been preserved, or what significance, if any, they may once have had, since they seem to have become detached from any organising framework.

It is probably simplistic to seek any single explanation for the dearth of memories from the early years of childhood. Generalised event representations are clearly present and are used to guide encoding and retrieval, but they are simple and skeletal in content, and specific episodes may be indexed with inappropriate tags so that they cannot be retrieved later. The existence of "trivia" memories also suggests the possibility that some specific memories are floaters that have drifted away from, or never been firmly linked to the relevant general event representation. These memories would then be difficult to access and retrieve. Since the amount and nature of the input to the system appears to be a crucial factor in the development of memory organisation, it is tempting to speculate that there is some optimal mix of routine and novel experiences. If experience were too narrowly confined to an unvarying routine, scripts would be few and poorly elaborated; if experience were constantly changing, it would be difficult for the child to abstract general event knowledge and build general event representations.

CONCLUSIONS

Memory for personal experiences, as this chapter has illustrated, includes a wide-ranging variety of different types of memory. Researchers are forced to rely on relatively informal ways of gathering their data and cannot exclude or control the many factors which influence the encoding, retention and retrieval of memories of personal experiences. In spite of these problems, theories and models developed in more formal cognitive studies are surprisingly successful at interpreting and making sense of the findings.

Although many aspects of autobiographical memory are still obscure, these studies have had considerable success, particularly in revealing the organisation and retrieval processes. The consensus of the findings indicates that organisation is both thematic and temporal with types of events or actions being represented at different levels of generality/specificity. When people try to recall a particular episode from the past, retrieval processes access the level of categorisation or time period which provides the optimum context for search. This optimum level of representation is one that is rich and specific enough to generate useful cues and reminders. Particular episodes which are sufficiently distinctive, novel, deviant or recent are not absorbed into generalised representations but are represented at the most specific level where they can be identified by specific tags, or stand out because they are distinctive.

There is good evidence that memories lose specificity over time and become more generalised; that older memories tend to be less vivid and less accessible; and accuracy declines with time and dating of memories is imprecise. False memories can be deliberately implanted and recognition tasks show a relatively high rate of false positive responses for false memories and false details of true memories. However, experimental paradigms tend to exaggerate the fallibility of autobiographical memory and underestimate the amazing quantity and quality of information that is retained over a lifetime.

7 Memory for Knowledge: General Knowledge and Metaknowledge

There is more to everyday memory than mundane matters like remembering to put out the milk bottles. Everyday memory involves retrieving and using stored knowledge of many different kinds in the appropriate contexts. These different kinds of knowledge include knowledge acquired formally from education or training, as well as knowledge that is picked up incidentally. In the course of daily life, a person may need to use knowledge of mathematics, of electrical wiring, of plant species, of cookery, of stock markets and many more specialised topics. Everyday memory is not just concerned with the trivial and the commonplace.

TYPES OF KNOWLEDGE

This chapter examines memory for general knowledge about the world rather than specific knowledge about personal experiences, semantic knowledge rather than episodic knowledge. As we noted in Chapter 6, p. 146, this is not a sharp distinction, as the kind of semantic knowledge that consists of generalised event knowledge is built up by abstraction from personal experiences. However, the important difference between the two kinds of knowledge is that semantic knowledge consists of objective general facts and episodic knowledge consists of subjective specific facts.

The knowledge stored in human memory forms a very large database (Nickerson, 1977) but nobody knows, as yet, how large it is. In any case, the most interesting questions concern what information is stored in memory, and how it is organised and retrieved, rather than how much information is in store. Within semantic knowledge, a number of distinctions can be made that are important when we come to consider how knowledge is stored and organised in memory.

Much of human knowledge is incomplete, inconsistent, vague and uncertain. Nickerson distinguished between fuzzy relational knowledge and absolute knowledge such as quantitative facts. Relational knowledge includes facts such as:

Potatoes are bigger than peas
France is north of Spain
Alexander the Great lived before Napoleon

which represent relative differences in magnitude, location, and temporal order. He pointed out that people are more likely to know these kind of relationships than to know actual sizes, dates, weights, speeds, ages, monetary values, or whatever. This observation lends support to Nickerson's contention that much of our knowledge is approximate rather than exact. The model of the world that we have in our heads is vague and inexact. And, as he convincingly points out, this kind of approximate knowledge is all that is needed for most decisions and actions in everyday life. For most purposes, we do not need to know precise numerical values. We need to be able to make rough estimates and fairly crude relational judgements. Much of our knowledge is also imprecise because it is probabilistic. Predictions about what the weather will be like tomorrow, when the plums will be ripe, the state of the bank balance next month, and the chances of catching a train, are couched in terms of probabilities. In these kinds of cases, precise knowledge would be more helpful, but is usually not available.

However much we know, we are constantly being confronted with demands for knowledge that we do not have, and, even when we do know it, we cannot always retrieve a given item of information when we want to. One of the most interesting and important questions, then, is how can we function with an information system that appears to have such serious shortcomings? Before we can begin to address this question, we need to make some further distinctions between different kinds of knowledge.

Inferential Knowledge

The amount of knowledge that can be retrieved far exceeds the knowledge that is actually stored in memory. This is because memory is not just a repository of facts, but a set of processes that allow further information to be inferred, calculated, estimated, or guessed. Nickerson emphasised the distinction between facts that have been learned explicitly, such as:

The sum of 2 and 4 is 6
Whales are mammals
The Aswan dam is in Egypt

and implicit, or tacit knowledge that consists of facts that are unlikely to
have been learned explicitly, but which can be inferred from other knowledge such as:

Julius Caesar had a mother
Giraffes have teeth
The Mississippi flows downhill

This distinction between explicit, pre-stored knowledge and implicit,
inferential or computable knowledge was evident when map knowledge
was analysed in Chapter 3, p.69. In any information system, whether it is a
computer or a human memory, information may be pre-stored and represented explicitly, or it may computable by the application of inferential
procedures to other information that is in store. There is a trade-off
between pre-storage and computation. Pre-storage is very expensive in
terms of storage space and, if large amounts of information are pre-
stored, very efficient search and retrieval processes are required to locate
and access particular items. For knowledge that is not very likely to be in
frequent use (like the example about Julius Caesar's mother) it is obviously
uneconomical to have it pre-stored. Having knowledge that is implicit, but
not pre-stored, saves space, but implicit information takes more time to
compute, and errors may occur if incorrect inferences are made.

Camp, Lachman, and Lachman (1980) demonstrated the psychological
reality of this distinction between pre-stored and computable knowledge.
They selected a set of questions likely to be retrieved by direct access.
These were questions like "What was the name of the flying horse in
mythology?" Subjects either know or do not know that the answer is
Pegasus. Many of the direct access questions involved proper names
because these are not computable—they cannot be inferred. Another set
of questions were inferential questions such as "What direction does the
Statue of Liberty face?" or "What US President was the first to see an
airplane?" Subjects were unlikely to know the answers to these questions,
but they could figure out the answer by inferential processes. Camp et al.
found that reaction times to respond "true" to answers to direct access
questions averaged 1.97 seconds, whereas reaction times to respond "true"
to answers to the inferential questions averaged 2.85 seconds. The additional retrieval time for inference questions reflects the reasoning processes
necessary to retrieve the answer. Explicit knowledge can be accessed
directly, implicit or tacit knowledge has to be retrieved by means of
inferential processes or computation.

Much of our everyday knowledge about the world is implicit and different kinds of inferences are used to access it. Graesser and Clark (1985) have described the way that some of these different kinds of inferences can be classified in "inference taxonomies".

Types of Inference

The first dimension of this taxonomy, pointed out by Collins (1979), distinguishes between *inferences based on knowledge* and *inferences based on metaknowledge*. Inferences based on knowledge include both deductive reasoning (e.g. Socrates is mortal because he is a man and all men are mortal) and inductive reasoning (e.g. Jane has a short skirt, and Anne has a short skirt, so short skirts must be fashionable). Inferences based on metaknowledge are inferences based on what you know about your knowledge (e.g. "It can't be true because I would have known it if it were true" or "Everybody knows that and I know what most other people know, so I must know it too"). The kind of negative inference based on "lack of knowledge", which is discussed on p.184, is also an example of an inference based on metaknowledge.

A second dimension in the taxonomy of inferences distinguishes between *functional inferences* and *set inferences*. Functional inferences include inferences about causes, consequences and goals (e.g. "It must have rained overnight because the road is full of puddles"). The most common kind of set inferences are deductions whereby we infer that a member of a subset must have the properties of the superordinate set. Subsets derive properties from their superordinates by a process known as "inheritance". We infer, for example, that a robin lays eggs because robins are a subset of the superordinate set of birds, and the superordinate concept "bird" has the property "lays eggs". So robins "inherit" the property of being able to lay eggs. Inductive generalisations are also inferences that operate on sets. When enough examples of a property have been noted in different subsets, it may be inferred that the property belongs to the superordinate set. If you find that Renaults are reliable and Citroens are reliable, you may infer that French cars are reliable. Another kind of set inference is an analogical inference whereby we infer that the properties of one set also belong to other sets that are similar. So, if oranges are good for you, you may infer that grapefruit, which are similar, are also good for you.

A third dimension in the taxonomy of inferences contrasts *spatial, temporal,* and *semantic inferences.* Spatial inferences about distance, location, and orientation were discussed in Chapter 3, p.69, and temporal inferences about the dates of events in Chapter 6, p.165. Some semantic inferences are based on knowledge about word meanings. So, for example from the statement that "John is a husband" it can be inferred that John is human, male, adult, and married. Another kind of semantic inference is based on knowledge represented in schemas, scripts, or generalised event knowledge structures. So, when we hear that John ate in a restaurant, we can infer that he paid for it and supply default values for the menu. The specific event "inherits" components from the script by inferential processes. Other kinds of semantic inference that occur in the comprehension and interpretation of discourse are discussed in Chapter 9, p.267.

More formal kinds of inference, such as those used in formal logic or in mathematical and statistical reasoning, are not so relevant to everyday memory for various reasons. The kind of fuzzy knowledge that is typical in real world situations is often not precise enough for the application of formal logical procedures. People have to be taught how to make these inferences and they are more applicable to solving artificial problems than to naturally occurring situations. However, although people do not use formal reasoning very readily or accurately (Braine, 1978), they do use rough and ready estimation and probabilistic reasoning to make rough and ready judgements about quantities and frequencies. The next section describes some of the more informal kinds of rough and ready inferences that are made in everyday situations and that serve to extend the range and scope of the explicit knowledge we have stored in memory.

Negative Inferences

A fourth dimension in the classification of inferences is the difference between *positive* and *negative inferences*. Because we seldom store negative information explicitly, most negative facts have to be inferred. Negative information is not usually stored in memory. Although some negative facts that are especially important may be stored explicitly (e.g. fatty food is not good for you; the pub is not open until 7 p.m. on Sunday), it would be uneconomical to devote a large amount of storage space to memory representations of what is not the case. Deciding that something is not true usually requires an inference. Collins, Warnock, Aiello, and Miller (1975) analysed the process and modelled negative inferencing in a simulation program called SCHOLAR that operated on a geography database, using this as an example of general world knowledge. They distinguished between closed and open sets of knowledge. Closed sets of knowledge are relatively rare, but if you know all the counties of England and Wales, or all the different species of gulls, then these are closed sets, and you can answer "No" to questions like "Is a tern a kind of gull?" or "Is Loamshire an English county?" by searching exhaustively through the relevant knowlege set. However, most sets of knowledge are open, either because the boundaries are ill defined or changing, or because a person's knowledge is incomplete. So, for example, if you do not know all the counties it would not be possible to give a negative answer with certainty. Or, if you were asked a question like "Is X a famous actor?", it would be difficult to answer negatively because the class of famous actors is ill defined and constantly changing.

However, people have a number of tricks or strategies that enable them to make negative inferences even if they cannot be certain to be correct. One of these is the *I would have known it if it were so* strategy, which Collins et al. call a *lack of knowledge inference*. I may decide that X is not a famous actor on the grounds that I don't know it and I would have known it if he were. To apply this strategy effectively, the following stages are required:

(1) I do not have this information in store. (This decision requires accurate knowledge of what I do and do not know.)
(2) My knowledge in this domain is complete or includes all the important facts. (This stage requires knowledge of the domain boundaries and of the relative importance of items of information.)
(3) This fact is important, so I would have encountered it and remembered it if it were part of the knowledge domain.

Other strategies for generating negative inferences rely on recognising that a putative fact cannot be true because it is directly contradicted by some other item of well-established knowledge, or because it is implausible in the light of other known facts.

Causal Inferences and Estimation Inferences

Knowledge about causal factors enables people to work out answers to specific questions when they do not already have the required information. They can extend their existing knowledge by making functional inferences that are probably true. In an example cited by Collins et al. (1975) a student was asked "Where in North America do you think rice might be grown?" and answered "Lousiana". When the teacher probed the reasons for this reply, it emerged that the student had used his knowledge that growing rice requires plenty of water, flat land, and a suitable climate, together with his knowledge of which states fulfilled these conditions, to generate the conclusion. Knowledge about causes allows people to infer the probable consequences and vice versa. If someone has food poisoning I can infer that he ate infected food; if he drinks a large quantity of alcohol I can infer that his driving will be impaired.

Mathematical inferences are commonly used in rough estimations of speed, distance, time, size, and weight. Camp (1988) reported that when an elderly man was asked "How far is it from Paris to New York?" he replied "Well, Lindberg flew there in about 36 hours with an average speed of about 100mph, so I'll say that it's about 3600 miles". Or, in an example cited by Collins et al., the question "How many piano tuners are there in New York City?" elicited the answer "Well, there are three or four in New Haven which has about 300,000 people. That's about one per 100,000. New York City has 7 million people so that would make 70. I'll say about 50 or 60". In arriving at this estimate, the respondent is assuming a roughly linear relationship between population size and number of piano tuners, and then correcting downwards to adjust for a deviation from linearity.

Analogical Inferences

In everyday life we use analogical reasoning to extend the explicit knowledge we have derived from past experiences so as to apply it to new experiences and handle novel situations. In the piano tuner example, the respondent used New Haven as an analogy for New York City. In everyday life we often work out how to cope with a current problem by recognising that it is similar to some other situation we have encountered before. Suppose, for example, that you are making strawberry jam and it fails to set. You remember that you had a similar problem previously when making raspberry jam and the solution was to add lemon juice. Recognising that making strawberry jam is analogous to making raspberry jam enables you to apply the same solution to the current problem. In this example the analogy is an obvious one because the two cases are very similar, but sometimes analogies are not so readily apparent.

Gick and Holyoak (1980) studied the ability of subjects to perceive a not very obvious analogy, and use it to solve a problem. They first read a story about a general who wanted to capture a fortress located in the centre of a country with many roads radiating outward from the fortress. All the roads have been mined so that, although small groups of men can pass along them safely, a larger force would detonate the mines, which makes a full-scale attack impossible. The solution is to divide the army into small groups and have them converge simultaneously on the fortress along different roads. Subjects were later given Duncker's (1945) radiation problem in which a patient has a malignant stomach tumour. It is impossible to operate, but the patient will die unless the tumour is destroyed. This can be done with rays only if they reach the tumour at sufficiently high intensity, but at this intensity they would destroy the healthy tissue surrounding the tumour. The solution is to focus low intensity rays from different directions, so that they converge simultaneously on the tumour site. On the surface, the two problems are totally dissimilar, but at a more abstract level they are analogous.

These examples highlight the fact that recognising analogies depends on the level of abstraction at which the two scenarios are represented in memory. If they are represented in too much detail the surface dissimilarities obscure the analogy. When they are expressed at a more abstract level, as a generalised event representation (the need to bring a high level of force to bear on an area plus some factor which only allows direct access to low levels of force), the analogy between the two problems is obvious and it is readily apparent that the simultaneous convergence solution, which solved the military problem, can also be applied to the tumour problem.

However, most of Gick and Holyoak's subjects were unable to perceive and make use of the analogy spontaneously, unless they were given a strong hint that it would be useful. In one experiment, some of the subjects were given the military story, and also a second analogue story about a fire at an oil rig. The firefighters needed to spray a large quantity of foam onto the fire, but did not have a hose large enough to deliver a sufficient quantity. The solution was to direct foam on to the fire from smaller hoses, spraying from different directions. Subjects who were given both of the analogue stories were more likely to perceive that the analogical solution could be applied to the tumour problem than subjects who only heard one of the analogue stories.

It is possible that in everyday life people also need to build up repeated similar experiences before they can abstract analogical inferences successfully. A current situation can only be perceived as analogous to similar previous experiences if people can recognise that it matches some previously encountered situation in relevant respects. Because two situations are never exactly identical, analogies rest on fuzzy matches. Knowing what degree and kind of similarity constitutes a useful analogy is an important aspect of everyday competence.

All these examples show that human knowledge, although limited, is extremely elastic. What we don't know we can infer, guess, estimate, or predict. We can produce a plausible, if uncertain, answer. It is relatively rarely that we are completely at a loss. In human memory, reliance on fuzzy knowledge and implicit knowledge, and on inferential processes rather than on direct access to explicitly pre-stored information, has the effect of making a limited amount of knowledge go a long way.

Case-based Knowledge

The view that reasoning is guided by rule-based inferential processes has recently been challenged by the development of case-based, or instance-based models of thinking. According to these models, reasoning is a matter of retrieving examples rather than applying rules. The shift from rule-based to case-based models is an important one because it entails a shift of emphasis away from the storage of abstract rules and generalised event representations in memory and toward an increased role for representations of specific events and specific experiences. Case-based reasoning is similar to analogical inferencing in that a previous situation is remembered and used to solve a new problem, but differs in that the previous experiences are represented as particular cases, not as generalised events. This means that case-based reasoning is more expensive in terms of storage, but may be more economical in terms of processing.

Case-based reasoning (CBR) is widely used in everyday life. Figure 7.1 shows an example where CBR is used to plan a meal (Kolodner, 1992). Here the particular experiences of previous meals are used to meet the demands of the new situation. This looks like being the dinner party from

---

A host is planning a meal for a set of people who include, among others, several people who eat no meat or poultry, one of whom is also allergic to milk products, several meat-and-potatoes men, and her friend Anne. Since it is tomato season, she wants to use tomatoes as a major ingredient in the meal. As she is planning the meal, she remembers the following:

> I once served tomato tart (made from mozzarella cheese, tomatoes, Dijon mustard, basil, and pepper, all in a pie crust) as the main dish during the summer when I had vegetarians come for dinner. It was delicious and easy to make. But I can't serve that to Elana (the one allergic to milk).
>
> I have adapted recipes for Elana before by substituting tofu products for cheese. I could do that, but I don't know how good the tomato tart will taste that way.

She decides not to serve tomato tart and continues planning. Since it is summer, she decides that grilled fish would be a good main course. But now she remembers something else.

> Last time I tried to serve Anne grilled fish, she wouldn't eat it. I had to put hotdogs on the grill at the last minute.

This suggests to her that she shouldn't serve fish, but she wants to anyway. She considers whether there is a way to serve fish that Anne will eat.

> I remember seeing Anne eat mahi-mahi in a restaurant. I wonder what kind of fish she will eat. The fish I served her was whole fish with the head on. The fish in the restaurant was a fillet and more like steak than fish. I guess I need to serve a fish that is more like meat than fish. Perhaps swordfish will work. I wonder if Anne will eat swordfish. Swordfish is like chicken, and I know she eats chicken.

FIG. 7.1.   Using case-based reasoning to plan a meal (from Kolodner, 1992). Reprinted by permission of Kluwer Academic Publishers.

hell, but the host is gamely trying to reconcile all the constraints by examining past solutions. As Kolodner points out, this example is typical of the kind of common sense reasoning in use in daily life. As we plan our activities we base our decisions on the memory of what worked out well and what was less than successful on previous occasions.

In addition to this use of CBR in informal everyday situations, it is also used in legal and medical decision-making and in the exercise of skills like car repairing. Lawyers are explicitly taught to use old cases as precedents for constructing and justifying arguments in new cases. Doctors base diagnoses and propose treatments of new cases on the basis of recollections of particular cases they have previously encountered, and car mechanics use much the same strategy.

The effectiveness of CBR depends on having a mental library of appropriate cases to draw upon, and these should include both successful and unsuccessful experiences so that the ones with successful outcomes can be used to suggest solutions to new problems and, importantly, the ones with unsuccessful outcomes can serve as warnings. The user of CBR must also be able to perceive the relevance of the new situation to the past experience, to adapt the previous solution appropriately, and to evaluate outcomes. Cases are used in two different ways: They provide "ballpark" solutions that can be adapted to the new situation, and they provide evidence for or against some solution that is being considered. CBR is also a learning mechanism. Users become more efficient with time because they build up their reference library of useful cases and because they become better able to avoid past mistakes. Cases need to be stored in memory together with information about the problem, its solution, pros and cons, and this whole package needs to be carefully indexed so that it can be recalled later when it is relevant to a new situation. The indexing of cases is a very important aspect of case-based reasoning and it is not at all clear how optimal indexing can be achieved.

The main advantages of case-based reasoning can be listed as follows:

(1) It provides fast ready-made answers to problems. It is usually quicker to adapt an old solution than to work out a new one from scratch.
(2) It allows us to find solutions in knowledge domains that we do not fully understand, or when a problem is poorly defined or a situation fraught with uncertainties.
(3) It enables us to avoid previous mistakes.

CBR has been implemented in computational models that plan meals, design landscapes, solve labour disputes, and diagnose medical and psychiatric conditions. A number of case-based legal reasoners have also been developed. HYPO (Ashley, 1988) is one of the most sophisticated, designed to simulate adversarial reasoning. Faced with a new problem, HYPO retrieves similar cases and classifies these as supportive or non-supportive. The support set is used to generate justifications and the nonsupport set is used to generate counter-arguments. Cases in the support set are then used to construct counters to the counter-arguments. Building programs such as this helps to understand the processes involved in CBR.

Researchers working with CBR argue that it is a simple and natural form of reasoning that closely reflects our everyday experience and conforms to our introspections. Others (e.g. Smith, Langston, & Nisbett, 1992) argue in favour of rule-based reasoning or hybrid models that combine both specific cases and general rules. However, the importance of the CBR work at present is as a corrective to models of knowledge representation that have emphasised abstraction and generalisation at the expense of specific instances.

METAKNOWLEDGE

Some of the insights about how general world knowledge is organised and retrieved from memory have come from the subjective self reports that are generated when people are required to answer factual questions, and, at the same time, to report on their memory processes. Recent studies have used this method to probe people's ability to know about their own memories. The general term "metamemory" has been used, but Cavanaugh (1988) has pointed out that three kinds of knowing about memory can be distinguished:

(1) *Systemic awareness* consists of knowing how memory works, what kinds of things are easy or difficult to remember, or what kinds of encoding and retrieval strategies produce the best results.

(2) *Epistemic awareness* consists of knowing what we know, knowing what knowledge is in store and being able to make judgements about its accuracy. This is metaknowledge.

(3) *On-line awareness* consists of knowing about ongoing memory processes and being able to monitor the current functioning of memory, as in prospective memory tasks (Chapter 2, pp.26–37). Cases of absent-mindedness occur as a result of failures of on-line awareness.

As Cavanaugh has noted, the three kinds of metamemory may be interrelated. In trying to recall a particular fact, epistemic awareness may be involved in knowing that the relevant information is in store; systemic awareness may guide the selection of search strategies and direct the search process; and on-line awareness might be involved in keeping track of the progress of the search.

Evaluating Memory Failures

One function of systemic awareness is that it provides us with standards against which to evaluate memory failures. People have quite clear expectations about what things they ought to be able to remember and what it is quite acceptable to forget. However, it appears that these expectations are tailored to the age of the person who is doing the forgetting, and also vary with the age of whoever is making the judgement. Erber, Szuchman, and Rothberg (1990) asked young and elderly subjects to evaluate other people's memory failures. The subjects were provided with written vignettes describing memory failures of different kinds. Examples are:

"Mrs X went upstairs to get a stamp and forgot why she had gone up."
"Mrs X was introduced to someone and shortly afterwards forgot the person's name."
"Mrs X forgot to buy one item of the three she intended to buy at the grocery store."
"Mrs X hid money in her house and next day could not remember where it was."

In some examples Mrs X was described as young (23–32 years) and in others as elderly (63–74 years). Subjects were asked to rate possible reasons for the memory failures, whether they were signs of mental difficulty, and whether they indicated a need for memory therapy or for medical evaluation. It was strikingly evident that the same memory failure that, when the protagonist was described as young, was dismissed as due to lack of attention and of no consequence, was seen as a sign of mental difficulty and need for memory training when the protagonist was described as elderly. Young subjects were also more severe in their judgements than the older subjects. These findings show that people have double standards about what level of memory efficiency is "normal" and their judgements are biased by negative stereotypes of ageing.

Knowing What We Know

In the recall of general knowledge it is the epistemic kind of metamemory, or metaknowledge, that has received most attention.

Our ability to know what we know, and, even more importantly, to know what we do not know, is such a commonplace feature of everyone's mental processes that we tend to take it for granted, and fail to realise quite how surprising and how puzzling an achievement it is. Given the enormous range and quantity of information that an adult accumulates and stores over a lifetime, it is surprising that when we are asked a question we can usually say at once and with reasonable confidence whether the answer is in memory or not. Paradoxically, we know whether the search for an answer will be successful or not before it has begun. An example of this ability comes from lexical decision tasks. People are able to decide that a letter string (such as *brone*) does not constitute a real word, and they make this decision so fast that it is hard to believe that they can be searching through the entire mental lexicon to find out whether *brone* is represented. The same ability to know what we know and what we do not know extends to facts as well as lexical items.

Knowledge on the Tip of the Tongue: The TOT State

Brown and McNeill's (1966) research into the tip-of-the-tongue phenomenon is a classic study of epistemic metamemory. When recall of knowledge is rapid and successful there is little or no conscious awareness of how that knowledge was retrieved. Direct access to information in the memory system is a fast and automatic process and is not accessible to introspection. Occasions when recall is slow, effortful, and indirect are much more illuminating to the researcher because people are able to report something about how they are searching and what fragments or items the search process turns up along the way.

Brown and McNeill focused on cases when a target is known but cannot be recalled. In these cases there is a temporary failure of the retrieval process, but recall is felt to be imminent. This phenomenon was called the TOT state because the target item is felt to be on the tip of the tongue, and Brown and McNeill described this feeling as like being on the brink of a sneeze. The material used in their study consisted of rare words, and their findings are therefore relevant to the storage and retrieval of lexical knowledge rather than factual knowledge, but the basic method they developed has been adapted and used in other studies examining retrieval of general world knowledge. They assembled a large group of subjects and read out questions such as "What is the word designating a small boat used in the river and harbour traffic of China and Japan?" and succeeded in inducing 233 TOT states. Of these, 65% were classed as positive because, when the target word was supplied by the experimenter, it was recognised as the one that had been sought, indicating that the feeling of having the word on the tip of the tongue was a valid reflection of what was in the memory store. As in the studies of name blocks, described in Chapter 5, p.130, people in the TOT state could often supply partial information about the target word, recalling the first letter, number of syllables, and location of primary stress. They also recalled candidate words that were not the target, but were similar in sound or meaning, and they were able to judge the relative proximity of these candidates to the target.

Brown and McNeill (1966) concluded that words are generically organised in memory into sets with similar meanings or with similar sounds.

Recall of partial information, and of nontarget candidates that resemble the target word, reflects this generic organisation. James and Burke (in press) have reported results that reflect links between phonologically related words. Pronouncing prime words that shared phonemes with the blocked target words helped to resolve the TOT because activating these related words strengthened activation of the target. These findings suggest that top-down search processes first access a class of semantically or phonologically related words, and may sometimes stop short at this point without locating the specific target. It is worth emphasising, however, that these findings apply to indirect retrieval processes. They do not apply to rapid automatic direct access to a designated target, which does not necessarily follow the same route as TOT searches.

The Feeling of Knowing: FOKs and the Knowledge Gradient

The Feeling of Knowing (FOK) is distinguished from the TOT state because it relates to a whole range of knowledge states from being sure you do not know something, to being confident that you could recall it if you were given enough time, or given suitable hints, to being quite sure that you do know the right answer. Retrieval attempts, whether successful or not, are accompanied by a subjective feeling of knowing that falls somewhere along this scale. There are two main questions to be asked about FOK judgements. The first question is concerned with their accuracy. How well does the subjective FOK correlate with objective measures of correct recall? Does the FOK predict actual performance? The second question, which is more controversial, concerns the underlying mechanisms on which the FOK is based.

The Accuracy of FOKs

Lachman, Lachman, and Thronesberry (1979) developed Brown and McNeill's (1966) insights using a more experimental technique for investigating epistemic awareness and the retrieval of general world knowledge. Their experiment used a method known as the RJR (Recall: Judgement: Recognition) paradigm in which testing is divided into three phases. In Phase 1 of Lachman et al.'s experiment, subjects had to answer general knowledge questions covering current events, history, sport, literature, etc. such as "What was the former name of Muhammed Ali?" or "What is the capital of Cambodia?". They were told not to guess, but to give the correct answer or respond "Don't know" as quickly as possible.

In Phase 2, subjects were re-presented with all the questions to which they had responded "don't know" and asked to make a "feeling of knowing" (FOK) judgement on a 4-point scale: 1 = definitely do not know; 2 = maybe do not know; 3 = could recognise the answer if told;

4 = could recall the answer if given hints and more time. In Phase 3, after a short delay, the subjects were given four multiple choice alternatives for each of the questions to which they had initially responded don't know, and had to select one of these alternatives and give a rating of confidence in the correctness of their choice. So, for example, the choices for the question about the capital of Cambodia were Angkor Wat, Phnom Penh, Vientiane and Lo Minh. The confidence-rating scale ranged from 1 = a wild guess; 2 = an educated guess; 3 = probably right; to 4 = definitely right.

The results showed that high FOK ratings were positively related to the probability of picking the correct alternative and to the level of confidence. The response times in Phase 1 were also systematically related to the FOK ratings. Subjects took longer to say "don't know" when they thought they might possibly know the answer, so high FOK ratings of 3 or 4 were associated with long response times. When FOK was low, "don't know" response times were fast. Confidence ratings in Phase 3 also reflected the correctness of the choice. Subjects were more confident when they chose the correct alternative and less confident when their choice was wrong. This experiment takes subjective self-ratings of FOK and of confidence, and validates them against objective measures of accuracy and response time. The results confirmed that there is not a simple two-state dichotomy such that people either know something or they do not know it. Instead, there is a gradient of knowing that is reflected subjectively in the FOK and confidence ratings, and objectively in the speed and accuracy with which a target piece of information can be retrieved.

Similar findings emerged from a study by Gruneberg and Sykes (1978). They asked subjects to name the capitals of 25 countries and to give FOK ratings when they could not answer. FOKs were classed as positive (do know) or negative (don't know). They found that if they supplied first letter cues for the missing names, the probability of correct recall was higher (0.38) if a positive FOK had been given, and lower (0.14) if the FOK had been negative. However, they also found that negative FOKs were associated with different probabilities of recall depending on whether the knowledge being queried was something known to most people in the group to which the subjects belonged. When the question related to information that is generally well known (e.g. a familiar capital city like Paris), a negative FOK was more likely to be wrong. The subject under-estimated the probability that he could recall it. If the question related to some little known information, a negative FOK was more likely to be accurate. The subjective FOKs of individuals were more accurate when they were consistent with an objective estimate of probability of recall based on group knowledge. Nelson, Leonesio, and Landwehr (1986) reached a similar conclusion using the RJR paradigm like Lachman et al. (1979). They compared three different predictors of memory performance.

The FOK supplied by an individual was a better predictor than the average FOK of all the subjects, but the best predictor was the objective probability of recall. These findings draw attention to the fact that, although it is generally fairly accurate, the FOK may sometimes be misleading. Krinsky and Krinsky (1988) found that when subjects failed to remember a state capital, their FOK for the unrecalled capital city was distorted by a tendency to recognise falsely other large cities as the capital. For example, your estimate of your ability to recall the capital of Kenya will be inaccurate if you think Dar-es-Salaam is the capital. People cannot always judge what they will or will not be able to retrieve from memory.

Theoretical Explanations of the FOK

Koriat (1995) distinguished two very different views about the processes underlying FOKs. According to the *Internal Monitor View,* sometimes called the trace-based view, there are two stages involved. The first stage is like looking up a directory listing of computer files, and this precedes the second stage of retrieving the desired item. The FOK is based on whether or not the monitor detects the target item in the listing. As Koriat has pointed out, there are some problems with this account. It is consistent with an all-or-none FOK, rather than the graded judgements that are reported, and is also difficult to reconcile with inaccurate FOKs. By contrast, *Inference-based Models* claim that the FOK is based on inferences. For example, you may believe that you know something because the topic is familiar or because you can remember the context in which you acquired the information originally. Reder and Ritter (1992) elicited FOK judgements for arithmetical problems and varied the amount of exposure to whole problems and to individual terms in the problems. Their results showed that the FOK increased with increased exposure to the terms of the problem. That is, the FOK was based on familiarity with the question not familiarity with the answer. This result appears to support an inference-based account of FOK.

Koriat's *Accessibility Model* (Koriat, 1993, 1995) is also an inference-based model. However, according to Koriat, the FOK does not precede retrieval, but is based on the products of retrieval. The products of retrieval may consist of the target item or of partial information about the target provided by the initial retrieval attempt. The FOK is determined by both the quantity and the quality of this information; that is, the amount of information, its intensity, and the ease of accessing it. The main difficulty in testing this model is that partial information may not be consciously available. Given a question like "What is the capital of Uganda?", fragments of the target may be retrieved but remain below the level of conscious awareness. Koriat carried out experiments examining FOKs for the recall of both four letter nonsense strings (1993) and general knowledge facts (1995). The letter strings allowed Koriat to measure the amount of partial information available when recall of the whole string failed (i.e. the number of letters that were recalled), but in the experiments with general knowledge, the amount of partial information recalled for a given question had to be estimated from normative data based on how many subjects could answer the question, that is, if more people could answer the question it was simply assumed that more partial information would be elicited. This method is therefore less satisfactory, although recall of general knowledge has greater ecological validity than recall of letter strings.

The model predicts that:

(1) FOK will be higher if a response is given even if it is not correct than when no response is given (because the amount of information available is greater).

(2) FOK will be higher if the response is correct than if it is wrong (because the quality of the information is more intense and it is accessed faster).

(3) FOK will be higher if there is more partial information than if there is little or no partial information.

(4) FOK will be higher for questions that many subjects can answer (on the assumption that more partial information is, normatively, available for these questions).

These predictions were supported by the results. The model is also consistent with the graded character of FOKs and the fact that they are not always accurate. In line with his view that the accuracy of the FOK depends on the accuracy of the information retrieved, Koriat showed that for questions that tended to elicit many wrong answers FOKs were overestimated. The quantity and ease of access of the information misled subjects into feeling overconfident that they knew the correct answer.

Some general points arise out of Koriat's model. He concluded that FOK formation occurs neither before retrieval nor after retrieval, but is part of an interactive on-line process contemporaneous with retrieval. This view blurs the distinction between retrieval and FOK, between knowledge and metaknowledge, which are both seen as part of the same process. Another point of interest lies in the potential applicability of Koriat's model to issues about the relationship between confidence and accuracy in eyewitness testimony described in Chapter 4. People almost always have some partial information when they recall an event they have witnessed, so perhaps this is why they are sometimes overconfident.

Decisions about Ignorance: Knowing that You Do Not Know

How do people know that they do not know something? According to Koriat's model, people decide that they do not know something when the retrieval attempt yields little or no partial information. According to the Internal Monitor View, they decide they do not know something when no listing is found for that item in the directory. A further possibility is that both types of decision process can occur. Glucksberg and McCloskey (1981) explored their intuition that there are two basic types of do not know decision. One type is a slow, low confidence decision. If, for example, someone is asked "Is Kiev in the Ukraine?" he or she may ponder for several seconds and eventually reply "Don't Know" hesitantly. In contrast, a question like "What is Jimmy Carter's favourite colour?" might elicit a fast, high-confidence "Don't Know".

Glucksberg and McCloskey considered that the two different kinds of response might reflect two different knowledge states. When a person has some knowledge that is relevant to the question (e.g. that Kiev is in the former USSR; that Ukraine is in the former USSR) this relevant knowledge is accessed and evaluated to find out whether an answer to the question is implicit and can be inferred from it. The slow don't know response is produced only after it is clear that the relevant knowledge will not yield an inference that answers the question. When a person has no knowledge relevant to the question (e.g. knows nothing at all about Jimmy Carter's taste in colour) a fast rapid response can be made. Because the initial search for relevant facts draws a blank, the process stops short. Subsequent stages of evaluation or attempted inferencing do not occur, so the response is faster. Glucksberg and McCloskey's ideas can be accommodated by subsequent theoretical explanations of the FOK. The slow response can be equated with the inference-based Accessibility Model and the rapid response with the trace-based Internal Monitor Model.

To test their intuitions Glucksberg and McCloskey ran several experiments. In one of these, the subjects learned a set of statements such as:

John has a pencil
John doesn't have a shovel
Bill has a bowl
Bill has a magazine

They were then presented with test sentences to which they had to respond True (e.g. John has a pencil); False (e.g. John has a shovel); or Don't Know (e.g. John has a magazine). As predicted, reaction times to respond Don't Know were fastest. For both the True and the False judgements subjects had some information in store (about John and a pencil or about John and a shovel) and had to evaluate whether the relationship in the stored statement matched the relationship in the test sentence. For the Don't Know judgement there was no information about John and a magazine that needed to be considered.

In another experiment Glucksberg and McCloskey compared reaction times to respond to different questions about real world knowledge. There were three types of question:

(1) Known questions, e.g. "Was John F. Kennedy a Democrat?". It was expected that most subjects would know the answer to these questions.

(2) Don't Know-Relevant questions, e.g. "Does Ann Landers have a degree in journalism?". It was expected that most subjects would not know the answer but would know the relevant fact that Ann Landers writes a syndicated advice column.

(3) Don't Know-No Relevant questions, e.g. "Does Bert Parks have a degree in journalism?". In this case subjects would not have any knowledge relevant to the question.

Responses to the Don't Know-No Relevant questions were, on average, 300 milliseconds faster than responses to the Don't Know-Relevant questions. These results confirm Glucksberg and McCloskey's (1981) model for the two different kinds of Don't Know response.

States of Awareness

A relatively new technique for studying the phenomenology of memory probes metamemory in order to shed light on the phenomenal experience of remembering. In recognition tests people are asked to say whether each positive response is accompanied by a conscious recollection of the experience of encountering that item before, or whether it is simply based on a feeling of familiarity without any specific recollection of its previous occurrence. These two "states of awareness" are classed as Remember responses and Know responses, respectively. The proportion of Remember to Know responses has been found to vary with age, the level of processing, the type of stimulus material, the allocation of attention, and the effects of drugs, (see Gardiner & Java, 1993, for a review). A general conclusion is that deeper, more elaborative encoding promotes more Remember responses, indicating conscious recollection. This interesting methodology has mainly been used in traditional laboratory tests for word recognition but is beginning to be applied to more naturalistic material such as memory for music (Java, Kaminska, & Gardiner, 1995). It offers intriguing possibilities of illuminating the nature of the mechanisms underlying different types of remembering.

Individual Differences in Metaknowledge

Individual differences in epistemic awareness have been explored by Perlmutter (1978). She examined the effects of age and of level of education on several aspects of metamemory in a study that tested old and young adults with different levels of education. She reasoned that with increasing age an individual would accumulate an increasing amount of world knowledge. Age deficits in fact retrieval could then arise if interference increased with the size of the knowledge base, or if strategies of retrieval were unable to handle the increased amount of information. Epistemic awareness might also decline in old age, because, as the knowledge base changes over time with the acquisition of new information and with forgetting old information, metaknowledge needs to be continuously updated. To express this idea in terms of the library analogy for knowledge storage is to suggest that the catalogue gets out of date in old age. Old people may then base judgements on what they previously knew rather than what they currently know.

Perlmutter also explored the possibility that age differences in systemic awareness might affect fact retrieval. Age differences in question-answering would arise if old people are less able to select and implement optimal strategies of retrieval. Among the battery of tests, Perlmutter included a systemic awareness component consisting of 60 questions probing subjects' knowledge of how their own memories functioned. Examples are shown in Fig. 7.2. There was also a general knowledge test of 24 factual questions and subjects were asked to give a confidence rating for their answers and, if they were unable to recall a fact, to predict their ability to recognise the correct answer. This was followed by a fact-recognition test, and again confidence ratings had to be supplied.

The results showed that the subjects did not differ in systemic awareness. They all thought it easiest to remember information that was related, organised, interesting, understandable, and concrete, and they reported using similar strategies. The elderly subjects remembered more facts in response to the general knowledge questions, but there were no age differences in the accuracy with which old and young predicted whether they would be able to recognise the correct answer, and no age differences in confidence ratings. Overall, there were significant correlations between confidence and number of facts recalled and between prediction accuracy and fact recall. People who knew more facts were also better at knowing what they knew. This finding is a clear indication that the efficiency of epistemic awareness does not decline with the size of the knowledge base.

Although in Perlmutter's study FOK accuracy did not appear to decline in old age, Hultsch, Hertzog, and Dixon (1987) noted that elderly people believed that their memory capacity was smaller than that of young adults;

When you can not remember something do you find it upsetting?
Do you have more difficulty remembering things when you are tired?
Do you have more difficulty remembering things when you are pressured?
Do you have more difficulty remembering things when you are anxious?
Are you more likely to forget things when your mind is preoccupied?
Over the years have you become more aware of your memory?
Over the years have you noticed any changes in your memory?
Do you use memory aids more often than you previously did?
Over the years has your memory improved?
Over the years has your memory become worse?
Do you think your memory will change as you get older?
Do you think your memory will get better when you get older?
Do you think your memory will get worse when you get older?
Do you think your memory will always stay as it is now?
Do you think you will forget things more easily when you get older?
Do you think you will remember more details as you get older?
Do you consciously try to memorise things more than you used to?
Do you remember some kinds of things better than others?
Do you find it easier to remember organised things than unorganised things?
Is it easier to remember visual things than verbal things?
Do you find it easier to remember bizarre things than usual things?
Do you find it easier to remember things you are most interested in?
Do you find it easier to remember concrete things than abstract things?
Do you find it easier to remember things that are related to each other than things that are not related to each other?
Are there some kinds of things that are really hard to remember?
Are you especially likely to forget unpleasant things?
Do you have more difficulty remembering details than generalities?
Do you find it more difficult to remember things you are not interested in?
Do you find it more difficult to remember unfamiliar than familiar things?
Do you find it more difficult to remember things you do not really understand?

FIG. 7.2. Items from a metamemory questionnaire (from Perlmutter, 1978). Copyright 1978 American Psychological Association. Reprinted by permission of the author.

that their memory had declined more and that they had less control over memory operations. Camp (1988) also reported that elderly people thought their ability to remember facts had declined, but that their ability to "figure out" answers by making inferences had improved. However, when they were tested and compared with young people, the results showed exactly the opposite. The elderly were better at fact recall but poorer at inferential retrieval. These results suggest that elderly people are not necessarily accurate in their assessment of their own memories.

It is not clear, therefore, whether metamemory ability declines in old age, but there is evidence that in children it improves with age. Flavell and Wellman (1977) found that 9-year-old children were better able to predict whether they would recognise correct answers than 5-year-old children. Other aspects of metamemory also show developmental trends. Kreutzer, Leonard, and Flavell (1975) asked children aged 4–10 years questions like "If you wanted to phone your friend and someone told you the phone number, would it make any difference if you phoned right away, or if you got a drink of water first?" and "Suppose your friend has a dog and you ask him how old his dog is. He tells you he got his dog as a puppy one Christmas but can't remember which Christmas. What could he do to help him remember which Christmas he got his dog?"

Awareness of appropriate strategies for remembering phone numbers or retrieving dates of events increased with age. The pattern of age effects in old and young suggests that metamemory efficiency improves with experience but is unaffected by the size of the knowledge base.

Knowledge Sources

Another aspect of metaknowledge involves knowing where your knowledge came from. This may seem to be somewhat irrelevant, but it is important when making judgements about the accuracy or authenticity of knowledge. Much of the information that comes our way in everyday life is incorrect and we are constantly confronted with the need to decide whether to accept it and modify our existing knowledge structures accordingly, or to reject it outright, or to seek some further confirmation. If you state some fact that other people find novel or surprising, they will often ask you "How do you know?" If you can remember that you acquired the information from a reputable source, such as a work of reference, an acknowledged expert or a person recognised to be knowledgeable, your statement is likely to be accepted. Similarly, you almost certainly apply the same kind of "source test" yourself when you encounter some new information before you accept it as true. McIntyre and Craik (1987) tested memory for the source of information. Their subjects were given general knowledge questions, but when they responded "don't know", answers were supplied by one or other of two experimenters. One week later the subjects were tested for recall of the facts and were also asked to state the source of the information (i.e. which experimenter had supplied the information). Young subjects recalled 60% of the sources correctly, but elderly subjects made more errors. In naturally occurring situations people may remember the general context in which they acquired some information even if they cannot state the source precisely. They may remember that the information was acquired from a television programme, during a course of study, or from somebody they met at a party. Knowing where knowledge came from provides a useful indication of its authenticity.

LONG-TERM MAINTENANCE OF KNOWLEDGE

The previous section focused on issues about the nature of knowledge, but interesting questions can also be asked about the maintenance of knowledge. How permanent is knowledge once acquired? In his 1978 talk at the Practical Aspects of Memory conference (see Chapter 1, p.2), Neisser suggested that one of the important questions that memory research should address concerns what people retain of the knowledge they acquired during the years of their formal schooling. Educators have studied children's memory for what they learn at school over relatively short retention intervals of months, rather than years, but when we come to assess the value of education in the longer term we want to know how much people remember in the years after they have left school. What, if any, of the information we acquire with so much effort in our schooldays constitutes permanent knowledge? Because these issues have to be studied over long time spans, they are outside the scope of traditional laboratory methods, and have been neglected until recently, when the more adventurous approach of everyday memory research has encouraged some psychologists to tackle them.

Studies of Long-term Retention of Knowledge

Spanish and Mathematics

Bahrick (1984b) has conducted a series of studies of long-term retention of Spanish learned at school. Surmounting formidable methodological problems, his landmark study spanned retention intervals of up to 50 years and attempted to identify the conditions of original learning that determine the longevity of the knowledge acquired. The subjects were 773 individuals who had learned Spanish in high school. The time elapsed between studying the language and being tested varied from 0 to 50 years. A control group of 40 subjects who had never received any instruction in Spanish was also included in the study to establish a baseline for performance that could be achieved by guessing, or by incidentally acquired knowledge. The subjects who had learned Spanish supplied information about the level of their original training (how many courses they had taken), the grades they had attained, and how much they had used the language during the retention interval. The tests included reading comprehension, and recall and recognition tests for vocabulary, grammar, and idioms. The results showed that retention was predictable from the level of original training. People who had learned more remembered more. When the recall test scores were expressed as a percentage of the original grades about 40% of the original performance was maintained after 50 years, and on recognition tests about 60% was maintained.

Interim use of the language was negligible, so that no effects of rehearsal were evident. The most interesting finding can be seen in Fig. 7.3. Three components can be discerned in the retention function. Knowledge declined exponentially for about 3–6 years, but after this retention stabilised, and there was little further loss for a period of up to 30 years before a final slight decline. This final period corresponds to a time when the subjects were 60–70 years old and may represent the effects of ageing rather than of the retention period. It is clear, however, that much of the original knowledge remains accessible even after 50 years.

According to Bahrick (1984b), this knowledge has entered the *permastore*. On the basis of the discontinuous character of the retention function, he argued that there had been a discrete transition of knowledge into the permastore and that a minimum level of original training was necessary for

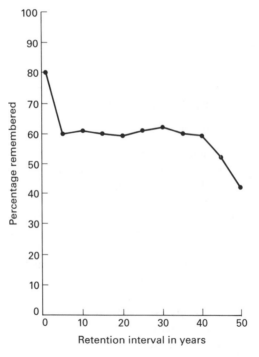

FIG. 7.3. Idealised retention curve for the very long-term retention of Spanish (adapted from Bahrick, 1984b).

this transition to take place. When the original training was insufficient, the knowledge would not be entered into the permastore and would only be retained for a shorter period.

Commenting on these results, Neisser (1984) suggested that there was no need to assume the existence of a knowledge permastore. Whereas Bahrick's explanation assumes that language-learning involves acquiring responses that are *reproduced* when retrieval takes place, Neisser argued that knowledge is *reconstructed*, rather than being reproduced. In his view, the enduring component of language knowledge does not consist of specific responses, but of generalised schemas, a structured system of knowledge of the Spanish language that enables people to reconstruct correct responses. Acquisition of knowledge schemas depends on the level of original training, as Bahrick's data confirmed. According to this interpretation, the information that is lost in the early years of the retention interval consists of isolated bits and pieces not closely related to the general schema. Neisser claims that retention of systematic schematised knowledge is enduring because it is protected from interference by its unique and specialised nature. Schema-based knowledge is not forgotten because other knowledge is not sufficiently similar to cause interference. On this interpretation, the discontinuity in Bahrick's retention curves does not reflect two different stores, a vulnerable store with a five-year span and a permastore, but two different kinds of knowledge, isolated items and integrated schemas.

Neisser's account is not wholly convincing. Although it is plausible to suppose that language-learning involves acquiring a schema for the grammar of the language that might enable people to reconstruct the grammar, it is not so clear that knowledge of its morphological and orthographic structure would enable them to "reconstruct" vocabulary. It might be expected, then, that knowledge of grammar would show a long-term retention plateau, but knowledge of vocabulary would be less well retained. However, in Bahrick's data, the retention function is similar in shape for both grammar and vocabulary.

In a follow-up to an earlier study, Bahrick and Phelps (1987) re-tested subjects who had learned 50 English-Spanish word pairs in laboratory conditions eight years earlier. They found that two variables predicted the likelihood of permastore retention. After eight years, memory for Spanish vocabulary was affected by the spacing of the original learning sessions and the number of presentations required for acquisition. The number of presentations reflects the ease of initial learning. Overall, about 10% of the originally learned words could still be recalled. Of words that had been learned easily 14% could be recalled, but of words learned with more difficulty only 2% could be recalled. Memory was also better when the intervals between the original study sessions were longer. These data indicate that long-term retention of knowledge (or in Bahrick's phrase, entry to the permastore) depends on the conditions of acquisition. On Neisser's view, schema acquisition would be dependent on the amount and depth of the original learning, and the type of knowledge, rather than on factors like spacing.

Bahrick, Wellman, and Hall (1988) designed an experiment to test Neisser's ideas. They measured speed of learning and retention for English-Spanish word pairs, and for pairs consisting of an English word and a Spanish nonword. They compared the performance of students who studied Spanish with students who studied other languages and had no knowledge of Spanish. The students of Spanish were assumed to have acquired general schemas of the language. It was expected that they would perform better with the English-Spanish word pairs, and, if having general schemas of a language allows people to guess or reconstruct vocabulary—as Neisser claims—they should also have done better with the nonwords, because these nonwords were constructed to conform to the characteristics of real Spanish words. The results showed that, although the students of Spanish did slightly better on the real Spanish words, they had no advantage on the nonwords. Bahrick et al. therefore concluded that people cannot use schemas to reconstruct vocabulary that they have forgotten.

Bahrick and Hall (1991) extended this research to the domain of mathematics and investigated long-term retention of mathematics by 1600 former students at retention intervals up to 50 years. They compared the performance of two groups, one who had studied up to the level of calculus and another group who had not reached this level. The two groups produced very different retention functions. Those who had studied to an advanced level showed very little forgetting; those who had not showed a steady decline. This study therefore confirms that the level of the original knowledge is a powerful determinant of subsequent retention.

Philosophy, Psychology, and Anthropology

Further studies have examined different knowledge domains. Naveh-Benjamin (1988) has studied retention of knowledge acquired in university courses of philosophy, psychology, and anthropology, comparing a zero retention interval with retention intervals of one and two years. He was particularly interested in how the knowledge structures changed over time. In order to examine this, he first asked the university teachers who had taught the courses to arrange different elements of knowledge into conceptual hierarchies, with general concepts at the highest level and specific concepts at the lowest level. When the subjects were tested, they were shown a conceptual hierarchy with some empty nodes and had to select items from a set of alternatives and place the correct item at the correct node. This test revealed a loss of information from 70% at the zero retention interval to 46% after two years. The loss of information was greatest at the lowest level of the conceptual hierarchy, whereas the higher-level concepts were better retained. The test also showed that the relationships between higher-order concepts and low-level specific examples were especially vulnerable to the effects of the passage of time. Knowledge became fragmented as people tended to forget the links between concepts.

Cognitive Psychology and Classic Novels

Conway, Cohen, and Stanhope (1991) studied retention of knowledge of cognitive psychology originally acquired as part of a university degree course, testing retention intervals up to 12 years. A range of tests probed memory for names and concepts, general principles and specific facts, and experimental design and statistics. The findings showed that, as in Bahrick's studies, there was a rapid loss of information over the first three years, after which knowledge remained stable (see Fig. 7.4). The results were also not altogether consistent with Neisser's schema-based account of knowledge retention. As in Naveh-Benjamin's study, general principles were retained better than specific facts, but a great deal of specific information was remembered. A test of memory for conceptual relations showed very poor retention, although this type of knowledge might be supposed to

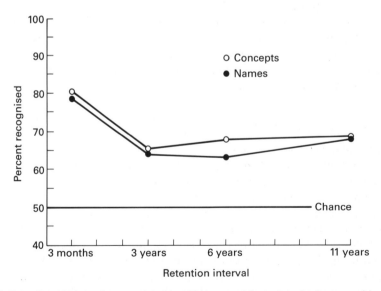

FIG. 7.4. Percentages of correct responses to names and concepts in the recognition test (based on data from Conway, Cohen, & Stanhope, 1991).

be inherent in a schema. On Neisser's account, concepts, which can be reconstructed from a schema, should be retained better than proper names, which cannot. The comparison of retention of names and concepts showed that memory for names initially declined more, but both types of knowledge subsequently stabilised at the same level. Interestingly, there was very little forgetting for the principles of experimental design and statistical analysis. Conway et al. (1991) reflected that this might be procedural knowledge because it was acquired and implemented in practical work, and suggested that procedural knowledge is more robust than declarative knowledge. Unlike Bahrick's subjects, all the former students in this study had received the same level of training, but, nevertheless, those who had achieved higher grades for coursework showed better long-term retention. Similar results were also obtained by Stanhope, Cohen, and Conway (1993) who examined long-term retention of classic novels studied as part of a university course. An initial decline was followed by stable retention. Memory for higher-level superordinate information was better than memory for very specific details, but a great deal of specific information was nevertheless retained and it is difficult to see how this could have been reconstructed from a schema.

Taken together these studies show that in a variety of knowledge domains a substantial amount of knowledge is retained over long periods of time even when it is not rehearsed or used. Factors that influence this long-term retention include the amount and spacing of original training; the level of expertise originally achieved; whether the knowledge is declarative or procedural, high-level general knowledge or low-level specific knowledge; and the extent to which it can be reconstructed from schemas. Conway, Cohen, and Stanhope (1992, p.480) speculated that it may be important to track the retention of knowledge and the retention of understanding separately: "the knowledge structures which support understanding may consist of integrative concepts or mental models that serve to cross-reference and organise the knowledge domain—our suggestion is that when a knowledge domain remains unused then the first type of knowledge to be lost is that of structures supporting understanding".

Knowledge Updating

Whether or not some of our knowledge is immutably lodged in a permastore, knowledge sometimes has to be revised. Some of the facts we thought to be true turn out to be false, or to need modification. New knowledge supersedes old knowledge that is outdated, or irrelevant, or contradicted. As in any information storage system, the information that is stored in memory needs to be corrected and updated.

Some researchers who have studied the process of knowledge updating have noted a *knew-it-all-along effect* (Fischoff, 1977; Wood, 1978). When people have been given new facts that contradict their previous knowledge they appear to be unable to remember what they originally believed, and claim to have known it (i.e. the new fact) all along. Apparently, the new knowledge is immediately assimilated with the previous knowledge, and any inconsistencies are eliminated so as to produce an updated version. An update-and-erase mechanism of this kind may be an efficient kind of information storage, but it represents a limitation of metamemory. The "knew-it-all-along" effect appears to indicate that, although people may know what they know, they are not very accurate at knowing what they used to know.

Hasher, Attig, and Alba (1981) examined the fate of discredited information in a complex experiment that involved asking subjects to rate a set of plausible statements about current affairs, the arts, sports, etc. on a seven-point true-false scale. Subsequently, they were given feedback about the truth or falsity of the statements, followed by further information either confirming or discrediting the feedback. Finally, when they were asked to reproduce their original ratings, it was apparent that these had shifted in line with the feedback. Even when the feedback had been discredited, subjects were still influenced by it. However, in a second experiment, Hasher et al. did succeed in inducing subjects to ignore disconfirmed information. It was more effectively discredited when they were told it had been deliberately misleading, not just a mistake. This time the re-ratings did not differ from the original ratings, showing that the subjects had returned to their original knowledge state. This finding suggests that old knowledge is not necessarily completely erased when it is contradicted, but can be recovered. The results also showed that it was easier to shift a belief from false to true than from true to false. People are more reluctant to change their views in response to falsifying evidence. A similar bias has been noted in studies of problem-solving (e.g. Wason, 1960) in which subjects generate a hypothesis in an attempt to solve a problem, and resist evidence that the hypothesis is false.

In everyday life, knowledge-updating is likely to be even more complex than in Hasher et al.'s experiment. There are three different processes that make knowledge-updating necessary. One of these is contradiction, as in the experiment. You may believe that the highest mountain in Britain is Snowdon until someone tells you this is not true. If the new information is sufficiently authoritative, you will probably discard the original belief. Another process that necessitates knowledge-updating is change. Little Willy changes from a small boy into a young man, or the neighbours trade in their Metro for a Volvo, or the new bypass is now the quickest route to the city. In these cases, the old knowledge is not so much wrong as obsolete.

Another process that enforces knowledge revision is the accumulation of counter-examples. A belief that cream and butter are good for you may need revising in the face of growing evidence that high-cholesterol foods are damaging to health. In some of these examples, knowledge-updating is a gradual process, with old knowledge being eroded over time, and gradually giving way to a new belief. While this process is going on a person may dither between two contradictory beliefs, or may be in a state of suspended disbelief, or may simply be confused. When knowledge-updating occurs as a result of change, the old knowledge is not necessarily forgotten or discarded, but may be maintained alongside the new knowledge. Naturally occurring knowledge-updating is much more complicated and variable than the kind of knowledge-updating that has so far been studied in laboratory experiments.

CONCLUSIONS

This chapter has emphasised that large amounts of knowledge are stored in semantic memory and the amount of knowledge available can be greatly expanded by inferential processes. Stored knowledge tends to be inexact, relative, or probabilistic but this kind of knowledge is "good enough" for most everyday purposes. Metaknowledge allows people to make the best use of what they know. They have a good practical grasp of how memory works and a fairly accurate assessment of what they know and what they do not know, so that effort can be directed to memory searches that are likely to be successful and not wasted on attempts that are doomed to failure. Although much of the knowledge acquired from formal education and not subsequently used or refreshed is lost from memory, a surprisingly substantial residue is retained almost indefinitely. There is also evidence that knowledge is not simply forgotten over time but may also be deliberately discarded or modified. These considerations emphasise the fact that knowledge structures are dynamic, not fixed. Knowledge structures change as expertise develops and fragment or become inaccessible as information is lost. Some types of knowledge are surprisingly well retained over long periods of time; other kinds of knowledge are lost more rapidly. Processes of revision, updating, and reorganisation are occurring continuously throughout our lives, and this is especially true of everyday knowledge. Whereas expert knowledge in domains such as chess or computer programming (discussed in the next chapter) is encapsulated, everyday knowledge domains tend to be interactive. Knowledge about transport is interwoven with knowledge about the environment, pollution, politics, and personal plans and activities, and changes in one domain force changes in the other domains.

8

Memory for Expertise

THE NATURE OF EXPERTISE

General world knowledge is the kind of information that is shared by many educated adults in the same culture. It includes miscellaneous and relatively superficial information about history, geography, science, literature, current events, and so on. Expert knowledge, on the other hand, consists of a body of tightly integrated, domain-specific knowledge about some particular defined area such as nuclear physics, eighteenth-century chamber music, computer programming, or French wines. The difference between the two kinds of knowledge is mainly one of depth and interrelatedness. Although the distinction is not a sharp one, expert knowledge is more detailed, more cohesive and integrated, and less likely to be common to the majority of the population. Expertise involves skills as well as knowledge but the balance of skill and knowledge varies with the nature of the domain of expertise. The role of skill is probably more important for expert typists and expert dancers; the role of knowledge is more important for expert historians or literary critics.

How does an expert differ from a novice? Ericsson and Pennington (1993) reviewed three different views about the nature of expertise: the *talent view,* the *knowledge view,* and the *acquired mechanisms view.* According to the talent view, people who become experts start off with special inborn capacities that allow them to develop superior performance. Ericsson and Pennington discount the role of talent in expert performance on two grounds. First, research has generally found that the superior level of ability in experts is confined to the domain of their expertise. For example, as we shall see in the section on chess expertise, the superior memory of chess experts is limited to meaningful chess positions (Chase & Simon, 1973). Second, a high level of expertise is invariably associated with a high level of practice. Nevertheless, it is arguable that some kinds of expertise do require innate characteristics whereas others do not. It is possible that anyone can become an expert cook or an expert bridge-player with sufficient motivation and practice, but physical skills in sport or dance may require specific physical characteristics that cannot be acquired. In other domains of expertise, such as music or art, the respective contributions of innate talent and training are more controversial.

The role of knowledge in expertise is undisputed. Nobody becomes an expert chess player or physician without acquiring a great deal of specialist knowledge and tests of knowledge are predictive of performance. When someone ceases to be a novice and becomes an expert in some particular knowledge domain, changes that are both qualitative and quantitative have taken place in the knowledge structures stored in memory. This is broadly true whether we are talking about formal knowledge domains like chess or computer programming, or less formal ones like birdwatching or cookery. Despite the fact that knowledge structures and reasoning strategies vary from one domain to another, some of the qualities that characterise an "expert", and some of the changes that are associated with expertise, are similar in different domains. It is, of course, almost tautologous to state that experts know more than novices about their area of expertise. They are also able to acquire and retain new information better than novices, and to utilise stored knowlege more effectively. It might be supposed that, as the amount of knowledge in store increases, search processes would be more complex and it would become more difficult to locate and retrieve particular items of information to order. However, this is not what happens. So, how does an expert manage to handle a greatly expanded amount of knowledge without being overwhelmed by it?

The answer lies in the *acquired mechanisms view* of expertise. Experts acquire cognitive mechanisms and cognitive strategies that allow them to handle the enlarged knowledge base effectively.

(1) Organisation and chunking. One of the most powerful of these mechanisms is chunking. Experts recode information into large, information-rich chunks and link the chunks with powerful associations.

(2) Selective encoding. Experts home in on the most important information and filter out irrelevant or unimportant details.

(3) Using strategies to extend basic capacity limitations.

The operation of these mechanisms is evident in the examples of different kinds of expertise considered in the rest of this chapter.

EXPERT MUSICIANS

The effects of expertise on memory is clearly evident in the domain of music. Memory for music has a number of special features that distinguish it from other forms of memory discussed in previous chapters. One of these is the enormous range of individual differences. Most people can remember simple melodies, but training and experience produce expert musicians with the ability to remember musical pieces that are many times greater in number, length, and complexity. In this respect, remembering music is quite unlike remembering language. Most people can remember some poetry and a few quotations, but individuals are not trained to be able to reproduce whole novels from memory (although a few mnemonists with exceptional memories may set out to learn telephone directories). Memory for music is also distinctive in that it needs to be complete, exact, and accurate. Memory for language most often takes the form of gist memory: The surface structure and verbatim wording are not retained after a few moments. In remembering language we retain the deep structure and can reconstruct the gist. Memory for music is more like memory for poetry in that ability to remember or reconstruct the exact surface form is crucial. It is generally agreed that music, like language, has a deep structure and that memory for the deep structure plays a part in reconstructing the original, but the relative contribution of memory for surface characteristics and memory for the deep structure is controversial. Krumhansl (1991a) stresses the importance of surface properties and suggests that memory for music may be more like memory for pictures than memory for language. Sloboda (1985), on the other hand, finds strong analogies between music and language. Both, he points out, have deep and surface structures; both have generative rules that allow the creation of unlimited novel sequences; both are universal and specific to humans. Children appear to acquire the ability to talk and to sing naturally from exposure without formal training and, in both language and music, cultural differences are superimposed on underlying universals. However, the existence of musical universals is disputed. Storr (1992) has argued that there are fundamental differences between different types of music and the characteristics of Western tonal music are far from universal.

Despite some parallels, there are striking differences between memory for music and for language. One of the most obvious is that for many untrained individuals music is a purely receptive ability. They may be able to remember and recognise familiar music, but are unable to reproduce it and are even more unlikely to be able to create new musical sequences.

This pattern of ability is not regarded as in any way abnormal. By contrast, the ability to reproduce language and to generate well-formed novel outputs is universal and inability is abnormal. Thus, several important differences emerge from this analysis. Memory for music is primarily receptive and there are huge variations in ability between trained and untrained individuals. Most of the memory activities described elsewhere in this book occur in a social context, but for those who are listeners, rather than performers, remembering music may be a solitary activity rather than a social one. Unlike language, the meanings that can be conveyed by music are limited, being largely confined to emotions and moods. Another distinguishing feature of music is its mnemonic potential. Many people, especially children, find it easier to remember songs than prose, and material like the multiplication tables is made memorable by being rhythmically chanted. Music provides a stable structure in which verbal material can be embedded.

Whereas some psychologists have stressed similarities between music and language, others have noted analogies between music and mathematics, both being concerned with creating order and elegance out of abstract patterns. Exceptional ability in music, like exceptional ability in mathematics, is highly specific and sometimes develops in early childhood. However, music is unlike mathematics in the way it arouses and engages the emotions, and the emotional and dramatic aspects of music are an important factor in its memorability.

Individual Differences in Memory for Music

One way in which individuals differ in their ability to remember music is in the possession of absolute pitch. If absolute pitch is a crucial component of expertise it is important to know whether it is an inborn gift or whether it is the result of training. Pitch is the main form-bearing element in Western music and this is true for classical, jazz, and pop music. Absolute, or perfect pitch is the ability to produce, name, or remember pitches on an absolute basis and is popularly believed to be an innate endowment. However, Sloboda (1985) claims that almost all musicians who begin training before the age of six have absolute pitch and almost none of those who begin training after the age of eleven have it, suggesting that there is a critical period for its development. Most untrained people have good memory for relative pitch, that is, the pattern of relationships between pitches, but have difficulty in retaining absolute pitch for more than a few seconds. However, Halpern's (1989) experimental findings suggest that this view needs to be qualified. She asked subjects to imagine humming a familiar tune and then hum the starting note or find it on a keyboard. Over repeated trials, extending over five days, subjects were remarkably consistent even when they were prevented from remembering their own output by hearing interfering notes and prevented from rehearsing by being made to chew gum. The accuracy and consistency of their memory for starting pitch suggests that familiar tunes are stored in terms of absolute, rather than relative, pitch, although Halpern differentiated between the good pitch memory shown by her subjects and "real" absolute pitch. Zatorre and Beckett (1989) tested 18 musicians with absolute pitch asking them to identify three piano tones by their letter names after up to 27 seconds of verbal interference (counting backwards by threes) or musical interference (singing scales). Recall was perfect, although the same subjects showed typical forgetting when asked to recall letter trigrams under the same conditions. This result suggests that the musical notes are not being encoded in terms of their letter names. Zatorre and Beckett concluded that their subjects were able to retain an auditory image of the sounds supported by mental representation of the movements involved in playing the sounds on instruments and by visualising them on a keyboard, and this multiple encoding made their memory for pitch resistant to interference.

Individuals who have exceptional musical skill combined with mental retardation have been described by Miller (1989). The proportion of musical savants among autistic children has been estimated at 10% but in mentally-retarded children as 0.06%. They are predominantly male, suggesting that the ability is sex-linked, and all of them have absolute pitch. However, as Miller points out, their talent does not emerge fully formed. Most of them have received some training and encouragement. This kind of exceptional musical skill is commonly linked with severe visual defects, language impairment, and generally low IQ with particularly poor ability in abstract thinking. Motor co-ordination may also be poor, but auditory short-term memory span is normal. This interesting pattern of impairment and spared ability tells us something about the characteristics required for musical skill. Miller carried out careful tests on Eddie, a five-year-old boy, and found that he and other savants did exceptionally well in tasks requiring retention of harmonic information, but were no better than other musicians in remembering material without any tonal element. He suggested that their superior memory for chords and melodies is due to having absolute pitch, which enables them to carry out rapid and accurate encoding, but he emphasised that musical savants are not like tape-recorders. The fact that they are better at remembering structured, meaningful musical patterns and show sensitivity to musical constraints suggests a more abstract, organised representation.

Among the normal population, differences in memory for music are obviously linked to degree of training, but some of the findings are surprising. In Russell's (1987) study, subjects heard 20 short pieces of modern jazz once each and then had a recognition test in which the jazz pieces were mixed with 20 distractor pieces. Subjects were asked to rate their musical competence, preferences, and listening experience. They ranged from those who could read music and play an instrument to those with virtually no competence at all, and those who listened a lot to those who hardly ever listened to music. The surprise finding was that although the musically competent were better at recognising pieces they rated as familiar, they were no better for the unfamiliar pieces. Russell believed that their advantage with familiar pieces was because they had schemas and labels for these, so, for example, they could label a piece like *O Grand Amour* by the Stan Getz Quartet as "a bossa nova melody with tenor sax". The fact that listening experience did not affect recognition performance may have been due to the fact that most of the subjects who listened to music a lot only listened to classical music, and not to jazz.

Apart from factors such as training and experience, Maylor (1991), in a naturalistic study, showed that ageing affects ability to recognise and name tunes. She tested the ability of older adults to recognise and name the theme tunes from past television programmes. Effects of frequency, recency and age were observed, with the effects of ageing being more marked for naming the tunes than for recognising them. This pattern of responses led Maylor to propose a model of sequential recognition shown in Fig. 8.1. As in Bruce and Young's (1986) model of face recognition, described in Chapter 5, recognition of familiarity precedes naming.

Differences Between Experts and Novices

Maylor's findings of age-related decline in memory for music contrast with examples of well-known expert musicians, such as Rubinstein or Solti, who retain their ability to remember music into late old age. Experts, in any case, represent music in memory differently from novices (Sloboda, 1985). Experts have hierarchical schemas capable of representing abstract higher-order groupings, whereas novices represent small-scale patterns of adjacent notes. A concert pianist may be required to produce over 1000 notes a minute for periods of up to 30 minutes (Chaffin & Imreh, 1994). How can this prodigious feat of memory be sustained? Performers establish multiple independent memory codes including motor, conceptual, auditory, and visual codes. The ability of expert performers to memorise a piece involves general knowledge of the principles of construction and the ability to encode the specific piece in terms of groupings and structures and to relate it to familiar styles and patterns. Experts are able to grasp the global structure and overall architecture of a composition. Bigand (1993) has identified two kinds of abstract musical knowledge structures. The first is a system of relations among musical categories such as pitch, duration,

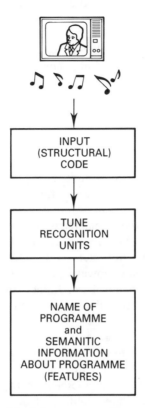

FIG. 8.1. A hypothetical model of the sequence of stages in recognising, naming, and recalling information about television programme theme tunes (from Maylor, 1991). © The Gerontological Society of America. Reprinted with permission.

loudness, and timbre. The second is a lexicon of abstract patterns that occur frequently. People who have substantial listening experience have knowledge of stylistic conventions and can extract general features such as recurrent melodies, the metrical construction, and harmonic framework, which helps them to reconstruct a piece. These differences in the way music is represented in memory underpin the huge gulf between the ability of expert musicians to remember music and the ability of the untrained novice. Novices and nonmusicians lack these higher-order abstract knowledge structures or have only a limited amount of knowledge that is implicit rather than explicit. Similar differences, described in the next section, have been found between expert and novice chess players, but the advantage conveyed by expertise is perhaps even more striking in the case of music.

One example is the often cited instance of the young Mozart being able to transcribe accurately the score of Allegri's *Miserere* after hearing it twice. It has been suggested that this feat reflects a kind of "eidetic" auditory memory, but Sloboda argued that it could be explained in terms of Mozart's general musical knowledge and the relatively simple structure of the piece. This latter explanation is consistent with the finding that the ability of expert chess players to reproduce board positions (see p.221) is not due to superior visual memory but to more abstract knowledge of the game.

Neural Organisation of Music

Musical expertise appears to be linked to particular patterns of neural organisation. There is ample evidence that the components of different cognitive abilities are localised in different areas of the brain. Whereas for most right-handed people the mechanisms controlling language are primarily, but not exclusively, located in the left cerebral hemisphere, nonverbal abilities are primarily, but not exclusively, mediated by the right hemisphere. It is far too simplistic, however, to conclude that musical ability is concentrated in the right hemisphere. Rather, the evidence suggests that some components of musical skill are right hemisphere-based and some are not.

Studies of patients following damage or surgery to right or left hemispheres have produced variable results. The consensus appears to be that right hemisphere damage has more disruptive effect on musical ability, but that there is left hemisphere involvement in rhythm, reading music and detailed musical analysis. The variability of the findings can be attributed to differences in the complexity of the tests that are administered and in the level of musical training in the patients. There is some evidence that left hemisphere involvment is greater in trained musicians (Bever & Chiarello, 1974). Kester et al. (1991) tested a group of patients who had right temporal lobectomy (RTLs) and a group with left temporal lobectomy (LTLs) carried out for the control of epilepsy, and compared these with a group of intact normal controls. None of the individuals had musical training. Prior to surgery, testing with the Musical Aptitude Profile and the Seashore Tonal Memory Test showed no differences between the RTL and LTL groups. After surgery there were changes in the profile of test scores. The scores of the RTL group declined on subtests requiring same-different judgements of tempo amd metre and judgements of style, but there was no change in their tonal discrimination. The group with left hemisphere lobectomy, like the controls, showed no differences between pre- and post-test scores on any of the subtests. Samson and Zatorre (1992) compared ability to learn and retain unfamiliar melodies and lists of nonsense words following right and left unilateral temporal lobectomy. Both LTL and RTL patients showed impairment, relative to controls, on both melodies and nonsense words, suggesting that both hemispheres were involved. However, on a recognition test after 24 hours' delay, the LTL group showed greater impairment for words than melodies and the RTL group showed the opposite pattern. Previous work had suggested that pitch interval is particularly important for delayed recognition and is likely to be disrupted by right hemisphere damage. The pattern of dissociations observed after brain damage or surgery is complex and not wholly consistent, but it serves to confirm that the neural representation of subcomponents of musical skill have some degree of independence and are not wholly lateralised to the right hemisphere. The variation in the results of different studies can be attributed, at least partly, to variation in the subjects' levels of musical experience.

The neural representation of songs is even more complex. Although it is common to find double dissociations of musical and verbal ability after unilateral brain damage, the words of a song and its melody are closely integrated and are not so clearly dissociable. The words and music of a song interact so that changing the phonetic patterns would change the melody. Samson and Zatorre (1991) produced evidence that words and tune are partially integrated in memory. They compared a group of RTLs, a group of LTLs, and a group of normal controls equated for level of musical experience. Twenty-four unfamiliar songs were presented successively. The recognition test included the original "old" songs, old words with a new tune, old tunes with new words, new tunes and new words, and a mismatch condition in which old words and an old tune were recombined. In favour of the integration hypothesis, all subjects recognised old tunes better when combined with the original old words than in the mismatch condition. The results also suggested a bilateral contribution to memory for songs as both LTL and RTL groups did worse than controls. A further experiment tested the hypothesis that the left hemisphere contribution was related to the words and the right to the melody. This time the recognition test consisted of a words-only condition and a tunes-only condition. Correct recognition of words was more disrupted by left temporal lobectomy, with scores of 93% (controls), 87% (RTLs), and 79% (LTLs). Correct recognition of tunes showed the opposite pattern, with scores of 70% (controls), 65% (LTLs), and 55% (RTLs). The findings are therefore consistent with the view that words and music are partially integrated; both hemispheres being involved, with the left contributing more to the representation of the words and the right to the representation of the tune.

Hyman and Rubin (1990) also reported findings consistent with integration in memory of words and music of songs. They carried out a naturalistic study of memory for the songs of the Beatles, including *Eleanor Rigby*,

Obladi Oblada, Can't Buy Me Love, etc. Subjects were asked to recall a song when cued with the title and first line or recall the title when cued with one line. Overall, 21% of lines were recalled, but the most interesting finding was that errors preserved the metre and rhythm of the original. For example, in attempting to recall the line "Rocky Racoon checked into his room" from the song *Rocky Racoon*, subjects substituted "stepped", "walked", or "went" in place of "checked". All these substitutions preserve the rhythm and illustrate the strong relationship beween words and music.

Factors Affecting Memorability of Music

Some music is intrinsically more memorable, but level of expertise interacts with structural characteristics of the music to determine memorability. Memory for music is most often studied by recognition tests or same-different discrimination tasks. Although a few studies have tested recall by requiring subjects to hum, sing, or reproduce notes on a keyboard, it is difficult with untrained subjects to distinguish between memory failure and incompetence. In recognition tests it is possible to discover what musical features are remembered by using foils that are transformations of the target items. The assumption is that it will be hard to reject a foil if the particular transposition is not important for musical memory. Some studies use synthesised musical sequences as target items in order to manipulate factors such as pitch and melodic contour, but these sequences are usually fairly brief and simple and may not be representative of memory for more complex "real" music.

Russell (1987), in his study of memory for modern jazz, set out to discover what makes some music particularly memorable. What does it mean to say that a tune is "catchy"? He selected target pieces that varied in rated complexity, memorability, familiarity, pleasingness, and melodiousness. The last three of these dimensions were highly intercorrelated, no doubt because pieces that are melodious are more pleasing and more likely to be listened to and become familiar. In addition to these subjective variables he included two objective ones, tempo and the number of instruments. Performance in the recognition test was negatively correlated to complexity and positively related to familiarity, pleasingness, and melodiousness, with each dimension accounting for around 30% of the variance. Prior to the experiment, independent raters rated more unusual pieces as more memorable, but in the test subjects' performance was unrelated to these ratings of memorability, perhaps because these pieces appeared less distinctive in the context of the foils. Overall, the results of this study suggest that memorability is determined by a complex interaction of musical characteristics, preference, and experience.

Sloboda (1985) has argued that composers construct music so that individual segments can be linked into larger units on the basis of similarity and connectedness. Given a sufficient level of expertise, music can be "chunked" and coded more economically if repetitions can be recognised, if similarities can be coded as variants, if underlying patterns and progressions are identified, and if the music has an emotional plot. These features facilitate reconstruction from a global representation. According to Sloboda, these conclusions are consistent with performance on tests of recall by singing, which revealed some errors on individual notes but retained the correct metrical structure and harmonic sequence. Palmer and Krumhansl (1990) used a discrimination task to test memory for temporal sequences and, like Sloboda, they concluded that music is recoded in terms of abstract knowledge of metrical structure. The pattern of memory confusions in their data confirmed that metre is represented in nested hierarchical levels. However, in another experiment Krumhansl (1991a) found evidence of memory for musical surface. Subjects heard the first half of a short piano piece by O. Messiaen that has an unfamiliar compositional structure. In a recognition test, subjects could identify excerpts from the part they had heard and also excerpts from the second half of the piece, which they had not heard, showing both accurate memory and ability to generalise. Krumhansl argued that because of the very unusual structure of the piece, subjects could not be relying on general schemas but must be relying on memory for surface characteristics. However, the experiment also revealed some limits to the ability to retain surface characteristics as some foils, for example transformations that maintained the melodic contour, could not be rejected. The ability of experienced listeners and musicians to recognise the expressive variation characteristic of particular performers playing particular pieces must also reflect memory for surface.

Dewitt and Crowder (1986) carried out recognition tests on short melodies systematically varying two features that define the melody; the contour information, or pattern of changes in pitch direction; and interval information, or ordered sequence of pitch distances. In the recognition tests, targets were mixed with foils that differed in contour or in both of these features. The results showed that contour information was more important at short delays of 1 second but interval information was more important at a longer delay of 30 seconds. Dewitt and Crowder concluded that contour information is more easily and rapidly encoded and so forms the basis for discrimination after a brief delay; the more abstract interval information takes longer to encode and is difficult to extract from very short melodies but becomes more important after longer delays.

The relative importance of the different factors that determine memorability has proved difficult to ascertain. Most researchers, such as Sloboda (1985) and Deutsch (1980), stress the importance of structure and cite the fact that pieces with hierarchical rule-governed structure are easier to recall than unstructured pieces, but Boltz and Jones (1986) found only weak effects of rule-based patterning and concluded that other factors, such as the number and timing of contour changes and and the relative position of melodic and temporal accents are more important. Factors appear to change depending on the length and type of sequence and the length of the delay before recognition is tested. Krumhansl (1991b) has pointed out that the factors affecting memorability include some that are not specific to music but influence the encoding of any acoustic inputs. There are general principles for segregating and organising acoustic inputs that also apply to music. However, it is clear that many of the factors that make music memorable depend on the listener having sufficient expertise to identify them and utilise them in representational and reconstructive processes.

Memory for music is an area where traditional laboratory testing has dominated the research and the results may not be very relevant to the ability of the average untrained person to remember music in natural everyday situations. The laboratory tests showing that memory varies with the type of music and the length of the retention interval suggest that differences will be greatly magnified outside the laboratory in the natural situation where a much greater range of music is experienced over a much greater range of retention intervals. In ordinary circumstances a considerable part of memory for music in nonmusicians may be implicit rather than explicit, and techniques for testing implicit memory for music need to be developed. Interesting questions about the nature of memory for music remain unexplored, and conventional models of memory have little to say about how music is represented, recognised, and recalled. How does memory for music develop and improve? What processes are involved when a piece of music is played "in the head"? Does this process resemble inner speech? Do different singing voices or different instruments vary in memorability? Is music more analogous to language, or to mathematics, or to picture memory or face recognition? A more naturalistic approach is needed to throw more light on memory for music in a real world context, and memory for music needs to be incorporated in cognitive models.

FURTHER DOMAINS OF EXPERTISE

Playing Chess

Chase and Simon (1973) carried out a classic study of the differences between expert and novice chess players. Three subjects with different levels of expertise, a beginner, a class A player, and a Master, were allowed five seconds to study a chess board with a game in progress, and were then asked to reconstruct the board positions from memory. If the reconstruction was not complete and accurate the original board was re-presented and viewed again, and the procedure was repeated until a perfect reconstruction was achieved. The Master needed fewer attempts to achieve a perfect reconstruction than the class A player or the novice. On average, the Master placed 16 pieces correctly at the first attempt to reconstruct a middle game. The class A player placed eight pieces correctly and the beginner only four. However, when the subjects were asked to reconstruct chess boards in which the pieces were placed at random, there were no differences between them. This result showed that the Master did not just have superior memory ability. Expertise does not improve memory in general; experts only have better memories for meaningful, properly structured information in their particular knowledge domain.

Chase and Simon believed that chess experts perceive board positions in terms of relations between groups of pieces, so, whereas novices have to memorise the position of each individual piece, the expert only has to remember the group. They tested this "perceptual chunking hypothesis" in a further study. Subjects again had to reconstruct board positions, but this time, instead of relying on memory, they were allowed to look back at the original board as often as they needed to. Monitoring the number of "looks" revealed the size and composition of the perceptual chunks. The expert player memorised larger chunks with each glance at the board, and each chunk represented a meaningful cluster of related pieces. The expert organised information into chunks in accordance with the relational patterns resulting from the attacking and defensive moves that occur in the game. Reitman (1976) obtained a similar result when she compared expert and novice Go players. Other researchers have confirmed that expert knowledge is more highly organised than novice knowledge, using different techniques to identify the chunks and studying different knowledge domains. De Groot (1966) maintained that expert chess players have acquired detailed knowledge of board positions and the best moves associated with them. This allows them to select a move without having to review large numbers of possible moves and consider the outcome of each. On this interpretation it appears that chess experts are using a form of case-based reasoning.

Further evidence that chess performance is not determined by general memory ability comes from a study by Chi (1978) who demonstrated that child chess experts could recall more pieces from a board position than adult chess novices despite the fact that the adults had a better working-memory span. However, Horgan and Morgan (1990) studied young players and showed that, although chess performance was highly correlated with the amount of experience, there was also a significant correlation between chess skill and scores on tests of spatial reasoning ability. This finding suggests that the *knowledge view* is not enough to explain chess expertise. The role of cognitive ability cannot be dismissed entirely.

Computer Programming

Adelson (1981) used a technique similar to Chase and Simon's to compare expert and novice computer programmers, and also demonstrated that they used different types of organisation. The subjects saw 16 lines of code taken from three different programs scrambled together. They had 20 seconds' viewing, followed by 8 minutes for free recall. As the view-recall sequence was repeated, differences in the organisation of recall began to emerge. Experts began to sort out the mixture and group together lines of code that came from the same programs. Novices grouped together lines that looked alike. The experts were using their knowledge to form meaningful higher-level chunks of information and were able to recall more.

In a further study, Adelson (1984) showed that the representations formed by programmers can be characterised as either concrete representations, which instantiate procedural information about how the program operates, or as more abstract representations instantiating declarative knowledge about the higher-level principles of the program. Experts were more likely to form the abstract type of representation spontaneously, although they could shift to the concrete form if required to do so. McKeithen, Reitman, Rueter, and Hirtle (1981) also tested expert and novice programmers' ability to recall a 31-line computer program presented either in normal or in scrambled order. Figure 8.2 shows that for normal programs, recall increased with level of skill, but when the programs were scrambled there was no difference.

When novices and experts were asked to recall key words from programs, novices appeared to use shallower processing, grouping items by first letters or by natural language associations (e.g. "long" "and" "short" "bits" "of" "string"), whereas experts grouped keywords according to their function in programming. The experts also showed much less variability than the novices. All of the experts tended to use similar groupings, whereas the novices differed from each other.

Electronics, Physics, and X-rays

Egan and Schwartz (1979) compared the ability of skilled technicians and novices to reproduce symbolic drawings of electronic circuits. First, they asked an independent expert to indicate how the elements in the display should be grouped according to function. In the test, they found that, for the skilled technicians, the order in which elements were reconstructed, and the pauses in the process of redrawing, both corresponded to the functional

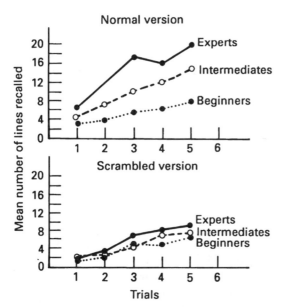

FIG. 8.2.   Lines of code recalled by experts, intermediate programmers, and beginners (from McKeithen et al., 1981).

groupings, but this was not true of the novices. Egan and Schwartz emphasised that the experts also imposed functional groupings on their recall even when the original circuits they had been shown were scrambled. They pointed out that this finding indicates that the organisation demonstrated by experts is conceptual chunking, rather than perceptual chunking, as Chase and Simon (1973) originally suggested. The experts are not so much perceiving patterns in the material, but rather are creating them by reorganisation in memory.

Similarly, in the domain of physics Chi, Feltovich, and Glaser (1981) showed that novices and experts use different principles to organise and group material. Given a set of physics problems to sort into groups, novices sorted on the basis of the items mentioned in the problem, such as pulleys or springs; experts took longer to analyse the problems and sorted them on the basis of the underlying principles, such as the conservation of energy or Newton's second law. Experts and novices also differ in their strategies for solving physics problems. Novices tend to proceed by reasoning backwards. Given a problem about velocity, they retrieve a formula yielding velocity and try to map it on to the information in the problem. Experts, by contrast, use forward reasoning, generating an initial representation of the problem and constructing a plan for solving it.

Studies of medical expertise and expertise in the interpretation of X-rays underline the way experts focus selectively on the most important information (Myles-Worsley, Johnston, & Simon, 1988; Patel & Groen, 1991). Both these studies showed that experts have better memory for pathological cases and for abnormal X-rays, but may even be inferior to novices in the recall of normal cases. Novice radiologists scanning an X-ray use the systematic bilateral comparisons they have been taught, but expert radiologists home in on features outside the range of normal variations (Carmody, Kundel, & Toto, 1984).

Waiters and Bartenders

Expertise influences the kind of strategies that are employed more mundanely by waiters and bartenders. Ericsson and Polson (1988) studied the memory organisation of a skilled waiter, JC, who could retain 17 menu orders in memory without writing anything down. In an experimental test of his ability, he could remember up to 8 orders, each consisting of a main course (8 alternatives with directions about how cooked), a starch (3 alternatives), and a salad with dressing (5 alternatives). The waiter mentally rearranged the orders into categorical groupings (e.g. one Blue cheese, two Oil and vinegar, One Thousand island) and used a first letters mnemonic to encode this as BOOT. Figure 8.3 shows a retrieval structure used by JC.

Beach (1988) compared the mnemonics used by expert and novice bartenders. Novice bartenders relied on verbal rehearsal of multiple orders, but the experts provided themselves with external cues by setting up the appropriate types of glasses for each drink along the bar as they heard each order. This strategy was more effective.

Attitudes and Interests

Similar findings also emerge from knowledge domains related to interests and hobbies. Expertise is often acquired because an individual has an absorbing interest in a particular knowledge domain such as football. In such cases, transformation of a novice into an expert is not just a matter of accumulating more and better-structured knowledge. The development of expertise brings about other changes that also affect memory for material in the knowledge domain. There are changes in emotional and motivational factors.

Football and Baseball

Morris, Gruneberg, Sykes, and Merrick (1981) carried out a study designed to show how knowledge of football (soccer) affects ability to remember scores. They measured level of expertise by administering a

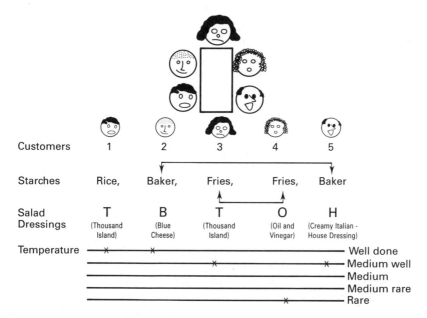

FIG. 8.3. A retrieval structure for dinner orders. The actual seating of five diners is shown at the top. Below are illustrated JC's category-based encodings for starches, salad dressings, and temperatures (adapted from Ericsson & Pennington, 1993). Reprinted with kind permission of Elsevier Science—NL, Sara Burgerhartstraat 25, 1055 KV Amsterdam, The Netherlands.

soccer knowledge questionnaire. There was a strong correlation between performance on the questionnaire and memory for new scores. It was not clear how the high-knowledge subjects were able to achieve superior recall as there is no obvious way to chunk or group a list of teams and their scores. The scores do not conform to learned patterns and even the most knowledgeable subjects were not able to predict them.

Morris, Tweedy, and Gruneberg (1985) explored this problem in a further series of experiments. Subjects were first given a questionnaire to measure soccer expertise. Then, general memory ability was tested by a free-recall test for a list of common words. Finally, free recall was tested for a set of real football scores and a set of simulated scores. Simulated scores were prepared by recombining teams and scores in a plausible way. An important feature of the design was that subjects knew which were the real scores, and which were simulated.

The results showed that soccer knowledge correlated at 0.82 with memory for the real scores, but only at 0.36 with the simulated scores. Free recall of common words correlated at 0.67 with memory for the simulated scores and not at all with memory for the real scores. Morris et al. concluded that for the high-knowledge individuals the real scores had real implications, and therefore aroused greater interest and activated processes of elaborative encoding. For example, the soccer expert would consider how the scores affected the teams' standing and future prospects. Simulated scores, although similar on the surface, failed to activate deeper-level encoding and were treated like the word lists.

In a second experiment, subjects were asked to rate their degree of support (positive or negative), their amount of knowledge about each team, the importance of each match outcome, and the predicted result. Memory for the actual scores was then tested and correlated with each of these ratings. Both degree of support and amount of knowledge were related to recall, but judged importance and accuracy of prediction were not related. This lack of relation between judged importance and recall caused Morris et al. to revise their view that elaborative encoding of the implications of the scores produced better retention. Instead, they argued that the emotional response aroused by support for particular teams seemed to be the crucial factor. High-knowledge individuals were more emotionally involved and therefore remembered the scores better.

A study of expertise in baseball showed that high-knowledge individuals were more likely to have goal-related knowledge structures. Spilich, Vesonder, Chiesi, and Voss (1979) compared individuals who had a great deal of knowledge about baseball with others who had little knowledge of the game. Subjects listened to an account of a baseball match lasting five minutes. Afterwards high- and low-knowledge individuals differed in the kind of information they recalled as well as the kind of errors they made. Free recall protocols of high-knowledge subjects showed that they recalled more of the actions that produced significant changes in the outcome of the game; they recalled more goal-related actions and these were integrated into sequences. Low-knowledge subjects recalled less information and made more errors in which they confused the players or confused different actions. For people who know little or nothing about baseball, memorising the commentary was like learning nonsense material. Because they did not understand how actions were related to goals, they were unable to differentiate important events that affected the outcome from irrelevant or unimportant events.

MENTAL REPRESENTATIONS OF EXPERT KNOWLEDGE

Different models of representation have yielded different accounts of the way knowledge structures change as novices become experts. This section outlines the accounts provided by models of categorical organisation, by schema theory and by production systems. All the models agree that the development of expertise is dependent on high levels of practice.

Categorical Organisation

There is good evidence that experts structure their knowledge differently from novices: forming different categories, using different attributes to distinguish between categories, and representing relationships between categories differently. Chess experts acquire a mental library of categories of patterns of board positions with associated moves. Expert musicians have categories based on conventions and rules of composition. Rosch et al. (1976) proposed that categories are organised in a conceptual hierarchy as shown in Fig. 8.4 Within a given hierarchy they distinguish a "basic level". The basic level is the one at which the concepts are most clearly defined and best differentiated from other related caegories. The basic level is also the one that is cognitively most accessible, the level at which we most often think and communicate with each other. In the furniture hierarchy, the concept of "chair" is basic, and the superordinate and subordinate levels are less accessible. However, Rosch et al. found some evidence that the basic level shifts with expertise, moving downward in the hierarchy. In their study, they encountered a subject who was an aeroplane mechanic, and who distinguished between many different types of plane, so that, whereas an ordinary person would identify an object as "a plane", he identified it as "a twin-engined Cessna". Similarly, for an expert on antique furniture, a chair is not just a chair, but a late Chippendale mahogany dining chair. For experts, the preferred, or basic level of

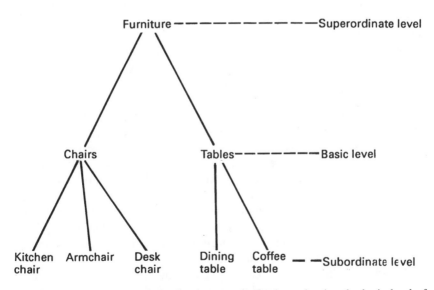

FIG. 8.4. A conceptual hierarchy for the category furniture showing the basic level of representation.

categorisation seems to be lower down the hierarchy, more specific, and more highly differentiated. Such a shift also necessarily entails an increase in the number of categories because the expert makes finer-grained distinctions.

Murphy and Wright (1984) set out to test some of these intuitions and observations in a systematic study comparing the knowledge structures of experts and novices. They studied four groups of people with different levels of expertise in clinical psychology. *Experts* were fully trained, with years of experience; *Experienced Counsellors* had less formal training but considerable experience; *Beginning Counsellors* had done voluntary work and taken undergraduate courses; and *Novices* were students just starting an introductory psychology course.

All the subjects were asked to consider three types of emotionally disordered child: the aggressive, the depressive, and the disorganised. They were asked to list as many as possible of the characteristics typical of each disorder. The results are shown in Fig. 8.5. As expected, the number of features listed increased with expertise, and the experts listed twice as many as the novices. Inter-subject agreement was also much greater among the experts. However, contrary to expectations, the experts' concepts had greater overlap with each other, as can be clearly seen in the figure. For the experts, the three types of disorder were actually *less* well differentiated because they listed more characteristics as belonging to more than one category of disorder.

Murphy and Wright confirmed this finding in a further test. The subjects were given a list of characteristics (e.g. "has low self-esteem"; "isolates self from others") and were asked to rate how well each characteristic described each type of child. These ratings again showed that the novices had simple, well-defined, distinctive concepts. They tended to think that characteristics were displayed by one type of child and not by the other types. The experts' concepts were less clear-cut and well-defined. They recognised that different types of child might exhibit the same characteristics, so that, for example, low self-esteem might be characteristic of both depressive and aggressive types. Although this finding seems counterintuitive, it does make a good deal of sense. The novice has probably learned a concept like "the depressive child" from textbook descriptions of proto-typical cases. The expert has encountered a much greater range and variety of cases and recognises that, in the real world, categories are not so sharply differentiated. Although in some knowledge domains expertise may bring about increasing precision of categorisation, in other domains concepts may become less distinctive with increasing knowledge.

A study by Chi and Koeske (1983) has attempted to plot qualitative differences in the structure of knowledge across different levels of expertise. They studied the knowledge base of a 4-year-old boy who had a

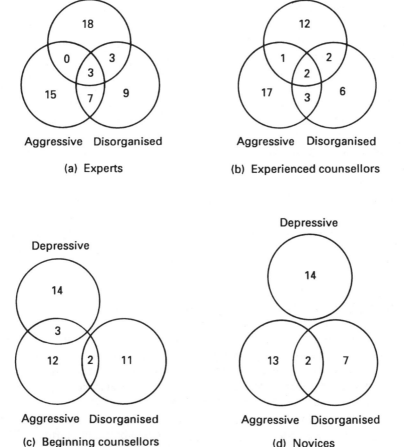

FIG. 8.5.   Venn diagrams representing the frequency of occurrences of common features in each diagnostic category as a function of level of expertise. Numbers in each area indicate the number of features agreed on by 25% or more of the subjects in that group (from Murphy & Wright, 1984). Copyright 1984 American Psychological Association. Reprinted by permission of the author.

consuming interest in dinosaurs. Numerous books on dinosaurs were regularly read to him by his parents and he had a collection of model dinosaurs. In a name-production task, they asked the child to produce the names of all the dinosaurs he knew and he eventually produced the remarkable total of 46 names. These were divided—on the basis of his mother's intuitions, and on the frequency with which they were mentioned in the books—into two lists, one of 20 well-known dinosaurs and one of 20 less well-known dinosaurs. In order to plot the child's knowledge structures, a guessing game was played. Either the experimenter listed two or three attributes (e.g. appearance, habits) and the child had to guess the name of the dinosaur with those attributes, or the roles were reversed.

The child's knowledge networks, illustrated in Figs. 8.6 (the well-known set) and 8.7 (the less well-known set), show the links between different dinosaurs (evidenced by the sequence of responses in the name-production task) and the links between dinosaurs and attributes (evidenced by responses in the guessing game). As the figures show, dinosaurs in the well-known set have more links between them, and the subgroups (shown by the dotted lines) of Armoured dinosaurs and Plant-eaters are more cohesive with more internal linkages. In the less well-known set the patterns of interlinkage are different. Fewer attributes are known and the subgroups are less cohesive. These differences in the structure of well-known and less well-known knowledge were correlated with memory performance. The well-known dinosaurs were better recalled in a memory test, and, when the child was re-tested one year later, they were better retained.

Schema Theory

Schema theory accounts for developing expertise in terms of the acquisition of schemas. The expert has schemas that are well developed, accurate representations of the generalised knowledge in the domain. Schemas supply frameworks that impose organisation and grouping on new information, and new knowledge can be economically stored by assimilation to this pre-existing framework. At retrieval, missing information can be derived from the schema by inheritance or by default (see p.78).

The novice starts off with only the most rudimentary schemas for the relevant knowledge domain. According to Rumelhart and Norman (1978) three processes are at work in producing the developed schemas of the expert:

(1) *Accretion*: New information is added to existing schemas so that the database is expanded without changing its basic principles. So, for example, basic chess-playing schemas for attack and defence might "grow" to accommodate new patterns as these become familiar.

(2) *Tuning*: Comparatively minor alterations may be made to existing schemas, gradually modifying, for example, the slots and values to conform to newly acquired knowledge. The restaurant schema (or script) may be tuned in this way to include paying at a check-out as well as paying the waiter at the table.

(3) *Restructuring*: This occurs when new knowledge is discrepant with existing schemas so that major changes are required. New schemas are

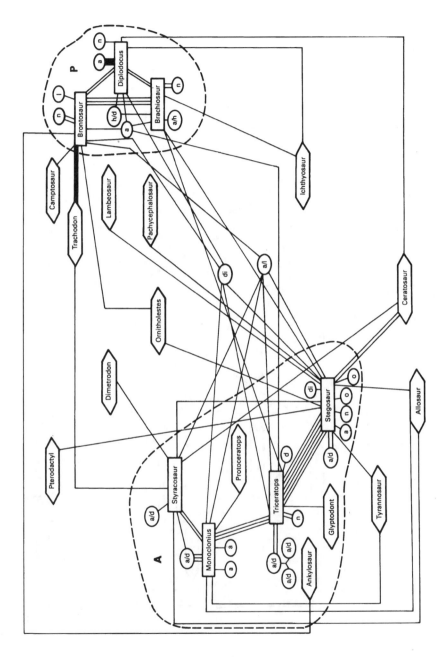

FIG. 8.6. Network representation for the target dinosaurs in the better known list (A – armoured; P – plant-eaters; a – appearance; d – defence mechanism; di – diet; h – habitat; l – locomotion; n – nickname; o – other) (from Chi & Koeske, 1983).

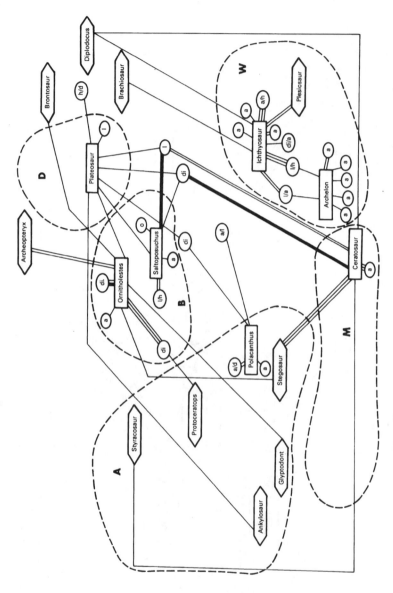

FIG. 8.7. Network representation for the target dinosaurs in the lesser known list (A – armoured; B – bird or egg eaters; D – duckbilled; M – giant meat-eaters; W – water dwellers; a – appearance; d – defence mechanism; di – diet; h – habitat; l – locomotion; n – nickname; o – other) (from Chi & Koeske, 1983).

created either by copying old ones and modifying them, or by deriving new generalisations from recurring patterns and building new schemas to instantiate these general principles.

As a result of these processes, the expert has more schemas than the novice, and has schemas that are more powerful and more widely applicable.

Production Systems

Production systems (Anderson, 1983) provide a general model of knowledge acquisition that specifies the changes that occur with increasing expertise more precisely than schema theory. In Anderson's ACT* production systems architecture two different kinds of knowledge are stored in long-term memory. Declarative memory stores factual knowledge, including temporal, spatial, and semantic information. Procedural knowledge consists of knowing what to do and how to act and this skill-based knowledge is stored in production memory and takes the form of production rules.

Productions are processing elements each consisting of a *condition plus action* rule. Each rule takes the form of an "IF" clause followed by a "THEN" clause. The IF clause specifies a state of affairs, the THEN clause specifies the action. When the pattern of a current state of affairs matches the pattern described in the IF condition, the production is activated and the action is elicited, as in:

IF the sink is full of dirty dishes
THEN do the washing up

A set of related productions constitute a production system, and goal-related productions are organised in hierarchies with higher-level goals and subgoals. Productions that are currently active are stored in working memory.

Production systems provide a general purpose cognitive system that can give an account of many different kinds of skill and knowledge. The chess player acquires a set of productions whereby patterns of pieces on the board form the conditions for making particular moves. The doctor acquires productions relating symptoms to treatments. According to this view, all experts have a repertoire of rules for recognising situations and taking appropriate actions. Note, however, that this rule-based account of expertise contrasts with the case-based account outlined on p.186, where the development of expertise consists in accumulating a library of relevant cases.

According to the production systems account, becoming an expert involves a number of processes. First, the novice acquires declarative knowledge by learning relevant facts. This stage is followed by gradual *proceduralisation* of the declarative knowledge, which is transformed from propositions into production rules. The novice medical student learns facts about the circulation of blood and the consequences of bleeding. At a later stage he or she acquires the production:

IF bleeding needs to be controlled
THEN apply pressure above the site of the wound

In Anderson's model, learning involves other processes as well as proceduralisation. New productions are added and old ones are modified. *Strengthening* occurs when productions are used frequently so that they are activated more readily. Correspondingly, productions that are seldom used lose strength and become harder to elicit. *Composition* takes place when sequences of productions, which reliably occur together and relate to the same goal, are integrated into a single higher-level production. The conditions of several separate productions are amalgamated into a single complex condition that triggers the whole sequence of actions. *Generalisation* is a process whereby the condition of a production is represented more generally so that the action has a wider range of applicability, and can extend to similar but novel situations. For example,the novice driver may learn:

IF the road surface is icy
THEN reduce speed

whereas the more experienced driver generalises the condition to include other kinds of dangerous road surface such as loose grit or oil slicks.

According to Anderson's ACT* model, the production overlap theory of transfer states that transfer between tasks depends on the extent to which the tasks share the same production rules. This theory predicts, therefore, that unless the tasks involve the same productions, no transfer will occur even if the tasks share a common base of declarative knowledge. These predictions were tested by Pennington, Nicolich, and Rahm (1995) who examined performance on two computer programming subtasks, the evaluation and generation of LISP instructions. Both these tasks have a common declarative base, but the overlap of productions is low. They found, contrary to the predictions, that there was a substantial amount of transfer. From a follow-up study in which verbal protocols were elicited they concluded that transfer was mediated by elaboration of declarative knowledge. The subjects were spontaneously generalising the conditions of use for functions and refining concept definitions. These findings suggest that the depth of conceptual understanding of the tasks is more important for transfer than simple redeployment of previously learned procedures.

However, production systems are versatile and flexible and this model can account for some of the observed differences in performance between novices and experts. Proceduralisation and strengthening make responses faster, and composition accounts for the higher-order chunking in memory that characterises expert performance. It does not account for the effects of emotional and attitudinal factors observed by Morris et al. (1985), or for the blurring of conceptual boundaries noted by Murphy and Wright (1984). The great advantage of this model, however, is the way it links knowledge to skill and helps us to understand how expertise influences what people do as well as what they know.

CONCLUSIONS

It seems evident that all three components of expertise—talent, knowledge, and acquired mechanisms—are involved to varying degrees in the different domains of expertise considered here. Interest, motivation, and long hours of persevering application and practice are also essential ingredients. Beyond these fairly obvious conclusions it is difficult to generalise across different areas of expertise. Both the nature of the underlying mental representations and the process of acquisition and development of expertise vary with the domain. The most striking common feature is the enormous advantage in memory that is conferred by expertise in any domain. The studies described in this chapter demonstrate, across a range of different knowledge domains, that experts organise information differently from novices. They are more likely to organise information into groups instead of treating it on an item-by-item basis. The groupings they use are in accordance with the functions, rules, or frequently occurring patterns of the knowledge domain, and this organisation into groups, chunks, or subsets of knowledge enables the expert to restrict search to relevant parts of the knowledge base when retrieving information. The superior memory of the expert is also due to the accumulated knowledge of the rules, patterns, and constraints that govern information in the knowledge domain. This allows the expert to infer missing information, or to reconstruct missing elements from partially remembered information. Because their knowledge is highly structured, experts remember vastly more than novices with less effort and fewer errors. These qualities extend the boundaries of expert knowledge and make it robust and relatively resistant to the effects of ageing and trauma.

9 Memory for Discourse: Conversation, Texts, and Stories

Much of the information that we store in memory is not acquired first hand through our own experience. It is acquired at second hand through reading or through listening to other people talk about their experiences. This chapter explores what is known about memory for information acquired in this way. Memory for spoken information and memory for written information are treated separately because they differ in important ways. Intake of written information is self-paced. The reader can pause, back-track, or take a coffee-break, but the listener must keep pace with the rate of speech, which is determined by the speaker. However, in both cases the input is sequential and both tasks place heavy demands on the working memory system, which must hold segments of the input temporarily until they can be related to what comes later. The meaning of the first part of a sentence often cannot be grasped until the rest of the sentence has been analysed. The meaning of part of a conversation or part of a story may be obscure until the rest has been processed. With any form of linguistic input, working memory has to function as a temporary holding store where new information can be related to previously acquired information and where parts of a message can be integrated with other parts. Memory for discourse therefore differs from many other kinds of everyday remembering in that the role of working memory is much more important. This contrasts with memory for faces and places, autobiographical experiences, witnessed events, and expert knowledge, where the emphasis is on long-term memory.

The first section of this chapter, which deals with memory for spoken information, emphasises the role of pragmatic factors such as intentions and attitudes. The second part of the chapter, which deals with written information, is more concerned with how this is structured in memory. Listening to speech usually takes place in a social context and is therefore strongly influenced by social and pragmatic factors like the intentions and personalities of the speaker and the hearer, the context of the utterance, and the social conventions that govern the exchange. These factors are of less importance when information is written. Reading is a more private and solitary occupation and much of written material is decontextualised. That is, the writer of the message may not know when, where, or by whom it will be read. Hence, written material must be much more formally structured, and must conform to accepted rules and formats, if it is to be intelligible to a range of potential readers. In conversation, the structure of the message is much less important because comprehension can be assisted by intonation, gesture, facial expression, repetition, and recapitulation.

SOCIAL REMEMBERING: THE DISCOURSE ANALYSIS APPROACH

The relationship between memory and conversation is twofold, including both memory *for* conversation and remembering *through* conversation. Conversation is not just something *to be remembered,* but can also be used as a *means of remembering.* In everyday life remembering is not necessarily a solo performance. If we cannot remember something, we commonly appeal to family, friends, or colleagues for assistance, and shared experiences are recalled collaboratively with different individuals supplying missing elements and cueing each other. Remembering in social contexts clearly plays a large part in everyday memory and the study of social remembering has assumed considerable importance in recent years. Social remembering differs from remembering individually in numerous ways. It serves different functions and is evaluated by different criteria using a distinct methodology known as discourse analysis.

The discourse analysis approach (Edwards, Potter, & Middleton, 1992) is concerned with how versions of events are constructed in conversation, how they are shaped and fitted to the particular context, and what the participants in the interaction accomplish. In strong contrast to other approaches to the study of memory, discourse analysis is not concerned with whether a memory is accurate or complete. The focus is on its function and its effect on the hearers. Issues of truth or falsity are simply irrelevant. These social memories are spontaneous descriptions of past events designed by the speaker as social actions. Thus, they may serve to establish the speaker's identity, to claim entitlement to membership of the group, to blame, to justify, to excuse, and so on. Discourse analysis researchers claim that their approach lies outside the information-processing tradition. They emphasise the multimodal nature of remembering whereby nonverbal experiences are translated by speakers into verbal descriptions that emerge from social interactions. Researchers transcribe and analyse these utterances in terms of the content, the sequential placing of the elements, the pattern of interaction, and the context of the conversation.

The theoretical background of discourse analysis is rooted in theories of social communication rather than theories of memory and, because it substitutes pragmatics for veridicality, it is closely related to work on conversational pragmatics. Grice's views on conversational implicature, and Searle's concept of speech acts, discussed in the following sections, can both be seen as forerunners of discourse analysis.

Pragmatics in Conversation

"Pragmatics" is the term used to describe the functional aspects of conversation. Conversation can have many different functions besides the exchange of information. For example, it may be designed to entertain, to advise, to annoy, to complain, and so on. The pragmatic aspect of the meaning of an utterance derives from the speaker's intentions and purposes. The intended meaning of an utterance may be quite different from its literal meaning. So, for example, the utterance "I'm tired" may be used to convey that it is no good asking the speaker to mow the lawn; that the speaker would like some sympathy and attention from the hearer; or that the speaker is justified in being unco-operative. Indeed, people sometimes say the exact opposite of what they intend the hearer to understand. If someone says "You've been a great help" when she has received no help at all, the utterance is intended to convey a reproach, and she is using sarcasm instead of a literal statement in order to underline the reproach.

Conversational Implicature

Complex implications like these run through everyday conversation. They cannot be derived by linguistic or by logical analysis, so how do we understand these implied meanings? The philosopher Grice (1967) claimed that conversation is normally governed by a *co-operative principle* consisting of a set of maxims or conventions observed by the speaker and the hearer. These are:

(1) *Quality*: A speaker should normally say what is true, and a hearer normally assumes that what he is being told is true.
(2) *Quantity*: The speaker should say as much as is necessary and neither more nor less.
(3) *Relation*: The speaker's utterances should be relevant to the topic. The hearer works on the assumption that what is said is in some way

relevant, and will try to work out the relevance if it is not immediately obvious.

(4) *Manner*: The utterances should be clear and orderly. The speaker normally aims to be understood and should not be obscure or ambiguous.

Grice's maxims are designed to explain the way people manage to exchange information in conversations, but, according to the discourse analysis approach, the exchange of information is only one of many functions of conversation. In practice, these conventions are often violated, either deliberately or involuntarily. Speakers may sometimes lie, mislead, joke, be sarcastic, verbose, ambiguous, irrelevant, or unintelligible, depending on the effect they are trying to have on their listeners. Nevertheless, hearers usually do make the default assumptions that what is said bears some relation to the truth, is in some way relevant, and that they ought to be able to understand it.

Speech Acts

The pragmatic aspect of the meaning of utterances has been analysed in terms of *Speech Acts* (Searle, 1969). Searle's idea that the speaker is performing an act by saying something, rather than simply making a statement of fact, is directly reflected in discourse analysis. The speaker who is promising, requesting, or blessing is *performing* a speech act. Speech acts like commanding, rebuking, or threatening are designed to produce some desired effect on the hearer. The function of such utterances is to convey the intentions of the speaker, or, in some cases, to bring about changes in the behaviour or state of mind of the hearer. Other kinds of speech act are expressives such as apologising, commiserating, deploring, which convey the speaker's state of mind. Speech acts are sometimes indirect. Instead of directly requesting "Please pass me the sauce" the speaker may use an indirect speech act, saying "Can I pass you the sauce?" Applying Gricean maxims, the hearer can work out that this is a request rather than an offer. He knows he already has the sauce, and he knows that the speaker knows he already has the sauce. By assuming that the utterance must be relevant in some way, he is able to infer the indirect intended meaning.

In one of Grice's own examples, a stranded motorist says "I'm out of petrol". A passer-by responds "There is a garage round the corner". The motorist needs to apply the maxim of relation to recover the conversational implicature that the garage sells petrol and is probably open. There are other principles that govern conversational exchanges, such as the *order of mention contract*, whereby events are normally mentioned in the order in which they occurred (as in "They bought a house and moved in"; "He borrowed a fiver and I never saw him again") unless otherwise indicated. The point to note about all these examples is that in conversational exchanges the actual words used convey only a part of the meaning. Conventions of interpretation supply additional elements over and above the literal meaning.

Studies in Discourse Analysis

Family Snaps

Edwards and Middleton (1988) studied remembering as a joint collaborative effort within the family. They recorded occasions when mothers, each with two young children, aged between two and six years, looked through the family photograph album together. Together, they identified the scene and people depicted, elaborated the details of the scene, placed it in context of time and place of occurrence, interpreted what was happening, and used inferential reconstruction to assign causes and consequences to the event. Children and parents compared reactions and contributed additional remembered information. Edwards and Middleton were particularly interested in two functions of these conversations. One of these functions was to teach young children how to remember. The mothers were leading and guiding the processes of elaboration, demonstrating how to draw out contextual inferences, as shown in Fig. 9.1.

The second function was concerned with affect, identity and relationships. The mothers interpreted the situations in the photographs so as to reinforce desirable affective relationships between siblings; they explained and underlined the continuity of the children's identities across changes of development and setting. Even when conversations are not designed, as these were, as collaborative acts of remembering, many everyday conversations also include explicit reminders, cues that reinstate shared memories, and appeals for help in remembering. Remembering through conversation is a common, naturally occurring phenomenon in everyday life.

Lawson and the Journalists

Edwards and Potter's (1992) study of a disputed conversation between the then Chancellor of the Exchequer, Nigel Lawson, and a group of journalists, is concerned with memory for a conversation, rather than remembering through conversation. The study highlights the way in which different versions of an event are constructed and the specific devices that are used to give an appearance of authenticity to a particular version. The journalists claimed that Lawson had said that universal pensions would be ended and

---

Modelling contextual inference

(1) With Helen (aged 2:3) and Sandra (4:11)
MOTHER: Who's that?
HELEN: I don't know.
MOTHER: Do you know where you were there?
HELEN: (. . .)
MOTHER: Whose house were you at there?/ Do you recognise . . . (. . .)
(*Looking at another picture.*)
SANDRA: Look there's Mummy on a boat/ I didn't go on boat (. . .)
'cause look there's (. . .)
MOTHER: Oh yes. I bet that was in Liverpool when we went on the
ferry boat.

(2) With Paul (4:3) and Rebecca (5:10)
MOTHER: Do you remember being on this beach?
PAUL: Yuk// No.
MOTHER: Don't you/ when we went to Jersey/ on the aeroplane// do
you not remember that?
PAUL: Is that Jersey?
MOTHER: Mm/ look Rebecca's wearing a hat that says Jersey on it.
(. . .) (*Looking at another picture*)
PAUL: Look/ what is that?
MOTHER: (. . .) probably a book. We were going to go on that/ boat/
for a trip down the river/ and we took one or two books to keep you
two occupied.

FIG. 9.1. Modelling contextual inference (from Edwards & Middleton, 1988). Reprinted by permission of Sage Publications.

replaced by pensions that were conditional on means-testing. Lawson at first challenged the accuracy of this report of what he had said, but later switched to denying the interpretation. He claimed to have spoken of targeting resources on the less well-off. The journalists interpreted this as meaning that he planned to redistribute the existing resources, basing their interpretation on past experience of what "targeting" usually implied and on knowledge of government policy. Lawson maintained that his remarks implied that *extra* resources would be distributed. The journalists sought to authenticate their recollection of what had been said, for example by including a lot of detail in their reports. One report stated: "Mr Lawson sat in an armchair in one corner, next to a window looking out over the garden of No. 11 Downing Street. The Press Secretary, Mr John Gieve, hovered by the door. The rest of us, notebooks on our laps, perched on chairs and sofas in a circle around the Chancellor" (*The Observer*, 13 November 1988). This is a device designed to establish credibility—when presented with so much detail how could we doubt the accuracy of the reported conversation? The journalists also tried to counter the objection that Lawson was unlikely to have made such a politically unwise statement by appealing to accounts of his personality as overconfident and arrogant. Lawson's own strategy was to claim that the journalists' version was dictated by their desire to produce a more sensational and newsworthy story. The study illustrates the way that a particular conversation may be remembered quite differently by different participants and gives some account of how these versions are pragmatically constructed and defended.

Reminiscence Work

A final example of discursive remembering comes from group reminiscence, which is commonly used as a form of therapy with elderly people, although it may also serve as entertainment or as a means of producing oral history. In a semi-organised setting, older people are encouraged to remember and re-tell experiences from their past lives. In the extract from Middleton and Buchanan, 1994 (see Fig. 9.2) a woman called Sue, in her seventies, is talking with the group about drinking habits and recounts a story of a visit from the parson. This extract illustrates a number of the functions of conversational remembering. Sue establishes her identity in relation to the social setting and social customs of the past and reinforces her group membership by engaging the interest of others in the group. She raises issues and invites comment about the cultural and moral ideas of the past, and her narrative constitutes what discourse researchers call an "entitlement claim" to the significance of her experience. Notice, too, how Sue includes direct verbatim speech in her narrative, which has the effect of making the memory appear more authentic.

Criticisms of Discourse Analysis

Many psychologists feel uneasy about an approach to memory that takes no account of truth or falsity. Most do recognise the importance and ecological validity of studying how people construct joint recollections, and admit that the influence of social, contextual, and motivational factors in shaping memory has been neglected, but nevertheless believe that considerations of accuracy remain a paramount aspect of memory. Discourse analysis represents an extreme constructivist view of memory that few cognitive psychologists find completely acceptable. It is also arguable that social remembering could usefully be studied using a more experimental approach. Critics point out that discourse analysis makes no attempt to examine how participants provide retrieval cues for each other, or to examine the effects of context by varying the context systematically; there is no attempt to quantify the data, or to control for researcher bias. It seems likely, therefore, that some combination of the methods of discourse

CONVERSATIONAL DATA

```
 1
 2   Sue:    I mean I've got nothing against drink/ if people enjoy drink I- I think they're
 3           entitled to it/ but erm/ it's not for me/ apart from er/ lemonade and/ shandy/ I
 4           don't mind that
 5           ((another conversation intrudes for some seconds at this point, until Sue
 6           continues))
 7   Sue:    I remember when er/ my father was alive/ he used to like a bottle of stout/
 8           used to ( ) bottle about like this/ and (&)
 9                                                            [
10   Rose:                     mm/ stout oh yes/ stout
11   Sue:    (&) er/ where we lived er/ we had a/ erm/ a/ firegrate with erm/ hobs I think
12           they called them (   ) hobs/ and er/ my (&)
13                                      [
14   ?f:                       ehh
15                                          [
16   Meg?:            yeah that's (yeah)
17                                                              [
18   Ted:                                             ah yeah
19                                                                       [
20   ?f:                                                        (  )
21   Sue:    (&) dad used to/ drink it out the bottle/ and er/ he used to stand it on the hob/
22           an- and he used to say it was beautiful(&)
23                                                            [
24   Ted:                                              warming
25   Sue:    (&)/ and er ((laugh)) a- you'll think (   ) and er/ I used to go to church in those
26           days/ and erm/ the parson/ we had a parson that used to visit/ and er/ I said to
27           me
28           dad/ the parson- / I said that the parsons coming/ (&)
29                   [
30   Ted:       is that why he kept it on the hob
31   Sue:    (&) I said that you won't drink your stout while he's here will you/ ooh my dad
32           was disgusted he said I will (&)
33                                           [
34   Ted:                     ((laugh))
35   Sue:    (&) drink me stout/ he said you ought to be ashamed of yourself/ and there it
36           stood on the hob y'know (&)
37                   [
38   ?m:           (  )
39   Sue:    (&) and in walked the parson with his/ dog collar on
40           I didn't know what to do/ and ((cough)) to make (&)
41           [
42   Rose?: ((laugh))
43   Sue:    (&) matters worse this erm/ stou:t was/ ch ch ch ch ((imitates noise of stout
44           bubbling)) you could hear it/ bubbling like (&)
45                                  [
46                         ((general laughter))
47   Sue:    (&)/ yeah and er/ me father said to him er/ ooh and er/ this parsons name was
48           a Mr Jackson he was a very very nice man/ and m- me father said er/ I don't/ I
49           don't think going to church is doing my daughter much good/ he said er/ she
50           asked me/ not to have my bottle of stout/ cos you were coming/ and Mr
51           Jackson said well I've never heard such a thing in me life he said/ I like one
52           meself
53           occasionally/ I never felt so bad after tha::t ((laughing tone))
54                         ((general laughter))
```

FIG. 9.2.   Conversational data from reminiscence work (from Buchanan & Middleton, 1995). Reprinted by permission of Cambridge University Press and the authors.

analysis together with experimental manipulations and controls could shed more light on the mechanisms of social remembering.

When objective methods of testing are employed some of the findings are counterintuitive. It might be expected that social remembering by a collaborative group would produce better recall than an individual remembering alone. Meudell, Hitch, and Kirby (1992) presented subjects with 24 unrelated words followed by immediate free recall. Three months later all subjects recalled the words again and were then assigned to either a joint-recall group or a solo-recall group. In the joint-recall condition pairs of subjects worked together collaboratively to recall as many words as possible; in the solo-recall group the subjects were asked to recall once more on their own. The results showed that, although pairs remembered more words than solos, this was simply the effect of adding together their individual scores. The number of new correct items generated by the joint collaboration was no greater than the number of new correct items generated by reminiscence in the solo subjects. Thus there was absolutely no evidence for social facilitation of recall, and Andersson and Ronnberg (1995), in a similar study of collaborative recall, found that social interaction actually inhibited remembering and collaboration had a negative effect.

MEMORY FOR CONVERSATION: THE COGNITIVE APPROACH

The cognitive approach is more concerned with the relationship between the original linguistic input and what is remembered, in particular with what is preserved and what is forgotten.

Memory for Wording and Memory for Meaning

When people remember conversations what do they remember? Empirical studies of memory for sentences, models of psycholinguistic processing, and models of memory, such as schema theory, all claim that memory for the surface form (the actual words and syntactic form) is lost very rapidly, and what is stored in memory is a more abstract representation of the meaning. The classic experimental demonstration of this phenomenon was carried out by Sachs in 1967. In her experiment, subjects listened to tape-recorded passages. One of the sentences they heard was "He sent a letter about it to Galileo, the great Italian scientist". A test sentence was presented after a delay of approximately 0, 25, or 50 seconds. The subject had to decide if the test sentence was identical with the original or if it had been changed. There were four kinds of test sentence:

(1) He sent a letter about it to Galileo, the great Italian scientist.
(2) He sent Galileo, the great Italian scientist, a letter about it.

(3) A letter about it was sent by him to Galileo, the great Italian scientist.

(4) Galileo, the great Italian scientist, sent him a letter about it.

Version 1 is identical. Versions 2 and 3 both preserve the meaning of the original although the wording has been changed. In Version 4, both the wording and the meaning are changed. Subjects could detect changes of wording (2 and 3) at the zero delay but after 50 seconds these judgements were at chance level. Memory for the original wording had been lost, but changes of meaning, as in (4) could still be detected with about 80% accuracy. This evidence suggests that verbatim wording (the surface form) is briefly stored in short-term memory, but only the semantic interpretation is retained in long-term memory.

According to this view, people remember the gist of a conversation, but after a few seconds they normally have little or no verbatim memory of what they have heard. Of course, it is recognised that people can remember speech word-for-word if they set out to memorise it and are given enough time and repetitions. People memorise poems and speeches in this way, but it is not considered the normal mode for remembering naturally occurring conversations. However, everyday experience does suggest that verbatim memory might be more common than Sachs' findings indicate. We are all familiar with verbatim raconteurs who report exchanges like "I said to her . . . , so she said to me . . .", in direct speech. Of course, this kind of recall may be only a quite inaccurate reconstruction, but we can sometimes quote the exact words someone has said. Several studies of memory for conversation have addressed the question of whether any verbatim memory persists, and under what conditions.

John Dean and Anita Hill

Neisser (1982a) analysed John Dean's memory for the conversations he had with President Nixon. Testifying to the Watergate Committee in June 1973, Dean described dozens of conversations with the President and with members of his Administration. Unknown to Dean, all the conversations that took place in Nixon's Oval Office were tape-recorded and transcripts were made available. Dean's recollection of these naturally occurring conversations could therefore be checked against the transcripts. Neisser analysed the recall of two conversations, one that took place nine months before the hearing and one three months before. The tape of the first conversation is shown in Fig. 9.3a. The President (P) and Robert Haldeman (H), the chief of staff, are discussing the fact that only five men and two minor White House officials (Hunt and Liddy) have been indicted for the Watergate break-in, so their efforts to conceal the involvement of higher officials seem to have been successful. Figure 9.3b shows Dean's recall of this conversation.

P: Hi, how are you? You had quite a day today, didn't you? You got Watergate on the way, didn't you?

D: We tried.

H: How did it all end up?

D: Ah, I think we can say well, at this point. The press is playing it just as we expected.

H: Whitewash?

D: No, not yet—the story right now—

P: It is a big story.

H: Five indicted plus the WH former guy and all that.

D: Plus two White House fellows.

H: That is good; that takes the edge off whitewash, really. That was the thing Mitchell kept saying, that to people in the country Liddy and Hunt were big men. Maybe that is good.

P: How did MacGregor handle himself?

D: I think very well. He had a good statement, which said that the Grand Jury had met and that it was now time to realise that some apologies may be due.

H: Fat chance.

D: Get the damn (inaudible).

H: We can't do that.

P: Just remember, all the trouble we're taking, we'll have a chance to get back one day. How are you doing on your investigation? (*Presidential Transcripts*, p.32)

P: Yes (expletive deleted). Goldwater put it in context when he said (expletive deleted) everybody bugs everybody else. You know that.

D: That was priceless.

P: It happens to be totally true. We were bugged in '68 on the plane and even in '62 running for Governor—(expletive deleted) thing you ever saw.

D: It is a shame that evidence to the fact that that happened in '68 was never around. I understand that only the former director [*J. Edgar Hoover, former head of the FBI*] had that information.

H: No, that is not true.

D: There was evidence of it?

H: There are others who have information (*Ibid.*, p.34)

D: Three months ago I would have had trouble predicting there would be a day when this would be forgotten, but I think I can that 54 days from now [*i.e., on election day in November*] nothing is going to come crashing down to our surprise.

P: That what?

D: Nothing is going to come crashing down to our surprise (*Ibid.*, p.36)

P: Oh well, this is a can of worms as you know, a lot of this stuff that went on. And the people who worked this way are awfully embarrassed. But the way you have handled all this seems to me has been very skillful, putting your fingers in the leaks that have sprung here and sprung there. The Grand Jury is dismissed now?

D: That is correct . . . (*Ibid.*).

FIG. 9.3a. John Dean's conversation on 15th September, 1972 (from Neisser, 1982a). Copyright 1982 W.H. Freeman & Co. Reprinted with permission.

On September 15 the Justice Department announced the handling down of the seven indictments by the Federal Grand Jury investigating the Watergate. Late that afternoon I received a call requesting me to come to the President's Oval Office. When I arrived at the Oval Office I found Haldeman and the President. The President asked me to sit down. Both men appeared to be in very good spirits and my reception was very warm and cordial. The President then told me that Bob—referring to Haldeman—had kept him posted on my handling of the Watergate case. The President told me I had done a good job and he appreciated how difficult a task it had been and the President was pleased that the case had stopped with Liddy. I responded that I could not take credit because others had done much more difficult things than I had done. As the President discussed the present status of the situation I told him that all I had been able to do was to contain the case and assist in keeping it out of the White House. I also told him there was a long way to go before this matter would end and that I certainly could make no assurances that the day would not come when this matter would start to unravel (*Hearings*, p.957).

FIG. 9.3b.   John Dean's recall of the conversation nine months later (from Neisser, 1982a). Copyright 1982 W.H. Freeman & Co. Reprinted with permission.

Neisser points out that, even considered as gist, hardly any of the recalled version is accurate. Nixon did not say the things he is reported to have said (e.g. asking Dean to sit down; that H had kept him informed of Dean's handling of the case; that he was pleased the case stopped with Liddy). Dean himself did not say that he could not take credit or that the matter might unravel later. Nevertheless, Neisser argues that Dean's account is correct at a much more general *thematic* level. They did discuss the cover-up and Nixon was clearly aware of it. Some of Dean's distortions, such as "The President asked me to sit down", can be seen as script-based intrusions, derived from an arriving-at-a-meeting script. Others are changes bringing the conversation into line with what (with hindsight) *should* have been said. For example, Dean would like to have warned the President that the cover-up might fall apart, because it eventually did. He would like the President to have appreciated what a difficult task he had. Under further interrogation, Dean repeated his statement in a way suggesting that he was recalling his earlier recall, rather than recalling the original conversation. Repeated reproduction, as Bartlett (1932) demonstrated, tends to produce constructive errors.

Dean's recall of the second conversation was more accurate. In this conversation, he made a more or less prepared speech warning the President of the precariousness of their position. Neisser points out a number of factors that might account for the superior recall of this conversation.

The original conversation took place only three months previously, so the time elapsed was shorter. Dean himself did most of the talking and had prepared what he wanted to say. There were only two participants instead of three. And, finally, the conversation conformed more closely to the way he wanted to present himself. It was apparent that Dean had often conflated or transposed different conversations. Many of the conversations were fairly similar in content, and were therefore remembered like repisodic events (see Chapter 6, p.148). Two findings emerge most strongly from this study. Firstly, recall is strongly influenced by motives, personality, and wishful thinking. Second, we need to distinguish several different levels of memory for conversation. Memory that is inaccurate at the lower levels of verbatim recall, and even at the level of gist recall, may still be correct at a much more general level of thematic recall.

Pezdek and Prull (1993) were concerned, in the wake of the Clarence Thomas-Anita Hill hearing, to assess gist and verbatim memory as a function of sexual explicitness and context. Subjects heard a five-minute dialogue between a man and a woman including target sentences that were either sexually explicit or neutral. The sentences were framed in either a consistent context (a singles bar) or an inconsistent context (a professional office). The researchers predicted that the sexual sentences would be recalled better because they would stand out from background sentences as surprising and distinctive, particularly in the inconsistent context. As predicted, and not too surprisingly, sexual sentences like:

"The girls in that movie had such tan bodies, creamy thighs, and breasts like watermelons"

were recalled and recognised better than neutral ones like

"It's said that it takes two lifetimes to master the art of fencing"

However, after a delay of 5 weeks, although the gist of sexually explicit sentences was still recognised well, verbatim recognition memory for both sexual and nonsexual material was very poor. The inconsistent context facilitated gist memory of sexual sentences, but not verbatim memory. The authors asked whether, based on these findings, it was likely that Anita Hill would have remembered sexual remarks made to her by Clarence Hill 10 years before. They suggested that, because the remarks were made in an office context, she might well have recalled the gist. However, to extrapolate from a delay of 5 weeks to one of 10 years seems risky.

Memory for Lectures and Seminars

In contrast to the study of John Dean's and Anita Hill's memory, other research has revealed that people do remember some kinds of utterance verbatim. Keenan, MacWhinney, and Mayhew (1977) examined memory for utterances made in the course of a linguistics seminar and discussion. They were interested in memory for pragmatic information, as well as memory for meaning and for surface structure. They distinguished between utterances with High or Low Interactional Content. Those with High Interactional Content (HIC) have a pragmatic role and a personal significance. They carry information about the speaker's attitude, beliefs, or relations with the listeners. Utterances with Low Interactional Content (LIC) are impersonal and factual. Examples are:

"I think you've made a fundamental error in this study" (HIC)
"I think there are two fundamental tasks in this study" (LIC)

The authors predicted that HIC utterances would be more memorable than LIC ones, and that people would be more likely to remember the exact wording of HIC utterances than LIC ones. This latter prediction was based on their intuition that the exact words are of critical importance in the interpretation of HIC exchanges, because choice of words determines whether such an utterance is polite or insulting, joking or serious.

Thirty hours after the seminar took place participants were given a recognition test with multiple choices including the original utterance reproduced verbatim (the target) and two foils, a true paraphrase of the original statement, and a new statement. As predicted, subjects recognised more HIC target utterances (56%) than LIC ones (19%). The difference betweeen recognition responses made to targets and recognition responses made to true paraphrases was taken as a measure of verbatim memory, because a true paraphrase can only be recognised as different from the original sentence if memory for the exact wording is preserved. For HIC sentences, recognition of targets exceeded recognition of true paraphrases by 38%. For LIC sentences, recognition of the verbatim target was only 1% more frequent than recognition of the paraphrase. In order to confirm that these differences were caused by the interactional role of the sentences, Keenan et al. (1977) carried out a control experiment. The HIC and LIC sentences from the original experiment were arranged in a list, and presented to new subjects who had not attended the original discussion. When the sentences were taken out of context in this way, they lost their interactional content, and this time the recognition test showed no difference between the sentences previously classified as HIC or LIC. Keenan et al. concluded that it is only when sentences have a pragmatic role and a personal significance for the hearer that they are remembered verbatim.

A similar result was obtained by Kintsch and Bates (1977) in two experiments on recognition memory for statements from a lecture. Figure 9.4 shows examples of statements made in two lectures, one on intelligence testing and one on psychoanalysis. These were divided into Topic statements, which made general points; Detail statements which supplied illustrative details; and Extraneous statements, which were jokes or announcements irrelevant to the main theme. These Extraneous statements, are similar to the HIC sentences in the Keenan et al. study in that they have interactional significance.

In Experiment 1, a recognition test was given two days after the lecture. Kintsch and Bates found that Extraneous statements were remembered better than Topic or Detail statements, which did not differ. Verbatim memory, as shown by the ability to distinguish between old statements and their paraphrases, persisted for all three types of statement, but, in line with the results of Keenan et al., subjects were more likely to remember the exact wording of Extraneous statements. A second experiment, with a five-day delay before the recognition test, produced substantially the same results, although verbatim memory was further reduced at this longer retention interval.

According to the predictions from schema theory, Topic statements should be remembered best because they are more important, more relevant and at a higher level of generality. However, Kintsch and Bates suggested a number of reasons why this did not turn out to be the case. In line with Brewer and Tenpenny's (personal communication, 1996) account of schema-based mechanisms (see Chapter 6), the Extraneous statements benefit from distinctiveness, standing out from the rest of the material. Both Detail and Extraneous statements are also more concrete than Topic statements, and, as can be seen from the example of an extraneous statement in the lecture on psychoanalysis, they may be richer in pragmatic information. The studies by Kintsch and Bates (1977) and by Keenan et al. (1977) converge in identifying pragmatic utterances as more likely to be remembered verbatim than factual ones.

Peper and Mayer (1978) studied the effects of note-taking on memory for lectures. In their study, one group of students took notes, the other group listened without taking notes. Those who did not take notes were better at remembering technical symbols and specific ideas, but the note-taking group were better at remembering the important general ideas, and their recall was more likely to include intrusions of relevant material acquired elsewhere. The act of note-taking therefore appeared to help the listeners to organise the material, to select higher-level information, and to integrate it with what they already knew. Those who listened passively were more likely to remember details verbatim, but had not grasped the main ideas so well. Kintsch and Bates did not report whether their students took notes during the lectures or not. Perhaps failure to recall the Topic statements was due to not taking notes.

An important point about memory for spoken information emerged from a study by Neisser (1988a). He held a series of weekly seminars and later tested students' ability to remember statements made in the seminars. Free

Sentence Category	Experiment 1	Experiment 2
	Topic Statement	
Old	The doctrine of natural biological evolution formed the rationale for Galton's study of the eminent families of Britain.	The closed energy model is still critical for the psychoanalytic approach to therapy.
Paraphrase	Galton compared the eminent families of Britain with the natural biological variations that figure so preeminently in the doctrine of evolution.	The psychoanalytic approach to therapy still depends critically on the concept of a closed energy system.
New	The inheritance of human intellect implied for Galton the practicability of supplanting inefficient human stock by better strains.	The concept of a limited energy system explains a great deal about neurotic development.
Paraphrase	None.	The development of neurosis can be explained in large measure by the concept of a limited energy system.
	Detail Statement	
Old	Galton was the brilliant younger cousin of Darwin.	Around 1887, Freud was working with Joseph Breuer, studying the method of free association.
Paraphrase	Darwin was the older cousin of the extremely intelligent Galton	Freud learned the method of free association from Joseph Breuer around 1887.
New	The phrenologists had tried to do the same thing before but failed.	In 1885, Freud spent time with Jean Charcot studying hypnosis as a clinical method.
Paraphrase	None.	Freud studied hypnosis as a clinical method under Jean Charcot in 1885.

Sentence Category	Experiment 1	Experiment 2
	Extraneous Statement	
Old	Isadora Duncan suggested to George Bernard Shaw that they should combine her beauty and his intelligence; Shaw however objected that the child might turn out with his looks and her brains.	Oh, speaking of anxiety, that reminds me. Marcia and I will not be able to answer questions between now and next Tuesday.
Paraphrase	Isadora Duncan told Bernard Shaw that she wanted a child from him in order to combine her beauty and his intelligence: Shaw, however, was afraid the child might get her brains and his looks.	Oh, speaking of anxiety, I forgot to mention that Marcia and I won't be answering questions until the exams are in on Tuesday.
New	The Spartans purposefully bred their strongest warriors with their most beautiful maidens, but in the end they became just as decadent as the Athenians, who had more fun all along.	In case I didn't mention it, Marcia and I will try to have the papers back to you a week from Tuesday.
Paraphrase	None.	Oh, if I didn't tell you before, Marcia and I plan to give you back the papers a week from Tuesday.

FIG. 9.4. Statements extracted from lectures on intelligence testing (Experiment 1) and on psychoanalysis (Experiment 2) (from Kintsch & Bates, 1977). Copyright 1977 American Psychological Association. Reprinted by permission of the author.

recall was tested first and cues were supplied if necessary, but students were able to respond "Don't Know" when they could not recall an item. The statements recalled were mostly at a general level, and specific information was less likely to be recalled. Although much of the material could not be remembered, subjects made very few errors. A recognition test was given after the recall test, and produced a very different pattern of results. When the subjects had to select an old target statement from two foils they made errors. Neisser also showed that recognition memory was distorted by attitude. Those students who, at a separate confidential interview, disclosed that they had a positive attitude toward Neisser as a teacher, selected foils in which he made helpful encouraging statements. Those who had negative attitudes attributed to him foil statements that were unhelpful and critical. This study underlines the fact that the recognition paradigm is an unnatural way to test memory for utterances and is liable to induce errors and distortions. If Kintsch and Bates had tested recall instead of recognition, they might well have found superior memory for Topic statements. If people are encouraged to report what they can remember and admit what they have forgotten, then memory may be sparse, but it is more likely to be accurate. Researchers tend to use recognition paradigms simply because these are much easier to score, but the memory that is elicited in recognition tests is more easily contaminated by attitudes, and by beliefs about what is plausible or probable.

Memory for Requests

Keenan et al. (1977) showed that pragmatic utterances were more likely to be remembered verbatim than purely factual statements that had no pragmatic function, and Kemper and Thissen (1981) obtained results showing that some kinds of pragmatic utterances are more likely to be remembered word-for-word than others. They focused on requests. The following examples show how these could vary in syntactic form (imperative, declarative, or interrogative); in the presence or absence of "please"; in the use of modal or auxiliary verbs like will, can, or should; and in the use of linguistic hedges and the indirect statement of wishes or needs. These factors combine to produce requests of varying degrees of politeness or directness:

Rake the leaves
Please rake the leaves
Would you rake the leaves
Why don't you rake the leaves
I think you should rake the leaves
I would like you to rake the leaves
I think the leaves need to be raked

Kemper and Thissen showed subjects cartoons. Each cartoon depicted a speaker-hearer pair of different status (e.g. a waiter-diner pair or a boss-secretary pair). In the caption a request was made for either an action or for money. When memory for the captions was tested, the results showed that the verbatim form of the request was most likely to be remembered if the wording violated normal social conventions, as in a low-status speaker using an impolite form to a high-status hearer (e.g. the waiter saying "Sit there" to the diner) or a high-status speaker using a super-polite indirect form to a low status hearer (e.g. the boss saying something like "I think it would be a good idea to type these letters"). These results indicate that pragmatic utterances that are surprising and distinctive are most likely to be remembered verbatim.

Memory for inferences

A study of memory for courtroom testimony by Harris (1978) showed that memory is influenced by pragmatic implications. In an earlier experiment (Harris & Monaco, 1976) sentences like:

The housewife spoke to the manager about the increased meat prices
The paratrooper leaped out of the door
were sometimes remembered as:
The housewife complained to the manager about the increased meat prices
The paratrooper jumped out of the plane

In these examples, the original version has been elaborated by inferential processes to unpack the pragmatic implications. When memory is tested, people often cannot remember what was explicitly stated and what was only implied. The same tendency was apparent in Harris' 1978 experiment simulating courtroom testimony. Subjects were told to pretend they were members of a jury, and listened to a five-minute account of a burglary. In a later recognition test, they claimed that statements were definitely true, and had been explicitly asserted, when in fact they had only been implied in the original testimony. These constructive errors occurred even when subjects were warned to avoid them. Explicit and implicit information appears to be integrated into a global memory representation of the meaning and cannot easily be distinguished. This phenomenon is further evidence of a bias toward remembering meaning and forgetting what has actually been said.

Memory Capacity for Spoken Information

How much information do listeners remember? How can information be structured or "put across" so that it is remembered better? What factors influence the amount of information that is recalled?

The Self-reference Effect

It is well established that recall is better for words that are judged with reference to the self than for words that are judged by other criteria, and it seems likely that the advantage for self-referring material extends to memory for conversation. Kahan and Johnson (1992) tested this idea. Pairs of female subjects held a conversation on general topics and then generated 20 adjectives, 10 that described themselves and 10 that described their companion. They reported these traits to each other and evaluated them as accurate or inaccurate. Two days later they were unexpectedly recalled and tested individually for free recall of the traits. They were also asked to recall who had generated each trait (the source) and who it referred to (the referent). Subjects recalled more of the traits they had generated themselves and their recall of what their partner had said showed a strong self-reference effect. That is, they remembered far more of what the partner had said about them than what the partner had said about herself, and even misremembered some traits that referred to the partner as referring to themselves. These findings confirm the intuition that the self-reference effect operates in conversation. People are particularly interested in what other people think of them and selectively remember what is personally relevant to themselves.

Weather Forecasts and Traffic Reports

Even when the information is impersonal, the amount that we recall may be affected by our interests and immediate concerns. Wagenaar (1978) has investigated how much people remember from radio broadcasts, using weather forecasts and traffic reports. Examples are shown in Fig. 9.5.

The weather report contains 32 idea units. The construction is complex. Information about time and place is interleaved, and there are no main

---

A weather forecast.
Forecast for tonight and tomorrow: In the evening in the southern part of the country a good deal of cloud, within the southeastern region some temporary rain, otherwise some cloudless periods but tomorrow, in the afternoon, some local showers, especially in the north and west regions. Wind moderate to strong, along the coast occasionally high to stormy earlier from the southwest, later veering to the northwest. Minimum temperature about 10°C, on the Wadden Shallows a few degrees higher. Maximum temperature from 16°C in the northwest to 22°C in the southeast regions.

A traffic report
On the following roads traffic jams are reported. A2 Den Bosch in the direction of Utrecht, between Outemborg and Vianen a jam of 6km. A27 Gorkum in the direction of Vianen, between Lexmond and Vianen, a jam of 3km. A29 Hellegatsplein in the direction of Rotterdam, at the entrance of Heinenoord tunnel a jam of 2 km . . .

FIG. 9.5.   Material used to test memory for radio broadcasts (from Wagenaar, 1978).

verbs. The traffic report (in full) contains 70 idea units and needs a detailed knowledge of geography to understand it. Memory was tested by cued recall, using cues like "clouds" or "location of jams". Memory for the weather report showed a ceiling of about eight idea units. The longer traffic report had a ceiling of 17 ideas. In general, the percentage of a message that was recalled declined with message length. Not surprisingly, drivers recalled the traffic report better than nondrivers.

A second experiment tested ability to remember preselected information. Before hearing the message, subjects were told they should try to remember those parts of the weather forecast relating to a particular region, or those parts of the traffic report relating to a particular route. The results showed that the subjects had difficulty in extracting and selectively storing the relevant parts of the weather forecast. Wagenaar (1978) pointed out that the complex structure made it difficult to select a part without first analysing the whole. Because of its simpler structure, selecting relevant information from the traffic report proved easier, and there was a 20% improvement in the amount recalled. The study highlights the importance of message structure and of prior knowledge in determining how much is remembered.

In another study of memory for weather forecasts (Wagenaar & Visser, 1979) compared a radio message (speech only) and three different kinds of television broadcast. The TV forecasts had different visual components, a talking head, a map with symbols appearing on it as the items were mentioned, and a map with a man pointing to the symbols. They found that the amount recalled was the same for the radio message and for the map with symbols. Both the talking head and the pointing man acted as distractors and actually impaired recall. The amount of information retained from weather forecasts is quite sharply limited and gimmicky visual aids are no help.

Doctor-patient Dialogues

Personal relevance and self-reference are not always enought to ensure good recall. When patients come away from consultations with their doctors they remember alarmingly little of the advice and information they have received. Ley (1978) has summarised the findings of various studies of memory for medical information and has shown that there are ways of presenting information that improve significantly the chances that it will be remembered. Estimates of how much people remember of what the doctor has told them range from 46% to 63%. Elderly people remember less than the young, and those with medical knowledge remember more than those who are medically naïve.

The patient's anxiety also affects how much is remembered. There appears to be a Yerkes–Dodson relationship between anxiety and forgetting.

Forgetting is greatest when anxiety is very low or very high, and intermediate levels of anxiety produce better recall. The amount of information given is linearly related to the amount recalled, with the percentage that is remembered declining as the total amount presented is increased. Although the perceived importance of the information does affect recall, patients do not seem to be very good at spontaneously selecting the most important elements of the conversation to remember. Memory for diagnostic information is best and memory for advice and instructions is poorest, although, in practical terms, this is the most important. This result appears to be largely due to a primacy effect. The first items of information are the best-retained, and many doctors present their diagnosis first. Ley's research showed that recall of advice and instructions could be improved from 50% to 87% if this information was presented first, and its importance was stressed. Accordingly, Ley generated six suggestions for doctors:

(1) Give instructions and advice first.
(2) Stress the importance of instructions and advice.
(3) Use short words and short sentences.
(4) Use explicit categories, stating, for example, this is the treatment you will need; these are the tests that will be done; this is what is wrong; this is what will happen to you; this is what you must do to help yourself. The doctor should announce each category in this way, and then supply the information.
(5) Repeat information.
(6) Be specific. For example, say "you must lose 7 pounds" rather than "you must lose some weight".

Four general practitioners adopted these suggestions and found a 10–20% increase in the amount of information retained.

Limits of Capacity

These studies reveal some of the constraints on memory for conversation. Speech is a rapidly fading continuous signal. The listener must perceive, interpret, and encode the message during the brief period it is available in working memory and before it has decayed or been displaced by the new material that is continuing to come in. Because conversations, lectures, and broadcasts almost always contain more information than people can remember or want to know, the listener must select what is important and discard what is redundant, irrelevant, or uninteresting. When the listener is equipped with prior schemas (e.g. the patient has medical knowledge, or the driver is familar with the routes), and when the new messages are well organised with the important elements clearly highlighted, this process of selective encoding can be achieved. When the message is poorly organised, the listener is forced to spend too long on interpretation and selection, and cannot keep pace with the input. In a lecture you can easily fall behind the speaker while trying to take notes and organise them under headings. In conversation, the listener has the additional task of generating contributions. You can easily miss what is being said while thinking of what you want to say yourself. On the other hand, interactive conversation has the advantage that you can ask the speaker to repeat the message or to speak more slowly. In dialogues, the speaker normally adjusts the style, amount, and rate of information to suit the listener.

MEMORY FOR TEXTS AND STORIES

We need to remember many different kinds of written information including poems and stories, factual texts such as newspaper articles or technical reports, letters, prayers, legal agreements, or instructions for operating the video-recorder or the washing machine.

The content of these different kinds of material spans the whole range of human experience and imagination and serves many different functions. Written information may be designed to entertain, to inform, to instruct, to convey emotions and states of mind, to preserve traditions and rituals. Most of the pragmatic functions of speech can also be served by writing. The speech acts described in the previous section should really be called *language acts* because they can be performed either in speech or in writing. Psychologists have rather lost sight of this pragmatic aspect of written language because research has concentrated on laboratory experiments, and has only explored a restricted range of written material, mainly consisting of formal texts. Memory for writen information in everyday contexts has been neglected. Outside the laboratory we use writing much more *pragmatically*. Consider the following examples:

IOU £30
4 pints, please
Gone to lunch, back at 2 p.m.
No Smoking
I am happy to accept you invitation . . .
I write to offer my sincere sympathy . . .

We use writing to promise, to request, to inform, to warn, to agree, to sympathise, just as, at other times, we use speech.

An important difference between laboratory research on memory for prose and stories and everyday life situations is that, in most experimental studies, subjects know that they will be tested so that learning is intentional. In everyday life we often read texts without deliberately trying to memorise what we read. Most of the information acquired from written material is acquired incidentally. Even when we read a newspaper article with interest, and with the intention of improving our knowledge of the topic, we do not always memorise as if preparing to be tested. Laboratory experiments usually test memory for short texts or stories of only a few hundred words after a single reading or a short study period, and testing usually takes place after a short interval. For these reasons, experiments on memory for prose and stories are not very similar to naturally occurring memory for written information and may not be representative.

There is obviously a close relationship between how we understand what we read, how we encode it, and how we remember it. The main focus of this chapter is on what is remembered, but the processes that create the memory representation have to be taken into account as well. Theoretical interpretations of memory for texts and stories are controversial and there are several different models that are currently debated.

The Role of Event Schemas

Recent studies of memory for texts and stories have emphasised the role of schemas. It is important, however, to distinguish between two different kinds of schema, which can be characterised as *event schemas* and *story schemas*. Event schemas consist of knowledge about the subject matter of the story. The event schemas activated in remembering a Trollope novel, for example, might include knowledge of Victorian social life and political history, foxhunting, country houses, and ecclesiastical preferment. Story schemas, however, consists of abstract, content-free knowledge about the structure of a typical story and are described in a later section. This section is concerned with the role of event schemas.

Some of the earliest studies of memory for stories were carried out by Bartlett (1932). He introduced the idea that schemas, or mental frameworks built up from prior knowledge and experience, are influential in shaping and moulding the memory of a story. In one of his experiments he asked people to read through a story about Indians in British Columbia, called *The War of Ghosts*. The last part of the story was:

> So the canoes went back to Egulac, and the young man went ashore to his house, and made a fire. And he told everybody and said: "Behold I accompanied the ghosts, and we went to fight. Many of our fellows were killed, and many of those who attacked us were killed. They said I was hit, and I did not feel sick".
>
> He told it all, and then he became quiet. When the sun rose he fell down. Something black came out of his mouth. His face became contorted. The people jumped up and cried. He was dead.

Below is a reproduction of the story, produced immediately afterwards:

In the evening he returned to his hut, and told his friends that he had been in a battle. A great many had been slain, and he had been wounded by an arrow: He had not felt any pain, he said. They told him that he must have been fighting in a battle of ghosts. Then he remembered that it had been queer and he became very excited.

   In the morning, however, he became ill, and his friends gathered round. He fell down and his face became very pale. Then he writhed and shrieked and his friends were filled with terror. At last he became calm. Something hard and black came out of his mouth and he lay contorted and dead.

Bartlett identified three schema-induced processes: sharpening, levelling out, and rationalisation. Examples of the changes resulting from these processes can be found in this reproduction. Sharpening can be seen in the details that are added by elaborative inferences (the young man being wounded *by an arrow*; the idea that his audience was composed of *his friends*; the fact that they *gathered round* and *were filled with terror*). Rationalisation is evident in the substitution of *had not felt any pain* for *did not feel sick* as being more consistent with an arrow wound. Some details (*the canoes, making a fire*) have been levelled out or omitted. According to Bartlett, the story has been revised in memory to fit with the cultural expectations and experience of the reader.

Representing Stories in MOPs

In a more recent development of Bartlett's (1932) ideas, the generalised knowledge structures conceptualised by Schank (1982b) as MOPs (see Chapter 6, p.144) have been applied to the representation of stories in memory. These more flexible schemas allow the information from different but related stories to be encoded within the same high-level MOP. Thus, the same high-level schema can guide the understanding and retrieval of information from similar but different lower-level schemas. Seifert, McKoon, Abelson, and Ratcliff (1986) initially tested this idea using stories that shared the same theme or TOP, but not the same schema or MOP. One story told of a graduate student who was treated badly by his college and decided to leave and enrol elsewhere; the first college then promised to treat him better but he had already fixed up to move. The second story concerned a secretary engaged to her boss; when the boss delayed setting a date for the wedding the secretary went off and married someone else although the boss then begged her to stay. Both stories are related by the common theme of "closing the barn door after the horse has bolted". Subjects read both stories followed by a list of test sentences for verification. Seifert et al. predicted that when a test sentence describing the resolution of one story was preceded by a test sentence describing the analogous resolution of the other story, verification would be faster, facilitated by the shared representation. No such facilitation occurred, so it was concluded that cross-story reminding does not occur at this high thematic level. However, in a follow-up experiment, McKoon, Ratcliff, and Seifert (1989) explored the effect of shared MOPs using stories that had a good deal of contextual and semantic information in common. An example can be seen in Fig. 9.6. In a recognition test, the target phrase "slowly strolled out into the cool ocean" was preceded by either a MOP-related prime from the same story (found an empty space for her blanket); a MOP-related prime from the other story (spread her towel in a dry place); or an unrelated prime (looked over the wine list and ordered Chablis).

The results showed that MOP-related primes from the different story produced as much facilitation as MOP-related primes from the same story, thus providing strong evidence that related stories share the same MOP and that cross-facilitation of retrieval can take place.

MOP: Going to the beach

First story
Linda decided to skip work on Thursday and go to the beach. At the beach, Linda found the parking lot to be surprisingly full for a weekday, but she eventually found a spot. The beach, too, was crowded, but Linda was still able to spread her towel in a dry place close to the water. Not wanting to get a sunburn, Linda put on some suntan lotion. After lying on her towel for some time, Linda was getting hot so she decided to take a dip, and dove into the refreshing water. After a short swim, Linda toweled off and packed up her things for the long walk to the car.

Second story
Because the sun was shining so brightly, Nancy decided to spend the day by the sea. When she had gotten to her favourite seaside spot, Nancy parked her car under a tree. Nancy walked quickly over the hot sand until she found an empty space where she could lay her blanket. Hoping to add some color to her pale skin, Nancy splashed on some baby oil. The sun was very strong, so Nancy decided to get up and go for a swim. Nancy slowly strolled out into the cool ocean. When she finally felt water-logged, she headed back to her blanket. She dried off for a while in the warm sun and then dressed for the trip home.

FIG. 9.6.   Two stories sharing the same MOP: Going to the beach (from McKoon, Ratcliff, & Seifert, 1989). Reprinted by permission of Academic Press, Inc.

Remembering without a Schema

The contribution of prior knowledge schemas to story recall has been strikingly demonstrated in several different experimental paradigms. The results are particularly dramatic when people are asked to remember a story for which they have no pre-existing event schema.

Bransford and Johnson (1973), in a classic series of experiments, showed that people remember very little of a text if they do not have an appropriate schema. Bransford and Johnson constructed two texts, which are reproduced here. The first text describes a situation so bizarre that without some clues the readers could not work out what was going on.

> If the balloons popped the sound would not be able to carry, since everything would be too far away from the correct floor. A closed window would also prevent the sound from carrying since most buildings tend to be well insulated. Since the whole operation depends on a steady flow of electricity, a break in the middle of the wire would also cause problems. Of course, the fellow could shout, but the human voice is not loud enough to carry that far. An additional problem is that a string could break on the instrument. Then there would be no accompaniment to the message. It is clear that the best situation would involve less distance. Then there would be fewer potential problems. With face to face contact, the least number of things could go wrong.

One group of subjects who were given no context and no title with this text remembered an average of only 3.6 ideas out of 14. Another group were shown a picture illustrating the text which made it clear that a guitar player standing in the street is trying to serenade a lady in the top floor of a high-rise building, and has used balloons to hoist a loudspeaker up to her level. Those who saw this picture *before* they read the text remembered 8 ideas. Using a "serenade" schema they were able to make sense of the text and encode a meaningful representation. Showing the picture *after* the text had been read failed to improve performance.

The second text describes a commonplace situation, but in such an abstract and obscure way that it was again difficult to know what it was about:

> The procedure is actually quite simple. First you arrange things into different groups. Of course, one pile may be sufficient depending on how much there is to do. If you have to go somewhere else due to lack of facilities that is the next step: otherwise you are pretty well set. It is important not to overdo things. That is, it is better to do too few things at once than too many. In the short run this may not seem important, but complications can arise. A mistake can prove expensive as well. At first the whole procedure will seem complicated. Soon, however, it will become just another facet of

life. It is difficult to foresee any end to the necessity for this task in the immediate future, but one can never tell. After the procedure is completed, one arranges the materials into different groups again. Then they can be put into their appropriate places. Eventually they will all be used once more, and the whole cycle will have to be repeated. However, that is part of life.

One group of subjects read this text with the title "Washing clothes" supplied before they read it; a second group had the title supplied after reading the text; a third group had no title at all. With no title, subjects recalled only 2.8 ideas out of 18. With the title supplied before reading the text, the score increased to 5.8 ideas, but the group given the title after reading recalled only 2.7 ideas. These results clearly indicate that when new information cannot be related to an appropriate schema, very little is remembered. Of course, the situation is a very artificial one. In everyday life there are normally plenty of contextual cues to tell us what schemas are appropriate for what we read. Written material comes with titles, headings, and illustrations, and the situation in which it is encountered also gives clues as to its content. Bransford and Johnson's (1973) material violates the co-operative principles by being deliberately obscure and failing to make clear what is being referred to.

Further evidence that possessing the appropriate schemas is crucial for recall comes from an experiment by Herrman, Crawford, and Holdsworth (1992), which showed that schemas can be gender-biased. A passage of text similar to that used by Bransford and Johnson was presented to male and female subjects;

> The procedure is actually quite simple. First, you rearrange the pieces into different groups. Of course, one pile may be sufficient depending on how much there is to do and the degree of design complexity. The next step is to get the necessary tools and implements. It is important not to overdo things. That is, work slowly and on one part at a time. In the short run this may not seem important but complications can easily arise. A mistake can be costly as well as time-consuming. At first, the whole procedure may seem complicated. However, after a while it will seem quite simple. Find the corresponding parts. Make sure they are the right pieces and attach them. At first they may not seem to fit. Do not worry, they will if you are patient, work carefully and follow our diagrams and directions. Once the smaller pieces are attached, the next step is to find which parts should now go together. Once you have done this, fit them together in the appropriate positions. Things should start to look good now. Add all the remaining pieces and extras—you now have your finished product.

Before they read the passage, half the subjects were given the title "How to make a shirt" and half were given "How to make a workbench". When recall was tested there was a clear gender bias. Women remembered more ideas if they had been given the title about shirtmaking; men remembered more if they thought it was about making a workbench. In addition to this kind of gender bias it has also been shown that schemas and scripts are culturally biased. Harris, Lee, Hensley, and Schoen (1988) presented four stories about people performing everyday activities. The stories concerned going on a bus, buying a record album, eating breakfast, and buying travel tickets, and they were either culturally consistent for the North American subjects or culturally inconsistent. For example, the "foreign" version of the "going on a bus" story described the Brazilian system of entering at the rear, paying a cashier seated in the middle, and exiting at the front. At subsequent testing, memory was distorted toward the subjects' culture-specific knowledge and this reliance on culturally-biased scripts was more marked when testing was delayed.

In theory, the use of schemas could facilitate several different stages of memory. At the encoding stage, the active schema guides the selection of relevant information, influences the interpretation, and integrates the new information with pre-existing knowledge. At the retrieval stage, schemas may facilitate recall by supplying an organisation or plan to direct search, and a framework that enables forgotten material to be reconstructed. The finding that schemas are only effective if they are activated before reading texts suggest that the role of a schema is to facilitate the encoding stage, and not to facilitate retrieval, but the results of other experiments suggest that the primary role of schemas is to aid retrieval.

Changing Schemas

Anderson and Pichert (1978) constructed an ingenious text that described how two boys played truant from school and spent the day at the home of one of them because the house was always empty on Thursdays. The text described the house as an older house set in attractive grounds well back from the road. Various possessions of the family such as a 10-speed bike, a colour TV, and a rare coin collection were mentioned, as well as features of the house such as its leaking roof and its damp basement. Altogether, the text contained 72 ideas that were rated by a separate set of subjects for importance to *either* a home-buyer (e.g. leaking roof, attractive grounds) *or* a burglar (coin collection, nobody home on Thursdays).

Half the experimental subjects were told to read the text from the point of view of a home-buyer, and half were told to read it from the point of view of a prospective burglar. After a 12-minute filled delay subjects were asked to recall the text in as much detail as possible. Following a further 5-minute delay, a second attempt at recall was made. This time, half the subjects were given a changed perspective. Home-buyers were switched to the burglar perspective, and vice versa. The rest of the subjects retained their original perspective and simply recalled the material again trying to retrieve more information.

The point of this design is that if schemas operate only at the encoding stage, supplying a new, different schema at the retrieval stage should not assist recall. In fact, however, subjects who shifted to a different schema recalled 7% more ideas at the second attempt than at the first. Those who did not change perspective actually recalled slightly less. In a follow-up experiment, Anderson and Pichert showed that the change of schemas influenced *which* ideas were remembered as well as the amount recalled. Recall of ideas that were important according to the new schema increased by 10%, and recall of ideas that were important to the previous schema, but not the current one, declined by 21%. Anderson and Pichert also recorded subjects' introspections about how they had studied and recalled the information. Most said they had selectively attended to the schema-relevant facts while they were encoding. However, the results demonstrated that they must also have encoded some schema-irrelevant facts because they were able to retrieve these later. The subjects reported that at retrieval they used the new schema to search memory and recover additional information. Why, then, did Bransford and Johnson's (1973) subjects fail to benefit when they were given the Serenade schema or the "Washing clothes" schema after reading the text at the time of recall? The answer must be that the Bransford and Johnson texts were too incomprehensible to encode at all. If information has not been encoded in the first place, then a schema supplied at the time of recall cannot guide retrieval.

Everyday experience suggests that the role of schemas is flexible and dynamic, and affects encoding, storage, and retrieval. If I read a newspaper article about government plans for changes in taxation, I encode the information within my pre-existing schema for the tax system. When I want to discuss it later with a friend, I use this schema to search for and retrieve the new information. But information that is originally encoded within one schema can sometimes be completely reinterpreted in the light of new information and transferred to a new schema. Films, novels, and television advertisements often have surprise twists built into the plot that require reorganisation of this kind. The apparently innocent nice guy turns out to be the villain, or what seems like a travelogue turns out to be an advertisement for beer. In these examples, changing schemas seems to involve recoding the information that is in store, rather than just using a different search plan to retrieve it.

Inferential Processes in Memory for Texts

Garnham (1985) distinguishes three kinds of inference that are made in comprehending texts:

(1) *Logical inferences* that follow from the meaning of words. For example, the statement that a robin is a bird logically entails that it is an animal.
(2) *Bridging inferences* that relate new information to previous information are made in understanding text as well as in understanding conversation.
(3) *Elaborative inferences* extend and enrich new information with previously acquired schema-based knowledge about the world.

Bridging Inferences

Clark and Haviland (1977) claimed that language users operate with a "given-new contract". An utterance (or a written statement) usually contains both given information (old information that is known to both the speaker and the hearer) and new information (information that is known only to the speaker). According to the given-new contract, the speaker or writer indicates the given information, making clear who or what is being talked about so that the hearer or reader can identify the topic, and then supplies some new information about it that is true and is not already known to the hearer, as in "Have you heard about Harry? He's gone to Majorca". Violations of the given-new contract (like just saying "He's gone to Majorca", without indicating the given information) are liable to elicit responses like "What are you talking about?" from the hearer.

Sometimes the hearer must refer back to a previous utterance in order to identify the given information. The utterance "Jane left early" refers back to the previous statement "The film was boring". The hearer has to infer that Jane left the cinema to escape further boredom. This type of inference that links new information back to a given topic is called a *bridging inference*. One of the main functions of a bridging inference is to identify what is being referred to. Sometimes, the bridge that has to be built is between one part of the text and another part and consists in *resolving an anaphor*. An anaphor is a word or phrase that has the same referent as an expression in another part of the text. The most common example is when a proper name or noun phrase ("Mr Biggs" or "the baker") is used initially and a pronoun ("he") is used later. Understanding that "he" and "Mr Biggs" refer to the same person is called resolving the anaphor. Resolving the anaphors is a necessary part of achieving *local coherence* within the text. Anaphors are often easily resolved by simple linguistic rules or conventions. Given the gender of the pronoun there may be only one possible referent. Where there is more than one possibility, the antecedent that immediately precedes the anaphoric expression is assumed to be its referent. In some cases, though, anaphors are more difficult to resolve and depend on prior knowledge of the topic, as in the example:

"Ann polished the wardrobe with a soft cloth and oiled its hinges."

The reader depends on knowledge of wardrobes and cloths to identify the referent of "its". Here is another example from the instructions for assembling a gas fire:

"For tapered inset fires place the four loose radiants in the gaps between the fixed radiants and the rear board turning them until they locate in their lower position."

It is (fairly) clear that "them" refers to the loose radiants because presumably the fixed radiants could not be turned.

Elaborative Inferences

Sometimes what is written is not intelligible on its own and inferences are required to elucidate the meaning. In today's *Times* the headline "Blue Berets Face Changing Role" would not make much sense unless I knew that the United Nations personnel wear blue berets and that the United Nations, after 50 years, is currently seeking to redefine its objectives. Prior knowledge is required to infer and make explicit what has only been stated vaguely or elliptically.

We also use prior knowledge to infer causes, consequences, and instruments as in the following examples:

The house burned to the ground (*it was on fire*).
The fragile glass was dropped on the stone floor (*it broke*).
She cut a slice of bread (*with a knife*).

It is not clear whether these kinds of inference are constructed on-line as the material is being read, or whether they are constructed later in order to answer questions or reproduce the information. The fact that people are often unable to distinguish between information that has been explicitly stated and information that has been inferred (as with the pragmatic implications discussed on p.255) suggests that inferences are built into the memory representations as they are encoded. However, the finding that inferred items can be effective cues for eliciting recall is more difficult to interpret. In a study of instrumental inferences, McKoon and Ratcliff (1981) showed that "ladle" was an effective cue for retrieving a sentence about stirring the soup, although it had been inferred, not explicitly stated. People may have inferred that the soup was stirred with a ladle when they first read the sentence, or they may have only made the inference when the cue was supplied. It is possible that we make some inferences at the time of encoding if they are obvious ones, or if they are necessary to make sense of the material. Other inferences, which are not so obvious or not so necessary, may only be made as a result of later probing.

Trabasso and Suh (1993) investigated how causal inferences are made. Causal inferences generally involve connecting two clauses and depend on the reader's knowledge of physical and psychological causality. Knowledge of goals and plans is thought to be central because they motivate people's actions. It has sometimes been claimed that causal inferences can only be made between sentences that are adjacent in the text but this study showed clearly that global causal inferences linking sentences that were distant from each other could be made. Trabasso and Suh asked subjects to read a story aloud and "talk aloud" their understanding of the story sentence by sentence. Verbal protocols from two subjects are shown in Fig. 9.7. Sentences from the text are shown in italics followed by the subjects' comments and interpretations. The protocols show elaborations of goals and intentions and causal explanations. These causal inferences constituted answers to "why" or "how" questions and included both local and global inferences. It was also noted that the occurrence of causal inferencing was the best predictor of long-term retention of the story. In this study, inferences were clearly being made on-line in working memory, but forcing subjects to talk aloud as they read may have induced comprehension processes that do not usually occur.

Whether inference-making is immediate or deferred, it is abundantly clear that what people remember when they have read a text goes beyond the words they saw on the page. The memory representation of the new information is integrated with prior knowledge of the topic and schemas supply missing information, probable values, and plausible interpretations.

Some Problems with Event Schemas

What Do We Remember?

When we remember written information, what is it that we remember? In the discussion of memory for conversation it was noted that, although people remember the meaning or gist of what has been said better than they remember the actual wording, they do retain the surface form of some utterances. Clark and Clark (1977) stated that memory for texts and stories is not so much memory for meaning as memory for the products of comprehension. This view fits well with some of the introspective evidence. When I try to recall a novel that I read a few months ago, I remember none of the exact words. My memory of the characters and events is detailed, but consists largely of products of comprehension

Talk-aloud protocols

Hierarchical version (Ellen)
Betty went to the department store.
Betty decided that, you know, something really fancy would suit, show her feelings toward her mother, instead of some homemade card that may or may not look any good.
Betty decided to knit a sweater.
Uhm . . . it's a very difficult gift to knit so it again shows that Betty really cared for her mother and wanted to give her something special, more than just a little rink-a-tink thing children with no money sometimes end up giving.
Betty selected a pattern from a magazine.
Well, this is her just going around and trying to find out exactly what type of sweater she's going to make.
Betty followed the instructions in the article.
This would be expected because if you are going to find a pattern for something to make you're going to follow the instructions.
Finally, Betty finished a beautiful sweater.
Well, she's done making her sweater now, that's it.
Betty pressed the sweater.
This shows that she really cares about how the sweater looks like, she wants to give her mother something special.
Betty folded the sweater carefully.
This is again, she really cared how the sweater looked. She felt it should mean something, giving it to her mother.

Sequential version (Maria)
Betty went to the department store.
She probably had money with her and with planning to buy a present at the department store.
Betty decided to knit a sweater.
She probably got the idea from seeing her friend, she thought wow that's really pretty what my friend is making, I'll make one too.
Betty selected a pattern from a magazine.
She probably went and looked through the magazine specifically and find the pattern knowing that that's a good place to find those.
Betty followed the instructions in the article.
So she started knitting the sweater. I can imagine her knitting it for someone else because it's right after the mother's birthday, but it doesn't necessarily follow.
Finally, Betty finished a beautiful sweater.
She is probably very proud of it. Probably wanted to show it to her friend.
Betty pressed the sweater.
I'm not sure what that is. Maybe that's to keep it from stretching or something.
Betty folded the sweater carefully.
O.K. She is probably gonna store it in the closet or something.

FIG. 9.7. Talk-aloud protocols from two subjects in the process of understanding a story. Ellen produced a hierarchical version and Maria produced a sequential version (from Trabasso & Suh, 1993). Reprinted by permission Ablex Publishing Co.

such as the visual images that I constructed from the author's descriptions, and the emotions that were produced by the story.

However, introspection also suggests that in some cases memory for the surface form of written information persists as well. When I try to remember the contents of a letter from a friend I remember some of the phrases exactly. I also remember the colour of the writing paper, the handwriting, and the pattern and position of words on the page. These introspections are inconsistent with a schema theory interpretation of memory for texts, whereby we remember only generalised ideas and not exact words or details.

Schema theory also has difficulty in accounting for experimental results that show that exact wording is sometimes retained. For example, Yeko-vich and Thorndyke (1981) found that some sentences from narrative stories could be distinguished from true paraphrases after a delay of one hour; and Hayes-Roth and Thorndyke (1979) found that a verbatim cue (i.e. one of the original words) facilitated recall of a sentence better than a synonym cue. Alba and Hasher (1983) have argued that the retention of lexical and syntactic information, and schematically unimportant details, as shown in these and other experiments, is not compatible with a schema theory account of memory for text. However, there are several different versions of schema theory.

The Schema-plus-Tag Model

The Schema-plus-Tag version developed by Graesser and Nakamura (1982) and described in Chapter 6, pp.139–141, can account for the fact that schema-irrelevant information is often retained better than schema-relevant information. According to this model, the memory trace of a text consists of a pointer to the relevant generic schema. This schema is copied into the specific memory trace that interrelates both the prior knowledge and the new knowledge, including what was explicitly stated and what was only implied, plus a set of tags, one for each item of atypical or irrelevant information. They tested this model in an experiment in which subjects read a restaurant script which contained both typical and atypical actions:

> That evening Jack wanted to go out to dinner so he called a friend who recommended several good restaurants. Jack took a shower, went out to his car, picked up his girlfriend and gave his girlfriend a book. He stopped the car in front of the restaurant and had the valet park the car. They walked into the restaurant and sat for a few minutes in the waiting area until the hostess escorted them to their table. They sat down at the table, the waitress introduced herself, and they ordered cocktails. Jack talked to his girlfriend and asked how her job was doing, and they decided what to eat. Jack cleaned

his glasses, paid the bill and bought some mints. Then they left the restaurant and drove home.

The schema-irrelevant, or atypical, actions in this script were judged to be:

Jack gave his girlfriend a book.
He asked his girlfriend how her job was doing.
He cleaned his glasses.
He bought some mints.

The other actions were judged to be typical in a restaurant script. (It is strikingly evident from this material that what is judged to be typical of a visit to a restaurant is highly culture-specific.) The results showed that recognition was better for atypical actions than for typical ones at all retention intervals. Recall was initially better for atypical actions, but after 3 to 4 days typical actions were recalled best. According to the model, typical actions are difficult to recognise as people do not know whether the actions are familiar because they were read in the test passage, or whether they are familiar because they are part of previously acquired schematic knowledge. Atypical actions that are specifically tagged are therefore easier to recognise. After short delays, atypical actions are also easy to recall, but, as the retention interval increases and memory for the passage decays, retrieval depends increasingly on schema-guided search, so schema-relevant actions are more likely to be recalled. This modified version of schema theory can therefore account for the fact that memory for schema-irrelevant facts, that are odd or unexpected, is sometimes superior to memory for facts that are more routine and predictable. However, it can be argued that the Schema-plus-Tag theory simply redescribes these findings, whereas Brewer and Tenpenny's (personal communication, 1996) explanation in terms of how schemas direct attention to inconsistent items and create a background that makes them distinctive (see Chapter 6) provides a better explanatory framework.

Word-perfect Memory

In memory for prose and stories, the general rule appears to be that the meaning, the gist, the most important and most relevant facts are best-remembered, although a few odd details may also be retained. The exception to this pattern is material that has been deliberately "learned by heart". In this case, verbatim memory can persist for a lifetime, although it may take numerous repetitions to acquire. Rubin's (1977) study of very long-term verbatim memory revealed that this type of memory is quite different from memory for the gist of texts.

During the course of their education, most people learn by heart some material such as prayers and psalms, poems, and speeches from Shakespearean plays. Rubin tested American college students' memory for the Preamble to the Constitution, the 23rd Psalm, and Hamlet's soliloquy. The students reported having memorised these items some time in the past, but had not recalled them during the past 3 to 4 years. When memory was tested, it was apparent that very long-term verbatim memory displays regular and distinctive characteristics. There were very few constructive errors. Recall was either perfect or it failed completely. For the Preamble and for Hamlet's speech, most people recalled about 20 words from the beginning and then came to a full stop. Recall of the psalm showed a less marked primacy effect, and was influenced by the rhythmic structure. Recall is clearly organised in terms of surface structure, as breakdowns occur at syntactic boundaries. The surface units are remembered as associative chains, and, if one link in the chain is missing, the rest is usually lost. However, where the material has a clear rhythmic structure, this can serve to reinstate items beyond the gap. This phenomenon, which appeared in Rubin's data, is also clearly seen when somebody is repeating a poem and fills a missing line with dummy syllables and then recovers the words on the next line as in:

Up the airy mountain,
down the rushy glen,
di dum, di dum, di dum,
di dum, di little men.

This very long-term verbatim memory acquired by arduous rote-learning is clearly quite different from the kind of memory for texts and stories that is acquired from a single reading.

Hunter (1979) has analysed the memory feats of story-tellers and singers in nonliterate societies. Theirs are not word-perfect verbatim recitals but reconstructions according to formulaic rules. The story-teller introduces new ingredients to suit the current audience while adhering to a traditional structure. The use of strong rhythms and group-chanting aids retrieval.

Mental Models

Johnson-Laird (1981) argues that stories are represented as mental models (described in Chapter 2, p.52). According to this view, the reader (or listener) constructs a mental model of the events recounted in the story. To construct a mental model of a story is to *imagine what was happening.* A mental model is a global representation integrating information from different parts of the story. It is constructed on-line as the story unfolds, and is a dynamic representation of the scene, characters, and events, incorporating spatial, temporal, and causal relations. Construction of the model depends on two factors, coherence and plausibility. Coherence is a function of the pattern of co-reference, which is the way that successive sentences are linked together in a chain of anaphoric references with, for example, a pronoun in one sentence referring back to a name or noun-phrase in the preceding sentence. Plausibility is the product of temporal, spatial, and causal relations that may be stated or inferred by the reader. The distinction between these factors is illustrated in the following Johnson-Laird examples:

Version A
Jenny was holding on tightly to the string of her beautiful new balloon. She had just won it and was hurrying home to show her sister. Suddenly, the wind caught it and carried it into a tree. The balloon hit a branch and burst. Jenny cried and cried.

Version B
She had just won it and was hurrying home to show her sister. Suddenly, the wind caught it and carried it into a tree. Jenny was holding on tightly to the string of her beautiful new balloon. Jenny cried and cried. The balloon hit a branch and burst.

Version C
Jenny had just won a beautiful new balloon and was hurrying home to show her sister. Suddenly, the wind caught it and carried it into a tree. Jenny was holding on tightly to the string of her balloon. She cried and cried. It hit a branch and burst.

Version A is coherent and plausible. The referents of "she" (Jenny) and "it" (the balloon) are perfectly clear. The temporal sequence of events, their causes and effects, are plausible in that they are consistent with prior knowledge. In Version B, the sentences are jumbled. The referential continuity is broken, and it is hard to resolve the anaphors, and the sequence of events seems implausible (she is still holding the string after the balloon has been carried away). In Version C, the referential continuity is restored by changing around the proper names or noun-phrases and the pronouns, but the sequence is still implausible.

Johnson-Laird reported experimental results that showed that stories in well-structured versions (like A) are remembered much better than those in jumbled versions like B. Stories like Version C are remembered slightly better than B, but still worse than A. There are also many other studies demonstrating that when stories are presented in a disordered sequence, they are re-ordered in memory and recalled in a more coherent sequence. Mandler (1978) presented the Beach story, shown in Fig. 9.8 in two different versions, a canonical one and an interleaved one. Subjects who

Canonical version
One day at the beach, a girl named Tammy was building a sand castle, while her friend Susan played with a frisbee. Suddenly, a big wave rolled right out of the ocean and splashed over the edge of Tammy's castle. Tammy thought her sand castle would be washed away and she wanted to save it. Quickly she took more sand and made the walls thicker. Then she made a ditch in front of the castle. The next wave filled the ditch but it didn't reach the castle. Soon the tide went out and Tammy's castle was safe from the waves. Meanwhile, a big black dog grabbed Susan's frisbee and started to chew on it. Susan was afraid of the dog but she wanted to get her frisbee back. She got a sandwich out of her lunchbox and held it out for the dog. The dog dropped the frisbee and ran off with the sandwich. Susan didn't get any lunch that day but she was happy that she had saved her frisbee.

FIG. 9.8a. Canonical version of the beach story (from Mandler, 1978).

Interleaved version
One day at the beach, a girl named Tammy was building a sand castle, while her friend Susan played with a frisbee. Suddenly a big wave rolled right out of the ocean and splashed over the edge of Tammy's castle. Meanwhile, a big black dog grabbed Susan's frisbee and started to chew on it. Tammy thought her sand castle would be washed away and she wanted to save it. Susan was afraid of the dog but she wanted to get her frisbee back. Quickly Tammy took more sand and made the walls thicker. Then she made a ditch in front of the castle. Susan got a sandwich out of her lunchbox and held it out for the dog. The next wave filled the ditch but it didn't reach the castle. The dog dropped the frisbee and ran off with the sandwich. Soon the tide went out and Tammy's castle was safe from the waves. Susan didn't get any lunch that day but she was happy that she had saved her frisbee.

FIG. 9.8b. Interleaved version of the beach story (from Mandler, 1978).

received the interleaved version tended to separate the sandcastle episode and the dog episode in their recall, and produced a version closer to the canonical one. Mandler interpreted these findings in terms of story schemas (see the next section), but they can also be taken as evidence for a mental model.

The mental model account has the advantage of relating verbal information to the real world. It also fits well with the introspective evidence that memory for stories includes visual images instantiating spatial relations. However, it does not account for the fact that some of the verbatim surface form of a story is sometimes retained.

Story Schemas and Story Grammar

A story schema consists of knowledge about the way stories are typically structured, which is derived from repeated experiences of hearing and reading stories. A limitation of story schemas is that they apply only to a subset of stories, like fairy stories, which follow a fairly traditional pattern, and not to other kinds of texts, like newspaper articles, essays, or novels and stories with a more innovative structure. Story schemas are content-free, that is, they are independent of the particular topic of the story. Unlike the mental model, which depends heavily on concrete knowledge of the real world, story schemas are highly abstract. They incorporate knowledge of story structure that reflects the existence of a story grammar. A story grammar is a system of rules that define the units of which a story is composed, and the relationships between these units. These are rewrite rules, which can be used to rewrite the story into its component units, and to rewrite each component into subcomponents. One version of these rules is shown later. Other, slightly different versions, have also been put forward, for instance by Mandler (1984):

> *Story*: setting + theme + plot + resolution.
> *Setting*: characters + location + time.
> *Theme*: goal.
> *Plot*: episode(s).
> *Episode*: event + reaction.
> *Resolution*: event or state.
> *Goal*: desired state.

These rewrite rules generate a hierarchical tree structure with subordinate nodes branching out from the superordinate node (Story). To illustrate this structure, take the story of Jenny and the balloon. This can be decomposed into the numbered statements:

(1) Jenny was holding tightly to the string of her beautiful new balloon
(2) She was hurrying home to show it to her sister
(3) A gust of wind caught it and carried it into a tree
(4) It hit a branch
(5) and burst
(6) Jenny cried and cried

Figure 9.9 shows how the rewrite rules generate a hierarchical tree structure for this story.

Story-grammar models generate several empirical predictions about memory for stories. The most important ones are that stories conforming

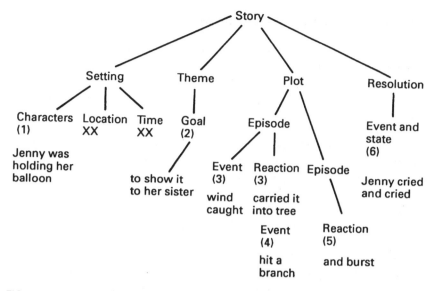

FIG. 9.9.   A hierarchical tree structure for the story of Jenny and her balloon.

to the canonical structure and the canonical rules will be remembered better; disordered stories will be re-ordered in memory; elements of the story that are higher in the hierarchy will be remembered better than elements at the lower or terminal nodes; and missing components will tend to appear as intrusions in recall. Mandler (1984) reviews experimental results that confirm these predictions and suggest that story schemas have psychological reality.

Hierarchical Models

The main objection to story grammars is, as we have already noted, that they only fit a restricted type of story. A more general hierarchical model, which applies to descriptive texts as well as stories, has been proposed by Kintsch and Van Dijk (1978) and Van Dijk and Kintsch (1983). The hierarchy in their model reflects the importance or generality of different propositions in the text. Instead of a text being fitted to a pre-existing, content-free framework based on knowledge of story structure, this kind of hierarchy is generated on-line by the semantic content of the particular text that is being read.

According to this model, sentences are analysed into propositions. The reader establishes local coherence by analysing the co-reference and relationships between adjacent sentences, and also establishes global coherence by extracting a set of *macropropositions*. These macropropositions constitute the summary, or gist, of the text and form the top level of the hierarchy. Macropropositions are the product of integrative processes that take place within a short-term memory buffer as the text is being read. Approximately three propositions are retained in the buffer at any one time and carried forward. These are the most recent and those judged to be most important. Attempts are made to integrate the buffer contents with successive incoming propositions by finding elements of overlap between them. If these fail, attempts are made to integrate the new propositions with knowledge stored in long-term memory. Inferences may be required to construct these integrative links. The macropropositions that are extracted by these processes are those that have the greatest amount of argument overlap with other propositions in the text and those that are judged most important. They have been retained in the buffer and carried forward through successive cycles of processing. The precise details of how the reader determines "importance" are not clearly specified, but may depend on the reader's own goals and expectations. In the hierarchical representation that results, important story elements, such as the theme and the resolution, are represented as macropropositions at high-level nodes. Detailed actions embedded in the plot are represented at low-level nodes.

Many studies have shown that people are more likely to remember the high-level propositions than the low-level ones (e.g. Meyer, 1975). Yekovich and Thorndyke (1981) undertook an investigation of this so-called *levels effect*. They designed their study to show whether the levels effect originates from preferential encoding of important propositions or from retrieval strategy. On the Kintsch and Van Dijk model, important propositions are remembered better because, at the encoding stage, they are continually being reinstated in the buffer and carried forward to a fresh cycle of processing. Alternatively, the privileged recall of high-level propositions might arise at the retrieval stage if the hierarchical representation functions as a top-down retrieval plan. If search starts at the top of the tree, retrieval probability would decrease as it progressed downward through the levels.

In their experiment, Yekovich and Thorndyke presented four stories that were similar in general structure, but different in content. The stories mapped on to hierarchies that had between 5 and 16 levels. Testing was either immediate or after a delay of one hour. A free-recall test was followed by a recognition test, in which subjects had to identify test statements as original, true paraphrase or false paraphrase. The results showed a clear levels effect in recall, but not in recognition. Figure 9.10(a) shows how the proportion of propositions recalled decreased from Level 1 (the top of the hierarchy) to Level 5+ (the bottom levels). But Fig. 9.10(b) shows that there is no clear relationship between levels and recognition. The finding that the levels effect is confined to recall shows that the hierarchy influences retrieval, not encoding. Differential

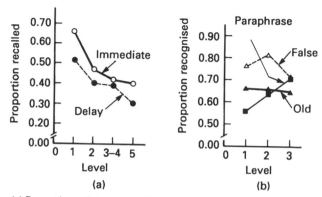

FIG. 9.10. (a) Proportions of correct recall of story propositions as a function of level in the organisation hierarchy. (b) Proportion of correct recognition of different item types as a function of level in the organisational hierarchy (from Yekovich & Thorndyke, 1981).

encoding would be reflected in recognition as well as in recall. Top-down search was also demonstrated by the finding that the probability of recalling a subordinate proposition, given that its superordinate had been recalled, was higher (0.63) than the probability of recalling a subordinate proposition, given that its superordinate had not been recalled (0.24).

In the data from the recognition test, shown in Fig. 9.10(b), the proportion of correct rejections of true paraphrases reflects the persistence of verbatim memory. This proportion was larger for propositions at the lowest levels of the hierarchy. Thus, although macropropositions are remembered in terms of their meaning, lower level specific details are more likely to be remembered verbatim. Overall, the results of this study are consistent with texts and stories being represented in a hierarchical organisation in memory, which is used to guide search when the material is recalled. It is interesting to note that a similar levels effect emerged when Stanhope, Cohen, and Conway (1993) tested very long-term retention of information from a novel. After delays of up to three years superordinate information was remembered better than subordinate information.

CONCLUSIONS

Memory for spoken and written material typically relies heavily on selectivity and interpretation. We select and remember the information that is personally important to us and we use the current context and prior knowledge to interpret the goals and intentions of the speaker or writer. We tend to remember the gist of what has been said or written rather than the actual words, but we also derive and remember the subtext that is composed of implications and nuances. In memory for speech, the social context influences the interpretation and emotion and motivation play an important part. Written texts are usually divorced from a contextual setting so that interpretation depends more on linguistic decoding. Event schemas contribute to the comprehension and recall of both spoken and written material, but more detailed models have been proposed to explain the representation of written material. Which account of memory for texts and stories is most convincing, mental models or hierarchical representations? Mental models have the intuitively appealing feature of treating memory for stories and memory for real world events as essentially the same. However, the temporal, spatial, and causal relationships represented in mental models are not necessarily hierarchical, so mental models have difficulty in accounting for the emergence of the levels effect in recall. In considering alternative models it should be emphasised that the type of representation may well vary with the aims and intentions of the reader. Most of the empirical findings come from experiments in which readers expect to be tested. One possibility is that hierarchical organisation is a mnemonic strategy developed to meet the task demands in this kind of situation. Mental models might give a better account of how we read a novel for interest and for pleasure in everyday life, when the aim is to understand rather than to remember. We want to make sense of what we read, to picture the scenes and events described, to evaluate the intentions and goals of the characters, to guess the outcome. We do not normally read stories in order to memorise them, or in the knowledge that we will be tested. Research on memory for written information needs to look at naturally occurring examples more closely before we can judge the power, scope and appropriateness of different models.

10 Memory for Thoughts and Dreams

It is a mistake to think of memory as if it were always a representation of the external world or a record of events and actions that really happened. Remembering is a private internal process that often consists of recalling thoughts, plans, imaginings, ideas, fantasies, and speculations. This aspect of everyday memory tends to be neglected and it is easy to see why. It is difficult enough to study everyday memory when it relates to real, objectively verifiable events, it is a great deal more difficult when it is concerned with subjective events that are only accessible by introspection. However, it is particularly impressive that ingenious and quite rigorous methodologies for studying internally generated memories have been devised and developed.

Even when memories are of external events they are often second-hand memories. That is, they are not the first original representations of the events but are re-recalled memories that may have been remembered and contemplated many times since the original experience. This chapter examines two examples of internally generated remembering. Both are concerned with the relationship between external reality and internally generated memories. Reality monitoring is concerned with our ability to distinguish between memories of real events and memories of events that have only been imagined, planned, or thought about. In memory for dreams, the issues centre on the relationship beween real life and the content of dreams and on the reasons why dreams are so difficult to remember.

REALITY MONITORING

What is Reality Monitoring?

In Chapter 2, the section on prospective memory examined factors that determine whether we remember to carry out an intended action, but that chapter did not include another important aspect of prospective memory— the ability to remember *whether* an action has already been performed or not. It is no good remembering to do something if you do not know whether you have already done it. You need to be able to distinguish between the memory of an action and the memory of an intention or plan to perform that action. Sometimes it may be difficult to distinguish these two kinds of memory, as, for example, when you are uncertain whether you actually locked the door or turned off the lights, or whether you intended to do so but have not in fact performed the actions. The ability to make such distinctions is part of a more general ability that has been called reality monitoring (Johnson & Raye, 1981).

Reality monitoring is the ability to discriminate between externally derived memories that originate from perceptions and internally derived memories that originate from imagination. External memories represent events that really occurred, objects that were perceived, actions that were performed, words that were spoken or written. Internal memories are of events that have only been imagined, actions that were planned, considered or intended, words that were thought but never uttered. The ability to distinguish between what goes on in the head and what goes on in the real world, between fact and fantasy, is a crucial aspect of competence in everyday life.

Reality monitoring is itself only part of a more general ability known as source monitoring (Johnson et al., 1993). In addition to the internal-external discriminations demanded by reality monitoring we often need to discriminate between memories derived from one external source and memories derived from another external source, as, for example, in remembering who told us a particular piece of information, or in which newspaper we read a news item.This kind of external–external source monitoring was also discussed in Chapter 7, p.200, but here we are concerned with internal-external source discrimination.

The distinction between internal and external memories may seem a trivially easy one. You may think that nobody in their right minds can fail to make it. But second thoughts bring to mind many examples of confusions and uncertainty. Many memories are in fact a mixture of perceived and self-generated material. When you remember events from your early childhood, for example, what you remember of the original experience is typically overlaid and interwoven with what you have heard other people tell you about it, and with your own imaginative reconstructions, which have filled in gaps, and may have transformed the original event. Similarly, we often hear someone telling an anecdote that improves with each retelling, being imaginatively embellished by the narrator until he or she can no longer distinguish truth from fiction. Cognitive psychologists are in agreement with these common sense observations. From Bartlett (1932) to Bransford and Franks (1972), the constructivist view of memory has emphasised the role of elaboration, interpretation, and reconstruction based on prior experience and stored knowledge. On this view, memory is not a direct copy of the physical information received through the senses. Remembering is not just a process of passively receiving impressions, but of creatively constructing a representation. Of course, some memories are much closer to an exact copy and some rely to a greater extent on construction, but most externally derived memories contain some elements that are reconstructions that have filled in the gaps and may have transformed the original event. As a result, the distinction between externally and internally generated memories is by no means clear-cut.

Failures of Reality Monitoring

Despite the fact that many memories are a joint product of external and internal elements, people are usually fairly competent at distinguishing fact from fantasy. Failures of reality monitoring are characteristic of schizophrenia, dementia, delirium, intoxication, and other states of mental abnormality that involve hallucinations or obsessions. In these disorders there is usually inability to distinguish between the real and the imaginary in current experience as well as in past experience. Developmental psychologists have also suggested that in early childhood the borderline between what is real and what is imaginary is not a clear one (Flavell, Flavell, & Green, 1983), and there is evidence that reality monitoring deteriorates in old age (Cohen & Faulkner, 1988b, 1989). However, failures of reality monitoring are not confined to abnormal or immature, or elderly individuals. In everyday life imperfect reality monitoring is quite common in normal intelligent adults, and is an important source of errors in judgements, in action, and in belief.

Some types of slips of action and failures of prospective memory occur because the memory of an action planned is confused with the memory of an action performed. For example, you may be uncertain whether you have added salt to the soup or only thought of doing so. Sometimes you may find yourself thinking "I know I thought I must remember to lock the back door but did I actually do it?", or you may be confused about whether you said something or only intended to say it. Misplacing objects can result from a similar kind of confusion. You thought you put the missing keys, diary, or whatever in the usual place, but in fact you only planned the action and never carried it out. Occasionally, you may be uncertain whether an event really happened or whether it occurred in a particularly vivid dream. We all have these experiences.

It is important to note that the direction of confusion affects the type of error that is made. When a plan or imagined act is mistaken for the memory of a real act, the consequence is an omission error. If you mistakenly think that you have already put salt in the soup or locked the door, the result is that the soup is left unsalted or the door unlocked. If, on the other hand, the memory of a performed action is mistaken for the memory of a plan, the result is a repetition error. The soup gets salted twice, or a second dose of medicine is taken, or you go to lock the door only to find it already locked. Everyday experience and questionnaire data suggest that these errors are more commonly associated with routine, frequently performed actions. With these actions the difficulty often lies in deciding whether a memory of performing the action is today's memory or yesterday's. (A colleague told me she often had to check whether her toothbrush was wet in order to decide whether she had brushed her teeth.) Strictly speaking, these are not errors of reality monitoring but problems of temporal dating. It is not so much a question of distinguishing between plan and action as between a recently performed action and a less recent performance of the same action.

Repetition Errors

Koriat, Ben-Zur, and Sheffer (1988) attributed repetition errors, when people repeat an action because they are unaware that they have already performed it, to defective output monitoring. He distinguished between two modes of output monitoring, on-line cancellation and retrospective judgements. On-line cancellation processes may operate to erase or tag a plan once it has been executed, just as I might strike out or tick the items on a shopping list when I have bought them. Or, executed plans may simply lose activation so that they are unlikely to be reactivated. In the absence of cancellation processes, retrospective checks may establish whether an act has been performed. These checks may be external or internal. We can check the external consequences by tasting the soup, examining the toothbrush, or trying the door handle. Alternatively, we can carry out an internal check, examining the memory trace of the act and making a reality-monitoring judgement about it.

Another type of reality-monitoring error affects judgements of frequency. The judged frequency of occurrence of a particular event may be inflated if that event is frequently imagined. The internally generated memories are added to the externally derived ones. Johnson (1985) suggests that people's subjective estimates of how often they have been ill or unhappy could be influenced by the frequency with which episodes of illness or unhappiness have been thought about: thus depression can reinforce itself.

Reality Monitoring and False Memories

The accuracy of reality monitoring is an issue that has assumed particular importance in the context of concern about recovered memories. When people "recover" memories of abuse that they suffered in childhood, they make a reality-monitoring judgement that these events actually occurred. In some cases it appears that these are false memories that have been constructed by the patient on the basis of suggestions from a therapist, and the claim that they are real recovered memories represents a failure of reality monitoring. This issue was discussed in more detail in Chapter 6, p.163.

Models of Reality Monitoring

Johnson and Raye (1981) have put forward a model to explain how reality-monitoring decisions are made, and they and their colleagues have tested the predictions of the model in a series of experiments. According to this model, there are two ways in which external memories can be distinguished from internally generated ones.

Evaluation of Qualitative Attributes

The first method depends on the evaluation of qualitative features of the memory trace. The differences between the two kinds of memory trace are illustrated in Table 10.1.

TABLE 10.1
Qualitative Differences between External and
Internal Memories

Attributes	Memories	
	External	Internal
Contextual attributes space and time	+	−
Sensory attributes visual, auditory, haptic	+	−
Detail and complexity	+	−
Coherence	+	−
Schematic Quality	−	+
Cognitive operations imaging, reasoning, decision processes	−	+

A plus sign indicates that an attribute is more likely to be present.

External memories are characterised by being relatively richer in sensory attributes such as sound, colour, and texture. They are set in a context of time and place of occurrence and other ongoing events, and are more detailed. Internal memories are more schematic and lacking in sensory and contextual details. They are also more likely to contain traces of the cognitive operations (such as reasoning, inferring, imaging) that generated them. According to the model, the origin of a memory can generally be determined by the extent to which it possesses these characteristics. Figure 10.1 shows how memories are evaluated according to the amount of contextual information they incorporate. However, qualitative differences would not invariably provide a clear indication of origin. Some internal memories can be unusually vivid and detailed. Shepard (1984) has pointed out that the memory representations generated for prospective planning must be accurate and detailed if they are to be any use. If you are mentally planning how to change the furniture around, or deciding whether you can get into a parking space, or whether a particular wallpaper would look well in your living room, you need to be able to generate internal representations that are a good match with external reality. And, of course, failures of reality monitoring confirm that internal and external representations can be sufficiently alike to be confused with each other.

Coherence and Plausibility

For memories that fall in the region of uncertainty in Fig. 10.1, Johnson and Raye (1981) suggested that different methods of evaluation could be employed. One method is to invoke criteria of coherence and plausibility. External memories ought to make sense in terms of our knowledge of

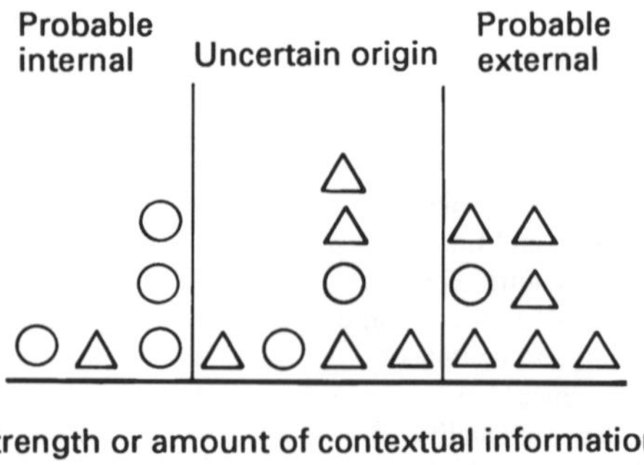

FIG. 10.1.   Representation of a set of decision rules for judging the origin of a memory on the basis of the amount of contextual information it includes (triangles – externally derived memories; circles – internally derived memories) (from Johnson & Raye, 1981).

the world. Internal memories, like fantasies and dreams, can sometimes be recognised because they violate natural laws or conflict with other knowledge. A dream in which you can fly or are invisible is unlikely to be true, and if the fantasy in which you tell your boss exactly what you think of him were a real event you would be out of a job. Similarly, recovered memories of being abducted by aliens in space ships lack credibility. People can sometimes check on the reality of a memory by trying to recall supporting context. If you can remember that when you locked the back door the key was stiff, and the cat was on the wrong side, the memory is probably of a performed action and not an imagined one. Another criterion is based on confidence. People appear to operate a strategy that has been called the "It had to be you" effect (Johnson & Raye, 1981). This strategy is used to determine whether a memory is of an action performed by oneself or by someone else. People assume that if the memory was something they had done or said themselves, they would be quite confident about its origin ("I'd know it if I'd done it"). If they are not confident they attribute the action to another person ("It has to be you").

Experimental Evidence

Johnson and her colleagues have tested this model of reality-monitoring processes in a series of experiments, manipulating the attributes of internal and external memories and observing the effects on reality-monitoring judgements.

The Effect of Qualitative Similarity

Johnson, Raye, Wang and Taylor (1979) tested the prediction that people who are unusually good at forming vivid and detailed visual images should be poor at making reality-monitoring judgements because the vividness of their self-generated images would make them qualitatively similar to externally derived memories. Conversely, people who are poor at imaging should be better able to distinguish their vaguer images from real memories. Prior to the experiment, subjects were divided into good and poor imagers on the basis of scores in a test requiring them to recall visual details of a picture they had seen. (In fact, this was a test of visual memory rather than of visual imagery and was not altogether appropriate for the rationale of this experiment.) In the experimental session, subjects were shown pictures of common objects, but interspersed with the pictures were trials in which they were given the name of an object and told to imagine it. The number of times a particular object was displayed as a picture, and the number of times it was imagined, was varied. Later, subjects were unexpectedly asked to judge the number of times each picture had been actually seen, ignoring the times it had been imagined. As predicted, for good imagers, the judged frequency was inflated by the number of times they had imagined the item. Poor imagers were less affected. Apparently, rich imagery makes reality monitoring more difficult.

The Role of Cognitive Operations

The cognitive content of memories has also been manipulated in several experiments. The experimenters worked on two assumptions:

(1) that the more difficult an item is to generate in thought, the greater the amount of cognitive operations that will be present in the memory trace; and

(2) that the greater the amount of cognitive operations in the trace, the more easily it will be recognised as self-generated.

In one experiment, Johnson, Raye, Foley, and Foley (1981) compared subjects' ability to identify which words they had generated themselves and which words had been generated by the experimenter. The words were instances (e.g. "dog") generated in response to category cues (e.g. "animal"). When a first letter cue was added to the category cue (e.g. "animal, d"), the identification of origin was less accurate. Johnson et al. (1981) argued that the added cue elicited the response automatically and so reduced the need for cognitive operations in generating the response, and the reduced cognitive component made the memory harder to identify as self-generated. This interpretation rests on the distinction between automatic and attentional processes described on p.39, and the idea that automatic processes occur without involving cognitive operations such as search and selection. In a further experiment, Johnson et al. found that it was also harder to identify the origin of highly typical (and hence more easily elicited) instances of a category than to identify the origin of more unusual instances. So, for example, a subject who generated the typical instance "apple" to the category cue "fruit" would be more likely to mistake its origin than one who generated "pomegranate".

Johnson (1985) pointed out that the recall of memories under hypnosis can be explained in terms of the reality-monitoring model. It has been shown (Dywan & Bowers, 1983) that attempts to enhance recall by hypnosis yield more false memories. Johnson suggested that memories generated under hypnosis may be like dreams. They have great vividness, but because they are produced without the exercise of cognitive control, they would lack any trace of cognitive operations. Internally generated false memories might then be indistinguishable from genuine externally derived memories.

Further evidence in support of the general principles of Johnson and Raye's (1981) model comes from Anderson's (1984) study. She compared Johnson's claim that errors in reality monitoring are caused by confusability of the memory traces, and an alternative explanation, whereby origin information is coded directly on the memory trace in the form of a tag and errors occur when the tag is lost. According to the confusability explanation, different kinds of self-generated memories, such as memories of performed actions and memories of imagined actions, are more similar to each other, and less similar to the other-generated memory traces derived from other people's actions. The confusability explanation predicts that errors should reflect a gradient of similarity. That is, the greater the similarity between origins, the greater the probability of confusing them. The origin tag explanation, on the other hand, predicts that all types of confusion would be equally likely because, once a tag is lost, origin identification must be pure guesswork. Her experiments used simple line-drawings as stimuli. Subjects had to trace the drawings (the Perform condition), imagine tracing them (Imagine), or watch someone else trace them (Look). She found that subjects were most likely to confuse the more similar self-generated memories (Perform and Imagine) than to confuse the self-generated memories with other-generated (Look) memories. She concluded that these results were consistent with Johnson and Raye's model. Subjects judged the origin of memories by evaluating qualities of the trace rather than by inspecting origin tags.

The Phenomenological Approach

Johnson and her colleagues have found further support for her model of reality-monitoring by studying phenomenological judgements about memories with different origins (Johnson, 1988; Johnson et al., 1988; Suengas & Johnson, 1988). They asked subjects to remember real or imaginary autobiographical events and then rate these memories for factors such as sensory qualities, emotions, supporting events, and spatial and temporal details. In another study they asked subjects to perform an action (having coffee, wrapping a parcel) or to listen to a description of these events and imagine doing them. Ratings of the memories for the real and the imagined actions were then compared. These ratings revealed clear differences. Real memories received higher ratings for sensory qualities and had more details of the setting. Differences were also apparent in the rate of forgetting and the effects of rehearsal. The clarity of imagined memories declined faster than the clarity of real memories and the difference between real and imagined memories increased over time, but rehearsal of the emotional quality of the memories blurred the difference. These studies demonstrate how phenomenological evidence can be strengthened by manipulating factors, such as retention interval and rehearsal, and noting whether the phenomenological ratings conform to the theoretical predictions.

Some of the effects reported by Johnson and her colleagues are not very large, and in some cases there is no independent evidence that the attempt to manipulate the nature of the mental representation and covert processes was successful. Nevertheless, a substantial body of confirmation for her model has accumulated.

Developmental Studies of Reality Monitoring

Some developmental studies have explored age differences in reality monitoring ability. Foley, Johnson, and Raye (1983) tested 6-, 9-, and 17-year-olds in a task that required them to discriminate between words that had been said and those that had been heard (Say vs. Listen), or between those that had been said and those that had been thought (Say vs. Think). The young children had no difficulty in the say-listen condition in discriminating between what they had said themselves and what someone else had said. They were also able to discriminate between words spoken by two different speakers (i.e. two external sources), but 6-year-olds were more likely to confuse the two self-generated sources, saying and thinking. Foley and Johnson (1985) also noted a similar developmental pattern in memory for the origin of actions. The younger children distinguished doing and watching, but not doing and imagining. It has been suggested that instead of being unable to discriminate between internal sources, young children have problems when two sources were very similar. To test this, Roberts and Blades (1995) devised a task in which the perform condition required children to hide counters under objects and the imagine condition required them to pretend to do so. This requirement was intended to ensure that the imagining did actually occur. Both conditions involve internal sources and both actions were very similar. In a surprise memory test the children were told the names of the objects and asked whether each was in a real or a pretend hiding place. The results showed no difference between children and adults in the proportion of confusions, so, clearly, children are not necessarily unable to distinguish between reality and fantasy and the preconditions for age effects in reality-monitoring judgements remain to be established.

At the other end of the developmental spectrum, Cohen and Faulkner (1988b; 1989) found that elderly people made more false positive errors in a reality monitoring task. They were more likely to misidentify actions they had only imagined, or actions that had not occurred at all, as ones they had performed themselves. There was evidence that elderly people have a lower criterion for deciding that a memory is a "real" externally derived one, but age-related deficits in the very young and very old may also be partly due to failure to encode distinctive features on the memory trace.

None of these experiments are very closely analogous to reality monitoring in everyday life, and Cohen and Faulkner noted that the self-rated incidence of reality-monitoring errors in daily life correlated only weakly with errors in their experimental task. In the laboratory tasks, when words are used as stimuli, they are isolated words occurring without context and do not form part of a meaningful message. When actions are the stimuli, they are not goal-directed and do not form part of an overall plan schema. Most of the experimental tasks are not sufficiently like naturally occurring instances of reality monitoring for us to be able to draw conclusions about how people normally distinguish internal and external memories in everyday life.

MEMORY FOR DREAMS

Dreams are a common element of everyday life, but are seldom mentioned in the literature on everyday memory. Yet most people are interested in the content of their dreams, puzzled by the elusive quality of memory for dreams, and fascinated by the strange relationship between the events they experience in real life and the echoes of these events in their dreams. Also, for the cognitive psychologist, interesting questions arise about how far memory for dreams conforms to the same theoretical principles as waking memory or whether it is fundamentally different. An account of memory in everyday life cannot be complete unless it includes memory for dreams because a substantial proportion of our everyday lives is spent in sleeping and dreaming. Moreover, a few cognitive psychologists are beginning to realise, somewhat belatedly, that the relationship between memory and dreaming poses many interesting and important questions that a comprehensive model of cognition should be able to answer. Memory is involved at three different stages of dreaming. First, memories of previously experienced real events are incorporated and represented within dreams, so memories form the content of dreams. Here, questions arise about what determines which particular memories are selected and reproduced in dreams and the extent to which they are distorted. Second, memory processes are at work within the dream, organising, sequencing, and monitoring the dream narrative. At this stage, the issues centre on how far these processes in dreams are similar to the same processes in waking cognition. The third role of memory comes at the stage of dream recall. On waking, we remember only a very small proportion of our dreams, so the most important questions are why dreams are so difficult to recall, and why some individuals remember dreams more often and in more detail.

Until the 1950s, the study of dreaming was largely confined to the psychoanalysts, notably Freud, Jung, and Adler. Their approach was primarily clinical and Freud is associated with his attempt to interpret dream symbolism in terms of sexual and aggressive impulses in infancy and anxieties about these impulses. However, Freud's classic work *Interpretation of Dreams*, first published in 1900, includes a surprisingly modern cognitive model of dreaming and a detailed review of the existing literature on dreaming that addresses many "cognitive" questions. Freud was concerned with cognitive issues about how dreams are generated and the degree of coherence within dreams. His observations included information about the content of dreams, the relationship of the dream content to the previous day's events, and to the life history and personality of the dreamer, as well as the psychological associations made by the dreamer to the dream content.

Despite these rich and perceptive observations, cognitive psychologists have been slow to interest themselves in dreaming, and in 1953 the neuroscientists took over from the psychoanalysts. Aserinsky and Kleitman (1953) published their ground-breaking findings about the association between dreaming and rapid-eye-movement (REM) sleep. REM sleep is found in all mammals. In humans, on average about two hours of a normal night are spent in REM sleep in periods lasting from 5 to 40 minutes and becoming longer later in the night. However, the physiology of REM sleep has not provided a complete explanation of dreaming as some REM sleep occurs without dreaming, and some dreaming occurs without REM sleep. On about 80% of occasions when people are woken from REM sleep they are able to report an ongoing dream. It seems likely, therefore, that some REM sleep occurs without concomitant dreaming, and this conclusion is reinforced by the fact that REM sleep is found in neonates and decorticates, where dreaming is thought to be improbable (Goodenough, 1978). Dreaming has also been found to occur in nonREM (NREM) sleep (Herman, Ellman, & Roffwarg, 1978), although the amount of dreaming is substantially less. It is also debatable whether dreaming takes place in the sleep-onset state. Vogel (1978) has noted that the borderline between dreaming and the kind of fantasising that takes place in the sleep-onset state is not a clear one: There is dream-like imagery, known as hypnagogic imagery, with decreasing control of mental activity and decreasing awareness.

What the discovery of the strong correlation between dreaming and REM sleep has achieved is to provide a methodology for dream research. Previously, researchers had to rely on diaries in which people recorded their dreams at home, but the accumulation of data by this method is slow because people typically report only two or three dreams each week. By contrast, when subjects are brought into the laboratory to sleep and are awakened during REM sleep, several dream reports can be collected each night. The laboratory method also has other advantages. Although home-dream reports tend to be of vivid, emotional, and bizarre dreams, these turn out to be misleadingly unrepresentative. REM-sleep wakings produce more mundane, realistic, coherent, and well-formed dreams which are nothing like the weird and strange dreams in the home-dream reports (Cavallero & Foulkes, 1993). In the laboratory, the conditions of recall can be controlled and manipulated so that the effect of distractions and delay intervals can be systematically assessed and pre-sleep stimulation can be presented so as to study its effect on dream content. It has become possible, therefore, to apply the methods of cognitive psychology to dream research and to search for commonalities between memory processes in waking life and memory processes in dreams. However, dream research is still entirely dependent on self-reports, and there is no way in which dreams can be judged as accurate or not accurate. Studies are usually restricted to very small numbers of subjects (perhaps because sleeping in a lab and being woken up several times a night is not an attractive prospect), and results have tended to vary from one laboratory to another. For whatever reason, cognitive psychologists have so far shown rather little interest in dream research.

The Origins of Dream Events

It is sometimes possible to trace the source of dream events to correspond-ing real events that have occurred in waking life. Thus, the dream is, at least to some extent, composed of memories. Alternatively, the dream event may be a reflection of a real event that is anticipated. Freud acknowledged that many dream events are echoes of experiences in recent days, including unsolved problems and preoccupations. Some have their origin in ongoing sensory or somatic events like a rattling window or a bout of indigestion, but, in his view, almost all dreams contain an element of wish fulfilment. Freud also emphasised that many dreams are related to childhood experiences and he cited cases where childhood memories that were completely inaccessible in waking life surfaced in dreams.

Researchers have studied the degree of correspondence between the real and the dream event and the temporal relationship between the two. Battaglia, Cavallero, and Cicogna (1987) compared the origins of dreams occurring in the sleep-onset state with REM dreams. The sleep-onset state is closer to real life on the continuum between waking and dreaming, and their research suggested that sleep-onset dreams contain more memories of recently experienced events that have an identifiable spatial and temporal context than REM dreams do: 10 subjects were awakened either within three minutes of falling asleep or in REM sleep and were asked by the experimenter "What was going through your mind just before I called you?" The dream report was recorded and divided into thematic segments. The dreamer was then asked to identify the origins of the dream events. These were divided into day residues (events that occurred the previous day), recent residues (events that occurred during the past year), and remote residues (events that occurred more than a year previously). Memories in sleep-onset dreams show a typical retention curve and most have clear origins in autobiograpical episodes of the last few days. REM dreams appear to be more like constructed narratives, less closely related to real life, and drawn from a wider time span.

A comparison between REM and NREM dreams by Foulkes, Bradley, Cavallero, and Hollifield (1989) also suggested that the different physiological states give rise to different types of dream. They compared two REM dreams and two NREM dreams reported by each of 16 young men. They concluded that REM dreams are more elaborated and include a broader range of mnemonic origins, including episodic memories, general knowledge, and self-knowledge. In their study, judges scored the degree of correspondence between the dream report and the real life source identified by the dreamer. They found that REM and NREM dreams did not differ in the number of identified sources but NREM dreams showed closer correspondence.

Of course, it is often impossible to identify any origin in waking life for the content of a dream. Antrobus (1978) pointed out that dream events may be, as Freud maintained, a symbolic or metaphorical representation of real events or, alternatively, the dream may be a distorted representation of the waking event. Freud's theory of dreaming claimed that "dream thoughts" were completely transformed by "dream work". In this case, there is scope to try to determine whether the distortion or transformation arises randomly or is due to systematic cognitive operations. Antrobus believes that the dream and the corresponding real event share common organisation and relational features, and has supported this view with evidence from a study in which subjects were trained, when awake, to associate a tone with a particular vignette. The tone was then presented when the subject was asleep and the sleeper was subsequently wakened and asked to provide a dream report. In one example, the subject learned to associate the tone with a vignette of a man cutting the bark of a tree with a cane knife. When the tone was presented during sleep the subject dreamed of himself cutting a pie with a kitchen knife, so here there was a high degree of correspondence between the pre-sleep event and the dream event. Cipolli, Battaglia, Cavallero, Cicogna, and Bosinelli (1992) also studied the incorporation of pre-sleep stimuli into dreams. They gave subjects lists of phrases to study before sleeping and found a high proportion were reproduced in subsequent dreams, although in a considerably distorted form. In one example, the phrase "the sword is pulled from the stone" gave rise to the dream report "I was trying to pull the cork from the bottle", thus preserving the relationship but changing the components. Antrobus has suggested that the distortion of reality that occurs in dreams can be accounted for if there is a disruption of the link between visual features and semantic features. Dreams often seem to contain bizarre and contradictory elements, and this hypothesised disruption might explain the kind of contradiction cited by Antrobus in which a dream character is identified by the dreamer as his brother but as having the appearance of a little girl. It is clear from these examples that methods exist for studying the mechanisms underlying the correspondence, or lack of correspondence, between dream and reality. Given the attention that cognitive psychologists are currently devoting to issues about accuracy and distortion in waking memory, it is of particular interest to speculate whether the same mechanisms operate in dreaming.

Organisation and Monitoring within Dreams

De Witt (1988) has argued against what he calls the "hallucinatory movie" view that characterises dreaming as a passive sensory experience so that dreaming is like watching a movie. This idea is consistent with introspective reports that dreams seem to be revealed or discovered rather than self-generated. Like a movie, dreams often have characters, places, and actions in meaningful scenarios, and there is often a narrative plot that has continuity and development. However, in opposition to the hallucinatory movie view, De Witt has put forward the "impaired consciousness model". According to this model, the dream is actively constructed and is at least partly under the dreamer's control, but normal processes of reality construction and reality monitoring are impaired or inoperative. De Witt's conclusions were based on students' responses to a questionnaire about characteristics of their dreams. Ten attributes of dreams are listed, and the percentage of respondents whose dreams exhibited these attributes are shown in parentheses:

(1) Visual images are vague and unstable (46%).
(2) Factual information is "just known" without any evidence (56%).
(3) Bizarre occurrences are accepted as normal (67%).
(4) Events are grossly misinterpreted (e.g. a group of people in a swimming pool was accepted as a maths class) (46%).
(5) There are abrupt shifts of continuity and scene changes (70%).
(6) The dreamer assumes different identities (59%).
(7) The dreamer has multiple points of view, often inconsistent with each other (62%).

(8) Prior events within the dream are invented (e.g. the dream began in a drug store but later the dreamer "remembered" it beginning in a sick friend's house) (46%).

(9) Earlier parts of the dream are distorted (36%).

(10) Events that are anticipated or feared turn into actual happenings within the dream (e.g. the dreamer saw a cliff-edge, was afraid of falling, then did fall) (60%).

These attributes are not consistent with dreams being passively experienced, but rather suggest construction and control processes that differ from those in waking life. In particular, the most striking feature is the absence of any attempt to maintain consistency either within the dream or between dream events and general knowledge. Within the dream, the characters, scenes, and events shift and change unpredictably and there are gross discrepancies between dream events and the dreamer's knowledge of the real world. Moreover, such discrepancies appear to be either unrecognised or unheeded by the dreamer. Some researchers (e.g. Cavallero & Foulkes, 1993) emphasise the continuity between cognitive processes in waking and cognitive processes in dreaming, but De Witt's data underlines some striking and important differences. It is paradoxical that, in the area of dream research, some studies are concerned to show the bizarre nature of dreams, whereas others (e.g. Montangero, 1991) stress that dreams are essentially coherent and orderly. It seems possible to support both views by judicious choice of examples.

Montangero has developed methods of analysis designed to discover the principles of sequential organisation in dreams. Dreams almost always have a sequence of actions and scenes so that questions arise as to the nature of the mechanism that regulates the progression from one scene to another, and whether dream sequences are organised in the same way as waking narratives. Montangero's subjects were wakened after about 10 minutes of REM sleep and asked to report their dream and then to reconstitute the precise order of events within the dream. The taped report was played back next day and they were asked if they recalled anything more. Dream events were then partitioned by two judges into semantic units at three hierarchical levels corrresponding to the main situation, steps within the situation, and subdivisions of these steps. Once the component units had been established, the type of connecting link between them was identified. Five main types of link were identified:

(1) Plausible continuation (e.g. "I go out—I meet a friend").

(2) Narrative links consisting of a triggering event, a desired outcome, and intermediate steps toward the outcome.

(3) Scripts in which events conform to a stereotypical sequence. These include dreams of visiting a restaurant or going on a plane.

(4) Teleonomic links in which successive events involve goals or intentions, means, and results. In Montangero's example, "I had to find a way to open up a secret passage. I pressed a tile and the passage opened before me".

(5) Causal links (e.g. "The rubber dinghy hit a stone, sprang a leak, and we fell into the water") .

Connecting links may exist between semantic units and also between sequences of units, but there may also be breaks between unconnected sequences. This method of analysis yields a dream description in terms of the number of semantic units and breaks, the length of the sequences, and the type of connections. However, the types of connections just listed are

---

1. Dreamer drives up a mountain road with her father, hears an alarming noise while her father says that there is a strange noise; they stop and see that they have a flat tyre. The father says that this is always happening to him. He decides to change the tyre.

2. Dreamer and her father decide to go to a mountain resort restaurant. Father says they must look for plates; dreamer gets porcelain plates; father says they are not suitable, paper plates will do.

3. Dreamer and members of her family sit down at a table in a mountain resort restaurant. A woman (her godmother) at another table gets up, goes towards them and kisses them. She says she has two boys. First boy comes up to their table, greets them and leaves. Dreamer thinks he is too young. Second boy comes and greets them, then leaves. His head is not visible, as in a badly framed movie picture.

4. Dreamer outside the restaurant.

5. Dreamer is sitting with a friend, in a room, looking at photographs. Dreamer pins the pictures on the wall. Friend makes a comment about a picture of herself. Suddenly the dreamer sees the real scene, as if she was standing beside the photographer who took the picture. Then dreamer and friend look at a picture of a horse. Again, dreamer sees the real scene and she notices that the photographer had not intended to photograph the horse, but a boy who was standing beside it. Dreamer laughs at the photographer's error.

FIG. 10.2. A dream narrative. Reproduced with permission of author and publisher from: Montangero, J. How can we define the sequential organization of dreams. *Perceptual and Motor Skills*, 1991, 73, 1059–1073. © Perceptual and Motor Skills, 1991.

clearly not mutually exclusive and particular examples may be difficult to classify. The following summary of a dream report cited by Montangero consists of five sequences:

As Montangero (1991) points out, this dream shows good continuity with only one major break, and includes plausible, script-based, causal, and teleonomic connecting links. The comparison of sequential organisation in dreams and in waking narratives is clearly a rich field of research, but the conclusions seem to be too dependent on the particular dream selected for analysis and the subjective judgements of the researchers. Dream experiences, as compared with normal waking experiences or stories generated when awake, are characterised by spatial and temporal discontinuity, by lack of plausibility, by frequent shifts of point of view and of scenario, and changes of mood and goals, by the actor's relative lack of control, by the vagueness and indeterminacy of the experience, and by the dreamer's acceptance of the inexplicable.

It is interesting to note, however, that there is evidence of a continuum of coherence when comparisons are made between waking fantasies, NREM dreams, and REM dreams. Reinsel, Antrobus, and Wollman (1992) compared dream reports when sleepers were wakened and waking fantasies that were generated by subjects relaxed in a quiet dim room. Judges then rated the resulting reports for bizarreness on the basis of discontinuities and improbabilities. Surprisingly, this measure of bizarreness was highest for the waking fantasies, next highest in REM dreams, and lowest in NREM dreams, decreasing with the level of cortical activation. The authors suggested a cognitive interpretation of these findings. When external stimulation is minimised and cortical arousal is low, then spreading activation is too sluggish to activate top-down processing and so impose the constraints of general knowledge. This explanation is in line with De Witt's view that normal operations of construction and monitoring are impaired during dreaming. The idea that memory in dreams and waking memory share the same cognitive mechanisms operating at different levels of efficiency is further supported by Kerr's (1993) observation that lesions in brain-damaged patients can cause parallel impairment of visual imagery in both waking life and in dreams.

Dream Recall

Why are dreams so difficult, in normal circumstances, to recall? It is clear from the huge discrepancy between the frequency of home-dream reports and the frequency of laboratory reports from REM sleep that we recall very few of our dreams and are usually unaware of having dreamed. Dream recall is extremely fragile and elusive.The slightest distraction on waking, or a brief delay before the recall attempt, is enough to disrupt the memory. Even if we do recall a dream on waking, it tends to vanish from memory later in the day and cannot be re-recalled. Goodenough (1978; 1992) reviewed two types of explanation for dream-recall failure. The first type of explanation centres on the content of dreams and the second on the nature of sleep and its effects on memory processes. .

Content-centred Theories of Dream-recall Failure

In support of this theory, Goodenough describes an experiment in which subjects classified as habitual dream reporters and as nonreporters were wakened at home by phone calls until they had each provided five dream reports. These reports were then presented to other subjects who were tested for recall of the dreams and found the dreams of the nonreporters harder to remember. This result suggests that the content of nonreporters' dreams influenced retrievability, but Goodenough points out that their initial dream reports may have been vaguer or less vivid, so that it was the nature of the report rather than of the dream itself that was affecting recall. There is evidence that dramatic, emotional, and salient dreams are more likely to be recalled and nonreporters do appear to have less salient dreams. Repression theories also centre on the content of dreams but, whereas the salience hypothesis predicts better recall of highly emotional dreams, repression theory predicts that intensely emotional dreams will be forgotten. There seems, however, to be no clear link between indices of repressive personality and dream-recall failure, and no link between repressive personality and the nature of dream content. Another content-centred explanation suggests that dreams are forgotten because, like scrambled texts, the content is disorganised. However, Goodenough noted that no relationship between ratings of disorganisation for initial dream reports and ability to re-recall the content had been found. It has also been suggested that the problem is motivational, and dreams are not remembered because we consider them to be unimportant and irrational. It is true that dream reporters tend to be more interested in their dreams than nonreporters, but this is more likely to be an effect than a cause of their superior dream recall.

Memory Process Explanations for Dream-recall Failure

According to this theory the ability to recall any dream, irrespective of its content, is impaired by the effects of sleep on memory processes. Memory process explanations point to the fact that dream recall exhibits several similarities with waking recall. For example, dream recall shows a recency effect, with dreams from later in the night being remembered better than those from earlier in the night, and a list-length effect, with a decline in re-recall when a larger number of dreams have been reported. On the assumption, then, that general memory processes are operating, it has been suggested that dream-recall failure may be explained in terms of state-dependency, with a mismatch of the sleep state and the waking state contributing to poor recall. Alternatively, it has been suggested that consolidation of memory traces is impaired by sleep. On this view, transfer to long-term memory does not take place, so recall is better if the dream is still in short-term memory when the sleeper wakes. However, against the consolidation hypothesis, there is evidence that the problem lies at the retrieval stage. Botman and Crovitz (1989) examined the effects of different types of cues on facilitating dream recall. They asked subjects to free-recall their dreams first, and then presented them with cues that were either:

(1) Cues relating to childhood events such as animal, car, fear, mother, house.
(2) Cues relating to the subject's experiences of the previous day.
(3) Colour words.

The childhood-event cues were ones that had been found effective in cueing real autobiographical memories. Both the childhood cues and the cues from the previous day facilitated additional dream recall. This finding fits with the everyday experience of being reminded of forgotten dreams by naturally occurring cues that bear some relation to the dream content. Botman and Crovitz put forward the interesting idea that the difficulty of retrieving dreams should be seen in terms of the context-plus-index model of memory (Reiser, Black & Abelson, 1985; see p.150) in which retrieval consists of accessing first the context and then the specific indices. Because dreams do not have contexts, this kind of retrieval process would be unable to access them.

Finally, further ideas about dream recall are offered by Ahsen (1992) and colleagues using a psychodynamic rather than a cognitive approach. They identify a type of dream they call 'lucid dreaming", in which the dreamer is engaged in an active struggle and may have the impression of being able to control the dream. They have developed a technique of dream recall known as "prolucid dreaming", which is designed to create in the waking subject a state similar to a lucid dream. The subject is encouraged to use imagery to re-experience the dream, and, simultaneously to interpret it. The subject is also enjoined to keep in mind the figure of a parent and this parental image is supposed to act as a "filter" producing heightened awareness and emotionality as in the example shown in Fig. 10.3.

It is possible that this method facilitates dream recall by associative cues or that recreating the dream state aids recall by means of state-dependency. However, the effects seem to be much more on enriching the interpretation than on actually recalling more of the dream content.

Dream: "Someone was chasing me with a knife. We had gotten into a disagreement in the dream. Most of the dream was chasing."

Conscious interpretation: "I do not know really what it means. I do not know the interpretation. There is no guess either. I draw a blank."

M-Dream (with the mother figure in mind): "I keep mother in mind and see the dream again. I feel kind of frozen and there is no movement in the dream."

F-dream (with the father figure in mind): "I keep father in mind and I see the dream again. I see more activity and instead of chasing there is more of challenging the person with the knife. I can see that I kick the knife out of his hand. There is less of fear in it."

Prolucid interpretation: As I keep mother or father in mind, the dream changes. I understand that there is an issue of being inactive and also being active, depending on which parent I keep in mind when I see the dream."

FIG. 10.3. The prolucid method (Ahsen, 1992).

As can be seen, there are too many explanations of dream-recall failure rather than too few. It is clear, however, that a satisfactory explanation must account for the fact that dreams can usually be recalled if the dreamer is wakened from REM sleep, but only seldom if waking occurs naturally. An explanation in terms of dream content cannot account for this. It seems more likely that characteristics of the physiological state that intervenes between REM sleep and natural waking are responsibile for the fragility of memory for dreams.

Individual Differences in Memory for Dreams

Individual differences in dream recall are marked—perhaps even more so than individual differences in waking memory ability. Those designated as homedream nonreporters only recall their dreams infrequently and also report dreams less frequently when wakened from REM sleep in the laboratory. It is not clear, therefore, whether they have poorer memory for dreams or whether they dream less often than those who are classed as home-dream reporters. Butler and Watson (1985) reasoned that dream quality determines the probability of recall. Highly salient dreams that are vivid, emotional, bizarre, and active are more likely to be recalled, so that the ability to recall dreams may be linked to the ability to generate salient dreams. Butler and Watson predicted that this ability would be linked to specific cognitive skills. To test this hypothesis, they woke subjects during every REM period and recorded the incidence of dream reports, rated the salience of the reported dreams, and correlated these measures with the subjects' scores on tests of cognitive ability. The results showed that subjects with low scores on the Wechsler Block Design test produced dream reports on 48.5% of wakings; subjects with high scores produced 83.5% dream recall. Significant correlations were also obtained between dream recall and subtests of the Wechsler Memory Scale and tests of visualisation ability. Kerr (1993) has also noted that scores derived from the Betts Questionnaire for rated vividness of visual imagery and ability to control and manipulate images correlated with frequent dream recall. These findings serve to emphasise the continuity between cognitive processes in waking life and those involved in dreaming.

Other factors besides differences in cognitive skills also contribute to individual differences in dreaming. Reinsel, Antrobus, and Wollman (1992) found that light sleepers reported 71% dreams in NREM sleep, whereas heavy sleepers reported only 21%. Heavy sleepers are thought to have insufficient cortical arousal to generate dreaming. Age and gender differences in dream reporting have also been observed. Kahn, Fisher, and Lieberman (1969) found that women recalled more dreams than men, and a group of elderly people aged 66–87 only recalled dreams on 55% of REM wakenings as compared to 87% for young adults. However, Waterman (1991), who studied the dream reports of 80 men and women aged between 45 and 75, found no age differences in dream frequency or in the length of the dream narrative. He measured general intelligence, visuospatial IQ, and, as a test of visual memory, recall from a silent clip of Bergman's film *Wild Strawberries*. All these scores, especially memory for the film, correlated significantly with the length of the dream reports but not with dream frequency. This pattern of results makes sense if the length of the report depends on the same memory processes as waking memory tasks, but the incidence of dreaming is controlled by other factors, such as physiological ones. An age-related decline in the emotionality of dreams is also likely to have a physiological explanation. One possibility that has not received much consideration is that home-dream nonreporters are more susceptible to distraction and interference so that their recall is more likely to be disrupted. On this assumption, dream reporting would be linked to measures of attentional capacity and distractibility.

Models and Functions

Antrobus (1991) and Fookson and Antrobus (1992) have explored the potential of connectionist modelling to provide a theoretical account of dreaming. There are two key assumptions that underlie their model. First, that the cerebral cortex is activated, and second, that sensory input is absent or inhibited. In REM sleep the cortex is apparently as active as it is in a waking state, yet there is little or no response to external stimulation. Both sensory and motor response subsystems are inhibited. Thus, during sleep, the pattern of distributed activation and inhibition is different from the waking state and, deprived of constraints from bottom-up sensory input, the system is dependent on its own self-generated reverberating activation. In the absence of external stimulation, rather than the conceptual modules controlling the production of visual images, image production by visual modules drives the interpretation by conceptual modules. When parallel distributed processing (PDP) networks are operating normally, bizarre combinations and bizarre sequences are not created because incompatible units are inhibited, but during sleep normal constraints based on the conditional probabilities of co-occurrence are not operating. Fookson and Antrobus have simulated the production of imagery and of sequences including bizarre and improbable combinations in their DREAMIT (Distributed Recurrent Activation Model of Imagery and Thought) models. DREAMIT-S is a single-layered network composed of 90 units representing features, objects, persons, and places, as well as abstract concepts such as values and roles. The network can create an integrated set of schemata integrating, for example, the "I-as-student" role with units for physics, college, and books, but cannot model sequence production. To achieve this, DREAMIT-BP, a multilayered model with back-propagation, was constructed. To mimic the conditions prevailing during sleep the output of the forward-propagation phase is folded back to the input layer. This model proved capable of generating sequences and also produced dream-like discontinuities and improbable combinations of features, as well as the repetitive loops that are sometimes experienced in dreams. This line of research, bringing together neural and cognitive analyses of dreaming, offers a valuable test-bed for further predictions.

The MEM model (Johnson, 1983, 1992; see Chapter 11) is comprehensive enough to encompass imagining and dreaming. Johnson's research on reality monitoring has analysed the differences between memories of perceptions and memories of imaginings. Internally generated thoughts and imaginings are distinguished by traces of constructive processes, and Johnson, Kahan, and Raye (1984) extended this idea to dreams. Pairs of subjects woke and gave each other reports of real dreams and made-up pseudo-dreams. Later, the subjects could distinguish between the pseudo-dreams they had made up when awake and real dream reports because the latter lacked traces of constructive processes. Although they are distinguishable, in Johnson's view, dreams, imaginings, and real memories are all products of the same cognitive system but vary in the contribution of different subsystems. Dreams are generated primarily by the reflective subsystem.

Ideally, models of dreaming should be linked to its function, but there is currently no agreement about the function of dreaming. Ellman and Weinstein (1991) distinguish four different accounts:

(1) According to Crick and Mitchison (1986), REM sleep is a sort of reverse learning whereby the neural networks are cleared.
(2) According to the opposite view, REM sleep is necessary for memory consolidation.
(3) REM dreams are considered to provide endogenous stimulation necessary to maintain cortical function.
(4) REM dreams are thought to fire a self-stimulation system that is positively rewarding. This would explain why REM sleep deprivation produces a rebound increase in dreaming.

Freud also considered the function of dreaming. He believed that dreams serve as a safety valve for desires that are censored during conscious waking life. Neither the DREAMIT model nor the MEM model offer a functional account of dreaming. However, although the DREAMIT model is difficult to reconcile with either the first or second of these views, it could be consistent with the third or fourth.

As dream research, using the approach and methodology of cognitive psychology accumulates, the similarities between dream cognition and waking cognition are increasingly being recognised. Brain disease and traumas have similar effects on waking memory and on dreams. Memory for dreams exhibits classic memory phenomena such as recency and interference. Retention functions for episodic day residues in dreams are similar to the functions seen in autobiographical memory. Memorability covaries with salience, and some kinds of waking memory ability, especially imaging ability and visual memory, correlate with memory for dreams. Although dreams also exhibit striking differences from waking cognition, particularly in lack of control and the inclusion of bizarre and improbable events, it seems likely that these can be understood in terms of existing cognitive theories.

CONCLUSIONS

Research on thoughts and dreams provides an excellent illustration of the strengths and weaknesses of everyday memory research. On the plus side of the equation, cognitive psychologists have risen to the challenge of investigating particularly inaccessible aspects of memory and have had considerable success in devising useful methodologies. Although ultimately dependent on the quality of people's self-reports, these methods incorporate experimental manipulations and the effectiveness of the manipulations in influencing the responses provides some validation for the self-reports. On the negative side, the theoretical accounts are weak: Models of reality monitoring are more descriptive than explanatory, but the development of connectionist models of dreaming holds promise for more powerful theorising. However, theoretical concepts derived from studies of memory for external stimuli and events have proved useful for interpreting internal memories. Interpretation of reality monitoring has employed concepts of visual imagery, automatic and attentional cognitive operations, and self-reference. Interpretation of dreaming has invoked concepts of interference, retention interval, salience, and narrative construction. This kind of theoretical overlap suggests that externally derived memories and internally derived memories can be accounted for within a unitary cognitive system.

11 Overview: Conclusions and Speculations

MODELS OF EVERYDAY MEMORY

In reviewing research on memory in the real world this book has included such a wide range of different memory functions and such a diverse collection of findings and observations that it is a difficult task to formulate any general conclusions or to incorporate them into a general model of memory. Some researchers, such as Tulving, have concluded that there is no single entity corresponding to "memory", but rather that memory consists of (Tulving, 1991, p. 25):

> a number of different brain/behaviour/cognition systems and processes that, through co-operation and interaction with one another, make it possible for their possessor to benefit from past experience and thereby promote survival.

Tulving proposed a number of criteria whereby separate systems could be distinguished.

(1) Different memory systems have different functions and handle different types of information.
(2) Different systems may employ different processes but need not necessarily do so.
(3) Different systems are mediated in different brain structures or mechanisms.

(4) Different systems have developed at different evolutionary stages.
(5) Different systems may have different forms of representation.

Applying these criteria, Tulving identified five separate but interacting memory systems:

(1) Procedural memory, which is involved in skills, actions and simple conditioning.
(2) The Perceptual Representation System, which is involved in perceptual priming of the identification of objects.
(3) Short-term memory, which is equivalent to working or primary memory.
(4) Semantic memory, for general knowledge of the world.
(5) Episodic memory, for conscious recollection of personal experience

Each of these five major systems includes multiple subsystems, as yet not fully identified. However, although there is general agreement that memory includes different systems and subsystems, there is no consensus about what these are and how they are related. Some researchers fear that a proliferation of different systems is conceptually untidy and empirically not confirmable. Johnson (1983; 1992) argued that there is a general system, but that multiple memory functions are served by a number of interacting subsystems. She formulated the multiple entry modular memory system (MEM), which was specifically designed to accommodate the diversity of memory functions displayed in everyday life. For Johnson (1983, p.81):

> the most impressive thing about memory is the range of functions it supports. The same memory system that recalls your vacation learns to play racketball. The same system that memorises a part in a play is startled by faces that resemble the mugger who got your wallet. The same system that can instantly classify a strange animal as a bird struggles to identify the pharmacist when you run into him in the grocery store.

In the MEM model the general system comprises three major subsystems:

(1) The sensory system, a low-level system for the detection of stimuli and the development of sensorimotor skills.
(2) The perceptual system, for recognising what is familiar, perceiving the relationships between objects, storage of complex patterns.
(3) The reflective system, for voluntary explicit free recall of events and for relating new information to stored information.

Any event creates multiple entries in all three subsystems, which can operate in parallel. The first two subsystems handle externally derived information, but the reflective system handles internally derived information allowing us to plan, reminisce, anticipate. The differential activation of the subsystems is controlled by attention.

The MEM model is both realist and constructivist and can therefore account for the fact that people have both accurate memories that are precise, specific, and detailed, and also inaccurate memories that are embellished, distorted, or edited. The sensory and perceptual subsystems store surface features and verbatim language, that is, copies of reality. The reflective system is constructivist and stores representations that are integrated, abstracted, and interpreted. According to this model, childhood amnesia can be explained by the later development of the reflective system, and Johnson also advances an evolutionary argument for the separate development of the reflective system. Emotion is primarily associated with the activation of the sensory and perceptual systems, and is weaker in the reflective system. This means, in Johnson's example, that we can reflect about tigers, anticipate their movements, and plan how to avoid them without being over-aroused by a full emotional response to tigers.

More recently, Johnson (1992) has developed the MEM framework further so that there are two perceptual systems (P1 and P2) and two reflective systems (R1 and R2), each with multiple component subprocesses as shown in Fig. 11.1. Applying this model to the issue of recollection, Johnson proposes that memory elements and features become bound into a complex memory trace as a result of reactivation. Reactivation can occur through repeated perception in the P system, or through being reflectively regenerated in the R system. Such reactivation binds memories together, welding context and content into a composite whole, and also strengthens the memory. Reflective reactivation may occur through the occurrence of chance cues or through the operation of *agendas*, which are basically programmes of mental operations designed to achieve goals. According to this model, memory for autobiographical episodes or for face-name pairs depends on reactivation that maintains clarity and detail and increases the probability of further reactivation. This formulation is particularly suited to everyday memories because it emphasises the complex configurational character of the representations.

One problem with models like Tulving's and Johnson's is that it is difficult to map all the different functions of memory in everyday life onto the proposed subsystems. Is there a case for adding more specialised subsystems for face memory or for spatial memory or memory for music? Once you start fractionating memory into separate subsystems it is difficult to know where to stop. There is also some confusion over the principle of classification. Johnson's subsystems represent different processes or stages

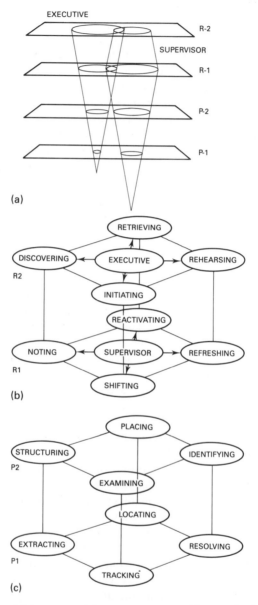

FIG. 11.1.   (a) A multiple-entry modular memory system with two reflective subsystems, R1 and R2, and two perceptual subsystems, P1 and P2. Reflective and perceptual systems can interact through control and monitoring processes (supervisor and executive processes of R1 and R2 respectively), which have relatively greater access to and control over reflective than perceptual subsystems. (b) Component subprocesses of R1 and R2. (c) Component subprocesses of P1 and P2. (Adapted from Johnson, 1992). Reprinted by permission of Plenum.

310

of processing: Tulving's classification seems to include both a process distinction (perceptual priming and short-term memory) and a distinction based on type of information (semantic memory and episodic memory).

So far, the diversity of memory in everyday life defies attempts to construct a fully comprehensive model. However, having surveyed most of the functions that an everyday memory system needs to perform, we are in a better position to identify the general characteristics that such a system needs to have. And if we cannot yet construct a satisfactory architecture of everyday memory, at least we can identify some of the concepts and theories that prove most useful in the interpretation of memory in the real world.

GENERAL CHARACTERISTICS OF EVERYDAY MEMORY

Characteristics of Encoding

Memory is Selective

Some characteristics of the memory system can be seen as resulting from the demands imposed on the system by the environment and by our way of life. Researchers tend to restrict consideration of everyday memory to here and now, that is, to urban Western society in the present day. It is instructive, however, to take a longer and broader view. In the kind of simple rural communities that were the norm a few centuries ago, and which still persist in remoter parts of the world, the demands on memory were relatively slight. People rarely encountered an unfamilar face. They carried out the same activities in daily and seasonal routines all their lives. They rarely travelled beyond the immediate well-known terrain. The same songs and stories were regularly repeated. Contrast this sort of life and the minimal demands it makes on the memory system with a twentieth-century urban lifestyle. We are continuously confronted with strange faces; we continually meet new people; we travel to new places and have to navigate in unfamiliar terrain. We have to learn new skills and perform new activities. We are bombarded with written and spoken verbal information almost every waking moment. The result is that in modern urban society the memory system is grossly overloaded.

We can support the overloaded memory system to some extent by the use of external aids. As life gets busier and more complicated, we rely more and more on information technology. We store information in data banks, in personal computers, in filofaxes, but memory is still overloaded. To cope with this overload the system must be selective. Selective attention and selective perception act to limit the inflow of information, but, even so, we still perceive far more than we could hope, or wish, to remember. In many laboratory experiments selectivity emerges as errors, but in the real world selectivity is both a virtue and a necessity. In everyday life, an ideally efficient memory system would make maximum use of external aids and selectively devote its resources to high-priority items, filtering out irrelevant or less important information. Memory does not necessarily need to be complete.

Memory is Elaborative

Although encoding is selective and selectivity may be seen as a strategy to achieve economy, the information that is selected for encoding is elaborated. We encode the context and the source of the information, we generate associations, we link it to pre-existing stored knowedge, scripts and schemas, and we set up cues and reminders. All these forms of elaboration are designed to enhance the retrievability of the information by providing indices that will locate and identify it. Elaborative encoding is also part of the process of comprehension. New information cannot be understood unless it is related in this way to its context and to the knowledge base already stored in memory.

Characteristics of Representation

Memory is Dynamic

Besides being enormously complex and rich in information, today's environment is also constantly changing. We move houses, change jobs, and travel around. The skills we learn need frequent updating. The media inform us daily of new events and offer new interpretations of old events. We need a dynamic memory system to cope with changing circumstances and a changing physical environment. We need to be able to update the knowledge we have stored and to transform the models of the world we construct in our heads. We have to revise the concepts we have acquired, or throw them out and acquire new ones. Fixed memory structures are liable to become obsolete or to be inappropriate for the current situation. We noted in Chapter 2 that the kind of mental models needed for planning or problem-solving are dynamic models, which are assembled as required. And Schank developed the idea of MOPs (Chapter 6) as part of a dynamic system that could draw on high-level general components and low-level specific components to construct appropriate memory representations on demand. Fixed memory structures are uneconomical to store because the same high-level elements need to be reduplicated in many different representations. Dynamic memories are readily revised, updated, and modified, whereas fixed memories would rapidly become redundant in a changing world.

Memory is Integrative

The most important function of memory in the real world is to link past, present, and future. Memory stores retrospective information, monitors current input and output, and constructs and stores future plans. This integration of past, present, and future in a unified personal history is achieved by interactive processes. New memories are stored within pre-existing knowledge structures; old memories are modified by new ones; prospective plans are built out of elements abstracted from past experience. This intricate interaction of past, present, and future allows us to maintain a coherent identity and to develop flexibly and adaptively in knowledge and experience. It is essential to the development and maintenance of a self-concept and thus is integral to autobiographical memory.

Memory is Able to Construct Hypothetical Representations

A distinguishing feature of the human mind is its capacity for "displacement" in thought. It is because we are able to think about things that are displaced in time and in space, and things that are not the case, that we are able to plan, to predict the outcome of actions and events, to prepare for eventualities. Our ability to construct detailed and accurate hypothetical representations of possible states of affairs is crucial for survival. To meet this requirement we have to have a constructive memory system. In the real world, a memory system that could only copy the information it received would be hopelessly maladaptive. It would also be incapable of invention, imagination, and creative art. Johnson's MEM model recognises and accommodates the need to incorporate both a real world and a constructed world.

Memory Can Store Both General and Specific Information

From a functional point of view it is easy to see the value of a memory system that abstracts and stores generalisations from experiences. Generalisation allows us to apply the knowledge acquired from one experience to a new experience that is similar but not exactly the same. It is the ability to store general memories that allows us to know what to do in a new restaurant or a different shop, to drive an unfamiliar car, or switch to a different job. Storing knowledge in a generalised form is also economical and reduces the information overload.

However, everyday memory also needs to store some information specifically, because in some situations general information is of little use. We need to remember specific names and specific faces. We need to remember precise information about routes and places and about where objects are located. It is probably true to say that specific information of this kind does not need to be stored for such a long duration as general information. It is not so important to remember names and faces from the remote past as those you have encountered more recently, and although general information about restaurants is always useful, there is not much point in remembering the menu and prices in a specific restaurant you dined in 10 years ago. Studies of autobiographical memory in Chapter 6 showed that repeated experiences tend to be collapsed into a generalised representation, and specific events are only stored if they are especially salient or unusual. Findings reviewed in Chapter 8 showed that memory for verbal information exhibits a similar mechanism, retaining a general representation of the gist of what has been read or heard, together with a relatively short-lived specific representation of the verbatim form. The usefulness of general information extends over an indefinite period, but a great deal of specific information can be discarded as life moves on.

Characteristics of Retrieval Processes

Explicit Memories are Retrievable

It is a characteristic of explicit memory that it can be recalled by a process of conscious effortful retrieval. As memories proliferate, retrieval must necessarily become more difficult. Retrieval is commonly driven by specific goals and may need to be translated into action, so the memory system must be linked to a response generating system as it is in production system models. Studies of retrieval in everyday life have revealed some of the main strategies used. The retrieval mechanism makes use of the way memory representations are organised in terms of categories, time periods, and levels of generality/specificity. When people search for remote memories, as described in Chapters 5 and 6, they use complicated search strategies such as partitioning the search context and searching relevant categories or relevant time periods, searching downwards from the higher levels of general schemas, or upwards from idiosyncratic markers placed on specific items at the lower levels. The striking difference that generally emerges between performance on tasks requiring recognition and tasks requiring recall suggests that retrieval is the most vulnerable aspect of everyday memory. One aspect of the memory system that results in economical storage is the way large amounts of information are only stored indirectly or inferentially, as described in Chapter 7. Explicit pre-stored knowledge is only the tip of the knowledge iceberg, much of which is submerged and consists of inferrable information. If we know that all men are mortal and that John Doe is a man, then the fact that John Doe is mortal is inferrable and does not need to be represented explicitly. The two forms of information storage are associated with different forms of retrieval—direct access and indirect search. Pre-stored, explicitly represented information can be retrieved directly, but inferrable information can only accessed indirectly by inferential reasoning

Recall May be Involuntary

In everyday life involuntary recall may occur spontaneously, bypassing the effortful processes of retrieval. Memories often come to mind without any deliberate attempt at recall and affect our behaviour and influence our thoughts, moods, and feelings. These involuntary memories are sometimes for targets (like people's names) that had resisted earlier attempts at retrieval but later pop-up into consciousness. On other occasions, involuntary memories are triggered by external perceptual or verbal cues or internal cues from current thoughts. A memory system that retrieves information involuntarily, as well as in response to deliberate recall attempts, is particularly suited to the demands of the real world. In many situations we cannot deliberately seek target information because we do not know what the target is. Involuntary memories, triggered by cues in the current situation, can be of analogous past experiences that contain useful hints, warnings, or reminders. Everyday life is full of reminders. For example, when planning a holiday, I involuntarily recalled a previous disastrous experience that reminded me to check the small print of the travel insurance document. Similarly, the sight of a petrol station reminds us to fill up the car, the autumn rainstorms remind us to get the roof fixed, and so on. A retrieval system that only provides information when you already know what it is you want to know is much less versatile.

Memory May be Implicit

Implicit memories are not consciously recalled but nevertheless influence behavioural responses. We can recognise faces, places, and objects as familiar without having any conscious recollection of previous encounters. Implicit memory primes and facilitates identification of current stimuli that have been experienced before. Implicit memory includes the skills and sensorimotor learning that we cannot describe or explain. It operates making minimal demands on cognitive processing capacity. Implicit memory is thought to be earlier in both evolutionary and ontogenetic terms, and also represents a sort of reservoir of memory that is better able to survive trauma and to resist the effects of ageing.

OPERATING CHARACTERISTICS OF EVERYDAY MEMORY

Memory Processes

Recent work has concentrated more on the nature of memory representations, so that the importance of memory processes has been underplayed. Most of the characteristics of the memory system that have been outlined so far are ones that have the effect of easing the burden on storage and placing greater demands on retrieval processes. Memories that are dynamic need to be assembled. Processes of transformation may be needed to rotate, align, expand, or contract the internal analogues we construct of the real world. Processes of selection, abstraction, and generalisation are needed to protect the system from overload. Hypothetical representations have to be constructed, and indirectly represented information has to be recovered by inferential processes. Complex matching processes are required to integrate new information with representations of past experience, and in order to perceive analogies between current problems and previously encountered ones. Elaborative encoding relies on processes of association and matching. All these processes need a temporary storage system like working memory which can maintain information in consciousness while these operations are taking place.

Metalevels of Memory

Metalevels of memory are needed to instigate, monitor, and control memory processes. The operations of working memory need to be driven by some form of central executive or supervisory attentional system linking memory to goals and actions. Retrieval from long-term memory is facilitated by metamemory awareness of what knowledge is in store and what kind of search strategies are most likely to be effective. Memories are more useful if people can make judgements about their accuracy. Metamemory processes also allow people to make judgements about what they *should* be able to remember and what other people should be able to remember. It is these different forms of metamemory that allow memory to be deployed purposefully in real life situations.

Memory Efficiency

Research has tended to emphasise the errors that occur in everyday memory functions. The picture that emerges is of an error-prone system in which memories are liable to be inaccurate, distorted, or fabricated. This emphasis is partly an artefact of research methodology. In experiments it is usually more informative to set task difficulty at a level where people make errors so that the nature of the errors and the conditions that provoke them can be identified. Diary studies such as those recording TOTs and slips of action have also concentrated on failures rather than on successes. People do make many naturally occurring errors in ordinary life situations, but, arguably, the methodology has produced a somewhat distorted view of memory efficiency. In daily life, memory successes are the norm and memory failures are the exception. People also exhibit remarkable feats of remembering faces and voices from the remote past, and foreign-language vocabulary, and childhood experiences over a lifetime. As well as such examples of retention over very long periods, people can retain very large amounts of information over shorter periods, as when they prepare for examinations, and sometimes, as in the case of expert knowledge, they acquire a large amount of information and retain it for a considerably long time. The conditions of laboratory testing provoke errors and magnify their importance. In everyday life people are not pressed to make forced-choice responses and can always admit ignorance or doubt, so that although omission errors may be more frequent, there are probably fewer commission errors. In any case, errors are the price of having a constructive memory that can fill gaps with best guesses. Considering how grossly it is overloaded, memory in the real world proves remarkably efficient and resilient.

References

Adelson, B. (1981). Problem solving and the development of abstract categories in programming languages. *Memory and Cognition, 9*, 422–33.

Adelson, B. (1984). When novices surpass experts: The difficulty of a task may increase with expertise. *Journal of Experimental Psychology: Learning, Memory and Cognition, 10*, 483–95.

Ahsen, A. (1992). The method of prolucid dreaming. *Journal of Mental Imagery, 16*, 1–84.

Alba, J.W., & Hasher, L. (1983). Is memory schematic? *Psychological Bulletin, 93*, 203–231.

Anderson, J.R. (1983). *The architecture of cognition*. Boston: Harvard University Press.

Anderson, R.C., & Pichert, J.W. (1978). Recall of previously unrecallable information following a shift in perspective. *Journal of Verbal Learning and Verbal Behavior, 17*, 1–12.

Anderson, R.E. (1984). Did I do it or did I only imagine doing it? *Journal of Experimental Psychology: General, 113*, 594–613.

Anderson, S.J., & Conway, M.A. (1993). Investigating the structure of autobiographical memories. *Journal of Experimental Psychology: Learning, Memory and Cognition, 19*, 1178–1196.

Anderson, S.J., & Conway, M.A. (Submitted). Why actions and contexts may not organize autobiographical memory: Further evidence against the activity dominance hypothesis.

Andersson, J., & Ronnberg, J. (1995). Recall suffers from collaboration: Joint recall effects of friendship and task complexity. *Applied Cognitive Psychology, 9*, 199–211.

Annett, J. (1991). Skill acquisition. In J.E. Morrison (Ed.), *Training for performance: Principles of applied human learning* (pp. 13–51). Chichester: Wiley.

Anschutz, L., Camp, C.J., Markley, R.P., & Kramer, J.J. (1985). Maintenance and generalisation of mnemonics for grocery shopping by older adults. *Experimental Aging Research, 11*, 157–160.

Antrobus, J.S. (1978). Dreaming for cognition. In A.M. Arkin, J. Antrobus, & S. Ellman (Eds.), *The mind in sleep* (pp. 569–581). Hillsdale, NJ: Lawrence Erlbaum Associates Inc.

Antrobus, J.S. (1991). Dreaming: Cognitive processes during cortical activation and high afferent thresholds. *Psychological Review, 98*, 96–121.

Aserinsky, E., & Kleitman, N. (1953). Regularly occurring periods of eye motility and concomitant phenomena during sleep. *Science, 118*, 273–274.

Ashley, K.D. (1988). Modelling legal argument: Reasoning with cases and hypotheticals. COINS Technical Report No. 88–01, Department of Computer and Information Science, University of Massachusetts, Amherst, MA.

Baddeley, A.D. (1982). Domains of recollection. *Psychological Review, 89*, 708–729.

Baddeley, A.D. (1993). *Human memory: Theory and practice*. Hove, UK: Lawrence Erlbaum Associates Ltd.

Baddeley, A.D., & Hitch, G. (1993). Recency re-examined. In S. Dornic (Ed.), *Attention and performance, Vol. VI* (647–667). Hillsdale, NJ: Lawrence Erlbaum Associates Inc.

Baddeley, A.D., & Wilkins, A.J. (1984). Taking memory out of the laboratory. In J.E. Harris & P.E. Morris (Eds.), *Everyday memory, actions and absentmindedness*. London: Academic Press.

Bahrick, H.P. (1984a). Memory for people. In J.E. Harris & P.E. Morris (Eds.), *Everyday memory, actions and absentmindedness*. London: Academic Press.

Bahrick, H.P. (1984b). Semantic memory content in permastore: Fifty years of memory for Spanish learned in school. *Journal of Experimental Psychology: General, 113*, 1–35.

Bahrick, H.P., & Hall, L.K. (1991). Lifetime maintenance of high school mathematics content. *Journal of Experimental Psychology: General, 120*, 20–33.

Bahrick, H.P., & Phelps, E. (1987). Retention of Spanish vocabulary over 8 years. *Journal of Experimental Psychology: Learning, Memory and Cognition, 13*, 344–349.

Bahrick, H.P., Wellman, C.L., & Hall, L.K. (1988). The effect of language schema on learning and retention of vocabulary. In M.M. Gruneberg, P.E. Morris, & R.N. Sykes (Eds.), *Practical aspects of memory: Current research and issues. Vol.1* (pp.390–395). Chichester: Wiley.

Baker-Ward, L.A. (1993). A tale of two settings: Young children's memory performance in the laboratory and the field. In G.M. Davies & R.H. Logie (Eds.), *Memory in everyday life: Advances in psychology, Vol.100* (pp.13–41). Amsterdam: North-Holland.

Banaji, M.R., & Crowder, R.G. (1989). The bankruptcy of everyday memory. *American Psychologist, 44*, 1185–1193.

Barclay, C.R. (1993). Remembering ourselves. In G.M. Davies & R.H. Logie (Eds.), *Memory in everyday life: Advances in psychology, Vol.100* (pp. 285–309). Amsterdam: North Holland.

Barclay, C.R., & Wellman, H.M. (1986). Accuracies and inaccuracies in autobiographical memories. *Journal of Memory and Language, 25*, 93–103.

Barsalou, L.W. (1988). The content and organization of autobiographical memories. In U. Neisser & E. Winograd (Eds.), *Remembering reconsidered* (pp.193–243). Cambridge: Cambridge University Press.

Bartlett, F.C. (1932). *Remembering*. Cambridge: Cambridge University Press.

Bartram, D., & Smith, P. (1984). Everyday memory for everyday places. In J.E. Harris & P.E. Morris (Eds.), *Everyday memory, actions and absentmindedness*. London: Academic Press.

Battaglia, D., Cavallero, C., & Cicogna, P. (1987). Temporal reference of the mnemonic sources of dreams. *Perceptual and Motor Skills, 64*, 979–983

Battman, W. (1987). Planning as a method of stress prevention: Will it pay off? In I.G. Sarason & C.D. Spielberger (Eds.), *Stress and anxiety, Vol.10*. New York: Hemisphere.

Beach, K.D. (1988). The role of external mnemonic symbols in acquiring an occupation. In M.M. Gruneberg, P.E. Morris, & R.N. Sykes (Eds.), *Practical aspects of memory: Current research and issues, Vol.1*. Chichester: Wiley.

Bekerian, D.A., & Bowers, J.M. (1983). Eyewitness testimony: Were we misled? *Journal of Experimental Psychology: Learning, Memory and Cognition, 9*, 139–145.

Bekerian, D.A., & Dennett, J.L. (1993). The cognitive interview: Reviving the issues. *Applied Cognitive Psychology*, 7, 275–297.

Berry, D.C. (1993). Slips and errors in learning complex tasks. In G.M. Davies & R.H. Logie (Eds), *Memory in everyday life: Advances in psychology, Vol.100* (pp.137–171). Amsterdam: North Holland.

Bever, T.G., & Chiarello, R.J. (1974). Cerebral dominance in musicians and nonmusicians. *Science*, 185, 537–539.

Bigand, E. (1993). Contributions of music to research on human auditory cognition. In E. Bigand & S. McAdams (Eds.), *Thinking in sound: The cognitive psychology of human audition* (pp.231–277). Oxford: Clarendon Press.

Bjork, R.A. (1978). The updating of human memory. In G.H. Bower (Ed.), *The psychology of learning and motivation: Advances in research and theory, Vol.12*. New York: Academic Press.

Boltz, M., & Jones, M.R. (1986). Does rule recursion make melodies easier to reproduce? If not, what does? *Cognitive Psychology*, 18, 389–431.

Botman, H.I., & Crovitz, H.F. (1989). Dream reports and autobiographical memory. *Imagination, Cognition and Personality*, 9, 213–224

Bower, G.H., Black, J.B., & Turner, T.J. (1979). Scripts in text comprehension and memory. *Cognitive Psychology*, 11, 177–220.

Braine, M.D.S. (1978). On the relation between the natural logic of reasoning and standard logic, *Psychological Review*, 85, 1–21.

Bransford, J.D., & Franks, J.J. (1972). The abstraction of lingustic ideas: A review. *Cognition 1*, 211–249.

Bransford, J.D., & Johnson, M.K. (1973). Consideration of some problems of comprehension. In W.G. Chase (Ed.), *Visual information processing*. New York: Academic Press.

Brewer, W.F. (1986). What is autobiographical memory? In D.C. Rubin (Ed.), *Autobiographical memory*. Cambridge: Cambridge University Press.

Brewer, W.F. (1988). Memory for randomly sampled autobiographical events. In U. Neisser & E. Winograd (Eds.), *Remembering reconsidered* (pp.21–90). Cambridge: Cambridge University Press.

Brewer, W.F. (1994). *The paradoxical role of schemata in memory accuracy*. Paper presented at the Third Practical Aspects of Memory Conference, Washington, DC, July.

Brewer, W.F., & Dupree, D.A. (1983). Use of plan schemata in the recall and recognition of goal-directed actions. *Journal of Experimental Psychology: Learning, Memory and Cognition*, 9, 117–129.

Brewer, W.F., & Tenpenny, P.L. (personal communication, 1996). The role of schemata in the recall and recognition of episodic information.

Brewer, W.F., & Treyens, J.C. (1981). Role of schemata in memory for places. *Cognitive Psychology*, 13, 207–230.

Bricker, P., & Pruzansky, S. (1966). Effects of stimulus content and duration on talker identification. *Journal of the Acoustical Society of America*, 40, 1441–1449.

Broadbent, D.E. (1958). *Perception and communication*. London: Pergamon.

Broadbent, D.E., Cooper, P.F., Fitzgerald, P., & Parkes, K.R. (1982). The cognitive failures questionnaire (CFQ) and its correlates. *British Journal of Clinical Psychology*, 21, 1–18.

Brown, N.R., Rips, L.J., & Shevell, S.K. (1985). The subjective dates of natural events in very long-term memory. *Cognitive Psychology*, 17, 139–177.

Brown, N.R., Shevell, S.K., & Rips, L.J. (1986). Public memories and their personal context. In D.C. Rubin (Ed.), *Autobiographical memory*. Cambridge: Cambridge University Press.

Brown, R., & Kulik, J. (1982). Flashbulb memory. In U. Neisser (Ed.), *Memory observed: Remembering in natural contexts*. San Francisco, CA: W.H. Freeman.

Brown, R., & McNeill, D. (1966). The "tip of the tongue" phenomenon. *Journal of Verbal Learning and Verbal Behavior, 5*, 325–337.

Bruce, D. (1985). The how and why of ecological memory. *Journal of Experimental Psychology: General, 114*, 78–90.

Bruce, V., & Young, A. (1986). Understanding face recognition. *British Journal of Psychology, 77*, 305–327.

Bruck, M., Ceci, S., Francouer, E., & Barr, R. (1995). 'I hardly cried when I got my shot!' Influencing children's reports about a visit to their pediatrician. *Child Development, 66*, 193–208.

Bryant, D.J. (1992). A spatial representation system in humans. *Psycholoquy*, 24th May, 1992.

Buchanan, K., & Middleton, D. (1995). Voices of experience: Talk, identify and membership in reminiscence groups. *Ageing and Society, 15*, 457–491.

Buckhout, R. (1982). Eyewitness testimony. In U. Neisser (Ed.), *Memory observed: Remembering in natural contexts*. San Francisco, CA: Freeman.

Burke, D.M., Mackay, D.G., Worthley, J.S., & Wade, E. (1991). On the tip of the tongue: What causes word finding failures in young and older adults. *Journal of Memory and Language, 30*, 542–579.

Burton, A.M., Bruce, V., & Johnston, R.A. (1990). Understanding face recognition with an interactive activation model. *British Journal of Psychology, 81*, 361–380.

Burton, A.M., & Bruce, V. (1992). I recognize your face but I can't remember your name: A simple explanation. *British Journal of Psychology, 83*, 457–480.

Butler, S.F., & Watson, R. (1985). Individual differences in memory for dreams: The role of cognitive skills. *Perceptual and Motor Skills, 61*, 823–828.

Byrne, R.W. (1979). Memory for urban geography. *Quarterly Journal of Experimental Psychology, 31*, 147–154.

Camp, C.J. (1988). Utilisation of world knowledge systems. In L.W. Poon, D.C. Rubin, & B.A. Wilson (Eds.), *Everyday cognition in adulthood and later life*. Cambridge: Cambridge University Press.

Camp, C.J., Lachman, J.L., & Lachman, R. (1980). Evidence for direct access and inferential retrieval in question answering. *Journal of Verbal Learning and Verbal Behavior, 19*, 583–596.

Campbell, R., Landis, T., & Regard, M. (1986). Face recognition and lipreading: A neurological dissociation. *Brain, 109*, 509–521.

Carmody, D.P., Kundel, H.L., & Toto, L.C. (1984). Comparison scans while reading chest images. *Investigative Radiology, 19*, 462–467.

Cavallero, C., & Foulkes, D. (1993). *Dreaming as cognition*. Hemel Hempstead, Herts: Harvester-Wheatsheaf

Cavanaugh, J.C. (1988). The place of awareness in memory development across adulthood. In L.W. Poon, D.C. Rubin, & B.A. Wilson (Eds.), *Everyday cognition in adulthood and later life*. Cambridge: Cambridge University Press.

Ceci, S.J., Baker, J., & Bronfenbrenner, U. (1988). Prospective memory: Temporal calibration and context. In M.M. Gruneberg, P.E. Morris, & R.N. Sykes (Eds.), *Practical aspects of memory: Current research and issues* (pp.360–365). Chichester: Wiley.

Ceci, S.J, & Bruck, M. (1993). The suggestibility of the child witness. *Psychological Bulletin, 113*, 403–439.

Ceci, S., Loftus, E.F., Crotteau, M.L., & Smith, E. (in press). Repeatedly thinking about non-events, *Consciousness and Cognition*.

Chaffin, R., & Herrman, D.J. (1983). Self reports of memory abilities by old and young adults. *Human Learning, 2*, 17–28.

Chaffin, R., & Imreh, G. (1994). *Memorizing for piano performance*. Paper presented at the Third Practical Aspects of Memory Conference, Washington, DC, July.

Chase, W.G., & Ericsson, K.A. (1982). Skill and working memory. In G.H. Bower (Ed.), *The psychology of learning and motivation: Advances in research and theory, Vol.16.* New York: Academic Press.

Chase, W.G., & Simon, H.A. (1973). Perception in chess. *Cognitive Psychology, 4,* 55–81.

Chi, M.T.H. (1978). Knowledge structures and memory development. In R.S. Siegler (Ed.), *Children's thinking: What develops?* Hillsdale, NJ: Lawrence Erlbaum Associates Inc.

Chi, M.T.H., Feltovich, P.J., & Glaser, R. (1981). Categorization and representation of physics problems by experts and novices. *Cognitive Science, 5,* 121–152.

Chi, M.T.H., & Koeske, R.D. (1983). Network representation of a child's dinosaur knowledge. *Developmental Psychology, 19,* 19–39.

Christianson, S.-A., & Hubinette, B. (1993). Hands up! A study of witnesses' emotional reactions and memories associated with bank robberies. *Applied Cognitive Psychology, 7,* 365–379.

Chung, M.-S., & Thomson, D.M. (1995). Development of face recognition. *British Journal of Psychology, 86,* 55–87

Cipolli, C., Battaglia, D., Cavallero, C., Cicogna, P., & Bosinelli, M. (1992). Associative mechanisms in dream production. In J. Antrobus & M. Bertini (Eds.), *The neuropsychology of sleep and dreaming.* Hillsdale, NJ: Lawrence Erlbaum Associates Inc.

Clark, H.H., & Clark. E.V. (1977). *Psychology and language: An introduction to psycholinguistics.* New York: Harcourt Brace Jovanovich.

Clark, H.H., & Haviland, S.E. (1977). Comprehension and the given-new contract. In R.O. Freedle (Ed.), *Discourse production and comprehension.* Norwood, NJ: Ablex Publishing.

Clifford, B.R. (1983). Memory for voices: The feasibility and quality of earwitness evidence. In S.M.A. Lloyd-Bostock & B.R. Clifford (Eds.), *Evaluating witness evidence.* Chichester: Wiley.

Cockburn, J., & Smith, P.T. (1988). Effects of age and intelligence on everyday memory tasks. In M.M. Gruneberg, P.E. Morris, & R.N. Sykes (Eds.). *Practical aspects of memory: Current research and issues, Vol.2.* (pp.132–136). Chichester: Wiley.

Cockburn, J., & Smith, P.T. (1994). Anxiety and errors of prospective memory. *British Journal of Psychology, 85,* 273–282.

Cohen, G. (1990). Why is it difficult to put names to faces? *British Journal of Psychology, 81,* 287–297

Cohen, G., & Burke, D.M. (1993). Memory for proper names: A review. In G. Cohen & D.M. Burke (Eds.), *Memory for proper names.* Hove, UK: Lawrence Erlbaum Associates Ltd.

Cohen, G., Conway, M.A., & Maylor, E. (1994). Flashbulb memory in older adults. *Psychology and Aging, 9,* 454–463.

Cohen, G., & Faulkner, D. (1983). Age differences in performance on two information processing tasks: Strategy selection and processing efficiency. *Journal of Gerontology, 38,* 447–454.

Cohen, G., & Faulkner, D. (1984). Memory in old age: "Good in parts". *New Scientist,* 11th October, 49–51.

Cohen, G., & Faulkner, D. (1986). Memory for proper names: Age differences in retrieval. *British Journal of Developmental Psychology, 4,* 187–197.

Cohen, G., & Faulkner, D. (1988a). Life span change in autobiographical memory. In M.M. Gruneberg, P.E. Morris, & R.N. Sykes (Eds.), *Practical aspects of memory: Current research and issues, Vol.1.* (pp.277–282). Chichester: Wiley.

Cohen, G., & Faulkner, D. (1988b). The effects of aging on perceived and generated memories. In L.W. Poon, D.C. Rubin & B. Wilson (Eds.), *Cognition in adulthood and later life,* Cambridge: Cambridge University Press.

Cohen, G., & Faulkner, D. (1989). Age differences in source forgetting: Effects on reality monitoring and eyewitness testimony. *Psychology and Aging, 4,* 10–17.

Cohen, G., & Java, R. (1995). Memory for medical history. *Applied Cognitive Psychology, 9,* 273–288.

Collins, A.M. (1979). Fragments of a theory of human plausible reasoning. In D.L. Waltz (Ed.), *Theoretical issues in natural language processing.* Hillsdale, NJ: Lawrence Erlbaum Associates Inc.

Collins, A., Warnock, E.H., Aiello, N., & Miller, M.L. (1975). Reasoning from incomplete knowledge. In D.G. Bobrow & A. Collins (Eds.), *Representation and understanding.* New York: Academic Press.

Conway, M.A. (1990). *Autobiographical memory: An introduction.* Milton Keynes: Open University Press.

Conway, M.A. (1991). In defence of everyday memory. *American Psychologist, 46,* 19–26.

Conway, M.A. (1993). Method and meaning in memory research. In G.M. Davies & R.H. Logie (Eds.), *Memory in everyday life: Advances in psychology, Vol.100.* North Holland: Elsevier.

Conway, M.A. (1995). *Flashbulb memories.* Hove, UK: Lawrence Erlbaum Associates Ltd.

Conway, M.A., Anderson, S.J., Larsen, S.F., Donnelly, C.M., McDaniel, M.A., McClelland, A.G.R., Rawles, R.E., & Logie, R.H. (1994). The formation of flashbulb memories. *Memory and Cognition, 22,* 326–343.

Conway, M.A., & Bekerian, D.A. (1987). Organisation in autobiographical memory. *Memory and Cognition, 15,* 119–32.

Conway, M.A., Cohen, G., & Stanhope, N. (1991). On the very long term retention of knowledge acquired through formal education: Twelve years of cognitive psychology. *Journal of Experimental Psychology: General, 120,* 395–409.

Conway, M.A., Cohen, G., & Stanhope, N. (1992). Very long term memory for knowledge acquired at school and university. *Applied Cognitive Psychology, 6,* 467–482.

Conway, M.A., Collins, A.F., Gathercole, S.E., & Anderson, S.J. (1996). Recollections of true and false autobiographical memories. *Journal of Experimental Psychology: General, 125,* 69–95.

Conway, M. (1990). On bias in autobiographical recall: Retrospective adjustments following disconfirmed expectations. *The Journal of Social Psychology, 130,* 183–189.

Crick, F., & Mitchison, G. (1986). REM sleep and neural nets. *Journal of Mind and Behaviour, 7,* 229–250.

Crovitz, H.F., & Schiffman, H. (1974). Frequency of episodic memories as a function of age. *Bulletin of the Psychonomic Society, 4,* 517–518.

Da Costa Pinto, A., & Baddeley, A.D. (1991). Where did you park your car? Analysis of a naturalistic long term recency effect. *European Journal of Cognitive Psychology, 3,* 297–313.

Davies, G.M., & Flin, R. (1988). The accuracy and suggestiblity of child witnesses. *Issues in Criminological and Legal Psychology, 13,* 21–34.

Davies, G.M., & Milne, A. (1985). Eyewitness composite production as a function of mental and physical reinstatement of context. *Criminal Justice and Behavior, 12,* 209–220.

De Groot, A.D. (1996). Perception and memory versus thought: Some old ideas and recent findings. In B. Kleinmuntz (Ed.), *Problem solving.* New York: Wiley.

De Haan, E.H.F., Young, A.W., & Newcombe, F. (1987). Face recognition without awareness. *Cognitive Neuropsychology, 4,* 385–415.

De Haan, E.H.F., Young, A.W., & Newcombe, F. (1991). A dissociation between the sense of familiarity and access to semantic information concerning familiar people. *European Journal of Cognitive Psychology, 3,* 51–67.

Deutsch, D. (1980). The processing of structured and unstructured tonal sequences. *Perception and Psychophysics*, *28*, 381–389.

Dewitt, L.A., & Crowder, R.G. (1986). Recognition of novel melodies after brief delays. *Music Perception*, *3*, 259–274.

De Witt, T. (1988). Impairment of reality constructing processes in dream experience. *Journal of Mental Imagery*, *12*, 65–78.

Dudycha, G.J., & Dudycha, M.M. (1941). Childhood memories: A review of the literature. *Psychological Bulletin*, *38*, 668–682.

Duncker, K. (1945). On problem solving. *Psychological Monographs*, *58* (whole no. 270).

Dywan, J., & Bowers, K. (1983). The use of hypnosis to enhance recall. *Science*, *222*, 184–185.

Ebbinghaus, H.E. (1885). *Memory: A contribution to experimental psychology.* Republished 1964, New York: Dover.

Edwards, D., & Middleton, D. (1988). Conversational remembering and family relationships: How children learn to remember. *Journal of Social and Personal Relationships*, *5*, 3–26.

Edwards, D., & Potter, J. (1992). The chancellor's memory: Rhetoric and truth in discursive remembering. *Applied Cognitive Psychology*, *6*, 187–215.

Edwards, D., Potter, J., & Middleton, D. (1992). Towards a discursive psychology of remembering. *The Psychologist: Bulletin of the British Psychological Society*, *15*, 441–446.

Egan, D.E., & Schwartz, B.J. (1979). Chunking in recall of symbolic drawings. *Memory and Cognition*, *7*, 149–158.

Einstein, G.O., & McDaniel, M.A. (1990). Normal aging and prospective memory. *Journal of Experimental Psychology: Learning, Memory and Cognition*, *16*, 717–726.

Einstein, G.O., & McDaniel, M.A. (1991). *Aging and time versus event-based prospective memory.* Paper presented at the 32nd Meeting of the Psychonomic Society, San Francisco, CA.

Ellis, H.D. (1975). Recognising faces. *British Journal of Psychology*, *66*, 409–426.

Ellis, H.D., & Shepherd, J.W. (1992). Face memory—theory and practice. In M.M. Gruneberg & P.E. Morris (Eds.), *Aspects of Memory, Vol. 1, The practical aspects* (2nd ed.). London: Routledge.

Ellis, H.D., Shepherd, J.W., & Davies, G.M. (1979). Identification of familiar and unfamiliar faces from internal and external features: Some implications for theories of face recognition. *Perception*, *8*, 431–439.

Ellis, J.A. (1988). Memory for future intentions: Investigating pulses and steps. In M.M. Gruneberg, P.E. Morris, & R.N. Sykes (Eds.), *Practical aspects of memory: Current research and issues, Vol. 1*. Chichester: Wiley.

Ellis, J.A., & Nimmo-Smith, I. (1993). Recollecting naturally occurring intentions: A study of cognitive and affective factors. *Memory*, *1*, 107–126.

Ellman, S.J., & Weinstein, L.N. (1991). REM sleep and dream formation: A theoretical investigation. In S.J. Ellman & J.S. Antrobus (Eds.), *The mind in sleep: Psychology and psychophysiology* (2nd ed.). New York: Wiley.

Erber, J.T., Szuchman, L.T., & Rothberg, S.T. (1990). Everyday memory failure: Age differences in appraisal and attribution. *Psychology and Aging*, *5*, 236–241.

Ericsson, K.A., & Pennington, N. (1993). The structure of memory performance in experts: Implications for memory in everyday life. In G.M. Davies & R.H. Logie (Eds.), *Memory in everyday life: Advances in Psychology, Vol.100* (pp.241–272). North Holland: Elsevier.

Ericsson, K.A., & Polson, P.G. (1988). An experimental analysis of a memeory skill for dinner-orders. *Journal of Experimental Psychology: Learning, Memory & Cognition*, *14*, 305–316.

Ericsson, K.A., & Simon, H.A. (1980). Verbal reports as data. *Psychological Review*, *87*, 215–251.

Evans, J.J., Wilson, B.A., & Baddeley, A.D. (1994). *An instrument for the clinical assessment of prospective memory.* Poster presented at the Third Practical Aspects of Memory Conference, Washington, DC, July.

Eysenck, M.W. (1992). *Anxiety: The cognitive perspective.* Hove, UK: Lawrence Erlbaum Associates Ltd.

Farah, M.J., Hammond, K., Levine, D., & Calvanio, R. (1988). Visual and spatial mental imagery: Dissociable systems of representation. *Cognitive Psychology, 20,* 439–462.

Fischoff, B. (1977). Perceived informativeness of facts. *Journal of Experimental Psychology: Human Perception and Performance, 3,* 349–358.

Fisher, R.P., Geiselman, R.E., & Amador, M. (1989). Field test of the cognitive interview: Enhancing the recollection of actual victims and witnesses of crime. *Journal of Applied Psychology, 74,* 722–727.

Fitzgerald, J.M. (1988). Vivid memories and the reminiscence phenomenon: The role of a self narrative. *Human Development, 31,* 261–273.

Flavell, J.H., Flavell, E.R., & Green, F.L. (1983). Development of the appearance-reality distinction. *Cognitive Psychology, 15,* 95–120.

Flavell, J.H., & Wellman, H.M. (1977). Metamemory. In J.W. Hagen (Ed.), *Perspective on the development of memory and cognition.* Hillsdale, NJ: Lawrence Erlbaum Associates Inc.

Flin, R., Boon, J., Knox, A., & Bull, R. (1992). The effect of a five month delay on children's and adults' eyewitness memory. *British Journal of Psychology, 83,* 323–336.

Flude, B.M., Ellis, A.W., & Kay, J. (1989). Face processing and retrieval in an anomic aphasia: Names are stored separately from semantic information about people. *Brain and Cognition, 11,* 60–72.

Fodor, J.A. (1983). *The modularity of mind.* Cambridge, MA: MIT Press.

Foley, M.A., Johnson, M.K., & Raye, C.L. (1983). Age-related changes in confusion between memories for thoughts and memories for speech. *Child Development, 54,* 51–60.

Foley, M.A., & Johnson, M.K. (1985). Confusions between memories for performed and imagined actions: A developmental comparison. *Child Development, 56,* 1145–1155.

Fookson, J., & Antrobus, J. (1992). A connectionist model of bizarre thought and imagery. In J. Antrobus & M. Bertini (Eds.), *The neuropsychology of sleep and dreaming* (pp.197–214). Hillsdale, NJ: Lawrence Erlbaum Associates Inc.

Foos, P.W. (1989). Age differences in memory for two common objects. *Journal of Gerontology: Psychological Sciences, 44,* 178–180.

Foster, R.A., Libkuman, T.M., Schooler, J.W., & Loftus, E.F. (1994). Consequentiality and eyewitness person identification. *Applied Cognitive Psychology, 8,* 107–121.

Foulkes, D., Bradley, L., Cavallero, C., & Hollifield, M. (1989). Processing of memories and knowledge in REM and NREM dreams. *Perceptual and Motor Skills, 68,* 365–366.

Franklin, N., & Tversky, B. (1990). *Mental spatial frameworks for different perspectives.* Paper presented at the Psychonomic Society Meeting, New Orleans, LA.

French, C.C., & Richards, A. (1993). Clock this! An everyday example of a schema-driven error in memory. *British Journal of Psychology, 84,* 249–253.

Freud, S. (1900). *The interpretation of dreams.* Republished 1955. New York: Basic Books.

Freud, S. (1916). Introducing lectures on psychoanalysis. In J. Strachey (Ed.), *The standard edition of the complete works of Sigmund Freud, Vol.2.* London: Pelican Books (published 1974).

Fruzetti, A.E., Toland, K., Teller, S.A., & Loftus, E.F. (1992). Memory and eyewitness testimony. In M.M. Gruneberg & P.E. Morris (Eds.), *Aspects of memory, Vol. 1, The practical aspects* (2nd ed.). London: Routledge

Galton, F. (1883). *Inquiries into human faculty and its development.* London: Macmillan.

Gardiner, J.M., & Java, R.I. (1993). Recognizing and remembering. In A. Collins, M.A. Conway, S.E. Gathercole, & P.E. Morris (Eds.), *Theories of memory*. Hove, UK: Lawrence Erlbaum Associates Ltd.

Garnham, A. (1985). *Psycholinguistics: Central topics*. London: Methuen.

Geiselman, R.E., Fisher, R., Mackinnon, D., & Holland, H. (1986). Enhancement of eye-witness memory with the cognitive interview. *American Journal of Psychology, 99*, 385–401.

Giambra, L.M. (1979). Sex differences in daydreaming and related mental activity from the late teens to the early nineties. *International Journal of Aging and Human Development, 10*, 1–34.

Gick, M.L., & Holyoak, K.J. (1980). Analogical problem solving. *Cognitive Psychology, 12*, 306–355.

Gilhooly, K.J., Wood, M., Kinnear, P.R., & Green, C. (1988). Skill in map reading and memory for maps. *Quarterly Journal of Experimental Psychology, 40*, 87–107.

Glucksberg, S., & McCloskey, M. (1981). Decisions about ignorance: Knowing that you don't know. *Journal of Experimental Psychology: Human Learning and Memory, 7*, 311–325.

Goldstein, L.H., Bernard, S., Fenwick, P.B.C., Burgess, P.W., & McNeil, J. (1993). Unilateral frontal lobectomy can produce strategy application disorder. *Journal of Neurology, Neurosurgery and Psychiatry, 56*, 274–276.

Goldstein, A.G., & Chance, J. (1971). Visual recognition memory for complex configurations. *Perception and Psychophysics, 9*, 237–241.

Goodenough, D.R. (1978). Dream recall: History and current status of the field. In A.M. Arkin, J.S. Antrobus, & S.J. Ellman (Eds.), *The mind in sleep: Psychology and psychophysiology* (1st ed., pp.113–140). Hillsdale, NJ: Lawrence Erlbaum Associates Inc.

Goodenough, D.R. (1992). Dream recall: History and current status of the field. In A.M. Arkin, J.S. Antrobus, & S.J. Ellman (Eds.). *The mind in sleep: Psychology and psychophysiology* (2nd ed., pp.143–171). Hillsdale, NJ: Lawrence Erlbaum Associates Inc.

Goodman, G.L., Aman, C., & Hirschman, J. (1987). Child sexual and physical abuse: Children's testimony. In S.J. Ceci, M.P. Toglia, & D.F. Ross (Eds.), *Children's eyewitness memory*. New York: Springer.

Goschke, T., & Kuhl, J. (1993). Representation of intentions: persisting activation in memory. *Journal of Experimental Psychology: Learning, Memory and Cognition, 19*, 1211–1226.

Graesser, A.C., & Clark, L.F. (1985). *Structures and procedures of implicit knowledge*. Norwood, NJ: Ablex.

Graesser, A.C., & Nakamura, G.V. (1982). The impact of a schema on comprehension and memory. In G. Bower (Ed.), *The psychology of learning and motivation: Advances in research and theory, Vol.16*. New York: Academic Press.

Greene, E., Flynn, M.S., & Loftus, E.F. (1982). Inducing resistance to misleading information. *Journal of Verbal Learning and Verbal Behavior, 21*, 207–219.

Grice, H.P. (1967). Logic and conversation: Willian James Lectures. Partly reproduced in P. Cole & J.L. Morgan (Eds.), *Syntax and semantics, Vol. 3: Speech acts*. New York: Seminar Press, 1975.

Gruneberg, M.M., & Sykes, R.N. (1978). Knowledge and retention: The feeling of knowing and reminiscence. In M.M. Gruneberg, P.E. Morris, & R.N. Sykes (Eds.), *Practical aspects of memory*. London: Academic Press.

Gruneberg, M.M., & Sykes, R.N. (1993). The generalizability of confidence-accuracy studies in eyewitnessing. *Memory, 1*, 185–189.

Halpern, A.R. (1989). Memory for the absolute pitch of familiar songs. *Memory and Cognition, 17*, 572–581.

Harris, J.E. (1980). Memory aids people use: Two interview studies. *Memory and Cognition, 8,* 31–38.

Harris, J.E., & Sunderland, A. (1987). Effects of age and instructions on an everyday memory questionnaire. *Canadian Journal of Psychology, 41,* 175–192.

Harris, J.E., & Wilkins, A.J. (1982). Remembering to do things: A theoretical framework and an illustrative experiment. *Human Learning, 1,* 123–136.

Harris, R.J. (1978). The effects of jury size and judges' instructions on memory for pragmatic implications from courtroom testimony. *Bulletin of the Psychonomic Society, 11,* 1129–32.

Harris, R.J., Lee, D.J., Hensley, D.L., & Schoen, L.M. (1988). The effect of cultural script knowledge on memory for stories over time. *Discourse Processes, 11,* 413–431.

Harris, R.J., & Monaco, G.E. (1976). Psychology of pragmatic implication: Information processing between the lines. *Journal of Experimental Psychology: General, 107,* 1–22.

Hasher, L., Attig, M.S., & Alba J.W. (1981). I knew it all along: Or did I? *Journal of Verbal Learning and Verbal Behavior, 20,* 86–96.

Hayes-Roth, B., & Hayes-Roth, F. (1979). A cognitive model of planning. *Cognitive Science, 3,* 275–310.

Hayes-Roth, B., & Thorndyke, P.W. (1979). Integration of knowledge from tests. *Journal of Verbal Learning and Verbal Behavior, 18,* 91–108.

Heckhausen, H., & Beckman, J. (1990). Intentional action and action slips. *Psychological Review, 97,* 36–48.

Herman, J.H., Ellman, S.J., & Roffwarg, H.P. (1978). The problem of NREM dream recall re-examined. In A.M. Arkin, J.S. Antrobus, & S.J. Ellman (Eds.), *The mind in sleep: Psychology and psychophysiology* (1st ed.). Hillsdale, NJ: Lawrence Erlbaum Associates Inc.

Herrman, D.J. (1984). Questionnaires about memory. In J.E. Harris & P.E. Morris (Eds.), *Everyday memory, actions and absentmindedness.* London: Academic Press.

Herrmann, D.J. (1991). *Super memory.* Emmaus, PA: Rodale Press.

Herrman, D.J., Crawford, M., & Holdsworth, M. (1992). Gender-linked differences in everyday memory performance. *British Journal of Psychology, 83,* 221–231.

Hitch, G.J., & Ferguson, J. (1991). Prospective memory for future intentions: Some comparisons with memory for past events. *European Journal of Cognitive Psychology, 3,* 285–295.

Holding, D.H., Noonan, T.K., Pfau, H.D., & Holding, C. (1986). Date attribution, age and the distribution of lifetime memories. *Journal of Gerontology, 41,* 481–5.

Horgan, D.D., & Morgan, D. (1990). Chess expertise in children. *Applied Cognitive Psychology, 4,* 109–128.

Hudson, J.A. (1990). The emergence of autobiographic memory in mother-child conversation. In R. Fivush & J.A. Hudson (Eds.), *Knowing and remembering in young children* (pp. 166–196). New York: Cambridge University Press.

Hultsch, D.F., Hertzog, C., & Dixon, R.A. (1987). Age differences in metamemory: Resolving the inconsistencies. *Canadian Journal of Psychology, 41,* 193–208.

Hunter, I.M.L. (1979). Memory in everyday life. In M.M. Gruneberg & P.E. Morris (Eds.), *Applied problems in memory.* London: Academic Press.

Huppert, F., & Beardsall, L. (1993). Prospective memory impairment as an early indicator of dementia. *Journal of Clinical and Experimental Neuropsychology, 15,* 805–821.

Hyman, I.E., & Rubin, D.C. (1990). Memorabeatlia: A naturalistic study of long term memory for song lyrics. *Memory and Cognition, 18,* 205–214.

James, L.E., & Burke, D.M. (in press). Tip of the tongue, phonological priming and aging.

James, W. (1890). *The principles of psychology.* New York: Holt.

Java, R.I., Kaminska, Z., & Gardiner, J.M. (1995). Recognition memory and awareness for famous and obscure musical themes. *European Journal of Cognitive Psychology, 7,* 41–53.

Jobe, J.B., Tourangeau, R., & Smith, A.F. (1993). Contributions of survey research to the understanding of memory. *Applied Cognitive Psychology, 7,* 567–584.

Johnson, M.K. (1983). A multiple entry modular memory system. In G. Bower (Ed.), *The psychology of learning and motivation, Vol. 17.* New York: Academic Press.

Johnson, M.K. (1985). The origin of memories. In P.C. Kendall (Ed.), *Advances in cognitive behavioral research and therapy, Vol. 4.* London and New York: Academic Press.

Johnson, M.K. (1988). Reality monitoring: An experimental phenomenological approach. *Journal of Experimental Psychology: General, 117,* 390–394.

Johnson, M.K. (1992). MEM: Mechanisms of recollection. *Journal of Cognitive Neuroscience, 4,* 268–279.

Johnson, M.K., Foley, M.A., Suangas, A.G., & Raye, C.L. (1988). Phenomenological characteristics of memories for perceived and imagined autobiographical events. *Journal of Experimental Psychology: General, 117,* 371–376.

Johnson, M.K., Hashtroudi, S., & Lindsay, D.S. (1993). Source monitoring. *Psychological Bulletin, 114,* 3–28.

Johnson, M.K., Kahan, T.L., & Raye, C.L. (1984). Dreams and reality monitoring. *Journal of Experimental Psychology: General, 113,* 329–344.

Johnson, M.K., & Raye, C.L. (1981). Reality monitoring. *Psychological Review, 88,* 67–85.

Johnson, M.K., Raye, C.L., Foley, H.J., & Foley, M.A. (1981). Cognitive operations and decision bias in reality monitoring. *American Journal of Psychology, 94,* 37–64.

Johnson, M.K., Raye, C.L., Wang, A., & Taylor, T. (1979). Facts and fantasy: The role of accuracy and variability in confusing imaginations with perceptual experiences. *Journal of Experimental Psychology: Human Learning and Memory, 5,* 229–246.

Johnson-Laird, P.N. (1981). Comprehension as the construction of mental models. *Philosophical Transactions of the Royal Society of London: The Psychological Mechanisms of Language.*

Johnson-Laird, P.N. (1983). *Mental models.* Cambridge: Cambridge University Press.

Johnston, R.A., & Bruce, V. (1990). Lost properties? Retrieval difficulties between name codes and semantic codes for familiar people. *Psychological Research, 52,* 62–67.

Jones, G.V. (1989). Back to Woodworth: Role of interlopers in the tip of the tongue phenomenon. *Memory and Cognition, 17,* 69–76.

Kahan, T.L., & Johnson, M.K. (1992). Self effects in memory for person information. *Social Cognition, 10,* 30–50.

Kahn, E., Fisher, C., & Lieberman, L. (1969). Dream recall in the normal aged. *Journal of the American Geriatric Society, 17,* 1121–1126.

Kassin, S.M., Ellsworth, P.C., & Smith, V.L. (1989). The general acceptance of psychological research on eyewitness testimony: A survey of the experts. *American Psychologist, 44,* 1089–1098.

Keenan, J.M., MacWhinney, B., & Mayhew, D. (1977). Pragmatics in memory: A study of natural conversation. *Journal of Verbal Learning and Verbal Behavior, 16,* 549–560.

Keller, F.S. (1953). Stimulus discrimination and Morse code learning. *New York Academy of Science, Series 2, 15,* 195–203.

Kemper, S., & Thissen, D. (1981). Memory for the dimensions of requests. *Journal of Verbal Learning and Verbal Behavior, 20,* 552–563.

Kerr, N. (1993). Mental imagery, dreams and perception. In C. Cavallero & D. Foulkes (Eds.), *Dreaming as cognition* (pp.18–37). Hemel Hempstead: Harvester Wheatsheaf.

Kester, D.B., Saykin, A.J., Sperling, M.R., O'Connor, M.J., Robinson, L.J., & Gur, R.C. (1991). Acute effect of anterior temporal lobectomy on musical processing. *Neuropsychologia, 29,* 703–708.

Kihlstrom, J.F. (1994). *Memory research: The convergence of theory and practice.* Paper presented at the Third Practical Aspects Conference, Washington, DC, July.

Kimberg, M., & Farah, M.J. (1993). A unified account of cognitive impairments following frontal lobe damage: The role of working memory in complex organized behavior. *Journal of Experimental Psychology: General, 122,* 411–428.

Kintsch, W., & Bates, E. (1977). Recognition memory for statements from a classroom lecture. *Journal of Experimental Psychology: Human Learning and Memory, 3,* 150–159.

Kintsch, W., & van Dijk, T.A. (1978). Toward a model of text comprehension and reproduction. *Psychological Review, 85,* 363–394.

Kirasic, K.C. (1991). Spatial cognition and behaviour in young and elderly adults: Implications for learning new environments. *Psychology and Aging, 6,* 10–18.

Klatzky, R.L. (1991). Let's be friends. *American Psychologist, 46,* 43–45.

Kolodner, J.L. (1992). An introduction to case-based reasoning. *Artificial Intelligence Review, 6,* 3–34.

Koriat, A. (1993). How do we know that we know? The accessibility model of feeling of knowing. *Psychological Review, 100,* 609–639.

Koriat, A. (1995). *Dissociating knowing and the feeling of knowing: Further evidence for the accessibility model.* (IIPDM Report no. 121) University of Haifa, Israel.

Koriat, A., Ben-Zur, H., & Nussbaum, A. (1990). Encoding information for future action: Memory for to-be-performed tasks versus memory for to-be-recalled tasks. *Memory and Cognition, 18,* 568–578.

Koriat, A., Ben-Zur, H., & Sheffer, D. (1988). Telling the same story twice: Output monitoring and age. *Journal of Memory and Language, 27,* 23–39.

Koriat, A., & Goldsmith, M. (1996). Memory metaphors and the real life/laboratory controversy: Correspondence versus storehouse conceptions of memory. *Behavioral and Brain Sciences, 19,* 167–228.

Kosslyn, S.M. (1981). The medium and the message in mental imagery: A theory. *Psychological Review, 88,* 46–65.

Kosslyn, S.M., Chabris, C.F., Marsolek, C.J., & Koenig, O. (1992). Categorical vs. co-ordinate spatial representations: Computational analysis and computer simulations. *Journal of Experimental Psychology: Human Perception and Performance, 18,* 562–577.

Kozlowski, L.T., & Bryant, K.J. (1977). Sense of direction, spatial orientation and cognitive maps. *Journal of Experimental Psychology: Human Perception and Performance, 3,* 590–598.

Kreutzer, M.A., Leonard, C., & Flavell, J.H. (1975). An interview study of children's knowledge about memory. *Monographs of the Society for Research in Child Development, 40* (No. 159).

Krinsky, R., & Krinsky, S.J. (1988). City size bias and the feeling of knowing. In M.M. Gruneberg, P.E. Morris, & R.M. Sykes (Eds.), *Practical aspects of memory: Current research and issues, Vol. 1.* Chichester: Wiley.

Krumhansl, C.L. (1991a). Memory for musical surface. *Memory and Cognition, 19,* 401–411.

Krumhansl, C.L. (1991b). Music psychology: Tonal structures in perception and memory. *Annual Review of Psychology, 42,* 277–303.

Kvavilashvili, L. (1987). Remembering intentions as a distinct form of memory. *British Journal of Psychology, 78,* 507–518.

Kvavilashvili, L. (1992). Remembering intentions: A critical review of existing experimental paradigms. *Applied Cognitive Psychology, 6,* 507–524.

Lachman, J.L., Lachman, R., & Thronesberry, C. (1979). Metamemory through the adult life span. *Developmental Psychology, 15,* 543–551.

Landau, B., & Jackendoff, R. (1993). "What" and "where" in spatial language and spatial cognition. *Behavioral and Brain Sciences, 2,* 217–238.

Leippe, M.R., & Romanczyk, A. (1987). Children on the witness stand: A communication/ persuasion analysis of jurors' reactions to child witnesses. In S. Ceci, M. Toglia, & D. Ross (Eds.), *Children's eyewitness memory* (pp.155–170). New York: Springer.

Lepper, M.R. (1995). Theory by numbers? Some concerns about meta-analysis as a theoretical tool. *Applied Cognitive Psychology, 9,* 411–422.

Ley, P. (1978). Memory for medical information. In M.M. Gruneberg, P.E. Morris, & R.N. Sykes (Eds.), *Practical aspects of memory.* London: Academic Press.

Lichtenstein, E.H., & Brewer, W.F. (1980). Memory for goal directed events, *Cognitive Psychology, 12,* 412–445.

Lindsay, D.S., & Johnson, M.K. (1989). The eyewitness suggestibility effect and memory for source. *Memory and Cognition, 17,* 349–358.

Lindsay, D.S., & Read, J.D. (1994). Psychotherapy and memories of childhood sexual abuse: A cognitive perspective. *Applied Cognitive Psychology, 8,* 281–338.

Linton, M. (1982). Transformations of memory in everyday life. In U. Neisser (Ed.), *Memory observed: Remembering in natural contexts.* San Francisco: Freeman.

List, J.A. (1986). Age and schematic differences in reliability of eyewitness testimony. *Developmental Psychology, 22,* 50–57.

Loftus, E.F. (1974). Reconstituting memory: The incredible eyewitness. *Psychology Today, 8,* 116–119.

Loftus, E.F. (1975). Leading questions and the eyewitness report. *Cognitive Psychology, 7,* 560–572.

Loftus, E.F. (1979a). *Eyewitness testimony.* Cambridge, MA: Harvard University Press.

Loftus, E.F. (1979b). Reactions to blatantly contradictory information. *Memory and Cognition, 7,* 368–374.

Loftus, E.F. (1987). *Remembering when.* Paper presented at the Second Practical Aspects of Memory Conference, Swansea, Wales.

Loftus, E.F. (1991). The glitter of everyday memory . . . and the gold. *American Psychologist, 46,* 16–18.

Loftus, E.F., & Burns, T.E. (1982). Mental shock can produce retrograde amnesia. *Memory and Cognition, 10,* 318–323.

Loftus, E.F., & Coan, D. (in press). The construction of childhood memories. In D. Peters (Ed.), *The child witness in context: Cognitive, social and legal perspectives.* New York: Kluwer.

Loftus, E.F., & Greene, E. (1980). Warning: Even memory for faces may be contagious. *Law and Human Behavior, 4,* 323–334.

Loftus, E.F., & Ketcham, K. (1991). *Witness for the defense.* New York: St. Martins Press.

Loftus, E.F., & Loftus, G.R. (1980). On the permanence of stored information in the human brain. *American Psychologist, 35,* 421–434.

Loftus, E.F., & Marburger, W. (1983). Since the eruption of Mount St Helens has anyone beaten you up? Improving the accuracy of retrospective reports with landmark events. *Memory and Cognition, 11,* 114–120.

Loftus, E.F., Miller D.G., & Burns, H. (1978). Semantic integration of verbal information into a visual memory. *Journal of Experimental Psychology: Human Learning and Memory, 4,* 19–31.

Loftus, E.F., & Palmer, J.C. (1974). Reconstruction of automobile destruction: An example of the interaction between language and memory. *Journal of Verbal Learning and Verbal Behavior, 13,* 585–589.

Loftus, E.F., Schooler, J.W., & Wagenaar, W.A. (1985). The fate of memory: Comment on McCloskey & Zaragoza. *Journal of Experimemtal Psychology: General, 114,* 375–380.

Loftus, E.F., Smith, K.D., Johnson, D.A., & Fiedler, J. (1988). Remembering when: Errors in the dating of autobiographical memories. In M.M. Gruneberg, P.E. Morris, & R.M. Sykes (Eds.), *Practical aspects of memory: Current research and issues, Vol. 1.* Chichester: Wiley.

Lutz, J., Means, L.W., & Long, T.E. (1994). Where did I park? *Applied Cognitive Psychology, 8,* 437–530.

Mackay, D.G., & Burke, D.M. (1990). Cognition and aging: A theory of new learning and the use of old connections. In T.Hess (Ed.), *Aging and cognition: Knowledge organization and utilization* (pp.1–51). Amsterdam: North Holland.

Mandler, G. (1967). Organisation and memory. In K.W. Spence & J.T. Spence (Eds.), *The psychology of learning and motivation: Advances in research and theory, Vol. 1.* London: Academic Press

Mandler J.M. (1978). A code in the node: The use of story schema in retrieval. *Discourse Processes, 1,* 14–35.

Mandler, J.M. (1984). *Stories, scripts and scenes: Aspects of schema theory.* Hillsdale, NJ: Lawrence Erlbaum Associates Inc.

Mandler, J.M., & Parker, R.E. (1976). Memory for descriptive and spatial information in complex pictures. *Journal of Experimental Psychology: Human Learning and Memory, 2,* 38–48.

Mantyla, T., & Backman, L. (1992). Aging and memory for expected and unexpected objects in real world settings. *Journal of Experimental Psychology: Learning, Memory and Cognition, 18,* 1298–1309.

Marshall, J.C., & Halligan, P.W. (1995). Seeing the forest or only half the trees? *Nature, 373,* 521–523.

Martin, M. (1986). Ageing and patterns of change in everyday memory and cognition. *Human Learning, 5,* 63–74.

Martin, M., & Jones G.V. (1984). Cognitive failures in everyday life. In J.E. Harris & P.E. Morris (Eds.), *Everyday memory, actions and absentmindedness.* London: Academic Press.

Maylor, E.A. (1990). Age and prospective memory. *Quarterly Journal of Experimental Psychology, 42A,* 471–493.

Maylor, E.A. (1991). Recognizing and naming tunes: Memory impairment in the elderly. *Journal of Gerontology, 46,* 207–217.

McCloskey, M., Wible, C.G., & Cohen, N.J. (1988). Is there a special flashbulb mechanism? *Journal of Experimental Psychology: General, 117,* 171–181.

McCloskey, M., & Zaragoza, M. (1985). Misleading postevent information and memory for events: Arguments and evidence against memory impairment hypotheses. *Journal of Experimental Psychology: General, 114,* 1–16.

McDaniel, M.A., & Einstein, G.O. (1993). The importance of cue familiarity and distinctiveness in prospective memory. *Memory, 1,* 23–41.

McDonough, L., & Mandler, J.M. (1994). Very long term recall in infants: Infantile amnesia reconsidered. *Memory, 2,* 339–352.

McGehee, F. (1937). The reliability of the identification of the human voice. *Journal of General Psychology, 17,* 249–271.

McIntyre, J.S., & Craik, F.I.M. (1987). Adult age differences for item and source information. *Canadian Journal of Psychology, 41,* 175–192.

McKeithen, K.B., Reitman, J.S., Rueter, H.H., & Hirtle, S.C. (1981). Knowledge organisation and skill differences in computer programmers. *Cognitive Psychology, 13,* 307–325.

McKenna, P., & Warrington, E.K. (1980). Testing for nominal dysphasia. *Journal of Neurology, Neurosurgery and Psychiatry, 43,* 781–788.

McKoon, G., & Ratcliff, R. (1981). Comprehension processes and memory structures involved in instrumental inference. *Journal of Verbal Learning and Verbal Behavior, 20*, 671–682.

McKoon, G., Ratcliff, R., & Seifert, C. (1989). Making the connection: Generalized knowledge structures in story understanding. *Journal of Memory and Language, 28*, 711–734.

McWeeny, K.H., Young, A.W., Hay, D.C., & Ellis, A.W. (1987). Putting names to faces. *British Jounal of Psychology, 78*, 143–149.

Meacham, J.A., & Leiman, B. (1975, September). *Remembering to perform future actions.* Paper presented at the American Psychological Association meeting, Chicago.

Meacham, J.A., & Singer, J. (1977). Incentive in prospective remembering. *Journal of Psychology, 97*, 191–197.

Means, B., & Loftus, E.F. (1991). When personal history repeats itself: Decomposing memories for events. *Applied Cognitive Psychology, 5*, 297–318.

Means, B., Mingay, D.J., Nigam, A., & Zarrow, M. (1988). A cognitive approach to enhancing health survey reports of medical visits. In M.M. Gruneberg, P.E. Morris, & R.N. Sykes (Eds.), *Practical aspects of memory: Current research and issues, Vol. 1.* Chichester: Wiley.

Meudell, P.R., Hitch, G.J., & Kirby, P. (1992). Are two heads better than one? Experimental investigations of the social facilitation of memory. *Applied Cognitive Psychology, 6*, 461–572.

Meyer, B. (1975). *The organisation of prose and its effect on memory.* Amsterdam: North Holland.

Middleton, D., & Buchanan, K. (1994). *Social remembering in conversation.* Paper presented at Memory: Toward a common vision, a multidisciplinary workshop at The Open University, Milton Keynes, September 1994.

Miller, L.K. (1989). *Musical savants: Exceptional skill in the mentally retarded.* Hillsdale, NJ: Lawrence Erlbaum Associates Inc.

Montangero, J. (1991). How can we define the sequential organisation of dreams? *Perceptual and Motor Skills, 73*, 1059–1073.

Morris, P.E. (1984). The validity of subjective reports on memory. In J.E. Harris & P.E. Morris (Eds.), *Everyday memory, actions and absentmindedness.* London: Academic Press.

Morris, P.E., Gruneberg, M.M., Sykes, R.N., & Merrick, A. (1981). Football knowledge and the acquisition of new results. *British Journal of Psychology, 72*, 479–483.

Morris, P.E., Tweedy, M., & Gruneberg, M.M. (1985). Interest, knowledge and the memorising of soccer scores. *British Journal of Psychology, 76*, 415–425.

Moscovitch, M. (1982). A neuropsychological approach to memory and perception in normal and pathological aging. In F.I.M. Craik & S. Trehub (Eds.), *Aging and cognitive processes.* New York: Plenum Press.

Murphy, G.L., & Wright, J.C. (1984). Changes in conceptual structure with expertise: Difference between real-world experts and novices. *Journal of Experimental Psychology: Learning, Memory and Cognition, 10*, 144–55.

Myles-Worthley, M., Johnston, W.A., & Simon, M.A. (1988). The influence of expertise on X-ray image processing. *Journal of Experimental Psychology: Learning, Memory and Cognition, 14*, 553–557.

Nakamura, G.V., Graesser, A.C., Zimmerman, J.A., & Riha, J. (1985). Script processing in a natural situation. *Memory and Cognition, 13*, 104–114.

Naveh-Benjamin, M. (1988). Retention of cognitive structures learned in university courses. In M.M. Gruneberg, P.E. Morris, & R.N. Sykes (Eds.), *Practical aspects of memory: Current research and issues, Vol. 2* (pp.383–388) Chichester: Wiley.

Neisser, U. (1978). Memory: What are the important questions? In M.M. Gruneberg, P.E. Morris, & R.N. Sykes (Eds.), *Practical aspects of memory.* London: Academic Press.

Neisser, U. (1982a). John Dean's memory: A case study. In U. Neisser (Ed.), *Memory observed: Remembering in natural contexts.* San Francisco, CA: Freeman.

Neisser, U. (1982b). (Ed.) *Memory observed: remembering in natural contexts.* San Francisco, CA: Freeman.

Neisser, U. (1982c). Snapshots or benchmarks? In U. Neisser (Ed.), *Memory observed: Remembering in natural contexts.* San Francisco, CA: Freeman.

Neisser, U. (1984). Interpreting Harry Bahrick's discovery: What confers immunity against forgetting? *Journal of Experimental Psychology: General, 113,* 32–35.

Neisser, U. (1986). Nested structure in autobiographical memory. In D.C. Rubin (Ed.), *Autobiographical memory.* Cambridge: Cambridge University Press.

Neisser, U. (1988a). The present and the past. In M.M. Gruneberg, P.E. Morris, & R.N. Sykes (Eds.), *Practical aspects of memory: Current research and issues, Vol. 2.* Chichester: Wiley.

Neisser, U. (1988b). What is ordinary memory the memory of? In U. Neisser & E. Winograd (Eds.), *Remembering reconsidered* (pp. 356–373). Cambridge University Press.

Neisser, U. (1991). A case of misplaced nostalgia. *American Psychologist, 46,* 34–36.

Neisser, U., & Harsch, N. (1992). Phantom flashbulbs: False recollections of hearing the news about Challenger. In E. Winograd & U. Neisser (Eds.), *Affect and accurcy in recall: Studies of "flashbulb" memories* (pp.9–31). Cambridge: Cambridge University Press.

Nelson, K. (1991). *Toward an explanation of the development of autobiographical memory.* Keynote address presented at the Internationational Conference on Memory, Lancaster, July 1991.

Nelson, K., & Gruendel, J. (1986). Children's scripts. In K. Nelson (Ed.), *Event knowledge: Structure and function in development.* Hillsdale, NJ: Lawrence Erlbaum Associates Inc.

Nelson, T.O., Leonesio, R.J., & Landwehr, R.S. (1986). A comparison of three predictors of individuals' memory performance: The individual's FOK vs. the normative FOK vs. base-rate item difficulty. *Journal of Experimental Psychology: Language Memory and Cognition, 12,* 279–287.

Nickerson, R.S. (1977). Some comments on human archival memory as a very large data base. *Proceedings of the Third International Conference on Very Large Data Bases,* Tokyo, October 1991.

Nickerson, R.S., & Adams, M.J. (1982). Long-term memory for a common object. In U. Neisser (Ed.), *Memory observed: Remembering in natural contexts.* San Francisco, CA: Freeman.

Nigro, G., & Neisser, U. (1983). Point of view in personal memories. *Cognitive Psychology, 15,* 465–482.

Nisbett, R.E., & Wilson, T.D. (1977). Telling more than we can know: Verbal reports on mental processes. *Psychological Review, 84,* 231–259.

Norman, D.A. (1981). Categorisation of action slips. *Psychological Review, 88,* 1–15.

Norman, D.A. (1988). *The psychology of everyday things.* New York: Basic Books.

Norman, D.A., & Bobrow, D.G. (1976). On the role of active memory processes in perception and cognition. In C.F. Cofer (Ed.), *The structure of human memory.* San Francisco, CA: Freeman.

Norman, D.A., & Bobrow, D.G. (1979). Descriptions: An intermediate stage in memory retrieval. *Cognitive Psychology, 11,* 107–123.

Norman, D.A., & Shallice, T. (1986). Attention to action: Willed and automatic control of behavior. In R.J. Davidson, G.E. Schwarts, & D. Shapiro (Eds.), *Consciousness and self-regulation: Advances in research and theory, Vol. 4* (pp.1–18). New York: Plenum Press.

Paivio, A. (1969). Mental imagery in associative learning and memory. *Psychological Review*, 76, 241–263.

Palmer, C., & Krumhansl, C.L. (1990). Mental representations for musical metre. *Journal of Experimental Psychology: Human Perception and Performance*, 16, 728–741.

Palmeri, T.J., Goldinger, S.D., & Pisoni, D.B. (1993). Episodic encoding of voice attributes and recognition memory for spoken words. *Journal of Experimental Psychology: Learning, Memory and Cognition*, 19, 309–328.

Parkes, K.R. (1980). Occupational stress among student nurses. *Nursing Times*, 76, 113–116.

Parkin, A.J. (1987). *Memory and amnesia: An introduction*. Oxford: Blackwell.

Patel, V.L., & Groen, G.J. (1991). The general and specific nature of medical expertise: A critical look. In K.A. Ericsson & J. Smith (Eds.), *Toward a general theory of expertise: Prospects and limits* (pp. 93–125). New York: Cambridge University Press.

Pennington, N., Nicolich, R., & Rahm, J. (1995). Transfer of training between cognitive subskills: Is knowledge use specific? *Cognitive Psychology*, 28, 175–224.

Peper, R.J., & Mayer, R.E. (1978). Note taking as a generative activity. *Journal of Educational Psychology*, 70, 514–522.

Perlmutter, M. (1978). What is memory ageing the ageing of? *Developmental Psychology*, 14, 330–45.

Perner, J. (1992). Grasping the concept of representation: Its impact on 4-year-olds' theory of mind and beyond. *Human Development*, 35, 146–155.

Pezdek, K., & Prull, M. (1993). Fallacies in memory for conversations: Reflections on Clarence Thomas, Anita Hill, and the like. *Applied Cognitive Psychology*, 7, 275–364.

Pillemer, D.B. (1992). Preschool children's memories of personal circumstances: The fire alarm study. In E. Winograd & U. Neisser (Eds.), *Affect and accuracy in recall: Studies of "flashbulb memories"*. Cambridge: Cambridge University Press.

Pollina, L.K., Greene, A.L., Tunick, R.H., & Puckett, J.M. (1992). Dimensions of everyday memory in young adulthood. *British Journal of Psychology*, 83, 305–321.

Poon, L.W., & Schaffer, G. (1982). *Prospective memory in young and elderly adults*. Paper presented at a meeting of the American Psychological Association, Washington, DC.

Price, E., & Cohen, G. (1995). *The effects of face-name congruence*. Unpublished manuscript.

Rabbitt, P.M.A., Maylor, E.A., McInnes, L., Bent, N., & Moore, B. (1995). What goods can self-assessment questionnaires deliver for cognitive psychology? *Applied Cognitive Psychology*, 9, 127–152.

Read, J.D. (1995). The availability heuristic in person identification: The sometimes misleading consequences of enhanced contextual information. *Applied Cognitive Psychology*, 9, 91–121.

Read J.D., & Bruce D. (1982). Longitudinal tracking of difficult memory retrievals. *Cognitive Psychology*, 14, 280–300.

Reason, J.T. (1979). Actions not as planned: The price of automatisation. In G. Underwood & R. Stevens (Eds.), *Aspects of Consciousness, Vol. 1*. London: Academic Press.

Reason, J.T. (1984). Absentmindedness and cognitive control. In J.E. Harris & P.E. Morris (Eds.), *Everyday memory, actions and absentmindedness*. London: Academic Press.

Reason, J. (1990). *Human error*. New York: Cambridge University Press.

Reason, J.T., & Lucas, D. (1984). Using cognitive diaries to investigate naturally occurring memory blocks. In J.E. Harris & P.E. Morris (Eds.), *Everyday memory, actions and absentmindedness*. London: Academic Press.

Reason, J.T., & Mycielska, K. (1982). *Absentminded? The psychology of mental lapses and everyday errors*. Englewood Cliffs, NJ: Prentice-Hall.

Reder, L.M., & Ritter, F. (1992). What determines initial feeling of knowing? Familiarity with question terms, not with the answer. *Journal of Experimental Psychology: Learning, Memory and Cognition*, 18, 435–451.

Reinsel, R., Antrobus, J., & Wollman, M. (1992). Bizarrness in dreams and waking fantasy. In J. Antrobus & M. Bertini (Eds.), *The Neuropsychology of sleep and dreaming.* Hillsdale, NJ: Lawrence Erlbaum Associates Inc.

Reiser, B.J., Black, J.B., & Abelson, R.P. (1985). Knowledge structures in the organisation and retrieval of autobiographical memories. *Cognitive Psychology, 17,* 89–137.

Reitman, J.S. (1976). Skilled perception in Go: Deducing memory structures from inter-response times. *Cognitive Psychology, 8,* 336–356.

Rhodes, G., Brennan, S.E., & Carey, S. (1987). Identification and ratings of caricatures: Implications for mental representations of faces. *Cognitive Psychology, 19,* 473–497.

Richardson, J.T.E. (1992). Remembering the appearance of familiar objects: A study of monarchic memory. *Bulletin of the Psychonomic Society, 30,* 389–392.

Richardson, J.T.E., & Chan, R.C.B. (1995). The constituent structure of subjective memory questionnaires: Evidence from multiple sclerosis. *Memory, 3,* 187–200.

Roberts, K.P., & Blades, M. (1995). Children's discrimination of memories for actual and pretend actions in a hiding task. *British Journal of Developmental Psychology, 13,* 321–333.

Robinson, J.A. (1976). Sampling autobiographical memory. *Cognitive Psychology, 8,* 578–595.

Robinson, J.A. (1992). Autobiographical memory. In M.M. Gruneberg & P.E. Morris (Eds.). *Aspects of memory, Vol. 1, The practical aspects* (2nd ed., pp.223–251). London: Routledge.

Robinson, J.A., & Swanson, K.L. (1993). Field and observer modes of remembering. *Memory, 1,* 169–184.

Rogers, T.B., Kuiper, N.A., & Kirker, W.S. (1977). Self-reference and the encoding of personal information. *Journal of Personality and Social Psychology, 35,* 667–688.

Rosch, E., Mervis, C.B., Gray, W.D., Johnson, D.M., & Boyes-Braem, P. (1976). Basic objects in natural categories. *Cognitive Psychology, 8,* 382–439.

Rossano, M.J., & Hodgson, S.L. (1994). The process of learning from small-scale maps. *Applied Cognitive Psychology, 8,* 565–582.

Rubin, D.C. (1977). Very long-term memory for prose and verse. *Journal of Verbal Learning and Verbal Behavior, 16,* 611–621.

Rubin, D.C. (1982). On the retention function for autobiographical memory. *Journal of Verbal Learning and Verbal Behavior, 21,* 21–38.

Rubin, D.C., & Baddeley, A.D. (1989). Telescoping is not time compression: A model of the dating of autobiographical events. *Memory and Cognition, 17,* 653–661.

Rubin, D.C., & Kozin, M. (1984). Vivid memories. *Cognition, 16,* 81–95.

Rubin, D.C., Wetzler, S.E., & Nebes, R.D. (1986). Autobiographical memory across the life span. In D.C. Rubin (Ed.), *Autobiographical memory.* Cambridge: Cambridge University Press.

Rumelhart, D.E., & Norman, D.A. (1978). Accretion, tuning and restructuring: Three models of learning. In J.W. Cotton & R. Klatzky (Eds.), *Semantic factors in cognition.* Hillsdale, NJ: Lawrence Erlbaum Associates Inc.

Rumelhart, D.E., & Norman, D.A. (1985). Representation of knowledge. In A.M. Aitkenhead & J.M. Slack (Eds.), *Issues in cognitive modelling* (pp. 15–62) Hove, UK: Lawrence Erlbaum Associates Ltd.

Russell, P.A. (1987). Memory for music: A study of musical and listener factors. *British Journal of Psychology, 78,* 335–347.

Sachs, J.S. (1967). Recognition memory for syntactic and semantic aspects of connected discourse. *Perception and Psychophysics, 2,* 437–442.

Salaman, E. (1982). A collection of moments. In U. Neisser (Ed.), *Memory observed: Remembering in natural contexts.* San Francisco, CA: Freeman.

Samson, S., & Zatorre, R.J. (1991). Recognition memory for text and melody of songs after unilateral temporal lobe lesion: Evidence for dual coding. *Journal of Experimental Psychology: Learning, Memory and Cognition, 17,* 793–804.

Samson, S., & Zatorre, R.J. (1992). Learning and retention of melodic and verbal information after unilateral temporal lobectomy. *Neuropsychologia, 30,* 815–826.

Schachtel, E.G. (1947). On memory and childhood amnesia. *Psychiatry, 10,* 1–26.

Schank, R.C. (1982a) *Dynamic memory.* Cambridge: Cambridge University Press.

Schank, R.C. (1982b). Reminding and memory organisation. In W.G. Lehnert & M.H. Ringle (Eds.), *Strategies for natural language processing.* Hillsdale, NJ: Lawrence Erlbaum Associates Inc.

Schank, R.C., & Abelson, R.P. (1977). *Scripts, plans, goals and understanding.* Hillsdale, NJ: Lawrence Erlbaum Associates Inc.

Schmidt, S.R., & Bohannon, J.N. (1988). In defense of the flashbulb memory hypothesis: A comment on McCloskey, Wible & Cohen (1988). *Journal of Experimental Psychology: General, 117,* 332–335.

Searle, J.R. (1969). *Speech acts.* Cambridge: Cambridge University Press.

Searleman, A.E., & Gaydusek, K.A. (1989). *Relationship between prospective memory ability and selective personality variables.* Paper presented at the annual meeting of the Psychonomic Society, Atlanta, GA.

Sehulster, J.R. (1988). Broader perspectives on everyday memory. In M.M. Gruneberg, P.E. Morris, & R.N. Sykes (Eds.), *Practical aspects of memory: Current research and issues, Vol.1* (pp.323–328). Chichester: Wiley.

Sehulster, J.R. (1989). Content and temporal structure of autobiographical memory: Remembering 25 seasons of the Metropolitan Opera. *Memory and Cognition, 17,* 590–606.

Seifert, C.M., McKoon, G., Abelson, R.P., & Ratcliff, R. (1986). Memory connections between thematically similar episodes. *Journal of Experimental Psychology: Learning, Memory and Cognition, 12,* 220–231.

Sellen, A.J., Louie, G., Harris, J.E., & Wilkins, A.J. (in press). What brings intentions to mind? An in situ study of prospective memory. *Memory.*

Semenza, C., & Sgaramella, T.M. (1993). Production of proper names: A clinical case study of the effects of phonemic cueing. In G. Cohen & D.M. Burke (Eds.), *Memory for proper names* (pp. 265–280). Hove, UK: Lawrence Erlbaum Associates Ltd.

Semenza, C., & Zettin, M. (1989). Evidence from aphasia for the role of proper names as pure referring expressions. *Nature, 342,* 678–679.

Shallice, T., & Burgess, P.W. (1991). Deficits in strategy application following frontal lobe damage in man. *Brain, 114,* 727–741.

Sheingold, K., & Tenney, Y.J. (1982). Memory for a salient childhood event. In U. Neisser (Ed.), *Memory observed: Remembering in natural contexts.* San Francisco, CA: Freeman.

Shepard, R.N. (1984). Ecological constraints on internal representation: Resonant kinomatics of perceiving, imagining, thinking and dreaming. *Psychological Review, 91,* 417–446.

Shiffrin, R.M., & Schneider, W. (1977). Controlled and automatic information processing. II: Perceptual learning, automatic attending, and a general theory. *Psychological Review, 84,* 127–90.

Shimamura, A.P., Janowsky, J., & Squire, L.R. (1991). What is the role of frontal lobe damage in memory disorders? In H.S. Levin, H.M. Eisenberg & A.L. Benton (Eds.), *Frontal lobe function and dysfunction.* New York: Oxford University Press.

Simon, S.L., Walsh, D.A., Regnier, V.A., & Kraus, I.K. (1992). Spatial cognition and neighbourhood use: The relationship in older adults. *Psychology and Aging, 7,* 389–394.

Skowronski, J.J., & Thompson, C.P. (1990). Reconstructing the dates of personal events: Gender differences in accuracy. *Applied Cognitive Psychology, 4,* 371–381.

Sloboda, J.A. (1985). *The musical mind: The cognitive psychology of music.* Oxford: Clarendon Press.

Smith, A.F., Jobe, J.B., & Mingay, D.J. (1991). Retrieval from memory of dietary information. *Applied Cognitive Psychology, 5,* 269–296.

Smith, E.E., Langston, C., & Nisbett, R.E. (1992). The case for rules in reasoning. *Cognitive Science, 16,* 1–40.

Spence, D.P. (1988). Passive remembering. In U. Neisser & E. Winograd (Eds.), *Remembering reconsidered: Ecological and traditional approaches to the study of memory.* New York: Cambridge University Press.

Spilich, G.J., Vesonder, G.T., Chiesi, H.L., & Voss, J.F. (1979). Text proceedings of domain-related information for individuals with high and low domain knowledge. *Journal of Verbal Learning and Verbal Behavior, 18,* 275–290.

Stanhope, N., Cohen, G., & Conway, M.A. (1993). Very long-term retention of a novel. *Applied Cognitive Psychology, 7,* 239–256.

Stevens, A., & Coupe, P. (1978). Distortions in judged spatial relations. *Cognitive Psychology, 10,* 422–437.

Storr, A. (1992). *Music and the mind.* New York: The Free Press.

Suangas, A.G., & Johnson, M.K. (1988). Qualitative effects of rehearsal on memories for perceived and imagined complex events. *Journal of Experimental Psychology:General, 117,* 377–389.

Sunderland, A., Harris, J.E., & Baddeley, A.D. (1983). Do laboratory tests predict everyday memory? A neuropsychological study. *Journal of Verbal Learning and Verbal Behavior, 22,* 341–357.

Tanaka, J.W., & Farah, M.J. (1993). Parts and wholes in face recognition. *Quarterly Journal of Experimental Psychology, 46A,* 225–246.

Taylor, H.A., & Tversky, B. (1992). Spatial mental models derived from survey and route descriptions. *Journal of Memory and Language, 31,* 261–292.

Tenney, Y.J. (1984). Aging and the misplacing of objects. *British Journal of Developmental Psychology, 2,* 43–50.

Thompson, C.P., & Cowan, T. (1986). Flashbulb memories: A nicer interpretation of Neisser. *Cognition, 22,* 199–200.

Thorndyke, P.W., & Hayes-Roth, B. (1982). Differences in spatial knowledge acquired from maps and navigation. *Cognitive Psychology, 14,* 450–89.

Thorndyke, P.W., & Stasz, C. (1980). Individual differences in procedures for knowledge acquisition from maps. *Cognitive Psycholgy, 12,* 137–175.

Trabasso, T., & Suh, S. (1993). Understanding text: Achieving explanatory coherence through on-line inferences and mental operations in working memory. *Discourse Processes, 16,* 3–34.

Tulving, E. (1972). Episodic and semantic memory. In E. Tulving & W. Donaldson (Eds.), *Organisation of memory.* New York: Academic Press.

Tulving, E. (1985). How many memory systems are there? *American Psychologist, 40,* 385–398.

Tulving, E. (1991). Concepts of memory. In L.R. Squire, N.M. Weinberger, G. Lynch, & J.L. McGaugh (Eds.), *Memory: Organization and locus of change.* New York: Oxford University Press.

Tulving, E., & Thomson, D.M. (1973). Encoding specificity and retrieval processes in episodic memory. *Psychological Review, 80,* 336–342.

Tversky, B. (1991). Spatial mental models. In G.H. Bower (Ed.), *The psychology of learning and motivation: Advances in research and theory, Vol. 27* (pp. 109–145). San Diego, CA: Academic Press.

Tversky, B. (1995). Memory for pictures, environments, maps and graphs. In D. Payne & F. Conrad (Eds.), *Practical aspects of memory*. Hillsdale, NJ: Lawrence Erlbaum Associates Inc.

Usher, J.A., & Neisser, U. (1993). Childhood amnesia and the beginnings of memory for four early life events. *Journal of Experimental Psychology: General, 122*, 155–165.

Valentine, T. (1991). A unified account of the effects of distinctiveness, inversion and race in face recognition. *Quarterly Journal of Experimental Psychology, 43A*, 161–204.

Valentine, T., & Bruce, V. (1986). The effects of distinctiveness in recognizing and classifying faces. *Perception, 15*, 525–536.

Valentine, T., & Moore, V. (1995). Naming faces: The effects of facial distinctiveness and surname frequency. *Quarterly Journal of Experimental Psychology, 48A*, 849–878.

Vallacher, R.R., & Wegner, D.M. (1987). What do people think they're doing? Action identification and human behavior. *Psychological Review, 94*, 3–15.

Van Dijk, T.A., & Kintsch, W. (1983). *Strategies of discourse comprehension*. New York: Academic Press.

Van Lancker, D.R., Cummings, J.L., Kreiman, J., & Dobkin, B.H. (1988). Phonagnosia: A dissociation between familiar and unfamiliar voices. *Cortex, 24*, 195–209.

Van Lancker, D., Kreiman, J., & Cummings, J. (1989). Voice perception deficits: Neuroanatomical correlates of phonagnosia. *Journal of Clinical and Experimental Neuropsychology, 11*, 665–674.

Vogel, G.W. (1978). Sleep-onset mentation. In A.M. Arkin, J.S. Antrobus, & S.J. Ellman (Eds.), *The mind in sleep: Psychology and psychophysiology* (1st ed.). Hillsdale, NJ: Lawrence Erlbaum Associates Inc.

Wagenaar, W.A. (1978). Recalling messages broadcast to the general public. In M.M. Gruneberg, P.E. Morris, & R.N. Sykes (Eds.), *Practical aspects of memory*. London: Academic Press.

Wagenaar, W.A. (1986). My memory: A study of autobiographical memory over six years. *Cognitive Psychology, 18*, 225–252.

Wagenaar, W.A., & Groeneweg, J. (1990). The memory of concentration camp survivors. *Applied Cognitive Psychology, 4*, 77–87.

Wagenaar, W.A., & Visser, J. (1979). The weather forecast under the weather. *Ergonomics, 22*, 909–917.

Wason, P.C. (1960). On the failure to eliminate hypotheses in a conceptual task. *Quarterly Journal of Experimental Psychology, 12*, 129–140.

Waterman, D. (1991). Aging and memory for dreams. *Perceptual and Motor Skills, 73*, 45–75.

Welford, A.T. (1958). *Ageing and human skill*. Oxford University Press.

West, R.L. (1984). *An analysis of prospective everyday memory*. Paper presented at a meeting of the American Psychological Association, Toronto.

West, R.L. (1986). Everyday memory and aging. *Developmental Neuropsychology, 2*, 323–344.

Wetzler, S.E., & Sweeney, J.A. (1986). Childhood amnesia: An empirical demonstration. In D.C. Rubin (Ed.), *Autobiographical memory*. Cambridge: Cambridge University Press.

White, P.A. (1988). Knowing more about what we can tell: 'Introspective access' and causal report accuracy 10 years later. *British Journal of Psychology, 79*, 13–45.

White, S.H., & Pillemer, D.B. (1979). Childhood amnesia and the development of a socially accessible memory system. In J.F. Kihlstrom & F.J. Evans (Eds.), *Functional disorders of memory*. Hillsdale NJ: Lawrence Erlbaum Associates Inc.

Whitten, W.B., & Leonard, J.M. (1981). Directed search through autobiographical memory. *Memory and Cognition, 9*, 566–579.

Wilding, J., & Mohindra, N. (1980). Effects of subvocal suppression, articulating aloud and noise on sequence recall. *British Journal of Psychology, 71,* 247–261.

Wilkins, A.J. (1976). A failure to demonstrate the effects of the retention interval. Cited in J.E. Harris, Remembering to do things: A forgotten topic, in J.E. Harris & P.E. Morris (Eds.), *Everyday memory, actions and absentmindedness.* London: Academic Press.

Wilkins, A.J., & Baddeley, A.D. (1978). Remembering to recall in everyday life: An approach to absentmindedness. In M.M. Gruneberg, P.E. Morris, & R.N. Sykes (Eds.), *Practical aspects of memory.* London: Academic Press.

Williams, M.D., & Hollan, J.D. (1981). The process of retrieval from very long-term memory. *Cognitive Science, 5,* 87–119.

Wilson, B.A., Cockburn, J.E., & Baddeley, A.D. (1985). *The Rivermead Behavioural Memory Test.* Bury St. Edmonds: Thames Valley Test Co.

Winograd, E., & Killinger, W.A. (1983). Relating age at encoding in early childhood to adult recall: Development of flashbulb memories. *Journal of Experimental Psychology: General, 112,* 413–422.

Wood, G. (1978). The knew-it-all-along effect. *Journal of Experimental Psychology: Human Perception and Performance, 4,* 345–353.

Woodhead, M.M., & Baddeley, A.D. (1981). Individual differences and memory for faces, pictures and words. *Memory and Cognition, 9,* 368–370.

Wright, D.B. (1993). Recall of the Hillsborough disaster over time: Systematic biases of 'flashbulb' memories. *Applied Cognitive Psychology, 7,* 129–138.

Yarmey, A.D. (1984). Accuracy credibility of the elderly witness. *Canadian Journal on Aging, 3,* 79–90.

Yarmey, A.D. (1993). Stereotypes and recognition: Memory for faces and voices of good guys and bad guys. *Applied Cognitive Psychology, 7,* 419–431.

Yarmey, A.D., & Bull, M.P. (1978). Where were you when President Kennedy was assassinated? *Bulletin of the Psychonomic Society, 11,* 133–135.

Yekovich, F.R., & Thorndyke, P.W. (1981). An evaluation of alternative models of narrative schemata. *Journal of Verbal Learning and Verbal Behavior, 20,* 454–469.

Yin, R.K. (1969). Looking at upside down faces. *Journal of Experimental Psychology, 81,* 141–145.

Young, A.W., & Bruce, V. (1991). Perceptual categories and the computation of 'grandmother'. *European Journal of Cognitive Psychology, 3,* 5–49.

Young, A.W., Hay, D.C., & Ellis, A.W. (1985). The faces that launched a thousand slips: Everyday difficulties and errors in recognising people. *British Journal of Psychology, 76,* 495–523.

Young, A.W., McWeeny, K.H., Ellis, A.W., & Hay, D.C. (1986). Naming and categorising faces and written names. *The Quarterly Journal of Experimental Psychology, 38A,* 297–318.

Zaragoza, M.S., McCloskey, M., & Jamis, M. (1987). Misleading postevent information and recall of the original event: Further evidence against the memory impairment hypothesis. *Journal of Experimental Psychology: Learning, Memory and Cognition, 13,* 36–44.

Zatorre, R.J., & Beckett, C. (1989). Multiple coding strategies in the retention of musical tones by possessors of absolute pitch. *Memory and Cognition, 17,* 582–589.

Zelinski, E.M., Gilewski, M.J., & Thompson, L.W. (1980). Do laboratory tests relate to self assessment of memory ability in the young and old? In L.W. Poon, J.L. Fozard, L.S. Cermak, D. Arenberg, & L.W. Thompson (Eds.), *New directions in memory and ageing.* Hillsdale, NJ: Lawrence Erlbaum Associates Inc.

Author Index

Subject Index